MW00887028

Robert Lindley Murray: The Reluctant U.S. Tennis Champion

Includes "The First Forty Years of American Tennis"

Roger W. Ohnsorg

Order this book online at www.trafford.com
or email orders@trafford.com

Most Trafford titles are also available at major online book retailers.

Cover Painting by Paul T. Hanover

Printed in the United States of America.

ISBN: 978-1-4269-4514-4 (sc)
ISBN: 978-1-4269-4513-7 (e)

Trafford rev. 01/27/2011

www.trafford.com

North America & international
toll-free: 1 888 232 4444 (USA & Canada)
phone: 250 383 6864 • fax: 812 355 4082

Contents

Acknowledgments

My thanks go first to the Niagara Falls Public Library in Niagara Falls, New York, the only source for researching the *Niagara Falls Gazette*, which contains the tennis exploits and business achievements of Robert Lindley "Lin" Murray from the time he came to Niagara Falls in 1916 until his death in 1970. Maureen Fennie and Linda Reinumagi of the Local History Department were particularly helpful with their collection of high school yearbooks, Hooker Electrochemical Company scrapbooks, and photographs, and also in scanning items of interest.

Joanie Agler at the International Tennis Hall of Fame and Museum Research Center in Newport, Rhode Island, was extremely helpful in providing and copying pertinent pages from lawn tennis annuals, *American Lawn Tennis* magazine, and Hall of Famer folders during and following my two trips to that wonderland out of the past, in addition to scanning and mailing pertinent pictures.

I would be remiss not to acknowledge Internet sources, particularly the Web site grandslamtennis.freeukisp.co.uk. This site contains, among other things, the complete draw sheets and results of every match played at the four major championships for men and at least from the quarters for women.

When the manuscript was nearing completion, I was fortunate to make contact with Lin Murray's descendants in California, specifically the daughter and granddaughter of Lin Murray's youngest sister, Lydia Huneke. Without their help I would not have been able to link Lin Murray with the Murrays of Murray Hill in New York City. Betty Buckman, the daughter, did much e-mailing and phoning to enable me to complete the genealogical charts. Chrissie Kremer, the granddaughter, provided family documents and several fabulous family photographs including one of her engraved gold pendant, which was awarded to Lin Murray for winning the 1918 U.S. singles championship.

Many thanks also to two friends who reviewed the manuscript with different viewpoints, Anne Brophy and Mary Chotoff.

Part I: The First Forty Years of American Tennis

Preface

Staten Island, at the southern tip of New York State, where I was born and raised and first played tennis, is the home of tennis in the United States. Major Walter Clopton Wingfield applied for a patent on a "New and Improved Court for Playing the Ancient Game of Tennis" on February 23, 1874. Wingfield called his new game *sphairistike* (σφάίρίστική in Greek), after the Greek word, meaning "ball game." That name was abbreviated to "sticky" and was soon replaced by "lawn tennis." Boxed sets of Major Wingfield's patented game of lawn tennis sold for five guineas (more than twenty-six dollars),[1] replete with plain rubber balls, four pear-shaped racquets, a net set, two net posts, stakes and mallet to anchor the poles, and a booklet of tennis rules entitled "*Sphairistike* or Lawn Tennis." The original court was hourglass-shaped.

Mary Ewing Outerbridge, on holiday in Bermuda, bought an original set of Wingfield's *sphairistike*, presumably in January of 1874 and, with the help of her brother A. Emilius Outerbridge, director of the Staten Island Cricket and Baseball Club, rigged up the net in a remote club corner.

Another of Mary's enterprising brothers, Eugenius H. Outerbridge, promoted a national championship at the club. The tournament began September 1, 1880, on a site very close to the bay on what became the ferry parking lot. The tournament was won by an Englishman, O. E. Woodhouse, who had learned about the tournament from a Chicago newspaper. Woodhouse won over I. F. Hellmuth, Canadian champion—and why not since earlier that year he had reached the final of the all-comers event of the England championships, losing to H. L. Lawford? The Wimbledon championships began in 1877.

It appears that Wingfield was marketing his boxed lawn tennis before the patent date.[2] The court dimensions and net height were continually changing, and imitators were entering the market despite patent protection. As a result, when players from Boston, Newport, New York, Philadelphia, and elsewhere descended on Staten Island for that first "national" tournament, some found balls, net height, rackets, and scoring different from what they had been accustomed to.

Three signatories to a May 5, 1881, call for organization and club representatives met in New York later that month to sort out the inconsistencies. The U.S. National Lawn Tennis Association was founded, and its members agreed to hold a national championship tournament for men in both singles and doubles on August 31 at the Newport Casino in Rhode Island.[3] The men's doubles moved to other sites in 1887. The women's singles championships were also established in 1887 at the Philadelphia Cricket Club, which also hosted the women's doubles event, beginning in 1889, and the mixed doubles championship, beginning in 1892.

The men's singles tournament moved from Newport to the West Side Tennis Club at Forest Hills in 1915, to the Germantown Cricket Club in Philadelphia from 1921 to 1923, and then back to Forest Hills in 1924. From 1884 through 1911, the tournament used a challenge system whereby the defending champion automatically qualified for the next year's final.

When I first came to Niagara Falls in March of 1966 after being transferred to Carborundum's headquarters here, my primary extracurricular concern was sifting out the local tennis players. I found out there was an Industrial Tennis League and contacted one or two of Carbo's players; the initial response was, "What? This is March!" I didn't care and started hitting up against the Hyde Park wall as soon as there was no snow.

Subsequently, players started showing up. I joined the Buffalo Racquet Club and played at St. Catharines where Ed Pickett, a member of the Niagara Falls Badminton and Tennis Club in Ontario, suggested I come over to play, which I did. My first serious recollection is of Ned Stafford inviting me to play singles. I expected tough competition in Buffalo with the wide variety of players, experience, and youth, but not as much from a comfortable and quaint club with somewhat "older" members. On one of those four "slippery" clay courts, Ned, (who was fifty-six years to my twenty-nine) proceeded to run me around to the tune of one or two games in three sets.

That was a humbling experience, as I thought my game was better than the results. I learned a lot that day and was determined to improve. I found out playing against Ned and others that you can't beat experienced players by just keeping the ball in play. They don't miss. You have to develop a driving game with well-placed ground strokes, overheads, and volleys. I did beat Ned two years later in the club championships, 7–5, 6–0, but what had he been like in his younger days?

There were also at the club at that time two other colleagues of Ned's, Eddie D'Anna and Harry Keating, who played mostly socially at that time. In their prime, they and Herb Peck were the "Four Horsemen" of tennis in Niagara Falls, New York. Eddie D'Anna had won the state high school singles title in 1926, while Stafford and Keating had won the state high school doubles title in 1929. They and Peck won several championships in the 1930s and 1940s.

Ned could occasionally be seen at the club, playing with a cigar in his mouth—usually unlit. When he coached tennis at Niagara Falls High, I've been told, Ned would drive the team to matches, puffing on one of his El Productos and causing his young entourage significant displeasure.

Ned, who had a sense of humor but was always gracious, said to me shortly after I first joined the club, "Let's play badminton with a couple of ladies." Not being a badminton player, yet deriving some confidence from the fact that it was another racket sport, I agreed, and we found ourselves badly trounced. I'd been set up. The two ladies were Ethel Marshall and Bea Massman (although they were about fifteen to twenty years beyond their prime). Ethel Marshall had won the U.S. National Badminton singles championship a record seven years in a row (1947–53) and the doubles in 1952 and 1956 with Bea Massman. In 1956 the Buffalo-based Marshall was among the first class of inductees into the U.S. Badminton Hall of Fame. In 1991 both Ethyl and Bea Massman were inducted into the Greater Buffalo Sports Hall of Fame, along with the Buffalo Bills running back, the infamous O. J. Simpson.

Stafford and others had mentioned a rather obscure name to me, R. Lindley Murray, a former tennis champion, who lived in Lewiston Heights. At the time I didn't pay much attention, as I wanted to hone my own game and pursue an engineering profession. But imagine what it was like for these men as youngsters (between the ages of about seven and eleven) to suddenly have the national indoor tennis champion from California come to town in late 1916 to work for Hooker Electrochemical and subsequently to win the national singles championship at Forest Hills in 1917 and again in 1918, beating the famous Bill Tilden in the final round.

What an inspiration to pursue the game, which D'Anna, Keating, Peck, and Stafford did successfully for at least two decades, with Ned winning the Canadian lawn tennis 45s and the U.S. lawn tennis doubles 70s. These Four Horsemen and others made Niagara tennis huge from the late 1920s through the 1940s.

In the late 1960s and 1970s, tennis started making a comeback in Niagara with the Niagara County closed and open tournaments. On my arrival in 1966 the only organized tennis was the Industrial Tennis League, which I learned had been initiated by R. Lindley Murray and his Hooker Electrochemical colleagues in 1919. A promoter extraordinaire, Murray joined the Industrial Athletic Council and in 1919 organized, promoted, and occasionally played in the tennis league, which hasn't missed a beat in over ninety years despite the waning industry and tennis players. It was the first of its kind in the country to find National Lawn Tennis Association sponsorship.

Murray brought some of the best national and international players to Niagara Falls for exhibition matches from 1917 through 1926. In addition, as a family man and Stanford University chemical engineering graduate, Murray undertook his employment at Hooker Electrochemical with his characteristic professionalism and became president and CEO, retiring in 1959.

He was always on hand to make speeches, referee matches, or present trophies to local tournament winners. An individual of this caliber deserves more than just a footnote, particularly among members of the present tennis community, most of whom I'm sure have never heard of him.

1
Beginnings

Lawn tennis (or tennis) had its origins in an ancient game known to the French as *jeu de paume*, and now called *real tennis* in Great Britain, *royal tennis* in Australia, and *court tennis* in the United States. Real tennis is still played on forty-two courts in the UK, Australia, the United States, and France. Of the nine courts in the United States, one is at the International Tennis Hall of Fame in Newport, adjacent to the grass court where Dick Sears won his first championship in 1881. The game is played in a building with high walls and a ceiling lofty enough for lobbing, with a playing floor about ninety-six by thirty-two feet. The courts are doubly asymmetric: each end, as divided by the net, as well as each of the court sides is different. The service is always made from the same court over a sagging net five feet at the ends and three feet in the center. The game still utilizes a cork-based ball two and a half inches in diameter weighing about two and a half ounces compared to the much livelier two-and-a-half-inch and two-ounce tennis balls. The twenty-seven-inch-long wooden rackets have slightly bent heads to make it easier to strike balls close to the floor and to facilitate slice. The features real tennis shares with lawn tennis are that the ball is struck back and forth over a net with a racket; the ball may only bounce once (When the ball bounces twice at the service end, the server does not necessarily lose the point. A "chase" is called, and the server later gets the chance to play off the chase from the receiving end.); two services are allowed; and lawn tennis has adopted the strange system of scoring by fifteens (with the exception of forty, which was shortened from forty-five). [1]

The origin of tennis terminology is thoroughly documented in Heiner Gillmeister's *Tennis: A Cultural History*. The earliest known name for the game, *jeu de bonde* ("the bouncing ball game") comes from around 1300,[2] which is earlier than *jeu de la paume* ("the game played with the palm of the hand"), the name for tennis in fashionable Paris.[3]

Tennis vocabulary was used by a contemporary minstrel or poet to describe the medieval Battle of Agincourt of October 1415, which was a victory for Henry V of England over a larger French army in the Hundred Years' War in which Henry invaded France and besieged the port of Harfleur.[4] The battle is also the centerpiece of the play *Henry V* by William Shakespeare. In a ballad titled "The Bataile of Agyncourt," the French Dauphin says:

'A tonne of tenys ballys I shall hym sende
For to pleye hym with all.'

The angered Henry replies with a more deadly counter-present:

'Swyche tenys ballys I shall hym sende
As shall tere the roof all of his all [= hall].'[5]

Tenys was the English term and *jeu de la paume* the French.[6] The ballad continues as a big gun's rally is described in tennis terms:

Tenys seyde the grete gonne,
How felawes go we to game.[7]

Thus a rally is announced by the call of *tenez*, meaning "take it," a call of warning from the server[8–10] from the French verb *tenir*, meaning "to hold."[11]

It appears that even in the game's early days nothing was known about the origin of the scoring method by fifteens. An advantage of two points was needed to win a game, as is true today. A *double victory* was one in which the opponent was not conceded a single point, and the *triple victory* was the ultimate achievement in which a player scored five consecutive points to snatch the game after trailing love–40. The five consecutive points necessary for the *vittoria rabiosa*, or "frenzied victory," inspired Scaino in 1555 to suggest "the most sensible explanation of the number fifteen would be to regard it as the product of the five successive points and the triple reward of the *vittoria rabiosa*."[12]

In addition to this explanation, "the division of the hour into sixty minutes, and the division of the circle into six segments of sixty have been considered."[13] In the first case four points are required for game: fifteen, thirty, forty-five, and sixty. In the second, a physical unit is the sixth part of a circle or sixty degrees, and fifteen degrees times four has the same value as a physical unit. Although a medieval match in France consisted of four games,[14] six such physical units are now required to win a set, thus completing a full circle.

The terms *advantage* and *deuce* must have existed since only a few decades after the Agincourt ballad. Jan van Berghe translated the French *avantage* into his native Dutch. He says that when both sides reach forty-five points, "two chases must be played. And if it then happens that one of the sides wins the first chase, this side calls out as loudly as possible *twoordeel/twoordeel* ('advantage/advantage')."[15]

As Gillmeister notes, *advantage* and *deuce* come together for the first time in linguist John Florio's *Second Frutes* of 1591:

> *H. You haue fortie then, goe to, plaie.*
> *T. And I a dewes then.*
> *H. I haue advantage.*[16]

So by the end of the sixteenth century the English had substituted the Latin prefix *ad-* for the French *a-* in *avantage* and shortened forty-five to forty. Being tied at forty-five each the tennis players were two points away from game which in Old French was *a deus* and in English *a deuce*, the indefinite article later dropped.[17]

The normal explanation of *love* goes back to the French *l'oeuf* (egg), a word which sounds fairly similar. In the English national pastime, cricket, a *duck's egg* (*duck* for short) was used for love or nothing. In the English language, the expression "neither for love nor money" existed in the Middle Ages; the winning player might have been considered the one playing for money and the loser for fun, or the love of the game.[18]

A political song written by Jeronimus van der Voort in 1583 describes a battle between the citizens of Antwerp and the French in terms of a tennis match in which people played either for money, pledges, or simply the honor. From the palace of the Duke of Anjou, the poet says, all that had been coming from the French were unwieldy balls and quality powder for loading guns. The Dutch or Flemish equivalent of the word honor is *lof.* "It looks as if the English expression for a player's failure to score a point owes its existence to an expression used in the Low Countries, *omme lof spelen*, 'to play for the honor.'"[19]

Love would be one of the sporting terms adopted from the continent as well as *set.* As a sporting term, the noun *set* seems to occur for the first time in John Florio's *Second Frutes* where a servant asks his masters if they want to play for money: "Will you plaie in set?" The pronoun *in* is the prefix of an underlying Flemish noun *inzet*, meaning stake.[20]

The old game of real tennis gave birth to another sport—rackets—in mid-eighteenth-century England. At London's Fleet and King's Bench debtors' prisons, the prisoners whiled away the hours by hitting balls up against the prison walls with tennis rackets. Originally the one front wall was used, but in time the game became popularized as a four-wall sport evolving into a sixty-by-thirty-foot enclosed court with a ceiling about thirty feet high. The ball may be played on a bounce or the fly and may also strike a side wall before hitting the front wall above a twenty-six-and-a-half-inch-high wooden board or telltale. The players use thirty-and-a-half-inch wooden rackets and a hard white ball weighing twenty-eight grams; games are to fifteen points unless tied at 13–all or 14–all. The game of squash rackets (or squash) began in the nineteenth century as an offshoot of rackets. The squash court, however, is much smaller—thirty-two feet long and twenty-one feet wide with a nineteen-inch telltale.[21]

A third game, badminton, can be traced to late-nineteenth-century India where British military officers brought the game back to England. Although the sport may be played outdoors, because the feathered projectile or shuttlecock is affected by wind, competitive badminton is best played indoors. The singles court is forty-four feet long and seventeen feet wide. The service courts are marked by a center line dividing the court's width and a short line six and a half feet from the net, which is five feet in height at its center. Unlike tennis the service boxes are in the backcourt, and players stand inside their service courts to serve and receive; a badminton serve must be hit below waist height. Like tennis the server and receiver stand diagonally opposite, the server in his right service court when the score is even and in his left service court when the score is odd. When the server loses a rally, the serve passes to his opponent.[22]

Major Wingfield applied for a patent (N° 685), dated February 23, 1874, for a "New and Improved Court for Playing the Ancient Game of Tennis." Wingfield's first edition of his booklet on "*Sphairistike*" (pronounced "shair-rist-ik-ee"), the Greek word meaning "ball game" or "play ball," which was soon contracted to "sticky" and then "lawn tennis," had six rules. The court was hourglass-shaped, sixty feet long (eighteen feet shorter than today), twenty-one feet wide at the net, and thirty feet at the baseline, compared to today's singles court width of twenty-seven feet.[23] A possible impetus for taking the game outside was the invention of vulcanized rubber by Charles Goodyear in 1844, later used to produce thin-walled bouncing balls, which Wingfield got from Germany.

Wingfield's game was a goulash of the other three. Like badminton, the service boxes were at the back of the court, and the server hit the ball over a high four-foot-eight net. Like rackets (and the period badminton), a point could only be scored by the server, and games were fifteen points. Like court tennis, it provided for a court with two sides, as divided by the net, that were not identical; and the serve was made from one side of the court only. The server stood in a marked space in the middle of the court. Imagine the overhand server's advantage from this position. Wingfield claimed that the hourglass shape of his court and the wing-nets stretched along the sidelines near the net were original features. Detractors said they were of no use to the game but just gimmicks.[24]

Wingfield was also marketing "A Portable Court for Playing Tennis" in a painted wooden box thirty-six by twelve by six inches, which contained the equipment and *The Book of the Game*. The package deal was priced at five guineas or a bit over twenty-six dollars. One of his exaggerated claims was that a "perfect court" could be put up on any croquet ground in five minutes.[24]

Others shortly took over the game and constantly altered it, while the major tried to keep up with the changes. In the fall of 1874 he issued a second edition of *The Book of the Game* now with twelve rules and a larger court, eighty-four by thirty-six feet. He lowered the net to four feet in the center, and provided for serving from either of the (now identical) sides of the net. The service courts were moved up to the fore court, near the net, and the server moved back to the baseline. The following spring he increased the width to thirty-nine feet but preserved his other dimensions.[26–28]

In May 1875 the Marylebone Cricket Club intervened as the governing authority of rackets and tennis and codified the rules. They retained the hourglass shape: seventy-eight feet long, thirty feet wide at the base, and twenty-four feet in the middle (the mean of which is the present dimension of twenty-seven feet). The net was five feet at the sides and four feet in the center. The service court extended twenty-six feet from the net (now twenty-one feet). Points (fifteen for a game, with deuce at 14–all) were scored only by the server, who served until he lost a rally, and two deliveries were allowed.[29]

The All England Croquet Club, experiencing financial difficulties, added a lawn tennis court, and the new game prospered. By 1877 the club's name was changed to the All England Croquet and Lawn Tennis Club, and a lawn tennis tournament—the first Wimbledon—was held starting July 9. The *Field* magazine, still in publication, provided a silver challenge cup worth twenty-five guineas.[30] By tournament time a rectangular court size (seventy-eight by twenty-seven feet) had been adopted; the wing-nets were gone; and the badminton-rackets scoring had been abandoned, supplanted by the court tennis system of games and sets. The service line remaned at twenty-six feet from the net, and a let on service was considered good, with two deliveries allowed. The balls were smaller and lighter than at present, and significantly, the net was still five feet at the posts, which were placed three feet outside the court but lowered to three feet three in the center. Six games comprised a set, and no advantage games were played.[31–32] Henry Jones, Julian Marshall, and Charles G. Heathcote proposed these changes and carried out all the arrangements for the first championship.

In that first 1877 championship the majority of players, the real or court tennis player, had every advantage; the net was high at the sides encouraging play corner to corner rather than down the sidelines, and the service line was so far back from the net as to give the heavily cut service a great advantage on balls covered with (white) flannel, which took more cut and bounded less.[33] The court tennis players used spoon-shaped rackets while the rackets players used rackets with small heads and long, thin handles. The services were either underhand or delivered from a point more or less level with the shoulder, the overhead service then unknown. There were two strokes: a sliced drive taken from rackets and a chop borrowed from court tennis.[34] As the high net at the sides encouraged play from corner to corner rather than down the sidelines, Spencer W. Gore, a twenty-seven-year-old rackets player, won the first Wimbledon, in a field of twenty-two as two hundred spectators looked on, by methodically serving, charging the net, and punching the ball back away from his opponents with little fear of being passed down the sidelines.

You would think the first lawn tennis champion would be enthusiastic, but in 1890 Gore wrote, "[I]n my opinion, it is its want of variety that will prevent lawn tennis in its present form from taking rank amongst our great games.... That anyone who has really played well at cricket, tennis, or even rackets, will ever seriously give his attention to lawn tennis, beyond showing himself to be a promising player, is extremely doubtful; for in all probability the monotony of the game as compared with the others would choke him off before he had time to excel in it."[35]

The 1878 championship introduced an entirely new style of play that lasted some three years termed the "pat-ball" period. P. Frank Hadow beat Gore in the challenge round by tossing or lobbing the ball over his head, and the volleying game was temporarily buried in obscurity. In 1878 A. T. Myers made a first attempt at an overhand service but was beaten in the quarters by eventual winner Hadow. By 1881 the overhand service came into general use.[36] By the second championship the net was lowered to three feet at the center and four feet, four inches at the posts; and the service line was moved in to twenty-two feet from the net. Henry Jones, as referee, periodically adjusted the net height and service line according to the number of service points won and lost on service. In 1882 the net height became three feet at the center and three feet, six inches at the posts with the service line twenty-one feet from the net, as it is today.

The 1879 championship was remarkable for the number of strokes per rally, forty or fifty not being uncommon. A large proportion of the competitors adopted the safe style of play introduced in 1878, with players not having the courage to hit hard or place the ball. John T. Hartley won in 1879 by defeating V. "St. Leger" Gould in the all-comers. Both made history: Hartley, who had to return to Yorkshire for Sunday duties between his semifinal and final, was the only clergyman to reach a Wimbledon final, and Gould was the only Wimbledon finalist to be convicted of murder (for which he was sent to Devil's Island in 1908).[37] Hartley won again in 1880 by hitting harder and placing the ball. The 1880 runner-up was Herbert Lawford who introduced a powerful forehand topspin ground stroke to the sport. Lawford, who won Wimbledon in 1887 over Ernest Renshaw and the all-comers five times (1880, '84, '85, '86, and '88), was a classic backcourt player. In 1880 the twin Renshaw brothers, Willie and Ernest, by attempting to volley at the net, were beaten in the third and fourth rounds respectively by O. E. Woodhouse but succeeded in winning the first of their seven doubles titles together.

Not until the emergence of the Renshaw twins did the era of pat-ball end. Dominating both singles and doubles throughout the decade, the Renshaws perfected the hard, deep volley from about the service line, and when lobbing was tried against them, they introduced a new stroke, which was for many years known as the "Renshaw smash."[38] The game from

1881 became a battle between two styles, represented by the backcourt player (e.g., Lawford) and the volleyer. That year nineteen-year-old Willie Renshaw won the first of his six consecutive singles titles by destroying John Hartley, 6–0, 6–1, 6–1. Lawford, Renshaw's senior by some ten years, lost to Willie in a tough five-set semifinal contest, 1–6, 6–3, 6–2, 5–6, 6–3. Willie declined to defend in 1887 because of an elbow injury, lost to Willoughby Hamilton in the 1888 quarters, and then won an incredible come-from-behind match against Harry Barlow in the 1889 all-comers final. He dodged six match points in the fourth set (trailing 5–2), and came back from 0–5 in the fifth to win, 3–6, 5–7, 8–6, 10–8, 8–6.[39] He defeated his brother Ernest for his seventh singles title, 6–4, 6–1, 3–6, 6–0. Ernest, hampered by his brother in the 1882, '83, and '89 challenge rounds, defeated Lawford for the 1888 title.

Evolution of Tennis Court Size and Net Height

Date	Court Length	Width at Baseline	Width at Net	Service Line from Net	Net Height, Posts	Net Height, Center	Court Shape	Post Position
Wing 1874	60 ft	30 ft	21 ft		5 ft[1]	4-ft-8	Hourglass	Sideline
Wing Fall 1874	84 ft	36 ft		18 ft[2]	5 ft[1]	4 ft	Hourglass	Sideline
Wing Spring 1875	84 ft	39 ft			5 ft[1]	4 ft	Hourglass	Sideline
MCC[3] 1875	78 ft	30 ft	24 ft	26 ft	5 ft	4 ft	Hourglass	Sideline
AECTC[4] 1877	78 ft	27 ft	27 ft	26 ft	4-ft-9[5]	3-ft-3	Rectangular	3 ft out
AECTC[4] 1878	78 ft	27 ft	27 ft	22 ft	4-ft-4	3 ft	Rectangular	3 ft out
AECTC[4] 1882	78 ft	27 ft	27 ft	21 ft	3-ft-6	3 ft	Rectangular	3 ft out

[1]Period drawings show net to be at uniform height (possibly four foot eight). In the *Field*, April 11, 1874, the net was seven yards long and four feet, eight inches high.

[2]Service courts were still in backcourt, but the server moved from service line to baseline, per November 28, 1874, issue of *Field*.

[3]Marylebone Cricket Club.

[4]All England Cricket and Tennis Club.

[5]The Encyclopedia of Tennis, p. 107.

2
American Men's Tennis

Early Years

The first tennis court in the Western hemisphere was in use in Bermuda no later than the end of 1873. Since Major Wingfield did not apply for a patent until February 23, 1874, perhaps he saw a threat to the game he was marketing and promptly sought a patent on the hourglass court. Twenty-one-year-old Mary Ewing Outerbridge had already learned of the game (no later than January 1874), for she arrived in New York February 2, 1874, on the SS *Canima* with her brother A. Emilius Outerbridge, as the passenger list shows, with a box of goodies from Bermuda.[1] To put American social life of the period in perspective, consider that only two days earlier the Jesse James Gang had held up a train on the St. Louis, Iron Mountain and Southern Railway at Gad's Hill, Missouri, making off with twelve thousand dollars.

The strange box and its tennis gear contents were confiscated by customs agents until A. Emilius, a shipping executive, used his pull to get the gear released. That spring a court was set up at the Staten Island Cricket and Baseball Club on the old Camp Washington grounds, later called St. George, by A. Emilius, a director of the club.[2] Miss Outerbridge is said to have practiced with her brothers and their friends.[3] Another brother, Eugenius Harvey Outerbridge, the first chairman of the Port of New York Authority, took the lead in promoting a national organization in May 1881, which later became the United States National Lawn Tennis Association (USNLTA).[4] In 1920 the USNLTA dropped "national" and became the

USLTA while in 1975 "lawn" was dropped, and now we have the United States Tennis Association (USTA).

It appears that the jury is still out on whether Mary Outerbridge was indeed the first to introduce tennis to America. The International Tennis Hall of Fame believes so, as Mary, "the Mother of American Tennis," was inducted in 1981.[5] Gillmeister doubts that Mary Outerbridge had Wingfield's boxed set with her when she disembarked in New York on February 2, 1874. His argument was that Mary "would hardly have acquired the *sphairistike* box without the rules." She departed Bermuda "on either 22 or 23 January 1874," and that "25 February 1874 has now and beyond all doubt been established as the date of the first printing of Wingfield's rules."[6] Gillmeister suggests it was in the spring of 1875 that Mary bought a set of Wingfield's *sphairistike.*[7] Wingfield's equipment was sold by his agents, Messrs. French and Co., 46, Churton Street, London, for five guineas, and competing sets were soon on the market despite patent protection.

However, Eugenius H. Outerbridge distinctly remembered his sister's first set of lawn tennis equipment and the hourglass-shaped court. He wrote to Dwight F. Davis on August 2, 1923, then president of the USLTA, that his sister's set was brought in from Bermuda in the spring of 1874. The letter was published for the USLTA's golden jubilee in 1931:

> To the best of my knowledge and belief it was in the spring of 1874 that my sister, Mary Ewing Outerbridge, brought from Bermuda a lawn tennis net, rackets and balls which she had obtained from the regimental stores through the courtesy of the colonel or some of the officers with whom she had played the game there.
>
> One of my older brothers, A. Emilius Outerbridge, was then a director of the Staten Island Cricket and Baseball Club, with its grounds at what was then called Camp Washington, later St. George, and through his assistance, she was given permission by the directors to set up a court on the grounds.[8]

Tennis was introduced to several other locations in 1874. The first documented instance at a most unlikely site: Indian territory at Camp Apache near present-day Tucson, Arizona, in early October 1874. Upon arriving at Camp Apache from San Francisco on October 4, Martha

Summerhayes, a young officer's wife, wrote: "The question of getting settled comfortably still worried me, and after a day or two, I went over to see what Mrs. Bailey had done. To my surprise, I found her out playing tennis, her little boy asleep in the baby-carriage, which they had brought all the way from San Francisco, near the court. I joined the group, and afterward asked her advice about the matter. She laughed kindly and said: 'Oh! You'll get used to it, and things will settle themselves. Of course it is troublesome, but you can have shelves and such things—you'll soon learn,' and still smiling, she gave her ball a neat left-hander."[9]

No mention is made of how or when the court got to Camp Apache. The how was likely by sea from England via San Francisco, brought either by an English diplomat or a London merchant. The when may have been on a previous trip by Ella Bailey or on Martha's first trip with Mrs. Bailey, which took about two months. In 1874 there were no railroads in Arizona, and Martha and her husband, Lieutenant Jack, embarked on the steamship *Newbern* from San Francisco on August 6 where she met Ella Bailey.[10] To get to Camp Apache they went by steamer down the coast, up the Gulf of California to Port Isabel, up the Colorado River some two hundred miles to Fort Mojave, and then overland across the Mojave Desert.

"Lawn tennis," as the game was officially known, did not necessarily require a lawn, only a flat surface, and it seems unlikely that Camp Apache had groomed, green turf. Warren Kimball, who served four years on the USTA Board of Directors, conjectures that tennis was first played in San Francisco.[11] That may be very likely, but it did take more than six years for the first lawn tennis club in California to be founded, in October of 1880 at San Rafael, a suburb of San Francisco.[12]

Back on the East Coast, William Appleton had a court laid down at his home in Nahant, a small seaside resort about ten miles from Boston, in August 1874. James Dwight and his second cousin Fred Sears, elder brother of Richard Sears, the first American champion, were the first to play there.

After James Dwight's graduation from Harvard College in 1874 he entered Harvard Medical School. But first, his father, a prosperous lawyer, gave him a trip to Europe as a graduation gift. Like Mary Outerbridge he returned with a boxed *sphairistike* tennis set. Noting that his uncle owned one of the smoothest lawns in Nahant, he prevailed on Mr. Appleton to let him mark out a court.[13] Another version of the story is that Appleton's son-in-law, J. Arthur Beebe, had "just brought the boxed set with him from London and had meant to present it to the Appleton's," but Dwight and Sears had beaten him to the punch and marked out a court in the side yard in August 1874.[14]

Dr. James Dwight later described the first tennis played in New England. The rackets were spoon-shaped and very light, about thirteen ounces, and the balls were large and uncovered, similar to those sold for children. The court was hourglass-shaped, and the service line was twenty-six feet from the net. As described by James Dwight,

> Mr. F. R. Sears, the elder brother of the champion, and I put up the net and tried the game. As we had no lines, and as we hit the ball in no particular direction, very naturally we could not return it. So we voted the whole thing a fraud and put it away.
>
> Perhaps a month later, finding nothing to do, we tried it again and this time in earnest. I remember even now that each won a game, and as it rained in the afternoon, we played in rubber boots and coats rather than lose a day.[15]

In August 1876 a round-robin tournament was held on Appleton's property, won by his nephew James Dwight over Fred Sears using the badminton-rackets fifteen-point system, 12–15, 15–7, 15–13. Reminiscing in 1890 Dwight said: "It was my first real match and I doubt if I ever worked harder. At the end of the game neither of us could go home."[16]

Sears's grandfather, David, owned property—partly in Brookline, partly in Boston—which he called Longwood, named after the house Napoleon Bonaparte stayed in while exiled to Saint Helena. Part of the property, which became the Longwood Cricket Club, he rented to a gang of cricketers for forty dollars a year in 1877. At the first U.S. Championships in 1881, Dick Sears wore the black-and-white striped cap and jacket of Longwood into the Newport Casino. In 1922 the club moved from the Sears Longwood property to a new site in Chestnut Hill near Fenway Park. Although it still bears the same name, the club is neither in Longwood nor is it a cricket club, the sport disappearing in 1911.[17–18]

Harry Wright, the first player-manager of the Boston Red Sox, and his brother, George Wright, played cricket for the United States and put Longwood on the sports map. George Wright, an American pioneer in baseball, was one of five men to play regularly for both the Cincinnati and the Boston Red Stockings until 1878, the latter winning six championships during his eight seasons. He was one of the principals of the famous sporting goods firm Wright and Ditson.[19]

George also brought tennis gear to Boston on his return from a baseball-cricket tour of England in 1874. A lawn tennis court was laid out at Longwood in 1878. The club held its first tournament in 1882, the Eastern sectional men's doubles in 1897, a national standalone tournament from 1917 to 1933, and the first Davis Cup, branded the International Lawn Tennis Challenge, in 1900.[20] George was the father of tennis great Beals Wright, a U.S. Championship winner and Olympic gold medalist, and also Irving Wright, not as successful as Beals, but nevertheless a U.S. top tenner in 1906 and 1907.

In the autumn of 1874, W. W. Sherman of Newport brought a set back from England, but the set was not put up until the following spring.[21] Two more were laid out at Newport in the early summer, and Dr. James Dwight recalled playing on Sherman's court in 1877 or 1878 as well as at several other residences in Newport including the court of a "Mr. Bennett,"[22] most likely the newspaper tycoon who built the Newport Casino in 1880.

Another set was used by the Millikens at Plainfield, New Jersey, and the first issue (vol. 1, no. 1) of *American Cricketer* of Philadelphia reported on June 28, 1877: "Lawn Tennis is very popular on the Germantown Cricket grounds."[23]

In New Orleans an Englishman organized a tennis club in December, 1876, "which was said to have been the outgrowth of considerable previous play."[24] New Orleans found a new use for tennis balls as recently as October 2009 when "Sheriff Marlin Gusman said investigators found drugs and other dangerous items being smuggled" into Orleans Parish Prison "via tennis balls thrown over walls into the jail recreation area."[25]

On July 15, 1874, Major Rowan Hamilton settled his account for Wingfield's tennis sets, purchased in May for use in Canada.[26] This may have given Canada a jump on the United States, as it was a Canadian, Isadore F. Hellmuth, who was a finalist in the Staten Island tournament against O. E. Woodhouse. Hellmuth had visited the Staten Island court and in 1874 established a club in Toronto that would come to be known as the Toronto Lawn Tennis Club two years later. In 1876, Hellmuth established a club in London, Ontario, where he had moved to practice law.[27]

Between Nahant and Staten Island, Malcolm D. Whitman in *Tennis Origins and Mysteries* makes a strong case for the latter's precedence. Dr. James Dwight wrote that a *sphairistike* or lawn tennis set was brought from

England in July 1875 and the game was played at Mr. William Appleton's place at Nahant in the late summer of 1875. Further substantiation of the year 1875 may be found in the description of the Nahant court. Dr. Dwight states that "the service line was 26 feet from the net" (see above), but that specification was not adopted until May 24, 1875, by the Marylebone Cricket Club (see table, chapter 1). In addition, the edition of *The Book of the Game* that accompanied each early set, first edition December 1873 and second edition November 1, 1874, made no mention of any line twenty-six feet from the net until the third edition, dated June 1, 1875.[28]

Regarding the Outerbridge date, although patents for the game were not applied for until February of 1874, other records reveal that the original tennis sets were obtainable in 1873. There is nothing improbable in the notion that some officer having taken the game to Bermuda, for it was "quite common for British army officers to be the first to introduce new sports into the Colonies."[29] Frank G. Menke, a well-known sports writer wrote that the Outerbridge set was imported from Bermuda in 1874, basing his conclusion on a published interview with a veteran customs inspector who was in the customs department when the duty on Miss Outerbridge's set was assessed. This inspector asserted that the inspection was made in 1874 and that he handled the first tennis apparatus ever seen in the United States.[30]

During the sport's first few years, lawn tennis was played under varying conditions, a fact that did not become apparent until open tournaments were held. The nets hung at different heights, the courts varied somewhat in size, and the balls differed both in size and weight. This was highlighted when Eugenius Outerbridge promoted a national championship at the Staten Island Cricket and Baseball Club. The tournament, which began September 1, 1880, on a site very close to the bay on what became the ferry parking lot, was won by an Englishman, O. E. Woodhouse, who had learned about the event from a Chicago newspaper. Only two months before he had beaten both William and Ernest Renshaw at Wimbledon before losing to H. F. Lawford in the all-comers. He astonished everybody with an overhead service, the first of the sort ever in the United States, and defeated Canadian champion I. F. Hellmuth in the final, using rackets scoring, 15–11, 14–15, 15–9, 10–15, 2–all in games but a winning margin of fifty-four points to fifty.[31]

Although Hellmuth still served underhand, he played an outstanding match against Woodhouse, who served a crushing overhead. Only one American, James Rankine in the opening round, even came close to the

Englishman, but Hellmuth matched Woodhouse point for point. "It was a promising beginning that offered false hope for Canada's future in the game."[32]

James Dwight and Richard Sears had come down from Boston to play the tournament but found the balls "lighter, smaller, and softer than the regulations demanded." They stayed out of the singles but were persuaded to play in the doubles and were beaten in the second round. James Rankine and W. M. Donald of Staten Island won the tournament, the heavy winds bothering the visitors. Later in the year, Philadelphia's Young America Cricket Club came to Staten Island for a match against the host club. The visitors lost, having been accustomed to a net six inches higher than that in use on Staten Island. What the game needed was standardization.[33]

A call for organization "for the purpose of adopting a code of rules and designating a standard ball, to govern and be used in all lawn tennis matches or tournaments throughout the United States" appeared in the May 5, 1881, issue of *American Cricketer* of Philadelphia. The three signatories were James Dwight, the subsequent "Father of American Lawn Tennis," representing the Beacon Park Athletic Association of Boston; Eugenius H. Outerbridge of the Staten Island Cricket and Baseball Club; and Clarence M. Clark, representing Philadelphia.[34]

The tennis convention was held May 21 at the Fifth Avenue Hotel in New York with representatives from nineteen clubs and proxies from fifteen others, none west of Pittsburgh. After the election of officers (General R. S. Oliver of the Albany Lawn Tennis Club as president) the United States National Lawn Tennis Association (USNLTA) was formed, and miscellaneous rules and regulations were passed, including (1) that the decision of the umpire was final, (2) that All England rules would be adopted and the English ball made by F. H. Ayres would be used, (3) that the service line would be pulled in to twenty-one feet from the net, where it has since remained, and (4) that the first championship would be held at the Casino in Newport on August 31.[35]

Newport Casino

Newport, on the Atlantic Ocean at the southern tip of Rhode Island, was already a preeminent social resort in 1881, with a number of palatial residences, referred to as "cottages." In the 1890s and early 1900s summer Newport became the social capital of America. Railroad baron William K. Vanderbilt's grand Marble House (completed in 1892) cost $11 million.

Built as a birthday gift for his wife, Alva, it set the precedent for the Gilded Age. Alva, apparently not impressed, divorced William in 1895, married Oliver Hazard Perry Belmont, and moved to his mansion down the street. Cornelius Vanderbilt's manse, the Breakers (completed in 1895), was the largest, most opulent house in a summer resort.

The Newport Casino had its origins in James Gordon Bennett Jr., publisher of the *New York Herald.* After Bennett's father, founder of the paper, turned control of the *Herald* over to his son in 1866, James provided the financial backing for the 1869 expedition by Henry Morton Stanley into Africa to find David Livingston for the *Herald's* exclusive account. Known for his flamboyant and sometimes erratic behavior, he left New York for Europe in 1877 after an incident that ended his engagement to socialite Caroline May. According to various accounts, he arrived late and drunk to a party at the May family mansion and then urinated into a fireplace in full view of his hosts.[36] The following year, so the story goes,

> Bennett was a member of the venerable Reading Room, then Newport's most exclusive club. He secured a guest card for a friend, an English Army officer [British Cavalry Officer, Captain Henry Augustus "Sugar" Candy], and then bet him he couldn't—or wouldn't dare—ride his horse up the Reading Room's front steps and into its front hall.
>
> The Englishman won his bet, and the irked Board of Governors of the Club notified Bennett that his guest card would no longer be honored. Bennett retaliated by building a rival club. He owned a house on Bellevue Avenue—on which many of the famed "cottages" were located—and now purchased the plot across the avenue from it, and commissioned architect Stanford White to build a new club on the site.[37]

The result was the Newport Casino, which today looks much as it did when it opened in 1880. The block on Bellevue Avenue, which runs roughly north-south, is divided into shops and nearer the north end is the only entrance to the Casino. Entering through the open corridor, guests may feel as though they are being transported into the pristine nineteenth-century tennis world. An oval, red-brick walkway surrounds an east-west grass display court. The Victorian buildings are covered in cedar shakes, now painted dark green; a restaurant sits to the left, and a short distance to the right along the path and up four narrow steps is the museum's gift shop. For a fee of ten dollars one can walk up a staircase to the museum proper, where a model of Major Wingfield in full regalia greets visitors on the left. Up another wide but short set of stairs are several large square pillars on each side of which are eight plaques featuring short biographies of Hall of Famers; in the center an interactive screen provides additional information and videos on the honorees. Beyond this room, the museum displays balls, costumes, rackets, trophies, a boxed tennis set, and much more from a bygone era. On the third floor are meeting rooms and the Information Research Center (IRC), a comprehensive tennis library opened in 2000 with over five thousand books, as well as yearbooks, periodicals, personal player memorabilia, and much more.[38–39]

At the end of the tennis court is the Horseshoe Piazza on which the stringed orchestra of John Mullaly played Offenbach and Strauss during Tennis Week.[40] The Casino has thirteen grass courts, four of which are directly east of the Piazza. Adjacent to the farthest court, where the earliest championship matches were played, is a two-story Victorian structure with a porch on both levels from which members of the gallery who were not seated around the courts viewed matches. The south side of this building contains one of the few "court tennis" courts in the United States, and on the north is the five-hundred-capacity, removable-seat Casino Theater, now being revived after more than twenty years through a $4.6 million facelift.[41–42] To the south of these courts on the other side of the walkway is the grandstand, directly in front of which are two grass courts; these were used for championship and special matches after the Casino ordered a portable grandstand from the Barnum and Bailey circus in 1892, which served its purpose for a time.[43]

As the Gilded Age drew to a close with the onset of the Depression, Newport fell by the wayside as a summer resort for the rich and famous, and by the 1950s the Casino was in sad shape financially. Fortunately, Casino president, James Van Alen, who would later introduce the tennis tiebreaker, stepped in and by 1954 had established the National Tennis Hall of Fame at the Newport Casino, which was officially sanctioned by the USLTA. Only Americans were inducted between 1955 and 1972, after which the field was opened to international players. In 1976 the National Tennis Hall of Fame and Tennis Museum was prefixed by "international," and that year also saw the inauguration of the Campbell's Hall of Fame Tennis championships, which is the last remaining professional tennis tournament played on grass in North America. In 1986 the International Tennis Hall of Fame was recognized as the sport's official Hall of Fame by the International Tennis Federation, the governing body of tennis.[44–46]

First Championship Closed to Foreigners

When the time for the first U.S. Championships arrived, twenty-five players turned up for singles, and thirteen pairs entered the doubles at the Newport Casino. Dr. James Dwight did not enter the singles that year but in the doubles paired with Richard D. Sears (the younger brother of Fred, with whom he had played at Nahant). The nets were four feet at the posts and three feet in the center, which led to playing cross court to avoid lifting the drives over the highest part of the net.

Dick Sears, using a sixteen-ounce racket, had taken up a mild form of volleying and, like the first English champion, Gore, "calmly tapped first to one side of the court and then to the other"[47–48] to win his first of seven consecutive singles titles before retiring undefeated in national play. As lobbing was then unknown, the harder his despairing adversaries drove the ball against the heavy racket, the harder it went back. Sears and a few others used a poor imitation of the overhead service, but most of the contestants used a plain underhand cut.[49]

Most of the doubles teams were made up on the spur of the moment with the result being little teamwork between partners. Clarence Clark and Fred Taylor of Philadelphia won the doubles title playing one man up and the other back,[50] defeating Dwight and Sears in the third round, 6–2, 6–1, and Newbold and Van Rensselaer in the finals, 6–5, 6–4, 6–5.

A large number of players wore knickerbockers, blazers, belts, cravats, and woolen stockings in their club colors. They all wore full-length shirts, a large majority rolling up their sleeves. The rubber-soled shoes were generally made of white canvas or buckskin, and each player wore a cap or round hat with a rolling brim. The rackets were generally slightly lopsided like the old court tennis bats.[51]

The nets were rather flimsy, not reinforced at the top, and the center strap was made of iron. The contestants played two of three sets until the finals, which were the best of five. No advantage sets were played, and the players changed courts at the end of each set.[52]

The U.S. Championships were initially closed to non-USNLTA members, possibly due to O. E. Woodhouse's win at Staten Island in 1880. In 1881 a Mr. J. J. Cairnes from Ireland, about the tenth player in

Great Britain, had made the trip to Newport to meet the best Americans but had been barred from competing. However, an open tournament was held a few days later to allow Cairnes to face the U.S. players. The issue finally narrowed to Cairnes and Sears, as had been desired, and Cairnes won easily, 4–6, 6–2, 6–1, 6–3, showing the superiority of British players at the time.[53–54]

In 1889 E. G. Meers, who had been ranked among Great Britain's top ten in 1888, reached the semifinal at Newport where he lost to Oliver Campbell in the semifinals.[55] The next non-American threat was Manliffe Goodbody, an Irish player of high rank, in 1894. He beat Fred Hovey (ranked third among U.S. players) after five sets in the third round and Clarence Hobart (ranked second) in the next round (quarters), with a score of 8–6 in the fifth after Hobart pulled out the third and fourth sets. Goodbody took out Larned in the final after the latter was up 2–1 in sets and 4–0 and 5–3 in the fourth.[56] Lefty Bob Wrenn saved the day for the United States by defending his title in the challenge round.

Before the 1897 season opened, the USNLTA issued a challenge to Great Britain, proposing an annual international match (pre–Davis Cup). The English authorities declined this challenge on financial grounds, but a team of British players came over on their own with the American clubs paying a share of their expenses. H. S. Mahoney, W. V. Eaves, and H. A. Nisbet (ranked second, third, and sixteenth, respectively, in Great Britain) played at Longwood, Hoboken, and Chicago. William Larned (ranked second among U.S. players) beat the visitors in all three events. At Newport, J. Parmly Paret beat Goodbody in the second round, and Malcolm Whitman (U.S. no. 8) beat Mahoney in the third round, while Eaves defeated Nisbet in the final. Robert Wrenn (U.S. no. 1) again saved the day by retaining his title in the challenge round over Wilberforce Eaves, 4–6, 8–6, 6–3, 2–6, 6–2.[57] At year's end the top five rankings were, beginning with the top spot, Robert Wrenn, William Larned, Wilberforce Eaves, Harold Nisbet, and Harold Mahoney.

Larned won the first two semifinal sets against Nisbet, and at 5–4 in the third, was twice within a single point of a straight-set victory. Nisbet managed to win the set by a score of 9–7, and the last two by 6–4, 6–4.[58] This was typical of Larned in important matches during his early years. Abroad in 1896, "he was three times within a single point of beating Mahoney, who won the All-England championships a month later, but lost in five exciting sets. At Wimbledon, Larned lost to Herbert Baddeley, after he had won the first two sets and seemed sure of victory."[59] Against

Baddeley, the English press said: "The way in which Larned went to work reminded one of nothing so much as Pim, for probably none else is capable of such clean, hard, and fearless hitting."[60] *Fearless* is the operative word, for nervousness or annoyance marred his concentration in the 1890s. His temperament and concentration improved throughout the 1900s, as will be shown later.[61]

The famous English Doherty brothers entered the 1902 U.S. Championships, Laurie defaulting to Reggie in the semis. Reggie beat Malcolm Whitman in the final but lost to Bill Larned in the challenge round, 4–6, 6–2, 6–4, 8–6. The Dohertys entered again in 1903; Reggie had won the Wimbledon title every year from 1897 through 1900, and Laurie won the title from 1902 through 1906. The Doherty brothers were drawn against each other in the quarters, and Reggie elected to default to his brother. Laurie, losing only two games in the semis, easily defeated William Clothier in the final and displaced Bill Larned in the challenge round to become the first foreigner to win the U.S. singles title. That wouldn't happen again until 1926 when two of the "French Musketeers" decided the final. Rene Lacoste beat Jean Borotra. (The Doherty brothers won the U.S. doubles title in both 1902 and 1903.)

Second and Subsequent Championships

The second championship of 1882 found all the players serving overhand with more or less speed, mostly less, with everyone coming in to volley on a good opening. Both Dwight and Sears had taken up lobbing, which had won the second English championship for Frank Hadow, and hit their volleys with greater pace. Sears had discarded his sixteen-ounce racket for one that weighed fourteen ounces. Sears again won the singles title, and in the doubles contest paired with Dwight. Their lobbing and volleying alongside each other was good enough to beat the one-up-and-other-back formation adopted by most of the teams. Sears would win the doubles title six successive years, and all but one of those (1885 with Joseph Clark) with Dwight, who was abroad at the time. In that second year (1882) the players still changed sides at the end of every set but could also change courts at the end of each odd game, providing the request was made before the toss; otherwise no odd game change was allowed until the deciding odd set.[62] It appears the option was rarely implemented, but around 1901 the odd game side change was stipulated. However, by mutual consent and notification of the umpire before the second game, the players could change sides instead at the end of every set. The deciding set was still an odd game change. It is again doubtful that alternative was ever implemented.

In June 1883 Joseph Clark of Philadelphia beat Dick Sears, the national champion, for the Harvard College championship. Competing in the first U.S. intercollegiate championship, which was held at a lunatic asylum in Hartford, Clark won the singles title and paired with Harvard freshman Howard Taylor to win the doubles. Sears, class of 1883, was unable to attend due to a bad knee. Some of the asylum inmates took pleasure in shagging balls; one of them tossed a ball back to Clark while he was getting ready to serve, hitting him on the back of the head.[63]

The Clark brothers, Clarence and Joseph, went to England in late June of 1883 with the consent of U.S. titlists Dwight and Sears, after beating them in a pair of trial matches, to play the first recorded international match at Wimbledon against the famous Renshaw twins, William and Ernest. British superiority was vindicated as the Renshaws won, 6–4, 8–6, 3–6, 6–1, on July 18 and, 6–3, 6–2, 6–3, on July 23. The Renshaws played two up or two back, the Clark brothers one up and one back. After this experience the Clark brothers adopted the English style of play.[64–65]

James Dwight had defaulted in the 1882 quarters but reached the national 1883 final, losing to Sears, 6–2, 6–0, 9–7, with advantage sets being introduced in the final round. In 1884 the net height at the posts was lowered from four feet to three feet six inches; the champion was barred from the all-comers contest (probably because Dick Sears had won the first three titles without losing a set); and the Bagnall-Wilde draw system was utilized, which brought all the byes into the first round.[66] According to Dick Sears, a new drawing was made after each round prior to the Bagnall-Wilde system whether there had been any byes in the completed round or not,[67] but there is no evidence of this in the matchups.[68]

R. B. Bagnall-Wilde of Bath in 1883 proposed the present system of having all byes in the first round so as to have the number of remaining players be a power of two,[69] and so as not to have three players arriving in the semifinals, as happened in five of the first seven Wimbledons. For example, with fifty-three entries the next power of two below that is thirty-two (2, 4, 8, 16, 32, 64), therefore the first or preliminary round must have twenty-one matches (42 ÷ 2 = 21) and 11 byes (53 – 42 = 11), five at the top and six at the bottom. The system was more or less implemented at the U.S. Championships in 1884 and at Wimbledon in 1885. In those days names were written on slips of paper, carefully folded, and put in a hat (of which there were plenty). They were then drawn one by one and written one below the other; the pairs that were to play together were bracketed.[70] This method sounds quite antiquated in today's computer age.

In the 1884 challenge round Sears finally lost a set to all-comers winner five-foot-four Howard Taylor from Yale, who reached the final on three subsequent occasions (1886–88). Steel points only ⅛ inch long appeared for the first time that year as Dwight and Sears found them commonplace in England.[71] Sears didn't play the 1884 Wimbledon, and Dwight lost in the second round to H. Chipp (7–5 in the fifth). Sears that year also brought out the so-called Lawford stroke, named by the press after Herbert Lawford, the 1884 Wimbledon all-comers winner. Sears had watched and played with Lawford and noted:

> He was a heavily built man who had not taken up the game until he was twenty-six years old. He was not very light on his feet, and certainly not an easy or graceful player. In spite of these handicaps, however, he was one of the greatest players of his time. He seldom came up to the net, but when he did so he generally killed the ball. His usual manner of playing this stroke was to wait until the ball was dropping; his racket was almost perpendicular to the ground with his wrist and hand slightly more forward than the head of his racket, and then hitting the ball with a great deal of force at the same time pulling up on it, he gave it a tremendous over-spin causing it to drop sharply after crossing the net and making it a very difficult stroke to volley successfully.[72]

Sears didn't think that anyone could have exactly copied Lawford and called it a "lifting stroke," which is known today as topspin. In 1885 advantage sets were implemented in all matches, and the Peck and Snyder ball was adopted in place of the Ayres English ball. In 1886 all matches were the best of five sets, but no advantage sets were played in these rounds unless the score reached two sets all.[73] Howard Taylor, finalist that year, and Dr. Dwight had a memorable second round (13–11 fifth set in Taylor's favor). The Peck and Snyder ball was given up and the Ayres ball reintroduced. At the next annual meeting the Ayers ball was again thrown out, and the Wright and Ditson ball was adopted.

There was no consistent following in of the service, as no rests whatever were allowed in the Sears's era. This perhaps led to some of the early players having a more evenly developed all-around game, as it would have been too enervating to continually rush the net in a five-set match between players of about equal ability.[74] And there were no chairs in the backcourt or next to the umpire's pedestal for the players to sit in during the crossover. The rest rule went through many alterations. In 1890 Rule 26 established that "play shall be continuous from the first service till the match be concluded; provided, however, that between all sets after the second set either player is entitled to a rest, which shall not exceed seven minutes."[75] That ruling became problematic in the first Davis Cup with Great Britain ten years later, as will be shown shortly.

After Dick Sears's run of seven, Henry W. Slocum Jr. from Yale won in 1888 against Howard A. Taylor. As it was known in advance that Sears was to default due to physical injury, even Dr. Dwight came out of retirement for a shot at the championship but was defeated by Slocum in the quarters. It was in the final round against Taylor that, as he changed sides at the end of a set, Slocum spied the stern face of his father peering into the court from the last row of spectators as if to say, "When are you going to start work as a lawyer?" Undoubtedly pleased with his son's victory, he was "plainly a little ashamed at having come from New York to Newport to see" Henry play.[76] Slocum noted that "the most beautiful women of the country graced the tournament with their presence."[77–78] That may have been true, but they, with their constant chatting and twirling, varicolored parasols, "were not there for the love of the game, and served only to make a moving background which was trying to the players."[79]

After working hard at his profession, Slocum returned to Newport in 1889 to successfully defend his title against a dashing left-handed player, Quincy A. Shaw. This necessitated another trip in 1890, and Slocum was beaten by a nineteen-year-old Columbia student from Brooklyn, Oliver S. Campbell, the youngest U.S. men's singles winner for a century, before Pete Sampras, a younger nineteen, won the title in 1990.[80] A net-storming volleyer, Campbell defeated Clarence Hobart, 2–6, 7–5, 7–9, 6–1, 6–2, for the 1891 title and Fred Hovey, 7–5, 3–6, 6–3, 6–1, for the 1892 title, making it three straight before his retirement. Campbell also won the doubles title three times: in 1888 with Valentine G. Hall and in 1891 and 1892 with Robert P. Huntington, the 1889 Yale intercollegiate champion.

With Oliver Campbell not defending in 1893, Robert D. Wrenn beat S. T. Chase in one semifinal, while Fred Hovey beat Clarence Hobart in the other. That week's issue of *Harper's Weekly* said, "No one for a moment doubted the superiority of these two players [Hobart and Hovey] over those remaining in the tournament."[81] Hobart won the all-comers in 1891, and Hovey won it in 1892, both later falling victim to Campbell. Wrenn's best previous showing was as an 1892 semifinalist. Hovey's memory of that final match was "that of an unending succession of steeple-high lobs from every corner of the court—smash after smash of mine coming back to me from all conceivable recoveries until my ability to put them away wore down. Wrenn's game that day was purely defensive, not the scoring lob but simply the high, position-saving stroke. How many miles he ran, how many lobs I tried to kill, no one knows."[82] Wrenn won, 6–4, 3–6, 6–4, 6–4, the first left-hander to do so. He would win three more times—in 1894 over Manliffe Goodbody from Great Britain, an 1893 Wimbledon quarterfinalist to champion Joshua Pim; in 1896 over Hovey; and in 1897 over Wilberforce Eaves from Great Britain.

Hovey beat Wrenn in 1895. Playing through the tournament that year Hovey beat C. B. Neel and William A. Larned, who forced the net consistently and had come to welcome the net charge of an opponent. Instead of taking the net against Wrenn as in 1893, Hovey stayed back with every confidence he could pass Wrenn, thus depriving the latter of his old attack, the steeple lob.[83]

Malcolm Whitman, 1896 Harvard intercollegiate champion and quarterfinalist in the 1896 and 1897 U.S. Championships, became convinced during 1898 that the key position was a volleying position, which he implemented successfully as the season progressed. In a quarterfinal round at Newport, his philosophy backfired on a soggy court against Clarence Budlong, a backcourt player with accurate ground strokes. The first set was cautiously played in the backcourt, both players slipping and sliding, and Whitman eventually winning, 11–9. As he had always beaten Budlong by forcing the net and also perhaps because he was a little overanxious, Whitman followed his serves and ground strokes in but, even with spikes, kept slipping near the service line. Budlong passed him over and over again, winning the next two sets. Whitman then abandoned his pet position and won the next two sets on the low-bounding muddy balls from the backcourt, illustrating the necessity of developing an all-court game. The score was 11–9, 4–6, 4–6, 6–2, 8–6.[84]

In the final, Whitman played lefty Dwight Davis, famous for the cup that subsequently bore his name. Davis took the ball near the top of the bound with a big, sweeping topspin stroke, making the ball drop suddenly so that it was hard to volley. Davis had a hot hand in the first set overcoming a 3–0 deficit with six straight games. As Whitman pressed forward to the volleying position, Davis began to hurry "his strokes just a little and they began to go just out instead of just in."[85] Whitman won the last three sets easily, 3–6, 6–2, 6–2, 6–1.

In 1899, Whitman, irritated at having to wait around for the all-comers winner, J. Parmly Paret, stayed back as usual to try out his ground strokes. He won the first two sets so easily he abandoned the volleying position entirely. Because the formula in a losing situation is to change tactics, Paret forced the net on every opportunity in the third set, caught Whitman off guard, and won the set. Having remained back so long, Whitman had lost his touch by the time he did go back to the net, but fortunately he recovered sufficient control to win a close fourth set and the match, 6–1, 6–2, 3–6, 7–5.[86]

As with Henry Slocum in 1888, Whitman had to first win a fight with his father, who wanted him to concentrate on law school (Harvard). Bill Larned was the 1900 all-comers winner. The Larned of the 1890s was a go-for-broke player and was unbeatable when his game was on. Whitman's change of pace game disturbed Larned, though, and except in the second set, when Larned's accuracy, grace, and power were invincible, Whitman won his third successive title, 6–4, 1–6, 6–2, 6–2, and the trophy for keeps.[87] The following year, when Larned learned to sacrifice brilliancy for safety on difficult shots, he became much more successful.

Davis Cup

In 1900 the first Davis Cup, initially titled the International Lawn Tennis Challenge, was played. The 1899 national champions in singles and doubles (Malcolm Whitman, Holcombe Ward, and Dwight Davis) and the national interscholastic champion Beals Wright (accompanied by his father George Wright, an American baseball pioneer and one of the principals of the famous sporting goods firm Wright and Ditson) played a series of exhibition matches on the Pacific Coast. So great was the feeling of good will that Dwight Davis of St. Louis, upon returning to Boston, consulted with Dr. James Dwight, then President of the USNLTA and former five-time national doubles champion with Dick Sears, about the idea of presenting a trophy to promote international team matches. Dr. Dwight enthusiastically approved the plan and after much correspondence with the English tennis authorities, the Davis Cup was born, deriving its name from the fact that Dwight Davis had donated a very handsome cup to represent the International championship.[88]

In 1900 Arthur W. Gore, Ernest D. Black, and H. Roper Barrett represented the British Isles in the first international matches played at the Longwood Cricket Club. In that inaugural match the United States won 3–0: Dwight Davis defeated Ernest Black, Malcolm Whitman won from Arthur Gore, and Davis and Holcombe Ward defeated Black and Barrett in doubles. According to Whitman, Gore had a formidable forehand but a weak backhand, allowing the former to exploit the weakest link with controlled returns to easily win in straight sets, 6–1, 6–3, 6–1.[89] It was in these matches that the "American Twist" service so perplexed the British that it was analyzed to death in English periodicals. The official English magazine *Lawn Tennis* reported:

> On absolutely reliable authority we are able to state that the service of the Americans, especially of Davis and Whitman, took our players completely by surprise. It was quite unlike anything which they had ever seen or dreamed of, notwithstanding that they knew well that Davis, Whitman, and Ward had made a specialty of the service, and were therefore on their guard. The main points about the service are its screw, spin, and pace. The ball often breaks a yard, and even when it is reached with the racket, the spin on it is so great that it is difficult to make a good return. Gore failed even to touch a great many of Whitman's services. Our players all admit that they would not believe it possible that any service could be invented which they could not return with a certain amount of force, but that the American service was impossible.[90]

The *Field*, in October 1900, said, "[I]t appears that the pace of these services is very great, that they bound to a height of some four feet from the ground, and that the ball becomes egg-shaped, breaks as much as a yard, and is still egg-shaped and spinning when the return stroke has to be made."[91]

In today's parlance for a right-hander, the ball is tossed to the left of the head, the racket head comes from below, meets the ball on the lower left surface, hits up and over it with a distinct wrist "kick," and ends on the right of the body. The service curves from right to left in the air but reverses on the bounce and goes from left to right or to an opponent's backhand.

The British players were not at all pleased with the Davis Cup for a variety of other reasons. Roper Barrett severely criticized the conditions at Longwood. "The ground was abominable." The grass was about twice as long as the longest grass on an English court. "The net was a disgrace to civilized lawn tennis, held up by guy ropes which were continually sagging, giving way as much as two or three inches every few games and frequently requiring adjustment."[92] Arthur Gore didn't like the American system of permitting a seven-minute rest after the second and subsequent sets.[93] In 1901 a seven-minute rest was allowed after the third set only for men and second set for women. By 1920 the rest was ten minutes. Barrett criticized the balls, which were softer and less resilient than those to which the British were accustomed. "The Americans' twisting serves," according to Barrett, "made these squashy tennis balls egg-shaped as they came over the net."[94] However, as Henry Slocum, the first U.S. champion after Sears, wrote in 1890 that "the most beautiful women of the country graced the tournament" at Newport,[95] Barrett ten years later conceded that the female spectators at Longwood were "not at all unpleasant to gaze upon."[96–97]

In 1902 the British challenged again and sent the formidable Doherty Brothers, Reggie and Laurie, and Dr. Joshua Pim to the colonies. Pim had won Wimbledon in 1893 and 1894, Reggie Doherty four consecutive years from 1897 through 1900; A. W. Gore won in 1901 and Laurie Doherty in 1902. Playing for the United States were Malcolm Whitman and William Larned in singles and Dwight Davis and Holcombe Ward in doubles. As Whitman's bar exams were to come shortly before the matches, his father was more averse than ever to his playing. But the pressure to represent the country prevailed, and Whitman played.

The matches were held August 6–8, 1902, at the Crescent Athletic Club in Brooklyn. Whitman played cautiously and very steadily against Pim, winning the first two sets before the match was stopped on account of rain. Whitman had a sleepless night, and all cramped up the next morning, Whitman lost the third set as easily as he had won the first two. His timing came back at the close of that set, both offensively and defensively, and he bageled Pim for the match. The lopsided score was 6–1, 6–1, 1–6, 6–0.

Whitman played Reggie Doherty in the afternoon and recalled varying speed and depth of serve, making it break into Doherty's body as much as possible and using his reverse serve as a change, especially in the deuce court. Doherty's heavily topped serve in the far corner of the advantage court broke high to Whitman's backhand. Since Doherty could easily volley a hard return about two feet above the ground on his net approach, Whitman was able to break a few of Doherty's serves by blocking the ball back with less pace, requiring Doherty to either volley lower to the ground or half-volley, giving Whitman time to get into an offensive position.[98] Whitman won, 6–1, 7–5, 6–4. Larned defeated Pim, 6–3, 6–2, 6–3, giving the United States the tie by 3–2. Reggie Doherty beat Larned in five sets, and the Doherty brothers beat Davis and Ward in four sets. The United States would not win the Davis Cup again until 1913 when "the California Comet" Maurice McLoughlin, Dick Williams, and Harold Hackett combined forces at Wimbledon.

Bill Larned

William A. Larned from Summit, New Jersey, duplicated Dick Sears's feat of winning seven U.S. Championships, not successively but over a career that spanned twenty-one years. Starting in 1891 he reached the third round. In 1892 he was an all-comers finalist and won the intercollegiate title for Cornell. A quarterfinalist in 1893, he reached the finals in the next three years; however, his aggressive style was too erratic to carry him to the pinnacle until 1901.

Larned refused to compromise with safety. He went after every shot and was unbeatable when on his game. There were times in those early years when he would easily win the first two sets of a five-setter, only to lose the match by going for winners off both wings with little margin for error. Larned was best known for his ground strokes, particularly his backhand, which he hit flat or with some top, and no player of Larned's day "had the variety, hid the direction so well, nor cut the lines as closely as he did."[99]

Larned was also very deadly on the forehand, which he hit with oppressive topspin. His direction, depth, speed, drop, and accuracy were equal to the best, but none were as deadly on the backhand. Many of the period's net-rushers were ruined by Larned's brilliant passing ability. An aggressive baseliner, Larned was nevertheless an accomplished volleyer and was much better in that department than on overheads. He put away short lobs effectively, though deep lobbing sometimes got him into trouble. He had a powerful service with a good deal of spin and accuracy.[100]

Like Tilden who also won seven U.S. Championships in the 1920s, six in a row, Larned was a late achiever, winning his 1901 title at age twenty-eight over Beals Wright. After beating Reggie Doherty in 1902, he wouldn't win again until 1907. His last title, ending a five-year string, was in 1911, the end of the challenge round, making him the oldest male singles champ at thirty-eight. He was ranked in the U.S. top ten nineteen times, starting with a ranking of sixth in 1892. He was eight times no. 1, five times no. 2, and four times no. 3. His name was missing from the elite list only once, in 1898, because he was away in the Spanish American War with Roosevelt's Rough Riders. Nineteen years was a record held for eight decades until it was topped by Jimmy Connors.[101]

Larned was a member of five Davis Cup teams. A winner in 1902, he lost in 1903 to Laurie Doherty in five sets, but in 1908, '09, and '11 he won all six matches against British Davis Cup opponents in the final, the round before the challenge round, the holders being the Australasians. Larned played only one of those matches, losing to Rodney Heath in 1911.

While serving in the 1898 war, Larned caught rheumatism in Cuba. His "health declined through the 1920s and he relinquished his New York Stock Exchange seat in 1922. That year he also formed the Dayton Steel Racquet Company to manufacture a steel tennis racket that he designed."[102] Partially paralyzed by spinal meningitis and unable to do any of the activities he loved most, he became depressed. On the evening of December 15, 1926, inside the private chambers of the exclusive Knickerbocker Club in Manhattan, the fifty-three-year-old Larned raised a .45 caliber pistol to his head and committed suicide.[103]

Maurice McLoughlin

When Larned wasn't winning in that four-year lapse between 1903 and 1906, Laurie Doherty, the younger of the Doherty brothers and a Wimbledon titlist for five successive years between 1902 and 1906, beat Larned in 1903; Holcombe Ward beat William Clothier in 1904; Beals Wright, son of sportsman George Wright, beat Ward in 1905; and Clothier beat Wright in 1906.

From 1912 on, the challenge round was abolished, and that year the first male Californian to win the U.S. Championships was Maurice McLoughlin (nicknamed Red or the California Comet). But it wasn't, however, an instantaneous climb to the pinnacle, and as with anything worth succeeding at, a learning curve and a lot of hard work were required. This one took four tries. As the opening statement in his Hall of Fame write-up states: "He came out of the West with a cannonball service, spectacular volleys and overhead smashes. He created great excitement in the East and abroad at Wimbledon with the violence of his attack. And more than anything else, [he] opened the eyes of the public to tennis as a demanding game of speed, endurance and skill."[104]

The hard courts of California produced a livelier, faster ball, and McLoughlin brought a certain measure of control to his speed. His philosophy simplistically put was to shorten points by having his opponents "play up" so he could "hit down." Bombing the service and following it to the net was how he got the job done. The Californians brought a faster pace to the court, quickly adapting to the grass.[105]

Californians Maurice McLoughlin, Melville Long, Thomas Bundy, two other men and Hazel Hotchkiss, first came east in 1909 to compete. When McLoughlin and Long met in the fourth round of the 1909 U.S. Championships, the pair was assigned center court as a gesture of courtesy. Maurice well remembered that the gallery was made up largely "of society people who plainly used the occasion as a social medium" and that the lack of interest and attention paid to tennis, especially by the fashionable front row occupants, was clearly evident. "There was always a continuous buzzing and gossiping during the rallies," he recalled with annoyance.[106] Newport obviously was not today's New York crowd, which gets involved. He also noted though, that as the match progressed, the "buzzing" subsided, and toward the end, "you could have heard a pin drop."[107] McLoughlin won that five-setter, 7–5, 6–2, 5–7, 2–6, 10–8. He reached the final, losing to William Clothier, who in turn lost to William Larned.

The following year McLoughlin lost to Beals Wright in the quarters while his subsequent doubles partner from Los Angeles, Tom Bundy, beat Wright in the final but lost to Larned in a five-set challenge round. McLoughlin beat Beals Wright in the 1911 final, but Larned captured his seventh and last—and fifth straight—championship in straight sets. Winning a major championship required more than a serve and volley. Reflecting, McLoughlin said, "What a lesson I did receive in how well the game could be played!"[108]

On the first day of the 1913 Davis Cup challenge round at Wimbledon on July 25, England and the United States split two singles matches. James Parke beat "Big Red" McLoughlin 7–5 in the fifth set, and Dick Williams beat Charles Dixon, also 7–5 in the fifth. The next day McLoughlin and Harold Hackett played Herbert Roper Barrett and Dixon. With the score two sets to one and 5–4 against the United States, McLoughlin serving at 30–40, match point for England, the Comet stepped up and served. There was a crackling noise as the linesman called fault: the racket had broken. McLoughlin slowly walked to the umpire's chair to retrieve a new racket, took a few swings through the air, and served a second ball ace. A few moments later, with England again at match point, the U.S. team put up a short lob, which was smashed between Hackett's feet. By some miracle his racket was there to produce a perfect lob to again deuce the score.[109]

The United States won that set 7–5 and the fifth set 6–4 for the match. Dick Williams was sitting with Wallace Johnson and Bob Wrenn and recalled "that during the last set Bob Wrenn chewed a perfectly good straw hat to pieces."[110] The United States needed one more win to take the Cup, and that was provided by McLoughlin over Dixon in straight sets, securing the third U.S. Davis Cup win and first since 1902.

Perhaps the pinnacle of his career was the 1914 Davis Cup challenge round at the West Side Tennis Club, August 13–15, against Australasia (Australia and New Zealand). Despite losing the tie by 3–2, McLoughlin defeated Tony Wilding in four sets and Norman Brookes in straight sets after an historic 17–15 first set, the most games ever played in a Davis Cup challenge round, tied by Bill Tilden and Dick Williams against Jim Anderson and John Hawkes of Australasia in 1923. Even though McLoughlin lost to Williams on September 1 in the U.S. final, he was given the top U.S. ranking.

Dick Williams

R. Norris "Dick" Williams won the 1914 and 1916 U.S. Championships over Californians Maurice McLoughlin and William Johnston, respectively. Williams, a go-for-broke player much like Bill Larned, was, according to his mixed doubles partner, Mary K. Browne, "at least ten years ahead of his time, for he was taking the ball on the rise, the method of stroking which the French perfected."[111] Henri Cochet was frequently a ball boy for Williams at Lyons and later said that he modeled his game after him, playing mid-court and taking the ball on the rise.[112]

Against McLoughlin, Williams (like Andre Agassi of the 1990s and early 2000s, arguably the best service returner in the history of tennis) stood about two feet inside the baseline to receive (and even farther on Red's twist service) and either hit the ball past him or at his feet when he came in. Williams also got to the net as soon as possible without waiting in the backcourt for an opportunity. "My game," he said, "was a drive for a line and, if at all possible, a follow in to half-volley from the service line or volley from the net."[113] Perhaps that aggressive all-or-nothing attitude reflected the new lease on life he had received after spending many hours in the freezing Atlantic as he watched so many around him, including his father, die after the RMS *Titanic* went down and having the RMS *Carpathian* doctor suggest amputating his legs.

Williams often served to McLoughlin's weaker wing, his backhand. On the other hand, serving to Red's strength in the deuce court left an opening on his backhand if Dick could get his racket on the return. He followed his serve in as far as possible every time, usually making the first return on a half-volley or volley.[114] Williams successfully applied these tactics to win the match, 6–3, 8–6, 10–8.

Against Billy Johnston in 1916, Williams used very little American twist, except on a second serve to keep it in. He usually served to Bill's forehand because in those days he had a relatively predictable return to the right court. As with McLoughlin, Williams "went in on almost every serve and, catching the ball on the service line, either on the volley or half-volley, tried to send it down the line or angle it off short."[115] Williams's fast serve didn't give him time to get beyond the service line on the reply, and he developed a good volley and half-volley game off both wings from that position.

Johnston usually served down the center. His serve was fast—but not fast enough for Williams to pulverize the ball using the speed of the server. With the 120 to 140 mph serves in today's game, it's easier to apply that speed to the return, a lesson learned nine to ten decades ago. Williams returned Johnston's serve down the line or sharply crosscourt and tried to get in as quickly as possible.[116] Williams won in five sets, 4–6, 6–4, 0–6, 6–2, 6–4.

Bill Johnston

Billy Johnston learned tennis in early 1906 at age eleven on the public courts in Golden Gate Park. The schools were temporarily closed after the great earthquake and fire of April 18. He picked up the California or Western grip on the hard cement courts, where the bound was high and partly because of his size (five foot eight and a half and 125 pounds at maturity), necessarily stood in to meet the ball on the rise. On the backhand Johnston hit with the same face of the racket as on the forehand, very unusual for a top player, but he shifted the grip about a quarter turn. "This grip produced a sliced drive rather than a topped drive," he said, "and was a natural grip for volleying either high or low balls with a fast slice."[117]

He served with a slice, not particularly severe but well controlled, and didn't necessarily charge the net. To Billy it depended on his opponent and the circumstances and how he served to do it. When he did go to the net, he didn't go in as far as fellow Californians McLoughlin and Lin Murray, as he felt vulnerable to the lob.

In receiving he stood near the baseline so as to return the ball at shoulder height, which the little man could hammer with his forehand. His topped forehand drive "was one of the most famous and effective shots in tennis history. No other player executed it as well as he did, taking the ball shoulder high and leaping off the ground on his follow-through."[118] He could return both forehand and backhand with great depth, and a net rusher would get the ball at his feet. His record speaks for itself, as he won two U.S. singles titles and was runner-up six other times, five of those to Tilden, and won the U.S. doubles title three times and the mixed once. He and Tilden brought the Davis Cup home in 1920 and kept it for seven years. He had as much fight as anyone and was the favorite of galleries.

Against Williams in the 1915 Forest Hills inaugural semifinal, Johnston served directly at his body and rarely followed his service to the net against him. In that match Johnston lost the first set after a big lead, split the next two, played more steadily in the fourth, and cut loose with everything in the fifth to win, 5–7, 6–4, 5–7, 6–2, 6–2.[119]

In the final against McLoughlin, Johnston played everything possible to his backhand, as Williams had done in 1914, and got to the net to beat McLoughlin to the punch. Johnston missed his shots by inches in the first set but improved appreciably in the second. In the third set Johnston was steadier and in the fourth pounded out thirty-two placements to win the title, 1–6, 6–0, 7–5, 10–8.[120]

In the U.S. Navy during World War I, Johnston didn't participate in 1917 and 1918 when R. Lindley Murray won the U.S. Championships but came back to defeat "Big Bill" Tilden in the 1919 final using the center theory in getting to the net and winning all his services. Johnston stood about on the baseline to receive Tilden's booming services, and, as he seldom came to the net, Johnston drove many of Tilden's serves down the center and took the net himself to win the match, 6–4, 6–4, 6–3.[121]

Tilden said that Johnston "showed not only the tennis world but my own pigheaded self what a vulnerable backhand I had."[122] As a result Tilden went indoors that winter in East Providence, Rhode Island, to hone that stroke to perfection and emerged in 1920 as the superman of the decade, winning both Wimbledon and the U.S. title, the latter against Johnston in a memorable five-set battle interrupted by a rain delay and a plane crash behind the crowded stand.

3
Women's Tennis

Women's tennis, like many other facets of women's life, was handicapped from the very beginning. This was still a time when women of wealth were breaking out of the stifling Victorian roles of wife and mother and taking up more active lives, yet the emphasis on fashion made them baubles on the tennis court. The first English men's championship was in 1877, the women's seven years later in 1884. In the United States the men's singles and doubles championships began in 1881 at Newport in late August; the women's singles contests began in 1887, doubles in 1889, and mixed in 1892, all at the Philadelphia Cricket Club in June.

Major Wingfield's first pamphlet showed mixed doubles being played on the hourglass court for which he applied for a patent in February of 1874. Wingfield shrewdly saw an opportunity to market a game that had "the advantage that it [might] be played in the open air in any weather by people of any age and of both sexes."[1] He saw the need for an outdoor game that would provide more exercise than croquet, "which of late years has monopolized the attention of the public."[2] And, remember, it was a woman, Mary Outerbridge, "the Mother of American Tennis," who first brought a boxed set of *sphairistike* back to the United States also in 1874 for which she was inducted into the International Tennis Hall of Fame in 1981.

When women sought to play tennis in a public tournament, the All England Club would have none of it. "For a game imposing so much strain on the human brain as well as on the body, a woman was simply too weak. As to the brains required in the process, hardly any woman would be capable of playing a game which meant very hard work even for a man."[3] As far as counting was concerned, one only needed to tell time, and regarding strength, from 1891 to 1901 women played the best of five sets in the U.S. Championships.

But a woman's biggest burden, once she was permitted to play competitively, was her tennis outfit. Gillmeister noted that "the fashionable lady wore the costume which the conventions of her time prescribed for her everyday routine: long skirts which reached the ground; several starched petticoats underneath and the obligatory corset tightly laced. All this was given additional support by a girdle adorned by a silver clasp; it terminated in a stiff whalebone collar around which a necktie was slung. No dress was without long sleeves. An extravagant broad-brimmed felt hat dominated the lady's head, and a sturdy heeled, elegant boot was considered a must."[4]

When the right was subsequently granted to the women to compete in public tournaments, they had to play at a different place or time. In 1879 the first Irish ladies' championships took place on one of the club's secluded courts.[5] At Wimbledon in 1884 "the ladies were admitted to the courts only after the gentlemen had finished their singles championship."[6] In 1887 the women finally began to play along with the men.

"From the start mixed doubles was regarded, by men, as … bordering, in some cases, on cruel and unusual punishment," except, of course, if one had an attractive enough partner for social tennis. In his 1893 edition of *Practical Lawn Tennis*, even Dr. James Dwight, the "Founding Father of American Tennis," remarked that "Ladies and Gentlemen's Doubles is not a game that I can speak of with much respect."[7]

Maud Watson was nineteen when she beat her sister Lilian, 6–8, 6–3, 6–3 to become the first All England champion in 1884. When the challenge round was instituted in 1886, she was toppled by Blanche Bingley, whom she had beaten in the 1885 final.

Lottie Dod

A fifteen-year-old "Lottie" Dod, the youngest of major champions, blew away the field in 1887 and successfully defended in 1888. In those two years she also won the intercollegiate singles and the Irish national singles titles. She won the British ladies golf championship in 1904 and was an Olympic silver medalist at archery in 1908.[8] Lottie returned to Wimbledon to win three successive titles, her final opponent being Blanche

Bingley-Hillyard each time, the latter winning in 1894 when Lottie Dod didn't compete.

Lottie was an outspoken critic of ladies' attire: "[F]or how can they ever hope to play a sound game when their dresses impede the free movement of every limb? In many cases their very breathing is rendered difficult. A suitable dress is sorely needed, and hearty indeed would be the thanks of puzzled lady players to the individual who invented an easy and pretty costume."[9]

Regarding a variety of derogatory remarks about the ladies' game, Lottie Dod sarcastically wrote in 1890: "Most of these suggestions were made through the medium of the *Field* newspaper, and the editor of that journal was thus for a time made the ruler of the game, as well as an arbiter of fashion, credited with the ability to regulate not only the weight of a lady's racket, but also the length of her skirt. For the moment, in fact, he was invested with the prerogative of an irresponsible despot."[10]

Lottie also deprecated the pat-ball game of her own sex. "Ladies should learn to run, and run their hardest, too, not merely stride. They would find (if they tried) that many a ball, seemingly out of reach, could be returned with ease; but instead of running hard they go a few steps and exclaim: 'Oh! I can't,' and stop."[11]

Lottie Dod was way ahead of her time in advocating a good style at the beginning: allowing no stiffness of arm or elbow; practicing against a wall to learn a stroke; keeping one's eye on the ball; avoiding running around the backhand to take the ball forehanded but instead practicing the former even though one risked losing points; presenting the body sideways to the ball, front foot forward, to allow a full and easy swing; practicing backhand strokes both down the line and crosscourt; changing the grip of one's racket both for forehand and backhand strokes. "When practicable, the ball should be taken with the head of the racket above the wrist."[12] These and many other sound advice elements are still being taught more than a century later. Does this suggest a woman's mind was incapable of mastering the game's counting method?

American Championships

As the first American championships were held at the Philadelphia Cricket Club, it was natural that the early winners were from its environs. At age twelve, Ellen Hansell and her cousins were driven by horse and buggy to the beautiful home of John Wanamaker in Jenkintown, near

Philadelphia. About 1882 he had brought from England a set of bats, balls, and a net. The kids leveled off a place for the court with a lawn mower, leaving the grass uncut where the lines ran, carved tree branches for net poles between which was stretched a clothesline. The bats were small, and the balls were uncovered, hard, black rubber.[13]

The big four of Philadelphia were Bertha Townsend, Margie Ballard, Louise Allderdice, and Ellen Hansell, the latter becoming the first U.S. champion in 1887 at age seventeen. They served with "a low, swift sidearm stroke, the twist making [the ball] skim along the turf with almost no bounce." The underhand lob was not used, and their rackets were roughly straight across at the top. The gallery, as Ellen recalled, was an "openly prejudiced crowd standing within two feet of the court lines, calling out hurrahs of applause, plus groans of disappointment" and some coaching suggestions. It was necessary to "grip our overdraped voluminous skirt with our left hand to give us a bit more 'limb' freedom when dashing to make a swift, snappy stroke," Ellen wrote.[14]

Ellen's Philadelphia friend Bertha Townsend defeated her in the 1888 challenge round and again won the title in 1889. In 1890 the attractive Roosevelt sisters, Ellen and Grace, first cousins of Franklin D. Roosevelt, were taken to and from Albany by their father. Ellen Roosevelt defeated Bertha for the singles title, and the sisters paired to win the ladies' doubles title that second year.

Starting in 1891 the women played best of five sets in the challenge round. That year Mabel Cahill, an Irish lady, beat Ellen Roosevelt, 6–4, 6–1, 4–6, 6–3. Elizabeth Moore, runner-up in 1892, '97, 1902, '04, and '06, won the singles title in 1896, 1901, '03, and '05. Recalling the 1892 championship, Moore said the girls were much cooler in their white "lawn dresses with leg-of-mutton sleeves, sailor hats, and ornamental tennis shoes." The temperature was ninety-seven degrees in the shade, and Moore played three matches that first afternoon.[15] Miss Cahill defeated Miss Moore for her second title, 5–7, 6–3, 6–4, 4–6, 6–2.

Beginning in 1894 the women were required to play best of five sets in both the final and challenge rounds. Helen Hellwig (challenger) beat Aline Terry (holder) in another five-set battle. Juliette Atkinson won over Hellwig in 1895, and Moore won her first title in 1896 in four sets over Atkinson, "a mite of a Brooklyn girl" who was good at several sports.[16]

Atkinson won two more titles, beating Moore in 1897 in five sets and Marion Jones from California in 1898, 7–5 in the fifth. From 1898 to 1900 Elizabeth Moore was out of championship tennis due to illness. Marion

Jones won in 1899 over Maud Banks, with Juliette Atkinson defaulting, while Myrtle McAteer easily defeated Edith Parker in 1900, with Marion Jones defaulting. Returning in 1901 Moore had a successful but tough go, defeating Miss Atkinson in a semifinal, 6–2, 9–7, and 1899 champion Marion Jones in the all-comers after dropping the first two sets and staving off a match point in the third, 4–6, 1–6, 9–7, 9–7, 6–3. She later remarked that after pulling "out the fourth set, Miss Jones didn't have much strength left."[17] I wonder why.

The next day Elizabeth Moore had to play 1900 champion Myrtle McAteer in the challenge round. McAteer had a well-directed slice, which was difficult to handle, but Moore was successful in covering court and volleying. Moore won another five-setter, 6–4, 3–6, 7–5, 2–6, 6–2. As a result of that match the tournament committee decided that those dainty and helpless females shouldn't be subjected to five-set marathons and reduced the 1902 and all subsequent championships to the best of three sets. Miss Moore retorted that it was "to considerable expressed dissatisfaction of the leading women players, including myself."[18] None of the modern lady champions seems to have expressed a desire to return to the three-out-of-five format.

In 1904 seventeen-year-old May Sutton of California gave everyone a lesson, including Miss Moore in the challenge round, 6–1, 6–2. Moore recalled: "Her California drive took such weird drops and bounds that none of us could handle it. And what seemed still more disconcerting, she would walk into the middle of the court and use that same California drive with which to volley balls from along the service line."[19]

Maud Barger-Wallach from New York, a very late bloomer, took up tennis at about age thirty. She had a painting studio on the outskirts of Newport, which Maud abandoned to play tennis with the ranking players who came to the Casino. She entered her first U.S. Championships tournament in Philadelphia in 1906. "With poor form and but little variety of strokes, success depended upon determination and accuracy," she later recalled. "My forehand was not powerful but steady. I struggled to keep the ball in play until I could work my opponent out of position and win a well-angled shot. Also, deep lobbing saved me in many pinches."[20]

With that steady forehand, it was grit and determination that carried her to the 1906 final, beaten by Helen Homans, 6–4, 6–3. With "an acute attack of cramps" Maud lost in a 1907 early round to Carrie Neely, who lost to Evelyn Sears in the all-comers.[21] In 1908 Maud beat Edith Rotch in the semis, Marie Wagner in the all-comers, 4–6, 6–1, 6–3, and lefty

Evelyn Sears in the challenge round, 6–3, 1–6, 6–3, at age thirty-eight. Molla Bjurstedt-Mallory took away her old-age record by winning in 1926 at forty-two.[22]

Hazel Hotchkiss

The year 1909 was the changing of the guard in women's tennis, dominated by Californians Hazel Hotchkiss from Berkeley and Mary Browne from Ventura County. Fifteen-year-old Hazel recalled first seeing two of the Sutton sisters—a three-month-older May and eighteen-year-old Florence, play at the Hotel San Rafael in 1902. "The rallies seemed endless, so accurate were the sisters." Soon afterward she watched Sam and Sumner Hardy play doubles. "Aside from their coordination as a team, which had enabled them to win the Pacific Coast doubles title five times" during the 1890s, Hazel was fascinated by "the speed of their rallies and their excellent volleying."[23]

Because of that impression and the fact that Hazel took up the game in her backyard where the surface was uneven, she began hitting the ball before it bounced and moved to the forecourt at every opportunity, becoming one of the first women to use the volley. As the only court in Berkeley was on the University of California campus, where girls were prohibited from playing after 8:00 a.m., she and her brothers started playing at 6:00 a.m.[24]

A few months later in December 1902, Hazel entered a girls' tournament at Golden Gate Park. Beaten by Miss Varney in singles, she paired with Miss Ratcliffe, whom she met on the train going to the Park, to win the doubles. Hazel had plenty of competition from three of her four brothers. Homer and Marius were Bay County doubles champions; Marius was interscholastic champion; and Miller, the oldest, played frequently.[25]

Hazel's first meeting with one of the Suttons was in 1903 against Violet, which she lost. In 1904 she defeated Ethel, who was by then Mrs. B. O. Bruce, 7–5, 6–0. She later defeated Florence Sutton, but it was not until the 1909 Ojai Valley tournament in April, shortly before she came east, that she was able to defeat May Sutton.[26] Hazel again beat May Sutton, 2–6, 6–4, 6–0, at the first interscholastic tournament held on Stanford University's asphalt courts in April of 1910.

When Nat Niles, Irving Wright (brother of 1905 U.S. singles champion Beals Wright), Wallace Johnson, and sportsman George Wright (father of Beals and Irving) visited California to extol the thrill of grass court play in

1908, Mr. Wright urged Hazel's parents to allow her to enter the national championships at Philadelphia. As a result, she and her father were on their way east a year later. "In those early years," she wrote, "the spectators were quite informal, sitting around the club house veranda chatting, while the contests were in progress on the courts close by."[27] Hazel had a three-setter with Louise Hammond in the final, 6–8, 6–1, 6–4, and beat Maud Barger-Wallach in the challenge round with the loss of a single game. Hazel also won the doubles with Edith Rotch and the mixed with Wallace Johnson.

After duplicating the hat trick in 1910, defeating Louise Hammond in the singles, 6–4, 6–2, and again in 1911, defeating fellow Californian Florence Sutton in a tough three-setter, 8–10, 6–1, 9–7, Hazel was allowed to remain in the East as a graduation present.[28]

In the final of the 1911 International tournament at Niagara-on-the-Lake, Ontario, national champion Hazel Hotchkiss pulled off the most amazing comeback of her career against 1907 Wimbledon champion May Sutton. After losing the first set at love, scoring only eight points, five of those on May's errors, and down 5–1 in the second, Hazel, playing the greatest tennis of her career, won twelve straight games, the first six with the loss of but six points. The final score was 0–6, 7–5, 6–0.[29]

Hazel married George Wightman of Boston in February 1912, and after only a few weeks' practice nearly two years later, she defeated then national champion Mary K. Browne, 6–3, 6–0, in the 1913 Longwood tournament. [30] Having to juggle tennis with birthing and raising five children, she responded to a challenge from her father to win after becoming a mother, a U.S. first. She lost to Molla Bjurstedt in the 1915 final, 4–6, 6–2, 6–0, but won the ladies' doubles and mixed titles. Bjurstedt was to win a record eight U.S. singles titles, her first in 1915, but in 1919 she lost to Marion Zinderstein in the semis. The diminutive 125-pound, five-foot, thirty-two-year-old Hazel reappeared that year to beat Zinderstein in the final, 6–1, 6–2, the year the challenge round was abolished for women.[31]

In addition to her four singles titles, she won the doubles seven times and the mixed six times. In 1924 she paired with one protégé, Helen Wills, to win the Wimbledon doubles, U.S. doubles, and Olympic doubles titles. Hazel won a second Olympic gold in 1924 with Dick Williams in mixed and paired with another protégé Sarah Palfrey to win the U.S. indoor doubles from 1928 through 1931, giving her a U.S. indoor total of ten doubles, two singles, and five mixed titles. Wightman earned the last of her record thirty-three U.S. titles in 1943 as she, at age fifty-six, and Pauline Betz won the U.S. indoor doubles championship.[32]

Wightman, known as "Lady Tennis," was instrumental in organizing the Wightman Cup between British and American women, first held in 1923. Hazel played five years on the U.S. team and was captain from its inception through 1948. The competition lasted through 1989.[33]

Mary K. Browne

After Hazel Hotchkiss-Wightman temporarily abdicated, Mary Browne (see profile in part III) from Ventura County (in the northwestern part of the Greater Los Angeles Area) came east alone in 1912 and became violently homesick. The Philadelphia Cricket Club had fifteen or twenty courts "laid out with portable backstops on a tremendous expanse of lawn," she recalled. "The only place from which to view the matches were the clubhouse porch and chairs arranged around the courts."[34] Like Hazel, this was her first time on grass. Shy, uncertain, frightened, and unaccustomed to both running in spikes and the low, slow bound off the grass, she nevertheless managed to win the title with her net play.[35]

The forehand drive was the prevalent weapon among women; all the other strokes paled by comparison. In the semifinals against Adelaide Browning, Mary had a narrow escape. Browning was very steady from the back court and returned almost everything and, after splitting the first two sets, led 5–4, 6–5, 7–6. Mary had changed from spikes to sneakers, and despite the slippery court she gained the net position, winning a couple of crucial points and the next three games for set at 9–7 and match. The score was 6–4, 3–6, 9–7.[36]

That morning Mary received a telegram from Dr. Sumner Hardy, president of the California Tennis Association, which said, "California expects you to win; don't disappoint us." Mary later said that telegram "really helped me win that match."[37]

Having played the great May Sutton, who possessed perhaps the best forehand passing shot in women's tennis, Mary's only hope was to get a return deep into her backhand court and come to the net. The lesson she learned from that match "was to cultivate steadiness from back court, to wait for a weak return for a kill and to work my way to the net with discretion."[38]

As with a great many of the California players, the five-foot-two right-hander had an extreme Western grip, a decided handicap on low balls but very effective on high bounding balls. The advantage she had over the Eastern girls at the time was that she could volley and smash overheads. Before the season was over she had shifted her grip slightly to drive the low balls.[39]

In those days all three championships—singles, women's doubles, and mixed—were played in one afternoon starting at three o'clock. Mary, entered in all three, won the 1912 singles over Eleonora Sears (see profile in part III), 6–4, 6–2, paired with Dorothy Green to win the doubles, 6–2, 5–7, 6–0, at which time it started to drizzle, and won the mixed title with Dick Williams over Eleonora Sears and William Clothier in another three-setter, 6–4, 2–6, 11–9, a total of eighty-two games. In the mixed doubles match, with the rain coming down steadily, there "was nothing to do but volley," she recalled. "Service was such an advantage that the last set went to twenty games before it was decided. During the last four games the rain was coming down in torrents, and still we went on, changing balls every three games, our rackets mushy and our clothes soaked."[40]

Players have frequently discussed the pros and cons of the challenge round whereby the previous year's titleholder did not take part in the tournament but merely stood about waiting to play the all-comers winner in the challenge round. The first men's champion, Dick Sears, thrived on it for four years until he retired undefeated. Mary Browne, however, was opposed to waiting about for two reasons. First, she "enjoyed competition and wanted to play as often as possible. Second, standing out does not put your game on edge."[41]

Mary duplicated Hazel's feat of three consecutive hat tricks by winning all three events in 1913 and 1914. She beat her 1912 doubles partner Dorothy Green in singles, 6–2, 7–5, and paired with Mrs. Robert Williams, another good volleyer, to win the doubles event, 12–10, 2–6, 6–3. In the mixed event, Mary partnered with Bill Tilden to win the latter's first major title. At this stage, seven years before he became champion, the press said Tilden "had great possibilities if he could only settle down." His service was devastating, but he was otherwise erratic.[42]

Because Mary was again in three finals, the tournament committee decided to hold the women's doubles final on Friday, leaving only two finals on the last day. In 1921 the mixed doubles event was transferred to Chestnut Hill, Massachusetts, along with the men's doubles tournament, which had been transferred there from Forest Hills in 1917.

Elizabeth Ryan

Another Californian Hall of Famer who never won a major singles title, but was a finalist at Wimbledon twice and at the U.S. Championships once, was Elizabeth "Bunny" Ryan of Anaheim, born February 8, 1892.

She lost to the invincible Suzanne Lenglen in 1921 and to Helen Wills-Moody in 1930 and lost a heartbreaker to Molla Bjurstedt-Mallory at the 1926 U.S. Championships, 4–6, 6–4, 9–7. Nevertheless, her major doubles record was magnificent—nineteen women's doubles titles and eleven mixed, most of those at Wimbledon.

Between 1914 and 1927 (there was no play during World War I, 1915–18), she won nine of ten Wimbledon doubles titles. Six of those were with Suzanne Lenglen, five times in a row. She and Lenglen never lost a Wimbledon doubles match, going 31–0. At forty-two, she won both the Wimbledon and French doubles titles in 1934. "Her 12 Wimbledon doubles titles (and 13 finals) are the tourney records, as are five straight with Lenglen.… She won a record seven mixed (of a record 10 finals) with five different partners."[43]

Ryan, a London resident most of her life, held the major tournament record of nineteen Wimbledon championships for forty-two years. Billie Jean King tied her record in 1975 by winning the singles. Ryan collapsed and died on July 8, 1979, at Wimbledon at the age of eighty-seven, the day before Billie Jean King got her twentieth title by winning the doubles event with Martina Navratilova.[44]

Molla Bjurstedt-Mallory

Molla Bjurstedt-Mallory (pronounced Boorstet; see profile in part III) first arrived in the United States in October 1914. A rugged Viking warrior, Molla was champion of Norway and won the bronze medal in the 1912 Olympics. In February 1915 she began seeing newspaper notices of the men's indoor championship at the Seventh Regiment Armory. She watched some of the matches and entered the women's national indoor tournament in March unheralded. Used to indoor play in Europe and with only three days practice, she met Marie Wagner in the final. According to Molla: "She had a better service than mine; nice clean strokes both forehand and backhand, and could volley or smash on occasion. But I was certainly faster on my feet and my forehand seemed stronger than hers."[45]

The biggest difference was that Molla, like R. Norris Williams, drove the ball before it reached the top of the bound which let her stand nearer the baseline. Molla was a punishing player from the baseline off both wings—some top on the forehand and slice on the backhand—and drove her shots from corner to corner. Molla dethroned the third ranked U.S. player, "Queen of the Boards" Marie, winner of six indoor singles titles, 6–4, 6–4.[46]

In the 1915 U.S. Championships Molla lost the first set to Martha Guthrie in the semifinals but won the match, 3–6, 6–2, 6–2. After again losing the first set to Hazel Hotchkiss-Wightman in the final, Molla won her inaugural title, 4–6, 6–2, 6–0, Mary Browne not defending. Hazel won the first set by getting close to the net to volley, but as Molla took the balls on the rise and Hazel began to tire, she could not get in far enough to handle them.[47]

Two weeks after the 1915 nationals Molla again beat Mrs. Wightman in the U.S. Clay Courts. Later in 1915 she went to California where she lost to Anita Meyers (see California Tennis 1915) after winning the first set at love. Meyers gave Molla "weird slices and chops" to disrupt the champion's rhythm to win the last two sets.[48]

Of all the women players Molla had met up to that time, May Sutton-Bundy was the best. "Her drive was the fastest and the … most difficult … to handle, because it dove suddenly to the ground and then jumped up unexpectedly with queer curves," she wrote. With an extreme Western grip, May had a powerful topspin forehand that made the ball dip and bound high. "When she could keep her drives near the baseline, they either forced me back farther than I had been accustomed to play or compelled me to make errors. She was also strong overhead when she came to the net and altogether had more power and effectiveness than any other woman tennis player of her time," Molla added.[49]

Way ahead of her time in taking the ball on the rise, Molla won a record eight U.S. singles titles between 1915 and 1926. She was a finalist to Marion Zinderstein in three sets in 1919, who in turn lost to Hazel Hotchkiss-Wightman the year the challenge round was abolished. Molla easily beat Helen Wills (seven U.S. singles titles) in 1922, the latter reciprocating in 1923 and 1924. With Helen Wills out of the 1926 championships, forty-two-year-old Molla defeated thirty-four-year-old Elizabeth Ryan for her eighth U.S. Open title.

4
California Tennis

The first lawn tennis club on the Pacific Coast was founded by a few English businessmen, who, finding the clear, exhilarating atmosphere conducive, set up a tennis court on the green turf at San Rafael, a suburb of San Francisco, in October of 1880. Very soon after the public found favor with the game, some fifty clubs sprang up on the coast, north and south. In the wake of the San Rafael Club came the California Lawn Tennis Club of San Francisco, which became the most prominent and powerful combination of tennis talent in the state in just a few seasons. "The immaculate white flannels and red sashes, striped blazers and caps show the club colors, and remind one of the gay picture which the tennis ground and the Casino galleries at Narragansett and Newport present."[1]

The California Lawn Tennis Club (or California Club) courts were built of "bituminous rock" containing a large proportion of sand. In fact, most of the period associations and clubs were suffixed with "Lawn Tennis Association" or "Lawn Tennis Club," in keeping with the nomenclature of the parent organization, the United States National Lawn Tennis Association (USNLTA), even though the preferred courts were bitumen (asphalt) or concrete. Since one afternoon's play could tear off the ball covering, a "double sewed and covered ball" was used. The Berkeley Tennis Club in Alameda was famous for its shell courts. According to *American Lawn Tennis* of 1899: "The California game differs somewhat from that played in the east, from the fact that all of the courts are bitumen, and the season is an endless one.... On account of the hard unyielding court the game is a fast one, and while there are several drawbacks to bitumen, principally because it tires the player, at the same time no balls are lost through an erratic bound, and the player seldom if ever slips. The dry summer makes turf courts altogether too expensive a luxury, while the bitumen court can be played on within an hour after a downpour in winter."[2]

The Southern California Lawn Tennis Association was organized in March of 1885, and the Pacific Lawn Tennis Association held the first tournament for the state championship in singles and doubles at Hotel del Monte, Monterey, on July 4, 1888. The right of the winner, William H. Taylor Jr., to be called state champion was disputed by R. Peyton Carter of Los Angeles. As the rivalry between Northern and Southern California at this time was particularly strong, a challenge was issued and then promptly accepted; and Carter, with many friends, journeyed to San Francisco to play Taylor on the California Club courts on October 18, 1888. Although Taylor lost the first set at love, he won the next three. The score was 0–6, 6–3, 8–6, 6–3.[3]

In order to settle the question, the California Club joined the USNLTA and received authority to hold a tournament for the Pacific Coast singles championship on July 4, 1889. Taylor again won the title over Valentine Gadesden and succeeded in capturing his third successive title in 1890 over challenger, C. R. Yates, 6–4, 9–7, 6–0, at the Hotel Rafael, San Rafael. By so doing Taylor won the Challenge Cup, valued at four hundred dollars, and the title "Pacific Coast Champion." Yates, the tournament winner, was awarded the California Club trophy valued at one hundred dollars.

The major California tournaments and their inaugural dates included the Southern California championship (1885) held in late July/early August in the Los Angeles area, the Pacific Coast (States) championship (1888) at Del Monte or San Rafael, the Ojai Valley (1896) and Southern California Interscholastic championship (1899) held in April at the Ojai Valley Tennis Club of Nordorff in Ventura county about eighty-five miles northwest of Los Angeles, and the California State championship (1901) in the San Francisco Bay area.

The big California Club in San Francisco was the real tennis center on the West Coast. Oakland, Alameda, and Los Angeles turned out numbers of players, but until 1899 the former of the three was the only one that had produced any champions. The top Californians in 1899 were Thomas Driscoll, Sam and Sumner Hardy from Oakland, George and Robert Whitney, Joseph Daily, and William H. Taylor Jr. of San Francisco.[4]

First Intercollegiate Rivalry

Stanford and California on the Pacific Coast inaugurated the first intercollegiate team versus team matches in 1892. Only dirt courts were available in the 1890s and early 1900s, and it was on one of these that Stanford first met California on June 3, 1892, at the Oakland Tennis Club. The Stanford Indians were victorious in their first meeting with the California Bears, winning 5–4, all singles. In this respect they were ahead of the East Coast, where team development would be a feature of the next decade.[5] For example, the 1908 Harvard tennis team, composed of six men for nine matches (six singles and three doubles), included C. C. Pell, Nat Niles, and A. S. Dabney, scheduled the Hartford Country Club, Princeton, and Yale while Princeton scheduled dual matches with Columbia, Cornell, Yale, Harvard, and Penn.[6]

The Stanford-Cal rivalry has continued ever since, now as part of the Pac 10 Conference founded December 2, 1915, and held in conjunction with the Annual Ojai Valley Tennis tournament. In 1894 both singles and doubles were played, with the Bears winning in 1894 and 1895 and the Indians in 1896. The scores were 5–1. The Bears won 5–3 in 1897, while from 1898 through 1905, only three matches were played each year and Stanford only won twice, in 1899 and 1900, by 2–1. In each of those years the Hardy brothers (Sam of Stanford and Sumner of California) tangled in both singles and doubles. Sam scored a sweep in 1899, and Sumner turned the tables on his brother in the 1900 singles event. The 1906 earthquake wiped out the tennis matches and almost everything else in the area, but Stanford bounced back to win 2–1 in 1907. From 1908 through 1911 the Bears scored four straight wins while the Indians eked out a 3–2 margin in 1912 under Captain R. Lindley "Lin" Murray.[7]

Carr and Sam Neel

In 1894 the Neel brothers, Carr and Sam, from the City of Oaks (Oakland), earned the right to play for the national doubles title by defeating Foote and Howland at Narragansett Pier, Rhode Island, but lost to the 1893 champions Hobart and Hovey at Newport. In 1896 Carr and Sam Neel won the Western doubles title at Kenwood in Chicago, defeated the Eastern champions, Hobart and Hovey, at Narragansett in five deuce sets, 4–6, 8–6, 4–6, 6–4, 6–4, after being down 4–1 in the fifth,[8] and then captured the national title at Newport in another five-setter over the holders Malcolm Chase and Robert Wrenn, becoming the first Californians to win a national title.

Carr Neel won the 1899 Western singles over Harold Hackett and J. A. Allen, two Yale experts from the East, in the semifinal and final rounds, Allen having defeated Sam Neel in the semis. Carr Neel beat Kreigh Collins (1899 U.S. no. 5) in the challenge round.[9]

Marion Jones

Marion Jones, the daughter of five-time Nevada Senator John Percival Jones, co-founder of the town of Santa Monica, was the first Californian to reach the singles final at the U.S. Tennis championships in 1898.[10] She won the national singles title in 1899 and 1902, the U.S. mixed doubles title with Ray Little in 1901, and the U.S. women's doubles with Juliette Atkinson in 1902. She also was the first American woman to win a medal at the Olympic Games. At the 1900 Paris Olympics, she won two bronze medals in tennis, one in singles and the other in mixed doubles, paired with the British star, Laurie Doherty. Her sister Georgina also competed in the 1900 Olympic tennis events.[11–12] Charlotte Cooper, already a three-time Wimbledon champion (she would win five times in all: 1895, '96, '98, 1901, and '08), took both singles and mixed doubles championships to become the first female Olympic champion.[13] In 1900, Marion Jones was the first non-British woman to play at Wimbledon, reaching the quarterfinals in the ladies' singles.

Jones married Robert Farquhar, but they divorced shortly thereafter. "From 1920 to 1961, she lived in Greenwich Village, where she was well known as a violinist and voice coach. She also translated opera librettos and for a short time was head of the New York Chamber Opera." Marion moved back to Los Angeles in 1961, where she lived until her death in 1965.[14]

East Meets West

For the fourth consecutive season, the Californians had endeavored to persuade the top Eastern players to make the trip. The first time, illness in Larned's family prevented him from going; the second occasion found business obstacles in the players' way; and the third year the Spanish American War took them from home. Then, of course, the great distance was always a drawback.[15] But finally, during the 1899 singles championship at Newport, a team of four Eastern experts was made up for a tour to the Pacific Coast. The Eastern team comprised current Canadian and U.S. champion Malcolm Whitman, U.S. doubles champions Dwight Davis and Holcombe Ward, and U.S. intercollegiate champion Beals Wright. The team left New York on August 24 and played its first match on September 5 after several days' practice on the Hotel del Monte courts at San Rafael.

The four Pacific Coast players were George Whitney, Pacific Coast champion; Samuel and Sumner Hardy, Pacific Coast doubles champions; and Robert Whitney, younger brother of George. In a round-robin event in which each of the Eastern men met each of the Western players in turn, the Eastern team won fourteen out of the sixteen matches played. Sumner Hardy accounted for the Pacific Coast's two wins over Ward and Wright, played a close five-set match against Davis, and won one set from Whitman. In the Pacific Coast doubles tournament, however, neither of the Eastern teams won the title. Whitman and Wright, after defeating the Whitney brothers in the final, lost to the Hardy brothers in the challenge round.

At the conclusion of the Del Monte tournament, the Eastern players made a trip through the northwestern United States and British Columbia, playing exhibition matches in Portland, Seattle, Tacoma, and Victoria. Subsequent three-time Canadian champion J. F. Foulkes participated in three of the events.[16]

Apparently inspired by their performance against the Eastern champions, Samuel and Sumner Hardy played the 1900 U.S. Championships; Samuel reached the third round by two defaults where he lost to Bill Larned (no. 3), and Sumner lost a five-setter in the second round.

1904

Alphonzo E. Bell of Los Angeles, winner of the 1903 Southern California and Pacific States singles titles, played the 1904 Eastern circuit, defeating such well-known players as E. B. Dewhurst, 1903 and 1905 intercollegiate champion; Robert LeRoy, 1904 and 1906 intercollegiate champion; and Dwight Davis. In addition, he played creditable matches with William Clothier (no. 3), Beals Wright (no. 4), and Holcomb Ward (no. 2). At the nationals he won four rounds before losing to Clothier in the quarters, 6–3, 7–5, 6–3, becoming the first Californian to be ranked in the top ten at no. 9. (Women's rankings began in 1913.)

Two subsequent Hall of Famers appeared in 1904 tournaments. In the California State championship sixteen-year-old Clarence Griffin lost in the final round to Drummond MacGavin while Hazel Hotchkiss won the ladies' singles title. The 1904 Pacific Coast rankings were as follows: Drummond MacGavin, no. 1; Alphonzo Bell, no. 2; Trowbridge Hendrick, no. 5; Simpson Sinsabaugh, no. 7; and Clarence Griffin, no. 8. Before May Sutton left on her Eastern tour, she beat her sister Violet for the Ojai Valley ladies' singles title.[17]

May Sutton

May Sutton won the 1904 national singles event. Born in 1886 in Plymouth, England, May Sutton and her family moved to a ranch near Pasadena, California, when she was six years old. It was there that she and her sisters Violet, Florence, and Ethel played tennis on a concrete court built by their father. At first May was an easy victim for her older sisters, but in 1900, at age thirteen, she won her first of nine Southern California titles. Her sisters accounted for another nine, and the tournament was nearly renamed the Sutton California championships. The saying in Southern California was "It takes a Sutton to beat a Sutton." She then went east in 1904 to win the coveted U.S. singles title at age seventeen against holder Elizabeth Moore, 6–1, 6–2. She also won the doubles title with Miriam Hall and was a mixed doubles finalist with F. B. Dallas.

May, a rugged five-foot-four-and-a-half, 140-pound, highly competitive right-hander with a powerful topspin forehand, started the emancipation from Victorian sports attire, wearing shorter skirts and fewer petticoats, shunning high-collared shirtwaists, and rolling up her sleeves. She made three trips to England and in 1905 became the first American and first non-British woman to win Wimbledon without the loss of a set, over two-time champion Dorothea Douglass. May lost to her in the 1906 challenge round, 6–3, 7–5, and defeated her again in 1907 when Douglass was Mrs. Lambert Chambers, 6–1, 6–4. She shocked English crowds at first by rolling up her sleeves to bare her elbows, heaven forbid, and wearing a shorter skirt than most, showing her ankles.[18]

Writing in 1931 May said: "In 1904 and 1905 the skirts were much too long, there were too many petticoats and they also wore long sleeves and sometimes high stiff collars (terrific!). Now they wear much shorter skirts, which is much more sensible. I really think the time will come soon when they will do without the skirt and just wear shorts and a pretty sweater."[19] Her prediction was correct when Helen Jacobs, 1932 U.S. singles and doubles champion, and Betty Nuthall of England set a new fashion for tournament play when they appeared in shorts at the 1933 U.S. Championships at Forest Hills stadium. And May was around in 1949 when Gertrude (Gussy) Moran appeared on the hallowed Centre Court on June 20 wearing a short tennis dress, designed by Ted Tinling, with ruffled, lace-trimmed knickers peeping out below the hem. The *United Press* noted Gorgeous Gussie's "lace-lined scanties gave England its gaudiest spectacle since the coronation."[20] The conservative members were outraged, but it did the club no harm in gate receipts. Tinling, a former tennis player of note turned fashion designer, was comparatively unknown. He subsequently became famous from the 1950s through the 1970s, designing daring and unusual tennis dresses for female tennis stars. [21]

In 1912 May married Tom Bundy of Los Angeles, who won the 1910 U.S. all-comers over Beals Wright. Alongside Maurice McLoughlin, Bundy took three successive doubles titles from 1912 through 1914. Firsts ran in the family, as their daughter, Dorothy Bundy Cheney, became the first American to win the women's singles title at the Australian championships, defeating Dorothy Stevenson in the final 6–3, 6–2. May's nephew and Violet's son, John Doeg, won the 1930 U.S. singles title over Frank Shields.

Returning to California after easily winning the 1904 U.S. singles tournament (6–1, 6–2 over Elizabeth Moore), May Sutton played the Pacific Coast championships beginning September 2. The women's event results were a repetition of the preceding years' outcomes, with the first prizes shipped to the Pasadena home of the Sutton sisters. *Wright & Ditson's 1905 Guide* said: "The pride of California, Miss May Sutton, had just completed her remarkable tour of the East, in which she met and conquered the best women players of the country and finished her phenomenal record by winning the National Championship in Singles for Women with the loss of but one or two games. It was not until she met her sister, Miss Florence, in the challenge match that she had to exert herself to defend her championship of the coast, defeating her in two close sets." May beat Hazel Hotchkiss in the final round and Florence Sutton in the challenge round. The 1904 Southern California championships were held in South Pasadena beginning on July 25. With May Sutton playing on Eastern courts, guess who the ladies' singles finalists were? If you said Sutton, you're right on both counts. Violet beat her sister Florence, 8–6, 6–4.[22]

Golden Gate Junior Tennis Club

The Golden Gate Junior Tennis Club was organized in the fall of 1904 for grammar and high school boys under seventeen years of age. Besides Maurice McLoughlin, a number of other talented youths regularly frequented the courts including Byron Batkin; the Strachan brothers, Bob and John; Clarence Griffin; and the Long brothers, Herbert and Melville. Bill Johnston found tennis to his liking in 1906 when the great earthquake and fire of April 18 closed schools.

As Johnston lived at 792 Clayton Street and McLoughlin lived across the street from him[23] and about six blocks from the Golden Gate tennis courts, it's not a stretch to imagine they might have hiked there together to practice. Bob Strachan and his younger brother, John, lived even closer, at 1449 Fifth Avenue. Clarence Griffin, at 106 Baker Street, was eight long blocks from the park and another two from the courts, while Mel and Herbert Long, at 21 Buena Vista Avenue, lived about two blocks further than Griffin. Roland Roberts lived on the other side of the city near what is now the San Francisco–Oakland Bay Bridge.

The Golden Gate Junior Tennis Club did a lot to democratize the game and produce players of championship caliber. Some of the youngsters became national champions and competed in Davis Cup play. The club consisted of four player classes, the fourth being for beginners. Stress was laid on an aggressive style of play as opposed to safe play. As a result a boy was rarely advanced to class III without having developed a respectable drive. Tournaments were held monthly in class singles, handicap singles, and handicap doubles. The latter two events encouraged the better players to develop ability and grit to come from behind against discouraging odds, while the younger boys benefited from being encouraged to attempt aggressive shots. Points were awarded for proficiency, good sportsmanship, and the observance of tournament rules.

The club shortly initiated two junior championship events—the Pacific Coast Junior championships played in the spring and the Bay Counties championship in the fall. A Grammar School championship in May of each year was later initiated.[24]

In the 1905 California Club championship held at Golden Gate Park, George Janes, the Pacific Coast champion, defeated Schmidt in the first class.[25] In this respect the Golden Gate Junior Tennis Club was way ahead of its time. The NTRP (National Tennis Rating Program) was established in 1978 whereby classifications between 1.0 and 7.0 in 0.5 increments were implemented so that players would compete with those near their own skill level.[26] Most club tournament players range between 3.5 and 4.5.

Maurice McLoughlin and Bob Strachan easily defeated John Strachan and W. Marcus in the 1905 Golden Gate Junior Club's handicap doubles.[27] At other 1905 venues George Baker won the Alameda County championship, Charles Foley the Bay Counties championship, and Carl Gardner the San Francisco title.[28]

This club developed some of the best players in the country over the next two decades in addition to Californians Tom Bundy, Trowbridge Hendrick, Ward Dawson of Los Angeles, and Lindley Murray of Palo Alto. U.S. singles titlists included Maurice McLoughlin (1912–13), Bill Johnston (1916, 1919), and Lindley Murray (1917–18). U.S. doubles titlists included Bundy–McLoughlin (1912–14), Clarence Griffin–Johnston (1915–16, 1920), and Howard and Robert Kinsey (1924). Singles finalists included McLoughlin (1909, 1911, 1914–15), Bundy (1910), and Johnston (1916, 1920, 1922–25). Doubles finalists included Carleton–McLoughlin (1909), Bundy–Hendrick (1910), Griffin–John Strachan (1913), Bundy–McLoughlin (1915), Ward Dawson–McLoughlin (1916), and Willis Davis–Roland Roberts (1920). Singles semifinalists included Elia Fottrell (1914), Griffin (1916), Strachan (1917), and Willis Davis (1921).

1906

In the 1906 Ojai Valley tournament in April, the men's singles final was between two San Franciscans. Carl Gardner beat Clarence Griffin. The interscholastic ladies' singles, doubles, and mixed events were won by the indomitable May Sutton.[29] Sherman Day Thacher, a graduate of the Yale School of Law in 1886, went to the valley at Ojai in 1887 and planted an orange grove on 160 acres of governmenjt land. Requiring financial assistance, he founded the Thacher School in 1889 and started tutoring in his stone house.[30] His brother, "William Thacher, the New England and intercollegiate tennis doubles champion while a junior at Yale University in 1886, came to the valley in 1890 for a family wedding, and stayed on to help with the school. In 1892, the first tennis court in the Valley was built on the school grounds. The first tennis tournament in Ojai was held on that court in 1893."[31] Competition in earnest started in 1896 as indicated earlier. The entry fee at the turn of the century was fifty cents. Today the fee is thirty-five dollars.

The 1906 California State championship was held in San Francisco at the California Club courts for the first time in early July, less than three months after the great earthquake and fire of April 18, and was won by Herbert Long who defeated Fred Adams, the titleholder. One of the best of the older players, Percy Murdock, beat Charles Foley, Carl Gardner, George Janes, and Melville Long, only to be defeated in the finals by Herbert Long. After defeating Melville Long by 7–5 in the third set that morning, he was in no condition to play a hard match with H. Long later that day. H. Long beat Murdock, 6–2, 3–6, 6–4, 6–1, and Fred Adams the holder, 6–4, 4–6, 7–5, 6–2. Hazel Hotchkiss won the women's singles. The San Francisco championship was won by Charles Foley of the Golden Gate Club over Carl Gardner, the holder, in a close match, 6–3, 6–2, 5–7, 1–6, 6–1.[32]

At the 1906 Pacific Coast championship at San Rafael in September, the surprises of the tournament were the defeats of Nat Browne, brother of Hall of Famer Mary Browne, Alphonzo Bell, Charles Foley, and Thomas Bundy in the final by sixteen-year-old Melville Long who won the championship by defeating George Janes in the challenge match, 6–2, 7–5, 6–2. Subsequent two-time national singles champion, a sixteen-year-old youngster from the Golden Gate Park, Maurice McLoughlin lost in the first round to Bell. Mel Long also won the junior title by defeating McLoughlin, Getz, and Batkin. Hazel Hotchkiss of Berkeley defeated Ethel Sutton, now Mrs. B. O. Bruce, in a semifinal and Gabriel Dobbins in the final. Hotchkiss had the distinction of being the first player outside of the Sutton family to defeat a Sutton in tournament play in some years. Hazel paired with Ethel Ratcliffe to defeat Gabriel Dobbins and Ethel Sutton-Bruce. Hazel first met Ethel Ratcliffe on the train going to Golden Gate Park in December 1902 to play her first tournament. The pair won the doubles event.[33]

The Bay Counties championship, held at the Golden Gate Club, was won by George Janes, who, after defeating Melville Long, champion of the coast, beat Charles Foley the titleholder in straight sets.[34]

All the 1906 Pacific Coast titles were won by Park players. Tennis was introduced in the Golden Gate Park in 1899 through a suggestion from Mr. George Wright, who visited that year with Dwight Davis, Holcombe Ward, Malcolm Whitman, and Beals Wright, son of George.[35] This was a big factor in early democratization of the game.

1907

Alphonzo Bell, who won the Southern California title from 1901 to 1903, won the April 1907 Ojai Valley singles and doubles titles with Simpson Sinsabaugh. Florence Sutton won the singles and the doubles events with fifteen-year-old Elizabeth Ryan from Anaheim. Elizabeth Ryan and Simpson Sinsabaugh won the mixed title. Elizabeth Ryan of Marlborough School, in Los Angeles, also won the interscholastic singles and doubles title, a new feature that year.[36] A magnificent doubles player and subsequent Hall of Famer Elizabeth Ryan long held the major tournament record for nineteen Wimbledon championships between 1914 and 1934, twelve ladies' doubles and seven mixed doubles.[37]

The seventh annual San Francisco City championship was concluded on the California Club courts on May 30. Maurice McLoughlin, who had lost in the first round in two 1906 tournaments, won the title. Every man he defeated in the tournament was of championship class. He first defeated Herbert Long (State champion), 6–3, 3–6, 6–2, and then George Janes (Bay Counties champion), 6–3, 8–6; he followed that up by taking the Coast champion, Melville Long, 6–3, 13–11. In the finals he beat Carl Gardner, ex-city champion, 2–6, 6–4, 6–3, 4–6, 8–6. In the challenge match McLoughlin defeated Charles Foley, 9–7, 6–0, 3–6, 6–2.[38]

The 1907 California State championship began on July 4 at the Golden Gate Club. Mel Long defeated Janes in the final and his brother, Herbert, in the challenge match. Hazel Hotchkiss successfully defended her title over Golda Myer, 6–4, 8–6. The Southern California championship was held at the Country Club of Ocean Park beginning on July 29. Melville Long, 1906 Pacific Coast champion, beat Carl Gardner in the quarters, A. E. Bell in the semifinals, and S. M. Sinsabaugh in the final, all without losing a set. In the challenge round Long beat Harold Braly the holder, 7–5, 2–6, 4–6, 7–5, 14–12. Seven times Braly needed but one point for match but did not have enough left to follow up. At 12–all they had been playing for over three hours, and Braly was so exhausted that he could not follow in his serve. Long was famous for his forehand crosscourt volley. In the ladies' singles Florence Sutton defeated Alice Scott in the final, 5–7, 6–3, 6–1. So highly regarded were the Suttons, it was noted that "Scott is the first lady other than a Sutton who has taken a set from any of the Suttons in a Southern California tournament." Florence defeated her sister, Ethel Sutton-Bruce, 1906 champion, in the challenge match, 9–7, 6–4.[39]

The Pacific States event was held in Del Monte instead of San Rafael beginning on September 1. "Red" McLoughlin beat A. E. Bell of Los Angeles in four sets, Bell showing better form than he had since he won the title in 1903. In the challenge round, McLoughlin beat Melville Long the holder in five deuce sets, 13–11, 6–4, 4–6, 5–7, 6–4. McLoughlin thus avenged his two 1906 first-round losses to Bell and Long and paired with George Janes to win the doubles. Little Bob Strachan won the junior event over Harold Getz in five sets while Florence Sutton beat Hazel Hotchkiss to win the ladies' singles and paired with her sister Ethel to win the doubles.[40] McLoughlin also won the final big event of the season, the Bay Counties tournament completed October 26 on the San Francisco Park courts. He beat Charles Foley in the final, 6–4, 4–6, 9–7, 6–2, and George Janes the holder more easily, 6–1, 7–5, 6–2. Carl Gardner and Mel Long won the doubles over Clarence Griffin and R. Hunt after five hard sets. Golda Myer turned the tables on Hazel Hotchkiss in the ladies' challenge match, 6–3, 7–5. The top 1907 Pacific Coast rankings were Maurice McLoughlin (no. 1), Melville Long (no. 2), Alphonzo Bell (no. 3), Carl Gardner (no. 4), Thomas Bundy (no. 5), and George Janes (no. 6).[41]

1908

The annual Ojai Valley tournament began April 9, 1908. Carl Gardner won the men's singles, Gardner and McLoughlin the men's doubles, and May Sutton the ladies' singles, while Elizabeth Ryan and May Sutton won the ladies' doubles title. In the interscholastic event Charles Rogers of Los Angeles won the boys' tournament while sixteen-year-old Elizabeth Ryan of Marlborough School won the girls' for the second time. On April 18 Herbert and Melville Long won the intercollegiate tennis championship of California for the University of California, defeating Stanford's men in both singles and doubles. Hazel Hotchkiss had an even easier time with her opponent and helped to add to the honors held by UC.[42]

The 1908 San Francisco championship began in late May at the California Club. In the semifinals Mel Long was forced to three sets by George Janes, while his brother Herbert fell to Carl Gardner in a tremendous three-set match that went to fifty games. Mel Long put the finishing touches on Gardner in the final, which his brother had started in the morning. Long started strongly in the challenge match by passing McLoughlin down the sides and with crosscourt shots when the latter came to the net. McLoughlin regained his confidence and, after winning the third set, closed out the match. The score was 4–6, 4–6, 6–3, 6–1, 6–3. This tourney was won in 1903 by J. D. McGavin, in 1904 by C. P. Murdock, in 1905 by C. R. Gardner, in 1906 by Charles Foley, and in 1907 and 1908 by M. E. McLoughlin.[43]

The California State title in July again changed hands as M. E. McLoughlin defeated M. E. Long. "McLoughlin went right to work in the first set and ... served, smashed and drove like a whirlwind." The score was 6–2, 12–10, 6–2. Janes and McLoughlin defeated Long and Gardner in the doubles finals, 6–1, 9–7, 10–8. Miss Mearns won the ladies' event and challenged Hazel Hotchkiss, who beat her, 6–1, 6–1, thus retaining her title.[44]

The twenty-fourth annual tournament for the Southern California championship was held on the new courts of the Hotel Virginia at Long Beach beginning on July 27. This tournament is the oldest fixed event on the Pacific Coast and began in 1885 on the old casino courts at Santa Monica. Thomas Bundy won the title over A. E. Bell in the final, 6–1, 6–2, 5–7, 6–1, because Mel Long of San Francisco, owing to summer school work, did not come down to defend his title. Bundy also won the 1908 Colorado, Long Beach, and Venice tournaments.

The presence of the redoubtable May Sutton lent the greatest interest to the ladies' singles tournament. Owing to her journeys eastward and abroad, she had not contested in any Southern California tourney for several years. As her sister Florence won the title in 1907, it was necessary for May to play through the tournament, which, as a matter of course, she won without the loss of a set. May lost no more than two games in any one match, defeating Ethel Sutton-Bruce in the final, 6–1, 6–1, and Florence in the challenge round, 6–1, 6–0. The closest match of the event was a preliminary round contest between two subsequent Hall of Famers, as Elizabeth Ryan beat Mary Browne, 6–3, 2–6, 8–6. Elizabeth Ryan and May Sutton won the ladies' doubles title, and May Sutton and S. M. Sinsabaugh won the mixed title.[45]

The 1908 Pacific States championship held on the asphalt courts of Del Monte the week of September 7 included such Eastern luminaries as Irving Wright (no. 9), Nat Niles (no. 8 for 1908), and Wallace Johnson (no. 9 for 1908). The Eastern visitors found the pace faster than what they had been used to on grass or dirt, but they adjusted nevertheless. The all-around play of Long, McLoughlin, Bundy, Gardner, and Janes was some of the best, particularly for Long and McLoughlin. Including a preliminary round, Mel Long beat Niles in the second round, 6–2, 6–4, while Johnson disposed of Janes, 8–6, 6–4, and Wright beat William Hunter of Stockton, 6–2, 6–4, in the third. The two remaining Easterners met in the semis, Johnson beating Wright, 6–1, 6–1, 6–1. In the final Long beat Johnson, 8–6, 6–2, 6–4, and then McLoughlin the titleholder in the challenge round after dropping the first two sets, 8–10, 6–8, 6–4, 11–9, 6–0.[46]

Niles and Wright beat A. E. Bell (Los Angeles) and L. R. Freeman (Pasadena) in the doubles final, 6–4, 6–3, 1–6, 6–4, but lost to Janes and McLoughlin in the challenge round, 5–7, 6–4, 6–0, 6–2. May Sutton beat Hazel Hotchkiss in the ladies' singles final and her sister Florence in the challenge round. Elizabeth Ryan and May Sutton won the ladies' doubles event over Ethel Sutton-Bruce and Florence Sutton. The junior singles title was won for a second year by Bob Strachan of San Francisco over Charles Rogers of Los Angeles. Byron Batkin and Bob Strachan won the junior doubles tournament, beating H. Fuchs and John Strachan.[47]

Tennis in and around San Francisco was growing rapidly. The Santa Rosa, Berkeley, and Oakland clubs had started since the first of the year, and all of the best players in the city and the Bay Area took part in tournaments held at Golden Gate Park. Four San Francisco players ranked by the PSLTA for 1908 were in the top five: Melville H. Long, no. 1; Maurice E. McLoughlin, no. 2; Carlton R. Gardner, no. 3; Thomas C. Bundy of Los Angeles, no. 4; and George J. Janes, no. 5.[48]

1909

The California State championship events were held in the Bay Area in June. In the men's singles event Carl Gardner beat veteran Alphonzo Bell in five sets. After winning a deuce fourth set and the first three games of the fifth, Bell could not stand the heat and the pace, and Gardner took six straight games and the match. Bell of Los Angeles, winner of the 1901 Coast championship, defeated the 1908 Coast champion Melville Long in straight sets. Gardner lost to McLoughlin in the challenge round in five sets.

In the afternoon Gardner and Long beat Bell and Tom Bundy. The following afternoon Gardner and Long faced Janes and McLoughlin, the titleholders, for the third time in the past year for a championship—and for the third time went down to defeat after winning the first two sets.

May Sutton played a magnificent game in the finals of the women's singles tournament by defeating her sister Florence without the loss of a single game. The greatest crowd in the history of the game in California gathered to see the challenge match between returning national champion Hazel Hotchkiss and May Sutton. The indomitable May Sutton prevailed in straight sets.[49]

The twenty-second annual tournament for the Pacific Coast championship began August 16 at Del Monte. Mel Long, singles champion, and Maurice McLoughlin, doubles holder with George Janes, were both absent, as were Tom Bundy, Carl Gardner, and Simpson Sinsabaugh, who were in the East, thereby reducing the strength of the field. However, several previous champions, cracks, and veterans such as Charles Foley, L. J. Freeman, Sumner Hardy, Percy Murdock, and Charles Rogers played. Charles Rogers, a youngster of great promise, was a bit nervous and impetuous, and George Janes won in four sets after dropping the first.

Although the Pacific Coast doubles title had been decided in July, won by Janes and McLoughlin for the right to play in the National Preliminaries, Freeman and Janes outclassed Hunt and Murdock. National champion Hazel Hotchkiss, having recently returned from the East, defeated Ethel Sutton-Bruce in two deuce sets but lost to Florence Sutton in the final. Hazel got a measure of revenge by pairing with Golda Myer to defeat the Sutton sisters, Ethel and Florence. In the mixed event Hotchkiss paired with Sumner Hardy to defeat Florence Sutton and L. J. Freeman. Charles Rogers beat John Strachan for the junior title.[50]

1910

Under the guidance of Stanford University the first interscholastic tournament was held on the university's asphalt courts in April 1910. In the singles final Elia Fottrell beat fifteen-year-old William Johnston, subsequent two-time national singles champion, in a close 4–6, 6–4, 7–5 encounter. The doubles title was won by the Fottrell brothers, Elia and Morgan, over Griffith (Griffin?) and Johnston, 6–1, 8–6. In mixed doubles Florence Sutton and Clifton Herd defeated Hazel Hotchkiss and Maurice McLoughlin, which was rather a surprise, but lost to Mary Browne and S. M. Sinsabaugh, 10–8, 4–6, 6–3. In the ladies' singles event Hazel Hotchkiss beat May Sutton, 2–6, 6–4, 6–0.[51]

The fifteenth annual tournament of the Ojai Valley Tennis Club began on April 21. M. E. McLoughlin won the singles title. In the finals of the men's doubles event, Sinsabaugh and Nat Browne, brother of Mary, defeated McLoughlin and Thacher, 6–4, 6–4.[52]

The 1910 San Francisco City championship began on June 4. The men's singles tournament was closed to all players except San Francisco residents. Maurice McLoughlin won the singles title for the fourth time, defeating his rival Melville Long in the challenge round, 6–4, 8–6, 6–4. These two local players were ranked respectively sixth and seventh nationally. Long and McLoughlin won in the doubles final over the Rogers brothers, Charles and Harry, 6–3, 7–5. Golda Myer won the ladies' singles event, while May Sutton and her future husband, Tom Bundy, won the mixed title.[53]

The twenty-fifth Southern California tournament took place on August 6, 1910, on the courts at Hotel Virginia in Long Beach. Nat Browne handily beat sixteen-year-old Elia Fottrell from San Francisco in the final but lost to Winifred Mace, the titleholder, 10–8, 4–6, 6–1, 3–6, 6–4. W. Dawson and S. Sinsabaugh beat A. Bell and N. Browne for the men's doubles title. Ethel Sutton-Bruce and C. Wayne beat Mary Browne and S. Sinsabaugh for the mixed title. May Sutton beat her sister Ethel in the ladies' singles final, and Elia Fottrell won the junior singles title, beating out V. A. Sheldon, 6–0, 6–2.[54]

The twenty-second Pacific States championship began in Del Monte on September 2. With three of the best players in Eastern tournaments—T. C. Bundy, C. R. Gardner, and M. E. McLoughlin—Melville Long had a rather easy task. Long and Sinsabaugh won the men's doubles title. The ladies' singles event touted a former national champion, May Sutton; a current national champion, Hazel Hotchkiss; and a future national champion, Mary Browne. In the first round Golda Myer beat Mary Browne, 6–3, 3–6, 6–3. In the second round May Sutton beat Ethel Sutton-Bruce, and Hazel Hotchkiss beat Golda Myer. May Sutton beat national champion Hazel Hotchkiss in a very close final, 7–5, 4–6, 6–4, and Florence Sutton in the challenge round, 6–1, 6–2. May Sutton and G. Young defeated Hazel Hotchkiss and Mel Long for the mixed title, 6–4, 8–6. Hazel Hotchkiss had won the 1910 national mixed title less than three months earlier with Joseph R. Carpenter over Edna Wildey and Herbert M. Tilden, the older brother of "Big Bill," 6–2, 6–2. Subsequent national champion Bill Johnston won the junior tournament.[55]

The first National Clay Court championship, held at the Omaha Field Club during the week of August 1, 1910, was won by Melville Long, San Francisco, who didn't lose a set. Long beat Drummond Jones of St. Louis in the semifinals, 6–4, 6–4, 6–3, and destroyed Walter Merrill Hall of New York in the final, 6–0, 6–1, 6–1.[56]

1911

In the twenty-third Pacific States championship, held in Santa Cruz during the week of June 19, 1911, Maurice McLoughlin lost his only set of the tourney to junior champion William Johnston in the third round. McLoughlin beat Charles Foley in the final and Melville Long in the challenge round. May Sutton won the ladies' singles title over Mary Browne, and the two paired to win the doubles. W. Johnston won the junior title over R. Greenberg, 6–4, 6–2, 6–2. Clyde Curley and Johnston won the junior doubles over R. Lindley Murray and J. Hutchinson, 6–2, 2–6, 10–8, 6–1.[57]

The Southern California championship was held August 1–5 in Long Beach. Ward Dawson beat Nat Browne in the final and successfully challenged Winifred Mace, the holder, for the singles title, but Dawson lost his doubles crown with Sinsabaugh to Browne and Duncan. Ethel Sutton-Bruce won three titles—singles, doubles, and mixed—while Elia Fottrell captured the junior singles title and the doubles title with Virgin Sheldon.[58]

The eighth annual Bay County championships at San Francisco, which began October 7, resulted in a victory for eighteen-year-old Elia Fottrell over sixteen-year-old John Strachan. The younger star leading, 6–8, 7–5, 6–2, 5–0, and 40–love defaulted in order to save his standing as a junior. In the junior event J. Strachan beat E. Fottrell in four sets but lost to W. Johnston the titleholder, 0–6, 6–2, 6–4, 7–5.[59]

1912

The annual intercollegiate contest between Stanford and the University of California was held April 5 and 6 on the California varsity courts in Berkeley. Stanford won the meet 3–2 by winning all three singles matchups but losing the two doubles. In singles Morgan (S) beat Frees (UC), 6–3, 10–8; R. L. Murray (S) beat Charles Rogers (UC), 4–6, 10–8, 7–5; V. Sheldon (S) beat H. Rogers (UC), 6–0, 6–3. In doubles Charles and Harry Rogers (UC) beat Murray and Morgan (S), 1–6, 6–2, 6–3, 4–6, 6–3; Breeden and Frees (UC) beat J. Hutchinson and V. Sheldon (S), 6–4, 6–1, 6–3.[60]

At the Stanford University interscholastic tournament in April, Johnny Strachan of Lowell High School repeated his performance of the previous year by winning the title from his old teammate, seventeen-year-old Will Johnston of San Francisco Polytechnic, 6–4, 6–8, 6–2, 6–2.[61]

The Central California championship, played at Stockton during the hottest spell of the year on asphalt courts heated to the boiling point, resulted in a win for Maurice McLoughlin, who had to play but one and one half matches, receiving three defaults en route. Carl Gardner and Bill Johnston won the doubles from Havens and McLoughlin, 6–8, 7–5, 6–1. Florence Sutton was successful in the ladies' singles, winning over Mary Browne, but in mixed doubles the latter retaliated by pairing with her veteran brother Nat to defeat Florence and Dr. Sumner Hardy in the finals.[62]

Maurice McLoughlin won the San Francisco City championship for the sixth time by defeating Mel Long in a four-set final, 2–6, 6–2, 6–3, 9–7. In the semis Mel Long beat his brother Herbert, 6–1, 6–4, 4–6, 6–4, while McLoughlin beat Johnston, 11–9, 6–2, 6–2.[63]

1913

William Johnston won the Coronado Country Club men's singles held February 7–11, 1913, over John Strachan, 8–6, 6–3, and paired with Nat Browne to win the doubles event over Clarence Griffin and Strachan, 6–1, 6–2, 6–2. Mrs. Ethel Sutton-Bruce won the singles tournament over her sister Florence, but Florence paired with Nat Browne to defeat Ethel and Roy Holland in the mixed event.[64]

The Ojai Valley championship took place April 24–26. W. M. Johnston won the men's singles title over J. R. Strachan, 6–4, 6–8, 6–2, and also won the all–San Franciscan final in the doubles event, paired with E. Fottrell, over A. Rosenberg and J. Strachan, 6–4, 8–6. Florence Sutton swept the ladies' singles, doubles, and mixed events. Lin Murray (Stanford) won the Pacific Coast intercollegiate singles over Newell (USC), 7–5, 3–6, 12–10, and paired with J. Hutchinson to win the doubles title over Herlihy and Montgomery (Occidental), 6–2, 6–1.[65]

William Johnston, McLoughlin's successor in several important titles won during the absence of the national champion, who was in England for the Davis Cup (U.S. won the Cup over Great Britain by 3–2) and Wimbledon (McLoughlin beat S. Doust in the final, 6–3, 6–4, 7–5, but lost to Anthony Wilding in the challenge round, 8–6, 6–3, 10–8), and gained another important victory in Del Monte, California, on June 21, 1913, when he won the title of Pacific States champion. Johnston was pressed by fellow San Franciscans fifteen-year-old Roland Roberts in the second round, 4–6, 8–6, 6–2, and teenager John Strachan in the final, 6–1, 6–1, 3–6, 4–6, 6–4. Elia Fottrell and Johnston beat Clarence Griffin and Strachan in the doubles, 10–8, 6–0, 2–6, 6–3. B. Detrick easily beat H. Van Dyke Johns for the junior singles title, 6–1, 6–1, 6–3, while Detrick and Johns paired to beat Henry and Roberts in the junior doubles event, 6–4, 1–6, 8–6.[66]

Thomas C. Bundy, the national doubles titlist with McLoughlin, won the Southern California singles tournament, held in Long Beach the week of July 28. Bundy beat Willis Davis in the final, 6–1, 4–6, 12–10, 6–4. In men's doubles Sinsabaugh and Wayne beat Bundy and Dawson in the final, 1–6, 6–4, 7–5, 6–2, and Browne and Duncan the titleholders, 3–6, 4–6, 8–6, 6–1, 6–4. H. V. D. Johns won the junior singles over Allyn Barber, 6–4, 6–3.[67]

At the California State championship in Oakland beginning on September 6, Bill Johnston beat Lin Murray for the men's singles title, 6–4, 5–7, 6–4, 6–4. In the semifinals Murray beat B. H. Batkin, 7–5, 6–2, while Johnston beat Elia Fottrell, 6–2, default. Murray paired with Willis Davis in the doubles but lost in the quarterfinals to Clarence Griffin and John Strachan, 6–4, 6–3, who in turn lost the title to Elia Fottrell and Bill Johnston, 6–3, 6–4, 6–2.[68]

1914

The California intercollegiate championship between Stanford and the University of California was held at UC's courts in Berkeley; UC won the event 5–0. Willis E. Davis (UC) defeated Herbert L. Hahn (S), 6–3, 7–5; Robert Lipman (UC) defeated Captain L. Sloss (S), 6–8, 6–4, 6–3; and E. P. Banker (UC) clobbered K. B. Uhls (S), 6–0, 6–3. In doubles Davis and Marshall Evans (UC) defeated Sloss and Hahn (S), 6–3, 6–4, 3–6, 6–4, while E. Breeden and H. Breck (UC) defeated F. S. Pratt and J. S. Hutchinson (S), 5–7, 6–4, 6–4.[69] This championship was nothing more than a meet between the two main universities in the state. Despite Hahn's losing both in singles and doubles, he won the Pacific Coast intercollegiate singles title at Ojai in April. *Spalding's 1915 Annual* said: "Had Lindley Murray, Stanford's best man, been able to compete, his university might have taken two of the five matches played."[70]

H. V. D. Johns of Lowell High School won the Stanford interscholastic singles title over L. Strauss, also of Lowell, 6–3, 8–6.[71]

The Pacific Coast championship took place on the courts of the Naglee Park Tennis Club in San Jose beginning June 22. Bill Johnston won the men's singles by defeating Clarence Griffin in the semis, 6–8, 6–1, 6–0, and Elia Fottrell in the final, 6–4, 6–0, 6–2. Johnston paired with Griffin to win the doubles event over H. Van Dyke Johns and Roland Roberts, 6–2, 6–2, 7–5. H. V. D. Johns won the junior singles title and paired with Roberts to win the junior doubles title.[72]

John Strachan beat Bill Johnston, 6–4, 6–2, Clarence Griffin, 6–4, 6–2, and C. B. Detrick, 6–1, 6–1, 6–3, to win the 1914 California State championship at Oakland beginning October 24. Strachan paired with his most formidable rival, Johnston, to win the doubles over fellow San Franciscans B. H. Batkin and Roland Roberts, 6–0, 4–6, 7–5, 6–3.[73]

1915

The Ojai Valley championship was held April 15–17, 1915. Ward Dawson won the men's singles tournament over H. Van Dyke Johns, who had just won the intercollegiate title. Dawson and Cliff Herd won the doubles title, while Florence Sutton captured the ladies' singles, doubles, and mixed doubles titles. H. V. D. Johns of Stanford won the Pacific Coast intercollegiate singles over Herbert Hahn, 6–0, 5–7, 6–1. In 1914, Hahn, also of Stanford, won the intercollegiate title, which Lin Murray had won in 1913. Johns partnered with Hahn to win the doubles crown in 1915.[74]

The seventeen-year-old San Francisco boy wonder Roland Roberts won the Southern California championship on Hotel Virginia's asphalt courts in Long Beach the week of July 26. En route Roberts beat experienced Eugene Overton in the quarters, Willis Davis in the semis, and Tom Bundy, three-time national doubles champion, in the final, 3–6, 3–6, 6–1, 6–2, 6–3. May Sutton-Bundy beat Mary Browne in the ladies' final and Florence Sutton in the challenge round.[75]

At the California State championship in Oakland September 2–9, Willis Davis of Belvedere joined the ranks of the major stars. The young University of California player defeated Carl Gardner in the second round and Roland Roberts in the semifinals and won a notable victory over the whirlwind player Lin Murray in the final, 3–6, 6–3, 6–4, 3–6, 6–3. Morgan Fottrell and Roland Roberts beat Willis Davis and Charles Foley for the doubles title.[76]

The 1915 Pacific States championship progressed through a series of astonishing upsets to a totally unexpected conclusion on the courts of the California Lawn Tennis Club in San Francisco the week following October 30. Herbert Hahn, the intercollegiate champion who had accompanied Lin Murray on his 1914 Eastern invasion, fell heir to the title despite the fact that among the contestants were two national champions—Johnston in singles and Griffin and Johnston in doubles. H. V. D. Johns beat Johnston in one semi, 4–6, 6–4, 6–3, 3–6, 7–5, while Hahn beat Griffin in the other, 4–6, 6–4, 4–6, 6–2, 6–3, and Johns in the final, 6–1, 6–4, 3–6, 6–1. Upsets also plagued the ladies' singles as Anita Meyers beat national champion Molla Bjurstedt in the semis, 0–6, 6–4, 6–4, while Hazel Hotchkiss-Wightman easily defeated Myers in the final.[77]

The 1915 Pacific Coast rankings were William M. Johnston, no. 1; John R. Strachan, no. 2; Clarence J. Griffin, no. 3; Willis E. Davis, no. 4; Robert L. Murray, no. 5; Carl R. Gardner, no. 6; Ward Dawson, no. 7; Roland Roberts, no. 8; H. Van Dyke Johns, no. 9; and Clifton B. Herd, no. 10.[78] All were from the San Francisco Bay Area, with the exceptions of Dawson and Herd, who were from Los Angeles.

1916

At the twenty-first annual Ojai Valley championship, no less than 259 players competed in the various events, including three former national champions—Maurice McLoughlin, Thomas Bundy, and Mary K. Browne. A new champion was named in every event, however, because most of the state's leading stars were on their way east. Emory Rogers won the men's singles title from Herbert Hahn, while Mary Browne easily won the women's singles title over Ethel Sutton-Bruce and paired with Mrs. L. R. Williams to beat the Sutton sisters, Ethel and Florence. Herbert Hahn of Stanford, who captured the 1914 intercollegiate singles title, won it again for 1916 over E. Warren.[79]

The national champion, Bill Johnston, cleaned up at the 1916 Pacific Coast championships at Del Monte during the week of June 17 with a loss of but two sets. He beat his national championship doubles partner Clarence "Peck" Griffin in four extended sets, 9–7, 7–5, 6–8, 8–6, and paired with Griffin to convincingly win the doubles. Roland Roberts, who had taken a set from Griffin in the men's semifinals, won the junior title over Griffin's younger brother Elmer.[80] Helen Baker beat Marjorie Thorn, 8–6, 6–4, to win the women's title, Thorn having disposed of Anita

Myers in the quarters in three sets. The spectacular women's singles feature was the quarterfinal between Laura Herron and Marjorie Wale, in which Herron outlasted Wale in a three-hour, two-set match, 10–8, 11–9.[81–82]

John Strachan of San Francisco won through a field of fifty-eight players in the annual California State championship, defeating Carl Gardner handily after losing the first set through wildness. At this championship last year Willis Davis had beaten both Gardner and Roberts on his way to the title. Playing with William Marcus, Strachan won the doubles title over Gardner and veteran Dr. Sumner Hardy, although the winners required the full five sets before victory was assured, 2–6, 6–1, 5–7, 12–10, 6–4. Anita Myers beat Mrs. J. C. Cushing, 2–6, 6–3, 6–4, in the women's singles event.[83]

Carl Gardner won the Alameda County title over Robert Lipman in four sets, while Mrs. J. C. Cushing captured the women's event by unexpectedly eliminating Anita Myers in the semifinal and Carmen Tarilton in the final with the loss of but three games each match.[84]

1917

Because of the war in Europe, all 1917 tournaments were "Patriotic" events in which no challenge cups, titles, or trophies were awarded; the net profits raised by entrance fees and gate receipts were turned over to the Red Cross.

The first of the Patriotic tournaments, which raised four hundred dollars, was held by the Ojai Valley Association in Nordhoff, California, April 8–12. Emory Rogers of Los Angeles won the men's singles in two 13–11 sets over Axel Graven. Maurice McLoughlin and Simpson Sinsabaugh won the doubles title, while Mary K. Browne won the women's singles title over Mrs. L. R. Williams; the two paired to win the doubles event.[85]

The Pacific States Patriotic tournament was held at the Claremont Country Club on Saturdays and Sundays beginning on June 14. In a field consisting of such notables as Byron Batkin, Clyde Curley, and Roland Roberts, three-time champion William Johnston swept the field, defeating John Strachan in a five-set final. After losing the first set 8–6 to Helen Baker, former national champion Hazel Hotchkiss-Wightman won the next two at love for the women's title.[86]

The doubles event overshadowed the singles tournament in the Pacific Coast Patriotic tournament held at Long Beach June 30–July 4. Mary Browne's brother Nat and Claude Wayne defeated former national champions Tom Bundy and Maurice McLoughlin. The Brownes dominated the event as Mary won the singles title over Florence Sutton and paired with her brother to win the mixed title over May Sutton-Bundy and her husband Tom, a rare case in which a Sutton didn't win.[87]

At the California State Patriotic tournament held at the Berkeley Tennis Club beginning on September 8, Ensign William Johnston won in both the men's singles and doubles events. In the former he started badly, due to lack of practice, but came back strong, defeating Roland Roberts in the semifinal and swamping Mervyn Griffin, the sixteen-year-old boy wonder and youngest brother of three-time national doubles champion Clarence. Griffin defeated Carl Gardner in his semifinal in five sets, 9–7 in the fifth. Helen Baker beat Anita Myers for the women's crown and paired with her foe to win the doubles crown. Mervyn Griffin captured the junior singles title over subsequent national doubles champion Howard Kinsey in five sets after dropping the first two.[88]

1918

With Willis Davis, Clarence Griffin, William Johnston, Lin Murray, and John Strachan away in the service of their country, the 1918 tennis tournaments in the vicinity of San Francisco were kept alive by the crack youngsters and vets. Mervyn Griffin, youngest brother of Lieutenant Clarence Griffin, and Roland Roberts carried off the major honors for the year. Prior to his enlistment in the army, Roberts annexed the San Francisco City and Pacific Coast titles, while Griffin took the Bay Counties, California State, and all the junior events, until his state title win made him ineligible for the junior championships. Seventeen-year-old Mervyn Griffin was the latest star developed on the San Francisco public courts.

Helen Baker of San Francisco established her claim as the best woman player in the Bay District. For several years Baker and Anita Myers had been dividing the local titles between them. Myers won the Coast title and Baker the California State, Bay Counties, and San Francisco City championships.

The Golden Gate Tennis Club, the Ladies' Park Tennis Club, and the Junior Tennis Club held their monthly tournaments as usual. Two local papers also sponsored tourneys. The San Francisco *Bulletin* held a handicap mixed doubles won by Helen Baker and Howard Kinsey over Helen Law and Robert Kinsey, while the San Francisco *Call* staged an ambitious handicap affair for the benefit of the World War Work Fund at the California Lawn Tennis Club. Howard Kinsey and Helen Baker won their respective singles events, and Mary Louise Potter and Robert Kinsey took the mixed doubles title.[89]

1920

At the 1920 April Ojai Valley tournament, Phil Neer won the men's singles while Morgan Fottrell and Ray Johnson won the doubles.[90] The All California intercollegiate tournament was also held at the Ojai Valley Tennis Club. James Davies defeated Wallace Bates in singles, 7–5, 4–6, 7–5, while Davies and Phil Neer defeated Bates and Edmund Levy in doubles.[91] Philip Neer attended Stanford University and in 1921 became the first player from a Western university and only the second non–Ivy League player (G. M. Brinley from Trinity, Connecticut, won in 1886) to win the NCAA intercollegiate singles and achieved a national ranking of no. 20. Neer defeated J. B. Fenno Jr. of Harvard, 3–6, 6–1, 6–4, 1–6, 6–1.[92] A year later he and Jim Davies won the NCAA doubles, the first non–Ivy League school to do so. On January 28, 1933, Neer played his friend and occasional mixed doubles partner Helen Wills-Moody, reigning Wimbledon champion, in an exhibition match in San Francisco. The twenty-eight-year-old Moody beat the thirty-two-year-old Neer, 6–3, 6–4, predating the "Battle of the Sexes" by forty years.[93]

In the San Francisco championships at the California Tennis Club beginning May 1, Roland Roberts beat Mervyn Griffin, father of the famous entertainer of the same name, 6–4, 6–3, 7–5. In the semis Roberts beat Robert Kinsey, while Griffin beat Howard Kinsey. Roberts paired with John Strachan to beat the Kinsey brothers in the doubles final in four deuce sets.[94]

At the Pacific Coast championship in Berkeley beginning on June 19, Willis Davis beat Clarence Griffin, 10–8, 6–4, 2–6, 6–3. In the men's doubles the Kinsey brothers, Howard and Robert, beat the Griffin brothers, Clarence and Merv.[95] The Kinsey brothers were ranked fourth nationally in 1920. Helen Wills won the junior girls' singles title.

Robert Kinsey won the Southern California men's singles at the YMCA Field Club beginning on July 27.[96] At the California State tournament, held in Berkeley September 4–12, Wallace Bates beat Merv Griffin. In the semifinals Griffin beat Phil Neer, and Bates beat Howard Kinsey. Helen Wills lost in the final round of the junior girls' singles event in that tournament.[97]

The Bay Counties singles championship at the Golden Gate Park Tennis Club, which began October 2, was won by Robert Kinsey over Elmer Griffin in four sets. Roland Roberts and John Strachan won the doubles event.[98]

The 1920 California rankings were Willis Davis, no. 1; Clarence Griffin, no. 2; Roland Roberts, no. 3; Robert Kinsey, no. 4; Wallace Bates, no. 5; Mervyn Griffin, no. 6; Howard Kinsey, no. 7; Morgan Fottrell, no. 8; Elmer Griffin, no. 9; James Davies, no. 10. William Johnston was not considered, as he did not compete. Helen Wills, who would win nineteen singles titles at the French, Wimbledon, and U.S. championships between 1923 and 1938, was ranked ninth in California for 1920.[99]

On the national scene in 1920 Roland Roberts paired with Willis Davis to reach the finals of the U.S. doubles, only to lose to fellow San Franciscans Clarence Griffin and Bill Johnston, while the Kinsey brothers defeated Australian Davis Cuppers Gerald Patterson and Pat O'Hara Wood for the 1924 U.S. doubles title. Paterson, who was the nephew of Australian opera singer Dame Nellie Melba, played with a steel racket in 1925 and was inducted into the International Tennis Hall of Fame in 1989 and the Australian Tennis Hall of Fame in 1997.[100] Howard Kinsey paired with Vinnie Richards to win the 1926 French doubles title over Jacques Brugnon and Henri Cochet. That same year he reached the Wimbledon final, losing to Jean Borotra after beating Brugnon in the semis, 7–5 in the fifth. Bill Tilden wrote of the Kinsey brothers that he had "seldom seen a team work together more smoothly than the Kinseys."[101–102]

Helen Baker, the Griffin brothers—Clarence, Elmer, Mervyn—the Kinsey brothers, and Roland Roberts are just a few period players in the USTA Northern California Hall of Fame.

5
A Few Notes on Men's Doubles

The dates and venues for the U.S. men's singles, women's singles, women's doubles, and mixed doubles events are reasonably straightforward and well-documented. The men's singles were played at Newport, Rhode Island, from 1881 to 1914. In 1892 the Newport Casino purchased a portable grandstand from Barnum and Bailey, which held about three thousand.[1] In 1915 the event moved to a much-needed larger stadium at the West Side Tennis Club in Forest Hills, Long Island, with stands to accommodate about ten thousand. For a brief period (1921–23) the tournament moved to the Germantown Cricket Club in Philadelphia, while the West Side Tennis Club built a concrete horseshoe stadium to accommodate fifteen thousand spectators. In 1968, Open tennis dawned, uniting amateurs and pros. Clay courts were installed in 1975 for the tourney's last three years at Forest Hills. In 1978 the U.S. Open moved a few miles to the USTA National Tennis Center in Flushing Meadows, which featured hard courts.[2–3]

The first U.S. women's singles championship was held in 1887 at the Philadelphia Cricket Club followed in 1889 by the women's doubles event and in 1892 by the mixed doubles tournament through 1920. In 1921 the women's singles and doubles championships were held at Forest Hills, the women's singles until 1977, and the women's doubles until 1933. In 1934 the women's doubles matches were played at Germantown, from 1935 to 1941 at the Longwood Cricket Club, from 1942 to 1945 at Forest Hills, and from 1946 to 1967 at Longwood.[4–5] From 1921 to 1933 the mixed doubles matches were played at Longwood, in 1934 at Germantown, from 1935 to 1941 at Longwood, and from 1942 to 1977 at Forest Hills.[6–7] All events, including men's doubles, combined in 1968 at the West Side Tennis Club and in 1978 at the USTA National Tennis Center.

By contrast, the men's doubles had complicated growing pains until 1917 after going full circle to become a stand-alone tournament at Longwood. The literature has simply said: "The doubles tournament has a wandering history" and "sectional doubles tournaments ... were staged at a variety of locations with the winners playing off for the title at Newport"[8]; or it indicates that matches were played at Newport, Rhode Island, from 1881 to 1919 (1914).[9]

The literature is very vague as to when and where the stand–alone championships were played, when they became sectionalized, where the sectional tournaments were played, and where the playoffs took place. Some of the tournaments were stand–alone; once the sectional winners played for the championship at Newport (1890); sometimes the sectional winners played off at Newport, the winners then meeting the previous year's champions after the challenge round began in 1891. A preliminary doubles tournament was subsequently initiated in which the sectional winners played off for the right to meet the holders at Newport or at the West Side Tennis Club. The doubles came full circle from its inception as a stand-alone tournament with the singles at Newport in 1881 to a stand-alone tournament at Longwood in 1917 to a stand-alone tournament with all the other events at the West Side Tennis Club in 1968. The following is an attempt to sort this out with a few examples and a table.

The first U.S. doubles championship was played at Newport in 1881, along with the singles, through 1886. As "it had been the custom at Newport to play a round of singles in the morning and a round of doubles in the afternoon, and as it had ... been decided [in 1887] that all sets both in singles and doubles should be the best of five 'vantage sets, it was decided to play the singles, only, at Newport, and the doubles were awarded to the Orange [Lawn Tennis] Club in Orange, New Jersey." Since the doubles at Orange were three weeks after the singles, the event was anticlimactic and not well attended.[10] Sears won his sixth and final doubles title paired with Dwight at that tournament.

In 1888 and 1889 the doubles were played at the Staten Island Cricket and Baseball Club—in September of 1888, three weeks after the singles, and in July of 1889. There had been a certain lack of interest among the players in September as they had neglected to keep in form or condition, and the play was horrendous. The move to July proved more successful, and although the entries were not much better than they had been in 1887, the play was much improved.[11] Oliver Campbell and Valentine Hall won in 1888; Henry Slocum and Howard Taylor beat Campbell and Hall in three close sets in 1889, 14–12, 10–8, 6–4.

In 1890 the doubles were sectionalized, whereby the Eastern titlists met the Western (or more correctly Midwest) titlists at Newport during the singles championship. The Eastern doubles were again played at the Staten Island Cricket Club on June 30, while the Western doubles were played at the Kenwood Lawn Tennis Club in Chicago on July 14. At the U.S. Championships in Newport, which began on August 27, the two winners met. The Eastern titlists, Valentine Hall and Clarence Hobart, beat the Western titlists, John Carver and John Ryerson, 6–3, 4–6, 6–2, 2–6, 6–3.[12]

In 1891 the doubles challenge round was inaugurated. The Eastern winners from Staten Island played against the Western winners from Kenwood in Chicago at Newport for the right to meet Hall and Hobart at Newport. The Western doubles continued to be played in Chicago through 1906. In 1892 the Eastern doubles were played at Saratoga, New York.,[13] along with the New York State singles championship. The Hall brothers, Edward and Valentine, earned the right to represent the East at Newport after a hard match with H. G. Bixby and F. H. Hovey. The Western champions J. W. Carver and J. A. Ryerson defaulted to the Eastern winners,[14] the latter losing to holders Oliver Campbell and Bob Huntington.

At the annual USNLTA meeting, held in February 1893, it was resolved that the doubles championship for the 1893 season would be held at Chicago as part of the World's Fair festivities, including the championship match between the tournament winners and the 1892 champions Oliver Campbell and Bob Huntington. The tournament was held at the St. George Cricket Club in Chicago beginning July 25 with sixteen pairs from the East, West, and Pacific Coast. Clarence Hobart of New York and Fred Hovey of Massachusetts, tournament winners, beat two Pacific Coast teams along the way—William Taylor and Joseph Tobin of San Francisco in the second round and the Neel brothers, Carr and Sam, in the semis—and the Western champions S. T. Chase and J. S. Clark in the finals. In the challenge round the champions of 1891 and 1892, Campbell and Huntington, used the same style of play that had been successful before. With Campbell at the net and Huntington, the expert lobber, near the baseline, they lost to Hobart and Hovey in four sets, 6–3, 6–4, 4–6, 6–2. This was the only time in the history of the U.S. Championships an event was held off the Eastern seaboard.[15–17]

In 1894, for example, when Manliffe Goodbody from Ireland played in the U.S. Championships, he paired with Valentine Hall in the Eastern tourney held at Narragansett Pier, Rhode Island, which was won by Arthur Foote and John Howland. The Western champions, the Neel brothers, Carr and Sam, defeated the Yale champions Foote and Howland at Narragansett, thereby qualifying to play for the championship at Newport against the defending champions, Hobart and Hovey.[18–19] Hobart and Hovey won. The Eastern doubles and the playoffs were again held at Narragansett Pier in 1895 and 1896.

For 1896 the Neel brothers from California, Carr and Sam, won the Western title at Kenwood on July 11, while Hobart and Hovey won the Eastern title on August 10. The Neel brothers then defeated Hobart and Hovey on August 14 in five deuce sets, 4–6, 8–6, 4–6, 6–4, 6–4, after being down 4–1 in the fifth.[20] The brothers captured the national title at Newport in another five-setter over the titleholders Malcolm Chase and Robert Wrenn.

In 1897 the Eastern doubles moved to Longwood. On July 31 Harold Mahoney and Harold Nisbet from Great Britain defeated Malcolm Whitman and George Wrenn in a long five-set match, 9–7, 9–7, 2–6, 4–6, 6–3, for the title.[21] In the Western doubles at Kenwood, George Sheldon and Leo Ware, two Eastern players who had gone West, beat E. P. Fischer and J. C. Neeley in five sets.[22] Sheldon and Ware then beat Mahoney and Nisbet at Newport after another exciting five-set match, 11–13, 6–2, 9–7, 1–6, 6–1, becoming national champions when the Neel brothers didn't defend.

In 1898 Dwight Davis and Holcombe Ward won the Western doubles played at Kenwood on July 18, while Malcolm Whitman and Robert Wrenn won the Eastern doubles played at Longwood on July 25. At Newport that year two matches were played: Davis and Ward beat Whitman and Wrenn, 6–2, 6–3, 4–6, 6–3, but lost to George Sheldon and Leo Ware, the defending champions, 1–6, 7–5, 6–4, 4–6, 7–5.[23–24] The same venue prevailed through 1906 with the Chicago and Longwood winners playing off at Newport and then meeting the titleholders.

The 1899 Western doubles at Kenwood, which began July 10, comprised twenty-four teams. J. A. Allen and H. H. Hackett, two Yale experts from the East, beat Myers and Waidner.[25] At Longwood nineteen teams competed in the Eastern doubles beginning on July 24. In the finals Dwight Davis and Holcombe Ward beat C. R. Budlong and B. C. Wright. [26] At Newport Davis and Ward (East) beat Allen and Hackett (West),

3–6, 6–3, 6–3, 6–2, and then toppled the holders George Sheldon and Leo Ware, 6–4, 6–4, 6–3.[27]

In 1903, Kreigh Collins and Harry Waidner, who had won the Western championship at Kenwood, met Holcombe Ward and Leo Ware, the Eastern championship winners at Longwood. The Westerners won the playoff at Newport the first day by a score of 6–3, 6–4, 7–5, but they lost to the famous English Doherty brothers, Laurie and Reggie, in the challenge round the second day, 7–5, 6–3, 6–3. In receiving, the English pair stood one up at the net and one back.[28]

In 1905 the Eastern champions Fred Alexander and Harold Hackett defeated the Western champions Kreigh Collins and Louis Waidner in straight sets but lost to the titleholders Holcombe Ward and Beals Wright in the challenge round in three 6–4 sets.[29]

As the Western champions were unable to be present in 1906, the usual match for the first day of the tournament did not take place. Instead, Holcombe Ward and Beals Wright, titleholders, defeated Fred Alexander and Harold Hackett, Eastern titlists, in four 6–3 sets.[30]

In 1907 the doubles championships were played for the first time in three sections—the East at Longwood, the West at Kenwood, and the South at Atlanta. The winners of each section played at the Crescent Athletic Club in Bay Ridge, Brooklyn, in a preliminary doubles tournament. In the first match Alexander and Hackett (West) beat Clothier and Larned (East), 6–3, 6–0, 6–4. The winners then played Wylie Grant and Nat Thornton of the South. This match was even more one-sided as Alexander and Hackett won, 6–2, 6–1, 6–1. As Beals Wright had already played in the Eastern doubles, there was no championship pair to defend the title, and Alexander and Hackett won the championship without even appearing at Newport.[31]

The same scenario prevailed in 1908 when the East, West, and South winners met on the fine grass courts of the Crescent Athletic Club in Bay Ridge beginning on August 13. In the first match Ray Little and Beals Wright (East) beat Whitehead and Winston (South), 6–0, 6–3, 6–2. The East then won a much closer match from the Western pair, Nat Emerson and L. H. Waidner, 7–5, 6–3, 6–4, but lost to Alexander and Hackett at Newport.[32]

When in 1909 the Far West or California played, the tournament was held on the Onwentsia Club grass courts in Lake Forest, Illinois, from 1909 to 1916. At the annual USNLTA meeting on February 9, 1917, the delegates voted to hold the national doubles championship at the Longwood Cricket Club in Chestnut Hill, Massachusetts, in *one* tournament; the champion team would play through, thereby abolishing the challenge round. The following resolution was adopted unanimously at the same meeting: "The Executive Committee is authorized to award the Sectional Championships to all the Sections of the country, one to the Middle States and New England as in the past, and one to each of the other Sections; *and each Section is urged to send a team to play in the National Doubles Championship*."[33] The national doubles were played at Longwood through 1933, at Germantown in 1934, at Longwood from 1935 to 1941, at Forest Hills from 1942 to 1945, and back to Longwood from 1946 to 1967.[34]

Men's Doubles

Date	Location	Venue
1881–86	Newport Casino, RI	Stand-alone tournament with singles
1887	Orange Lawn Tennis Club, Orange, NJ	Stand-alone tournament September
1888	Staten Island Cricket Club, NY	Stand-alone tournament September
1889	Staten Island Cricket Club, NY	Stand-alone tournament July
1890	Sectionalized; East at Staten Island; West at Kenwood Lawn Tennis Club, Chicago	East vs. West at Newport
1891	Challenge round inaugurated; East at Staten Island; West at Kenwood	Playoffs at Newport; winners played 1890 champions at Newport
1892	East at Saratoga, NY; West at Kenwood	Playoffs at Newport; winners played 1891 champions at Newport
1893	St. George Cricket Club, Chicago, IL	Stand-alone tournament July; winners played 1892 champions at Chicago
1894–96	East at Narragansett Pier, RI; West at Kenwood, playoffs at Narragansett	Winners played previous year's champions at Newport
1897–1906	East at Longwood Cricket Club, MA; West at Kenwood	Playoffs at Newport; winners played previous year's champions at Newport
1907–08	Preliminary doubles tournament played at Crescent Athletic Club, NY; East, West, and South winners played off	Winners played previous year's champions at Newport

1909–14	Preliminary doubles tournament played at Onwentsia Club; East, West, South, and Pacific Coast winners played off	Winners played previous year's champions at Newport
1915	Preliminary doubles tournament played at Onwentsia Club; East, West, South, Pacific Coast, and Northwest winners played off	Winners played previous year's champions at West Side Tennis Club
1916	Preliminary doubles tournament played at Onwentsia Club; East, West, South, Pacific Coast, Northwest, Middle Atlantic, Missouri Valley, and Southwest winners played off	Winners played previous year's champions at West Side Tennis Club
1917–33	Challenge round eliminated; Longwood Cricket Club, Chestnut Hill, MA	Stand-alone tournament July

The Preliminary tournament winners from 1909 to 1916 were:

1909 George Janes and Maurice E. McLoughlin
1910 Thomas C. Bundy and Trowbridge Hendrick
1911 Raymond D. Little and Gus F. Touchard
1912 Thomas C. Bundy and Maurice E. McLoughlin
1913 Clarence J. Griffin and John R. Strachan
1914 George M. Church and Dean Mathey
1915 Clarence J. Griffin and William M. Johnston
1916 Ward Dawson and Maurice E. McLoughlin

In 1911 and 1914, when the Pacific Coast team did not win the right to compete in the nationals, the Coast winners were Bundy and McLoughlin, and Griffin and Johnston, respectively.

1909

The 1909 Pacific States doubles tournament was held July 1–5 on the new cement courts of the Hotel Virginia in Long Beach. This event had usually been played in conjunction with the singles championship held in September at Del Monte, but in order that the winners might reach Lake Forest, Illinois, in time to compete in the preliminary national doubles event, beginning on August 2, it was necessary to select an earlier date. Of the nineteen teams entered, Alphonzo Bell and Tom Bundy won the tournament by defeating Nat Browne and Simpson Sinsabaugh, 6–4, 2–6, 6–4, 6–4. In the challenge round George Janes and Maurice McLoughlin, both San Franciscans, defeated Bell and Bundy in a terrific five-setter, 5–7, 4–6, 6–3, 6–3, 6–4.[35]

On August 3–4, teams representing the East, West, South, and Pacific Coast met on the Onwentsia Club's grass courts in Lake Forest, Illinois. It was the first time in sixteen years that Chicago was allotted a meeting of national import, the last being the 1893 World's Fair stand-alone tournament. The South's representatives Theodore Pell and Wylie Grant, both New Yorkers, defeated the West's Trux Emerson of Cincinnati and R. A. Holden Jr., 1910 Yale intercollegiate champion, 6–3, 6–2, 8–6. Immediately following that match the Pacific Coast team of Janes and McLoughlin defeated the Eastern combination of Nat Niles and A. S. Dabney Jr. Despite being down 5–2 in the first set, the Pacific Coast team rallied to win, 7–5, 6–4, 6–3, McLoughlin's services and Janes's smashes foretelling the eventual outcome in the first set. The Coast players defeated the Southern pair for the right to play in the nationals by a score of 5–7, 6–2, 6–3, 6–3.[36] Janes and McLoughlin, in their first nationals, were easily defeated by the great doubles combination of Fred Alexander and Harold Hackett, 6–4, 6–4, 6–0.

1910

The 1910 doubles championship of the Pacific States, held July 1–5 on the cement courts at Long Beach, was won by Thomas Bundy and Trowbridge Hendrick over Melville Long and Maurice McLoughlin, 7–5, 6–8, 6–2, 3–6, 7–5, giving the champions the right to represent the Far West at Lake Forest, Illinois, to contend in the preliminary doubles against the East, South, and Mid West teams; the winners would meet the national champions at Newport.[37] The preliminary tie between the East, South, Mid West, and Far West resulted in Bundy and Hendrick defeating Waidner and Gardner from the Mid West, 5–7, 6–4, 6–4, 6–3.[38] Bundy and Hendrick reached the national final but lost to Fred Alexander and Harold Hackett, 6–1, 8–6, 6–3, giving the latter their fourth straight national doubles title.

1911

Maurice McLoughlin and Thomas Bundy won the 1911 Pacific Coast doubles championship and the right to play in the national preliminaries by defeating Hardy and Foley, 16–14, 4–6, 6–1, 6–1, at Long Beach. The winners were among sixteen star teams starting July 4.[39] The winners of the four sectional tournaments, Little and Touchard from the East, the Doyle brothers from the South, Cull and Martin from the Mid West, and McLoughlin and Bundy from the Pacific Coast, met on the Onwentsia Club courts August 1–2. R. D. Little and G. F. Touchard beat T. C. Bundy and M. E. McLoughlin, 6–4, 6–4, 7–9, 3–6, 10–8, and then C. B. and H. E. Doyle, 6–4, 4–6, 6–4, 1–6, 6–3.[40] The winning pair then dethroned Hackett and Alexander, champions the past four years, for the national title.

1912

The representatives for the Pacific Coast at the 1912 national preliminaries held on July 30 and 31 were Tom Bundy of Los Angeles and Maurice "Comet" McLoughlin of San Francisco. Walter Hayes and James Winston of Chicago (West) defeated William Clothier of Philadelphia and George Gardner Jr., of Boston (East) in five deuce sets totaling sixty games, 6–4, 5–7, 8–10, 6–4, 6–4. Meanwhile Bundy and McLoughlin (Pacific Coast) demolished Carleton Smith and Nat Thornton (South), 6–2, 6–1, 6–1, after the South started with a 2–1 lead. In the final round McLoughlin and Bundy defeated Hayes and Winston, 6–0, 7–5, 6–3. "Throughout the match Bundy and McLoughlin demonstrated that they are without question fifty percent stronger than when they met Touchard and Little a year ago in the heart-breaking five-set match.... Their team work is still not all to be desired, but even in this department they have improved vastly over their last year's form. Their net work, however, was easily the best ever seen in the West, and they presented a stonewall defense fully the equal of Hackett and Alexander's in the latter's palmy days."[41]

After four years of persistent effort, the Californians won the national doubles championship. Each had reached the challenge round on two other occasions. In 1909 McLoughlin and Janes lost to Hackett and Alexander "and in 1910 Bundy and Hendrick met the same fate at the hands of the same pair."[42] This year the challengers, Bundy and McLoughlin, defeated

Ray Little and Gus Touchard of New York, 3–6, 6–2, 6–1, 7–5, the latter pair having deposed four-time champions Hackett and Alexander in 1911.

1913

Clarence Griffin and John R. Strachan, both of San Francisco, earned the right to represent the Pacific States in the 1913 national preliminaries at Lake Forest, Illinois, by decisively winning the Pacific Coast doubles held July 1–5 at the Los Angeles Country Club. Thirty-two teams entered the struggle to represent the Far West. The logical favorites were the four San Francisco boys who met in the semis. Griffin and Strachan defeated Bill Johnston and Elia Fottrell in the semifinals, 6–3, 6–1, 6–2, and Clifton Herd and Ward Dawson of Los Angeles in the finals, 7–5, 6–1, 7–5.[43] Griffin and Strachan, fresh from their victory in the National Clay Court event, played throughout the national preliminaries in a whirlwind fashion by defeating J. B. Adoue and R. F. Shelton from the South and Gus F. Touchard and Watson M. Washburn from the East, 6–1, 8–6, 6–4.[44] In an all-California national final, they lost to 1912 champions Maurice E. McLoughlin and Thomas C. Bundy, 6–4, 7–5, 6–1.

1914

Spalding's 1915 Annual colorfully noted that "W. M. Johnston and Clarence Griffin dropped jauntily in at the Hotel Virginia, Long Beach, Cal., on July 1, and four days later emerged twice as jauntily, with the title and privilege of representing the Pacific Coast at Lake Forest, Ill." In one semifinal "McCormick and Barber bit the dust to the score of 6–1, 6–0, 6–1, hardly giving Johnston and his stubby partner a try-out." In the same round Nat Browne and Claude Wayne beat Winifred Mace and Simpson Sinsabaugh, 6-1, 6-3, 6-3. In the final round Johnston and Griffin beat Browne and Wayne, 6–1, 6–4, 6–3. "Browne and Wayne played Griffin two-thirds of the time, but that gentleman was right at the top and simply ate up all that came his way. Johnston, too, was deadly and the outcome was never in doubt from start to finish of the match."[45]

Johnston and Griffin, however, lost to Theodore Pell and Karl Behr (East), 4–6, 6–2, 1–6, 7–5, 6–3, in the semifinals at Lake Forest, Illinois. In the finals George M. Church and Dean Mathey (West) defeated Pell and Behr (East), 6–3, 6–4, 4–6, 7–5.[46] McLoughlin and Bundy retained the national title for the third time by defeating Church and Mathey in straight sets, 6–4, 6–2, 6–4.

1915

The 1915 Pacific States doubles championship opened July 1 on the courts of Hotel Virginia at Long Beach with twenty-five teams entered. The original plan was to have Strachan play with Johnston, but the former was unable to make the trip east; so at the last moment, Griffin was selected, and history shows how well the substitution worked out. The pair defeated Browne and Wayne in the finals, 6–3, 6–4, 6–4.[47] At the national preliminaries five doubles teams, representing as many sections of the country, including the newly organized Northwest division, battled at Lake Forest, Illinois, August 10–14. The strongest contenders were drawn against each other at the outset. The Pacific Coast stars, Johnston and Griffin, met and defeated the Eastern title winners, Williams and Washburn, in five long sets, 6–8, 6–3, 7–9, 6–4, 6–4. Johnston and Griffin then beat the Northwest titleholders, Church and Mathey, 8–10, 8–6, 7–5, 4–6, 7–5, in the semis and Hayes and Burdick of the West in straight sets.[48] Bundy and McLoughlin had defeated Church and Mathey for their third consecutive national doubles title in 1914 at Newport but were dethroned by Johnston and Griffin in an all-California 1915 final at Forest Hills, 6–2, 3–6, 4–6, 6–3, 6–3.

Johnston and Griffin went undefeated in 1915, winning the U.S. Championships over fellow Californians Bundy and McLoughlin, Pacific Coast, Preliminary Doubles, Newport, and Southampton. They beat Herd and Dawson, Browne and Wayne, Williams and Washburn (no. 3), Church and Mathey, Hayes and Burdick, LeRoy and Bull, Wright and W. F. Johnson, Little and Alexander, Pell and Prentice, Church and Hall, and McLoughlin and Bundy.[49]

1916

Among twenty-eight teams competing in the Pacific Coast doubles championship begun June 30 on the Hotel Virginia courts at Long Beach, Maurice McLoughlin (with a brand new partner, Ward Dawson of Los Angeles) captured the twenty-ninth annual championship by defeating lefthanders Tom Bundy and Clifton Herd in the finals, 9–7, 5–7, 6–3, 6–8, 6–2.[50]

Seven other sections were represented at the preliminary doubles competition that year at Lake Forest. In addition to the East, West, South, and Northwest, there were three new sections: Middle Atlantic, Missouri Valley, and Southwestern. Only two teams were considered serious contenders—McLoughlin and Dawson and George Church (Princeton) and Willis Davis (San Francisco) representing the East. After receiving a default in the first round Church and Davis overcame a two-set deficit to defeat W. T. Hayes and R. H. Burdick (West), 3–6, 6–8, 6–4, 6–3, 6–2. In the final round McLoughlin and Dawson beat Church and Davis, 4–6, 7–5, 7–5, 6–3. Church and Davis "were not consistently effective enough to overcome the whirlwind attack" of McLoughlin, who "was very nearly up to his old time form and carried his team through to victory in hard fought sets."[51]

William Johnston and Clarence Griffin once again retained their championship laurels by decisively defeating McLoughlin and Dawson in another all-California title match, 6–4, 6–3, 5–7, 6–3. McLoughlin was his old-time brilliant self only in flashes and obviously missed the steadying effect of his old partner, Tom Bundy, with whom he had won the title from 1912 to 1914. The most consistently brilliant player of the quartet was the twenty-eight-year-old "Griffin, who not only made openings by remarkably clever placing, but was extremely effective in finishing off the points, which in former years he would have left for his hard-hitting partner" Johnston.[52]

1920

The Pacific Coast played a sectional doubles tournament beginning July 2 even though a win wasn't necessarily required for the nationals. In the final Willis Davis and Clarence Griffin beat the Kinsey brothers, 4–6, 2–6, 7–5, 6–3, 6–4.[53] Qualifications for entry in the national doubles championship included:

1. A sectional doubles championship winner. If the winners could not compete, the runners-up could take their place.
2. Players who had been ranked by the USLTA during the prior five years, or who had at any time been ranked in the first twenty in singles or the first ten in doubles.
3. Players who have been semi-finalists or better in any two USLTA-sanctioned tournaments in the previous three years.

4. Players who had made a reasonably good record in not less than three sanctioned tournaments in the current season.[54]

And so it went that any reasonably good team could enter. At the 1920 U.S. Doubles Championship at Longwood beginning August 16, Willis Davis paired with Roland Roberts and Clarence Griffin paired with William Johnston with whom he had won the 1915–16 titles. The best match of the tournament was the semifinal between Davis–Roberts and Charles Garland–William Tilden, the former winning, 7–9, 6–4, 3–6, 6–4, 6–2. This match seemed to take the edge off Davis and Roberts, who lost to a team of seasoned players and good court generals, Griffin and Johnston, in an all–San Francisco final.[55]

Clarence Griffin had two tennis-playing brothers. Mervyn Griffin, father of the famous entertainer of the same name, was ranked seventy-sixth, and Elmer was ranked eighty-sixth in 1920. Also that year, three of the top four doubles teams were San Franciscans—Clarence Griffin and William Johnston, no. 1; Willis Davis and Roland Roberts, no. 2; and the Kinsey brothers, Howard and Robert, no. 4.[56]

The Golden State floodgates opened in 1909 at the U.S. Championships for both genders, with the women being initially more successful. Hazel Hotchkiss won her first of three successive U.S. singles titles in 1909 and defeated Florence Sutton in the 1911 challenge round, 8–10, 6–1, 9–7. In her Eastern debut, Florence defeated Eleonora Sears in the final, 6–2, 6–1. Hazel also won the women's doubles and the mixed titles each of those three years. Mary K. Browne of Los Angeles duplicated Hazel's feat of winning three consecutive hat tricks—the singles, women's doubles, and mixed doubles championships for the years 1912–14. The transplanted Viking warrior from Norway, Molla Bjurstedt, living in Brooklyn, won from 1915 to 1918, and Hazel Hotchkiss, now Mrs. George Wightman, won the 1919 title. When the first women's rankings appeared in 1913, Mary K. Browne was no. 1; Ethel Sutton-Bruce, no. 2; and Florence Sutton no. 3. Hazel Hotchkiss-Wightman was no. 2 in 1915 and 1918 and no. 1 in 1919. Even though well past her prime, May Sutton-Bundy was ranked fourth in 1921 and fifth in 1922, eighteen years after winning the U.S. singles title. She was age thirty-five and thirty-six, respectively. Had the Sutton sisters—Ethel, Violet, Florence, and May—played the U.S. Championships during the first decade of the twentieth century, it's likely they would have dominated women's tennis.

Five California men played in the 1909 Eastern tournaments and qualified for the nationals—Thomas C. Bundy, George C. Janes, Maurice E. McLoughlin, Melville H. Long, and Simpson M. Sinsabaugh. Bundy had defeated A. E. Bell for the 1908 Southern California title. Janes won the 1905 Pacific Coast singles title and the 1907 and 1908 doubles titles with McLoughlin. McLoughlin won the 1907 Pacific Coast singles and doubles events, the 1908 Ojai Valley doubles event with Carl R. Gardner, and the 1908 California State singles title and the doubles title with Janes. Long won the 1906 Pacific Coast junior singles, the 1907 California State and Southern California singles, and the 1908 Pacific Coast singles. Sinsabaugh, a doubles specialist, won many men's and mixed doubles titles between 1904 and 1908. In order to qualify for the nationals or be ranked, a player had to compete throughout the Eastern circuit in three or more sanctioned events. Sinsabaugh and Janes lost in the second round, Janes in five sets; McLoughlin defeated Long in the fourth round, 7–5, 6–2, 5–7, 2–6, 10–8 and reached the first of six U.S. finals, where he lost to William Clothier (no. 4); Bundy lost to Clothier in the semis. At year's end Maurice McLoughlin was ranked sixth and Melville Long ranked seventh.

The Pacific Coast men traveling east in 1910 to play in the nationals were Thomas C. Bundy, Carl R. Gardner, Trowbridge Hendrick, Maurice E. McLoughlin, and A. Thacher. Thacher unfortunately had a bye in the first round, a default in the second, and won only one game in the third. Hendrick had a good five-set win over Watson Washburn (future top tenner) in the third round but lost in the fourth. Gardner lost in the fifth, and McLoughlin lost to Beals Wright in the quarters. Bundy won the all-comers over Beals Wright, 6–8, 6–3, 6–3, 10–8, but lost to William Larned in the challenge round, 6–1, 5–7, 6–0, 6–8, 6–4. This was Larned's sixth U.S. singles title and fourth in a row. Four California stars reached the top ten—Tom Bundy (no. 2), Maurice McLoughlin (no. 4), Mel Long (no. 5), and Carl Gardner (no. 10).

The 1911 West Coast contingent included a resurrected A. E. Bell, Tom Bundy, Carl Gardner, Maurice McLoughlin, and Melville Long. Long lost in the fourth round to Nat Niles, Gardner to Gus Touchard in the quarters, Bundy to Beals Wright in the semis. McLoughlin won the all-comers over Wright but lost to William Larned in the challenge round, 6–4, 6–4, 6–2, Larned making it five in a row at the 1911 U.S. Championships, the last year of the challenge round, thus tying Fred

Sears with seven U.S. singles titles. The rankings for 1911 were Maurice McLoughlin, no. 2; Tom Bundy, no. 3; and Mel Long, no. 5.

In 1912 Tom Bundy and Maurice McLoughlin represented California. After one default and three easy wins, Bundy defaulted to George Church in the fifth round while McLoughlin beat Dick Williams in the quarters, William Clothier in the semis, and Wallace Johnson in the final, earning him the first of three successive no. 1 rankings. Bundy and McLoughlin won their first of three successive doubles titles.

In addition to Tom Bundy of Los Angeles and Maurice McLoughlin, two outstanding San Franciscan teenagers, Bill Johnston and John Strachan, played in the 1913 U.S. Championships. That year on the Pacific Coast, Johnston had beaten Strachan three times in singles events and four times in doubles matches. Johnston lost to Dick Williams (no. 2) in the fourth round, while Strachan beat fellow Californian Tom Bundy (no. 6) in the third round but lost to Wallace Johnson (no. 3) in the quarters. McLoughlin beat William Clothier in the quarters, Wallace Johnson in the semis, and Dick Williams of Philadelphia in the final for his second successive title. McLoughlin would be a finalist in 1914 to Williams and in 1915 to fellow San Franciscan, Bill Johnston. McLoughlin, "the California Comet," was thus in the final in five successive years, winning twice. Williams defeated Johnston in the 1916 final while R. Lindley Murray from Palo Alto won the 1917 and 1918 titles, the latter over Bill Tilden, while Bill Johnston won the 1919 title over Tilden. During the period 1910–19, Californians won six singles titles and five second-place finishes in the men's division. In doubles Tom Bundy and Trowbridge Hendrick from Los Angeles were 1910 finalists, while Bundy and McLoughlin won from 1912 to 1914. Clarence Griffin and Johnston, both San Franciscans, won in 1915, '16, and '20. In 1913, '15, '16, and '20, all-California national doubles titles were at stake. The finalists in those years, respectively were Griffin–Strachan, Bundy–McLoughlin, Ward Dawson (Los Angeles)–McLoughlin, and San Franciscans Willis Davis–Roland Roberts.

Such was the dominance of California tennis, especially among Bay Area players, at the U.S. Championships during the second decade of the twentieth century. The tournament records show that several California players beat national champions, would-be national champions, and U.S. top tenners. For example, after winning the 1915 U.S. singles event and the doubles title with Clarence Griffin, Bill Johnston came home to play in the Pacific Coast championship only to lose to H. Van Dyke Johns in one semi, while Griffin lost to Herbert Hahn in the other. Hahn and Johns were, respectively, 1914 and 1915 Pacific Coast intercollegiate titlists for Stanford. In 1914 Johnny Strachan beat both Griffin and Johnston in the California State championships.

For one reason or another—distance and financial and other obligations—the majority of California players never competed in the nationals. Yet it may be fair to say that a tournament of only San Francisco players could have compared favorably with the U.S. Championships at Newport or Forest Hills between about 1910 and 1920. Of the few players who did go east, the successful ones returned to play or stayed. Tom Bundy of Los Angeles was the oldest of those going east in 1909 at almost twenty-eight, yet he won the 1910 all-comers and took three consecutive doubles titles alongside Maurice McLoughlin from 1912 to 1914. A listing of the Californians in the U.S. top ten from 1910 to 1920 follows. All but Tom Bundy were Bay Area players.

1910: Tom Bundy, no. 2; Maurice McLoughlin, no. 4; Melville Long, no. 5; Carleton Gardner, no. 10. Gardner stayed East, working in downtown Manhattan.

1911: Maurice McLoughlin, no. 2; Tom Bundy, no. 3; Melville Long, no. 5. Mel Long studied medicine at Penn, returning to San Francisco as Dr. Long.

1912: Maurice McLoughlin, no. 1; Tom Bundy, no. 6.

1913: Maurice McLoughlin, no. 1; William Johnston, no. 4; John Strachan, no. 10.

1914: Maurice McLoughlin, no. 1; R. Lindley Murray, no. 4; William Johnston, no. 6; Elia Fottrell, no. 10.

1915: William Johnston, no. 1; Maurice McLoughlin, no. 3; Clarence Griffin, no. 7.

1916: William Johnston, no. 2, R. Lindley Murray, no. 4; Clarence Griffin, no. 6; Willis Davis, no. 8.

1917: No rankings.

1918: R. Lindley Murray, no. 1.

1919: William Johnston, no. 1; R. Lindley Murray, no. 4; Roland Roberts, no. 7.

1920: William Johnston, no. 2; Willis Davis, no. 5; Clarence Griffin, no. 6; Roland Roberts, no. 11.

Part II: Robert Lindley Murray

6
Family Genealogy

The genealogy of Robert Lindley Murray in the United States can be traced back to two early eighteenth-century immigrants whose names he shared: Robert Murray, a Presbyterian turned Quaker, born in Ireland of Scottish parents, and Thomas Lindley, a Quaker born in Ireland. The Murray motto—"Furth, Fortune, and Fill the Fetters," which roughly translates to go forth against your enemies, have good fortune, and return with hostages and booty—was certainly appropriate, as the first and subsequent generations became quite prosperous.

John Murray of the Scotch Murrays of Blair Atholl, County of Perth, where lies Blair Castle with its thirteenth century roots at one of Scotland's finest settings in the heart of Highland Berkshire,[1] fled, seeking political asylum, with his wife, sons, and their families to County Armagh, Northern Ireland between 1720 and 1721. His son, Robert Murray, was born in Armagh in 1721. Robert and his brother, with their father, John, traveled to America in 1732, settling in what is now Dauphin County in Pennsylvania, where the state capital Harrisburg is located. John Murray bought over two hundred acres on the Swatara Creek, then in Hanover Township, from 1732 to 1733. Robert became proprietor of the family's prosperous mill there while still in his teens.[2–3]

Robert Murray married Mary Lindley (1724–80) in 1744, after he converted from a Presbyterian to the Society of Friends as a Quaker. Mary Lindley's father, Thomas Lindley (1684–1743), had been born into a Quaker family in the village of Ballincash in County Wicklow, Ireland, later moving to Ringsend, County Dublin. Soon after immigrating to Philadelphia in 1719, Thomas applied to Dublin for clearance to marry Hannah Durborow, daughter of a Philadelphia brewer, an occupation frequently taken up by Quakers both in Britain and the colonies.[4–6] Thomas quickly became connected with the richest and most powerful men in Pennsylvania. As a blacksmith and anchorsmith, Thomas became a founding owner of the prosperous Durham Furnace workshop on the Delaware River in Bucks County with fellow Quakers in 1727, a six-thousand-acre iron ore site, and one of the leading forges in the colonies. About 1733, Thomas Lindley bought 480 acres of land in Paxtang Township in Lancaster County, a few miles from Robert Murray's residence in Swatara. In 1738 he became a justice of the peace and served in the Pennsylvania Assembly from 1739 until his death in 1743.[7–8]

From at least 1745 on Robert Murray was operating as a merchant and making trading visits to the West Indies, capitalizing on his position as a miller. Flour and wheat were Pennsylvania's major exports to the West Indies.[9] After a brief sojourn (1751–53) in North Carolina, the family returned to the north in 1753, where Robert settled in lower Manhattan bounded by Queen (now Pearl) Street on the west, Pine Street on the north, the East River, and Wall Street to the south,[10] with his home at the corner of Queen and Beekman Streets.[11] In little more than a decade and a half he became one of the city's wealthiest and most influential citizens. With a population of around 12,500, New York City was to experience an economic boom.[12] The French and Indian War between England and France erupted in North America in 1754, two years before the general conflict known as the Seven Years' War. Between 1754 and 1759, the customs value of imported English goods increased by 453 percent.[13]

This boom made Robert Murray's fortune from an array of businesses, the most important of which was shipping and overseas trade; he owned three vessels and an interest in a fourth by 1764. Along with the Franklins, he fitted out a sloop for whaling that sailed from New York in 1768. Robert Murray built a wharf on the lower East River at Wall Street, which was commercially active for many years afterward. It was the scene of the "New York Tea Party" in 1774, and at the end of the Revolution, George Washington debarked from Murray's wharf on his way to being sworn in as the first president.[14] Of necessity Robert was in the marine insurance business. He "dealt in indigo with the Delaplaines, and sold imported goods from the store of Murray and Pearsall on the waterfront." The store sold a wide assortment of goods: fashionable textiles, hardware, foodstuffs, clocks and watches, primers, spelling books, and young man's companions, required reading for young clerks.[15]

In about 1762, Murray leased land from the municipality and built a farming estate called Inclenberg, derived from a Dutch prominence, or the French equivalent, Belmont, on a since-leveled hill known as the Murray Hill neighborhood of Manhattan at what is today Park Avenue and Thirty-sixth Street.[16–17] In that fine house the Murrays entertained practically every dignitary who visited the city. In the family lore Mrs. Robert Murray, although a (teetotaling) Quaker, "was not above others imbibing at her parties. To do something different at one soiree, she asked the barman to go to the barnyard and bring back feathers from the tails of roosters to adorn the guests' glasses: hence the term 'cocktail.'"[18]

Although Robert Murray was a loyalist and continued to engage in trade with the British, Mary was sympathetic to the American cause. Many members of her family served in General Washington's army during the Revolutionary War. After the British won the Battle of Brooklyn Heights, Washington fell back to the Murray estate, where he had his headquarters for a brief time, and from its upper floor watched the movement of British ships in the East River.[19] Prior to his retreating toward Harlem Heights, Washington dispatched Captain Nathan Hale to find out what the British were doing on Long Island. A Tory kinsman betrayed Hale, and he was hung the following morning (September 22, 1776) at which time, with unfaltering voice, Hale famously uttered, "I only regret that I have but one life to lose for my country."[20]

On September 15, 1776, British troops led by General William Howe crossed Kip's Bay and occupied New York, intending to trap General Israel Putnam, whose headquarters were at No. 1 Broadway, before he could rejoin Washington. With Putnam's troops within a mile of her home, Mary and her young daughters, Beulah and Susannah, waited at the gates of their home on the Boston Post Road (also known as the Kingsbridge Road), approximating today's Lexington Avenue, to welcome the gallant Sir William with a "courteous invitation to alight and partake of refreshments."[21] This they did, while in an upstairs cupola, a maid watched as General Putnam's forced march on a very sultry day "encumbered by women and children and all kinds of baggage" safely passed by amid clouds of dust on the Middle Road (also the Bloomingdale Road) west of the home.[22–23]

For Mary's act of patriotism, the Knickerbocker Chapter of the Daughters of the American Revolution erected a monument to her memory in 1903 at Park Avenue and Thirty-seventh Street. In addition, the legend of Mary Lindley Murray was developed into two Broadway plays: *Dearest Enemy* in 1925 and *A Small War on Murray Hill* in 1957.[24]

A depiction of Mary Lindley Murray's heroism at Murray Hill in the Revolution on pages 74–75 of an unknown source.

(Courtesy Chrissie Kremer)

Lindley Murray

Robert and Mary's first child, the famous grammarian Lindley Murray (1745–1826), was born in a house near his father's mill on Swatara Creek, about a mile from what is today Harper Tavern near Route 22, eighteen miles northeast of Harrisburg.[25–26] After Lindley's formal education at Franklin's Philadelphia academy in 1756–57, Robert placed him in the counting house of his mercantile business,[27] the drudgery of which the young man resented. After a year's work in the Philadelphia counting house of the prominent Quaker merchant Robert Waln in 1762, the sixteen-year-old returned to New York where he remained in the routine of commercial affairs.[28]

Lindley had a clash with his father, entered the Burlington Academy in New Jersey to learn French for a short time,[29] and then returned home to a private tutor in classical knowledge and science, which was to his liking. His subsequent interest in law school led to Robert having him study at the Golden Hill office of the eminent lawyer Benjamin Kissam (c. 1737–80) in 1763. He was eighteen and just got in under the wire, since in January 1764 the new rules of the New York bar required two years of study at a university as well as a clerkship of two hundred pounds, which Robert Murray likely paid anyway.[30] Although the clerkship entailed much the same drudgery as the counting house, "Lindley persevered, finished his legal studies, and entered practice in 1767, at about the age of 22." In Lindley's second year at Kissam's, John Jay, subsequent first chief justice of the United States, arrived, and Lindley was made senior clerk. Murray and Jay continued an acquaintance throughout their lives.[31]

By 1767 the boom time was over, and New York City had endured an economic depression. The fall of Quebec and Fort Niagara cut off the French Frontier forts to the south and west. (The French and Indian War ended in September 1760 with the capitulation of Montreal.) From the pre-Revolution high in 1759 the customs value of imports had plummeted by 1761 to about the same value as it had been in 1754 before the boom.[32] During 1765 or early 1766, Robert went to London to revive his fortunes. Lindley joined him there after finishing his legal studies, accompanied by his new wife, Hannah Dobson, a Friend from Flushing, Long Island. The couple married on June 22, 1767. Her father, Thomas Dobson, and his wife, Catherine Bowne, were prominent Quakers; Catherine was a descendant of the famous seventeenth-century Quaker proselytizer John Bowen.[33]

Robert Murray went into business with fellow Quaker Philip Sansom of London, under the firm name Murray & Sansom. Robert returned to New York in 1768; Lindley and Hannah returned in late 1771.[34] Lindley began to represent the family on important New York bodies charged with enforcing on colonial merchants the nonimportation agreements in the wake of the Townshend Acts,[35] a series of acts beginning in 1767 enacted to tax the colonies for the specific purpose of raising revenue for the debt incurred following the Seven Years' War.[36] Parliament's passage in 1774 of what colonists were calling the "coercive acts" in response to the Boston Tea Party, roused anti-British fervor that led to the First Continental Congress (from September 5 to October 26), which forbade importation and use of British goods.[37]

Robert had two separate firms, Murray & Sansom and Robert Murray & Co.; his brother (younger by some twenty years), John Murray, conducted affairs in New York during Robert's absence in Britain. In 1771 the former "firm's name was changed to Murray, Sansom & Co., apparently reflecting John Murray's rise" as a junior partner.[38] The latter business handled mainly domestic investments. One store in Elizabethtown, New Jersey, "was operated by Ichabod Barnet, who was married to Robert's oldest daughter, Mary." John Murray also became a junior partner in that business.[39]

Lindley was caught between a rock and a hard place. Robert was a Loyalist merchant while Lindley represented the family on New York's Committee of Sixty, which was empowered to enforce nonimportation.[40] A major maritime event and an attempted cover-up by Robert and John Murray caused deep embarrassment for the family. "It gave the Murrays a wide reputation for opposing the patriot cause and almost resulted in expulsion of Robert and John Murray from New York City." The *Beulah* affair "was also likely an important factor in the exile of Lindley Murray from New York a decade later."[41]

On February 17, 1775, the Committee of Sixty prevented the *Beulah*, a merchant ship named after Robert Murrays's second daughter and carrying European goods belonging to his firm Murray & Sansom, from entering the port area. The *Beulah* lay in the Narrows between Staten Island and Brooklyn for three weeks and then moved to Sandy Hook off New Jersey on March 5. When a squall forced the committee's patrol boat to seek haven, the *Beulah* made way to Staten Island, under cover of darkness, where a previously arranged boat from Elizabethtown, New Jersey, just west of lower Staten Island, was waiting.[42] Samuel Lee, hired by Ichabod Barnet, had leased the boat where he, John Murray, Barnet, and two employees offloaded the goods and shipped them to Barnet's store in Elizabethtown.[43–44]

The zealous Isaac Sears of the committee of inspection found out about the clandestine offloading, and when the Elizabeth nonimportation committee called in Lee and Barnet for questioning, they "tried to stonewall and deceive the committee." Lee confessed on March 13, followed by John and Robert Murray's deposition March 15.[45] The Murrays promised to reship the goods unloaded from the *Beulah* and pledged two hundred pounds toward repairing a hospital in Elizabeth. In New York, Alexander McDougall, a leader of "Friends of Liberty" and Sears wanted "the Murrays banished from the city."[46] An impassioned letter from Mary Lindley Murray averted the banishment of her husband and brother-in-law.[47]

Just what Lindley Murray's role was as a member of the pro-patriot Committee of Sixty is unclear. According to Monaghan, "Lindley stayed politically neutral on the committee, but simply concentrated on defending his family's commercial interests."[48] After the battles of Lexington and Concord on April 19, 1775, the Committee of Sixty became the more radical Committee of One Hundred. Lindley initially continued membership but soon after went into exile with his wife at Islip, Long Island, until 1779.[49]

While on Long Island, Lindley may have been trading with the British,[50] and with patriot raiders on the island, Lindley, as a perceived loyalist, returned to the safety of Manhattan. Lindley and his wife Hannah lived at 209 Water Street, not far from the Murray wharf where he undoubtedly exported warehoused merchandise.[51] Within a few years Lindley made a fortune, and in 1784 he took over an estate located near the East River at what is today Twenty-fifth Street. It was called Bellevue and is now the site of Bellevue Hospital.[52]

The surrender of General Cornwallis on October 19, 1781, ended the military phase of the Revolution, and the British army finally evacuated New York City on November 25, 1783, almost three months after the Treaty of Paris on September 3. As intimidation and pressure on loyalists grew, Lindley departed for Pennsylvania, first to the Friends' stronghold in Bristol and then to Bethlehem, headquarters of the

Moravian sect, where he appeared to be very happy.[53] Robert visited Lindley at Bethlehem around June of 1784, apparently bringing the distressing news that "in an arrangement with the political authorities to protect the family property from seizure, Lindley would be forced into exile abroad."[54]

Lindley probably could have lived in Bethlehem indefinitely, but his desire "to forestall possible confiscation of the Murray family's property" weighed heavily on him.[55] Lindley and Hannah sailed from New York about December 1, 1784, and after some five weeks reached London, England, subsequently settling at a Quaker community in Holdgate near York.[56] Lindley had served as "a sacrificial lamb for his father's actions and had acted to protect his own and his family's property in New York City."[57]

In his exile, Lindley began his literary career. His first book, *The Power of Religion*, published in 1787, consisted of well-chosen, wide-ranging anthologies of readings; he followed the same format in compiling his reading textbooks.[58] His *Grammar of the English Language*, published in 1795, was an immediate success, followed by *English Exercises* and *A Key to the Exercises* in 1797, the *English Reader* in 1799, and *An English Spelling Book* in 1804.[59] Though successful in Britain, Murray's textbooks had their largest sales in the United States, "partly because no international copyright agreement existed and the books could be reprinted without royalties being paid."[60]

"From 1801 through 1840, Murray's total published output of literary textbooks in the United States was about 12.5 million copies," exceeding the output of Noah Webster in those years. His total output of some 15.5 million copies (including the British figures) made him the best-selling producer of books during the first four decades of the nineteenth century.[61] His most popular work was his *English Reader*, full of selections from the liberal-minded writers of the Scottish Enlightenment, most notably the Reverend Hugh Blair. Abraham Lincoln praised the *English Reader* as "the best schoolbook ever put in the hands of an American youth." The book utterly dominated the American market for readers for over a generation from 1815 into the 1840s. It was replaced mainly by the McGuffey Readers, a series of reading texts, which began to appear in 1836.[62]

Lindley Murray.
(From D. Rice and A. N. Hart. *The National Portrait Gallery of Distinguished Americans.* Philadelphia, 1854.)

John Murray

Since Lindley and Hannah had no children, the focus of this biography of Robert Lindley Murray, the tennis player, must fall to Robert and Mary's only other surviving son, John Jr. In addition to Lindley and John (1758–1819), Robert Murray and Mary Lindley had three daughters: Mary (born 1752), Beulah (1762–1800), and Susannah (1764–1808).

John Murray Jr. was born in New York on June 3, 1758. In 1768 he sailed with the family for Europe, where he received the balance of his education.[63] He married Catherine Bowne at Flushing, New York, in 1783. She was the daughter of James Bowne, descendant of John Bowne (1627–95), who built the celebrated "Bowne House" in 1661 at Flushing.[64] Prior to 1945, when the Bowne family deeded the property to the Bowne Historical Society,[65] it was "the only house in the United States of that period" that had never been out of the family. It had some of the original furnishings, many of which were made in the house.[66] The Bowne House was listed on the National Register of Historic Places in 1977. The house reportedly served as a stop on the Underground Railroad prior to the Civil War,[67] and it was in this house that George Cox, founder of the Society of Friends in England in the late 1640s, stayed when visiting Flushing from 1671 to 1672.[68]

John built his city residence at 335 Pearl Street, where he lived for forty years, and his country home on a portion of his father's estate at what is now the southeast corner of Thirty-seventh Street and Fifth Avenue.[69] He made his fortune in commerce while still a young man in New York City, and before the Revolution, he had opened a brewery which continued in business for decades. It was located at 13 Oliver Street and in 1803 was extended through to Catherine Street. Supposedly, General George Washington drank ale from John's brewery while in New York.[70] John gave much of his life to benevolent works, earning for himself the title of John Murray the "Philanthropist."[71] John was elected governor of the New York Hospital in 1782 and continued in its service for thirty-two years, three years of which he was secretary.[72] In 1795 he and a few others sought to improve the condition of the New York State Indians "by instructing them in agriculture and the useful arts."[73] In 1796 Mr. Murray and some others applied to the Legislature for a repeal of the disproportionate penal code. As a result Chief Justice Spencer introduced legislature requiring the building of two state prisons in New York. In 1797 John was "appointed one of the five commissioners to build Newgate Prison at Greenwich Village," the first state penitentiary in New York.[74]

John was one of the founders of the New York Historical Society (November 20, 1804), and he, with other founders of this society, seeing the need to educate the multitude of immigrant children drifting to their shore, met at John's house on Pearl Street.[75] The result was the New York Free School Society, founded by Mr. Murray and Thomas Eddy in February 1805. John served as vice president from the time of its establishment until his death on August 4, 1819.[76–77] (DeWitt Clinton, mayor of New York City and subsequent governor of New York, was its first president.) After Murray's death Thomas Eddy published a thirty-one-page tribute, *Memoir of the Late John Murray, Jun., Read Before the Governors of the New-York Hospital*, September 14, 1819. In it he said, "[Murray's] benevolence and liberality, would not permit him to confine the distribution of his estate, to his family and relations. As in life, so in death, his charities abounded." Likewise, George Trimble, secretary pro tempore of the New York Free School Society had a memorial printed in the Daily Almanac of October 2 and 4, 1819.

Robert I. Murray

Robert I. Murray, the eldest son of John and Catherine, was born at his father's country home on Murray Hill in 1786.[78] He was a fun-loving, adventurous youth and rebelled against the conventions of authority. At fourteen he was sent to school in Burlington. According to Sarah Murray, one summer's afternoon he and other students went to the river for a swim. The boys dared young Murray to swim around a large vessel just weighing anchor. Accepting the challenge, Murray reached the ship and dove beneath her coming up on the other side. He stayed with the vessel and out of sight of his companions until the vessel was opposite an obscure point. He then swam to shore, reached home in advance of his companions, changed his clothes, and seated himself at his studies. His companions, believing he had drowned, ran back to the house with the alarming news only to find him quietly at his lessons.[79]

At the age of twenty-two he went into the wholesale drug business with a Benjamin Collins. "On the retirement of Mr. Collins his brother became a partner, and for some years the firm was Robert & Lindley Murray."[80] At twenty-six he married Elizabeth Colden (1795–1828), daughter of Cadwallader David Colden and great-granddaughter of Cadwallader Colden, the next-to-last colonial governor of New York.[81] Cadwallader David Colden (1769–1834) practiced law in New York City and from 1798 to 1801 was assistant attorney general for the First District, comprising Suffolk, Queens, Kings, Richmond, and Westchester counties. He was District Attorney of the First District from 1810 to 1811, a member of the New York State Assembly in 1818, and mayor of New York City from 1818 to 1821.[82] His grandfather Cadwallader Colden was born in Ireland of Scottish parents. He studied at Edinburgh University to become a minister and continued his studies in physics, anatomy, chemistry, and botany. In 1710 his aunt invited him to Philadelphia, where he started his practice in medicine.[83] He was acting governor on four occasions: 1760–62, 1763–65, 1769–71, and 1774–75 (during William Tryon's trip to England).[84]

In 1816, Robert, like his father John, was elected a governor of the New York Hospital, continuing his connection with it until his death forty-two years later in 1858. For twenty-four years he occupied his father's previous position of secretary of the board. "He was also a Manager of the House of Refuge and of the Institution for the Blind."[85]

He retired from active mercantile life in 1826,[86] and after a marriage of fifteen years, his wife and two sons died in the winter of 1828.[87] In 1830

Mr. Murray married Hannah Wilson Shotwell of Rahway, New Jersey. Robert died on January 26, 1858, at age seventy-two of what the doctor called *erysipelas*, five days after attending a meeting of the directors of the Bank of North America. He left four children: Mary M. Ferris, David Colden, Robert Lindley, and Sarah S. Murray (the daughter of Robert I. and Hannah Shotwell.)[88] Sarah Murray was the author of two books, *Under His Wings* in 1876 about her half brother Robert Lindley Murray[89] and *In the Olden Time* in 1894 about the descendants of John Murray, the 1732 immigrant. Sarah's mother Hannah S. Murray died on May 15, 1877, in her eighty-eighth year.[90]

Robert Lindley Murray

Robert Lindley Murray, the youngest son of Robert I. and Elizabeth Colden, was born on Cliff Street in New York City on November 11, 1825. "When only three years old, his mother and two little brothers died of a malignant sore throat." He was described as a very attractive child: "his flaxen hair fell in long curls, while his fair complexion and rosy cheeks formed a beautiful setting to the deep blue eyes."[91] In 1838 he entered Haverford College, but dyspepsia or indigestion caused him to return home in 1840.[92] Founded in 1833 in Haverford, Pennsylvania, a suburb of Philadelphia, Haverford is the oldest college or university in the United States with Quaker origins.[93] On May 3, 1849, Robert Murray married Ruth Sherman Taber of New Bedford, Massachusetts, daughter of William C. Taber,[94] a former president, secretary, and treasurer of the New Bedford Institution for Savings.[95]

Owing to the anti-slavery principles of Friends, New Bedford early became a station on the Underground Railroad. Having made his escape from slavery, Frederick Douglass (1817–95), the famous black abolitionist, diplomat, and orator, made his way to Newport, Rhode Island, in 1838 with his free bride, Anna Bailey. William C. Taber, perched on top of a coach filled with "women Friends" on their way home from the New England Yearly Meeting, observed the forlorn couple and invited them aboard. Douglass climbed up beside him. Taber paid his fare, "brought him to his own house, and found work for him on the wharves, as he had been a stevedore at the South. While in New Bedford, he was taught to read by Charles Taber."[96]

Robert was a wool merchant in New York City and general agent of the Provident Life and Trust Company of Philadelphia in New York City, a bank and insurance company founded in 1865 by members of the Society of Friends. He was manager of Haverford College (1855–58), president of the Alumni Association (1864–66), minister in the Society of Friends, clerk of the New York Yearly Meeting, and president of the New York Bible Society.[97–98] The collapse of his wool firm in the financial crisis of 1857 brought on a severe depression or illness, from which his convalescence was slow.

Robert Lindley Murray and the Society of Friends were sought after by oppressed minorities. In the spring of 1860, an Indian princess emissary, Nah-nu-bah-wequa ("the upright woman") from Canada met with the Friends in New York. The Canadian government had taken Indian lands and offered them for sale. The tribes desirous of purchasing them back were informed that Canadian law forbid Indians to hold real estate, and the Indian princess was anxious to plead her cause before Queen Victoria in England. As recorded by R. L. and Sarah S. Murray, the Friends raised the required funds, provided introductory letters, and sent the Indian woman on her way. She was cordially received by the queen and returned to New York after nearly two years.[99]

In the early part of 1862 a fugitive slave by the name of Joseph Richardson, anxious to minister Christianity in Africa, came to the house of Robert Lindley Murray, where he received asylum. With the assistance of Friends, Richardson made arrangements for his passage to England for more education, as it was not safe for him to enter a school in the United States.[100]

In 1865 R. L. Murray purchased a country home at Chappaqua in Westchester County, where the family spent summers. One August evening nine years later "he went to attend the annual meeting of the New Castle Bible Society of which he was President." As he passed his house on the way to the stable he was thrown from his carriage and broke his leg. A surgeon soon after set the limb; but tetanus set in, and he died four days later on August 31, 1874, "in his fiftieth year, leaving six children—Robert I., Charles Taber, Anna Taber, Elizabeth Colden, Frances King, and Augustus Taber Murray."[101] His wife Ruth died in Palo Alto, California, in 1908 at the age of eighty-one.[102]

His brother David Colden Murray (d. 1885) and cousin Lindley Murray (1821–97), son of Lindley Murray and Eliza Cheesman, both entered Haverford, David in 1834 and Lindley in 1833. David was a shipping merchant and secretary of the New York Hospital, while Lindley was a wholesale druggist as was his uncle, Robert I. Lindley was also editor of the *Literary Periodical*, president of the Fire Insurance Company, and a real estate agent.[103] Lindley Murray's half-brother, Joseph King (b. 1836), son of Lindley Sr. and Mary Ann King, entered Haverford's junior class of 1859. He studied in the Harvard Law School and was vice president of the Alumni Association in 1887.[104]

Augustus Taber Murray

After the immigrant Robert Murray, Augustus Taber Murray, son of Robert Lindley Murray and Ruth Taber Murray, became the next patriarch of the Murray clan. Born October 29, 1866, in the old family home on Murray Hill, he, along with many of his predecessors, attended Haverford College, graduating in 1885. Five years later he received the degree of doctor of philosophy from the Johns Hopkins University. The following year Augustus studied at the universities of Leipzig and Berlin. For two years, from 1888 to 1890, he was a professor of Greek at Earlham College in Richmond, Indiana, founded in 1847 by the Quakers, and for one year, from 1891 to 1892, at Colorado College. In 1892 he came to Stanford where, except for two absences, he spent the remainder of his academic life until 1932.

Leland Stanford Junior University, commonly known as Stanford University or simply Stanford, was founded in 1885 by the former governor of California and future U.S. Senator Leland Stanford. He and his wife, Jane Lathrop Stanford, named the school after their only son, Leland Stanford Jr., who died of typhoid in Europe a few weeks before his sixteenth birthday. Stanford's Department of Classics dates back to the first year of classes in 1891. At that time, there were already ten students majoring in Greek and eighteen in Latin, with two faculty members.[105] Dr. Murray was visiting professor at the American School of Classical Studies at Athens, Greece, from 1922 to 1923 and for more than thirty years served as a member of the school's managing committee.

During World War I, Augustus was federal food administrator for the northern unit of Santa Clara County. He was a member of the American Philological Association, the Archeological Institute of America, and the Phi Beta Kappa Society. As a member of the Society of Friends, Augustus initiated the Friends' Meeting of Palo Alto in the late 1890s, which continues to this day. As minister one of his early parishioners was Herbert Hoover. In what was to have been a great celebration of Herbert Hoover's nomination for the presidency, Palo Alto received her distinguished son in silence, out of sympathy for the death of Mrs. Hoover's father, Charles D. Henry. The services were conducted by the patriarchal Augustus T. Murray on July 20, 1928. The old Hoover home on campus is now the residence of the Stanford president. Dr. Murray was president of the College Park (San Jose) Association of Friends from 1920 to his death in 1940. His eminence as a spiritual leader matched his eminence as a classical scholar, and in 1929 he took a five-year leave of absence from Stanford to become religious advisor to his close friend President Herbert Hoover and minister of the Friends' Meeting in Washington, DC, which the President attended.[106]

Dr. Murray authored numerous articles on classical and philosophical subjects, including interpretations of Homer, Theocritus, and Greek tragedy. His larger studies include a *Greek Composition*, a college edition of Xenophon's *Anabasis*, *Translations from Greek Drama*, and *Four Plays of Euripides*. For the Loeb Classical Library he translated the *Iliad* and the *Odyssey* of Homer and three volumes of *The Private Orations of Demosthenes* (the fourth was left unfinished).

One dominating feature of Greek education that Augustus admired was its love of athletics—the Hellenic combination of sanity, soundness of body, and intellect. At Haverford Dr. Murray was tennis champion, fullback on the varsity eleven, and a member of the baseball team. In tennis he was active until his seventieth year and his tall, straight figure was frequently seen on the Stanford courts, where his eldest son, trained by the father, won fame as national singles champion in 1917 and 1918. Another son won international laurels as a hurdler in the Olympic Games of 1920.[107–108]

Within a month of his death the Academic Council wrote in tribute on April 5, 1940:

> How well [Dr. Murray] realized the role that education with its energy, its spiritual and dynamic powers could play! And looking again to the Greek past, he saw clearly the lesson there to be learned—an intelligent subordination to the common good—and repeatedly, in writing and lecturing, his plea was to cherish the best visions of the people, and to guard democratic ideals. For education, he wrote, must give to the mind of the individual a sense of fairness and a breadth of sympathy. Man must live by work, by imaginative effort and sacrifice, in humbleness of mind and with no thought of self.[109]

The Murray House, built and dedicated to Augustus T. Murray in 1983, is one of seven focus theme houses at Stanford where both faculty and students with an active interest in a specific field live and explore their theme together in a residential setting.[110] The Murray House currently focuses on "Comparative Studies in Race and Ethnicity (CSRE)" and is home to about sixty students and resident staff.[111]

Monument in front of Murray House on Stanford campus.
(Courtesy Chrissie Kremer)

Robert Lindley Murray's Siblings

Augustus Taber Murray (October 29, 1866–March 8, 1940) married Nella Howland Gifford (July 5, 1868–October 1938), daughter of merchant Frederick Seymour Gifford, in New Bedford, Massachusetts, September 2, 1891. Nella has a rich ancestral history in her own right as a descendant of Henry Howland, who came to this country with his brother Arthur in either the *Fortune* in 1621 or the *Ann* in 1623. Another brother, John Howland, "had preceded them to Plymouth as one of the Mayflower Pilgrims in 1620."[112]

In 1893 Professor Murray built one of the first ten homes at Palo Alto, which, although no longer in the family (it was converted into apartments), still stands at 1019 Bryant Street about two miles from the Stanford campus. It is included in the local "Professorville" tour.[113–114] It was in this house that three athletic boys and two beautiful girls with classic Grecian names were raised—Robert Lindley (b. November 3, 1892), the firstborn and primary subject of this work, Frederick Seymour (b. May 15, 1894), Francis King (b. September 18, 1895), Minerva (b. February 27, 1898), and Lydia (b. October 25, 1905).

Frederic Seymour "Feg" Murray graduated from Stanford in 1916 with a degree in graphic arts. He was editor of the university paper and also his class yearbook.[115] At five feet eleven and 146 pounds Feg was a three-year letterman on the Stanford track and field team from 1914 to 1916 as well as team captain his 1916 senior year.[116] In the 1915 Pacific Coast intercollegiate meet he won the 100-yard dash in 10.4 seconds, finished second in the 220-yard event, and won the 220-yard (200 meter) low hurdles. In the 1915 National AAU championships held at the Panama-Pacific Exposition in San Francisco, Murray pressed Fred Kelly (1912 Olympic champion in 15.1 seconds) so hard in the 110-meter high hurdles that Kelly knocked down four hurdles, and Feg won, tying the world record time of 15.0 seconds.[117–118] He won the 200-meter low hurdles the same afternoon in the world record time of 23.6 seconds, "but the time was not accepted by the authorities because of a strong wind." At the Far Western championships Murray again beat Kelly in the low event in 23.8 seconds.

At the national intercollegiate championships held at Harvard Stadium in May 1916, Murray won the 110-meter high hurdles in the record intercollegiate time of 15.0 seconds and also the 200-meter low hurdles in 24.2 seconds.[119] Feg was also 1916 National AAU low hurdle champion in 24.0 seconds.[120] He competed for the United States in the 1920 Summer Olympics in Antwerp, Belgium, in the 110-meter hurdles and won the bronze medal in 15.1 seconds.

Feg and his younger brother, Francis, went to France in September 1917 as members of the Friends' (Quakers') Reconstruction Unit of the Red Cross. In April 1918 they enlisted in the camouflage section of the American Expeditionary Force, where they served in the trenches.[121] After the war Fred Murray served as the head coach of the Stanford track team for a year. He then studied at the Art Students League in New York City, after which he began a career specializing in sports-related cartoons for the *Sun* and *United Media*, a comic strip newspaper syndication service. In his spare time he worked himself back into shape at the New York University track for the 1920 Olympics in Antwerp at which he won the aforementioned bronze medal. Feg returned to California in 1934 and for eighteen years worked in Hollywood for the *Los Angeles Times*, where he was a sports cartoonist and columnist, and for *King Features Syndicate* as the creator of the cartoon *Seein' Stars*, in which Feg showcased Hollywood celebrities in full color with brief anecdotes about them. *Seein' Stars* appeared in hundreds of newspapers between 1941 and 1953. Around 1943 he did a feature called

"True Stories About Stamps" in *True Comics*.[122–123] Born May 15, 1894, Feg died in Monterey, California, July 16, 1973.[124]

Francis King Murray, according to his son Doug, spent his abbreviated life being called "Bay," which resulted from young Feg trying to say "baby." He grew into a sturdy six foot five athlete, and his intellect grew proportionately. Following in the footsteps of his father, he attended Haverford College in Pennsylvania for a year, but missing his family too much, he transferred to Stanford, where his 1917 diploma in the classics bears not only his name but that of his father, the department head. He graduated Phi Beta Kappa and lettered in track as a hammer thrower and in rugby.[125] He went to France with his brother Feg and like him resigned from the Red Cross to enlist in the camouflage section of the American Expeditionary Force. Francis taught at the Phillips-Andover Academy of Andover, Massachusetts, and died at age thirty-three of kidney disease on April 15, 1929, leaving a widow (aged thirty) and three children. His funeral was attended by President Hoover.[126]

Minerva Murray, named after the child of Zeus, broke the family tradition by not going to college,[127] and on December 19, 1920, she married Leland Rice Skelton, a 1917 Stanford graduate. As a member of a Stanford ambulance unit, Skelton served six months in the Balkans.[128] The couple had four children, including a set of twins. Minerva divorced and returned to 1019 Bryant with her children during the Depression. She remarried quite late and lived out her life in peaceful harmony.[129]

Lydia Murray attended Miss Harker's School in Palo Alto, St. Mary's Academy in Garden City, New York, Stanford University, and the Traphagen School of Art in New York City.[130] She married Albert Hussey Huneke, whom she met while at Miss Harker's, where Huneke was a teaching tennis pro. Albert, Stanford class of '24, earned a bachelor's degree in history, and because of his involvement in sports (he played baseball and tennis and was a "Yell" leader), the family had a water fountain erected with his name on it in front of the Sunken Diamond field.

Albert and Lydia were married in Stanford Memorial Church on January 2, 1929.[131] Mrs. Leland Skelton was the matron of honor; Mr. and Mrs. Robert Lindley Murray and their seven-year-old son, Tad, were in the bridal party. According to Doug Murray, just "before Lydia's wedding, her very staid and conservative mother took her aside and said 'Lydia, there is something I must tell you about marriage. We have never talked about this before.' Lydia had been the quintessential flapper throughout the roaring 20s and wise to the ways of the world by then. With innocence oozing out of every pore she said 'Yes mother. What is it?' 'Well dear. Never interrupt your husband while he is reading the sports page.'"[132]

Lydia became a pianist of concert ability and a professional fashion artist. After marrying Albert Huneke, she moved to Los Angeles, where she drew fashion illustrations for the *Los Angeles Times*. Following the death of her Albert in 1968, she married Thomas Moss. The couple lived in Menlo Park and South Carolina, and Lydia returned to the Bay Area after his death. Lydia died at age ninety, on February 14, 1996, the last surviving member of one of Palo Alto's earliest families.[133]

More of the Stanford and tennis line followed through two of Lydia and Albert's four children. John Murray Huneke (1929–2005), class of '53, earned a BS in mechanical engineering and an MBA in 1955; he was also the tennis team captain. John was a senior executive with Bechtel Investments in San Francisco and also helped spearhead the Bay Area Sports Hall of Fame into which Lin Murray was inducted. John's brother Albert H. Jr., earned a BS in business administration from UC Berkeley in 1961; his sister Elizabeth Christine (Betty Buckman) received a BA in English literature from UCLA in 1958, and his sister Frances King (Noura Durkee), class of '60, earned a BA in humanities honors/fine arts and an MA in fine arts in 1961. Frances also received the Lloyd W. Dinkelspiel Award in its inaugural academic year, 1959–60. Frances, a senior, was one of three people to receive the honor, given to either faculty or students. For Frances it was entitled "Award made to the female in the graduating class of 1960 with the most outstanding contributions to undergraduate education at Stanford University." Betty, now living in Torrance, California, had a long human resources management and administration career, including many years in the aerospace/aircraft industry.

Two of John Murray Huneke's three children attended Stanford: Murray C., '83, earned a BA in economics from Stanford and an MBA from Harvard University; Christine (Chrissie) Kremer, '84, holds a BA in international relations from Stanford and an MBA from UCLA's Anderson School of Management in 1990; and Lorraine (Lori) graduated from UC Berkeley with a BA in Far Eastern studies. Murray is a managing director and co-head of the investment banking, consumer, and industrial growth groups at Piper Jaffray. Chrissie worked in advertising and marketing, and Lori currently lives in China. It was initially through contacting Murray C. and then subsequently his sister Chrissie Kremer and their aunt Betty Buckman (Lydia's daughter) that I received much of the above family history and priceless photographs.

The Augustus Murray family, probably shortly after R. L. Murray's marriage to Ramona on May 9, 1916. Standing left to right: Minerva, Frederic Seymour (Feg), Robert Lindley, Ramona McKendry (Robert's wife), Dr. Augustus Taber Murray, Francis King (Bay), and Lydia (below). Seated in black is R. L. Murray's maternal grandmother and beneath Augustus is his wife, Nella Howland Gifford.
(Courtesy Chrissie Kremer)

The Murray homestead at 1019 Bryant in Palo Alto, as it appears today.
(Courtesy Chrissie Kremer)

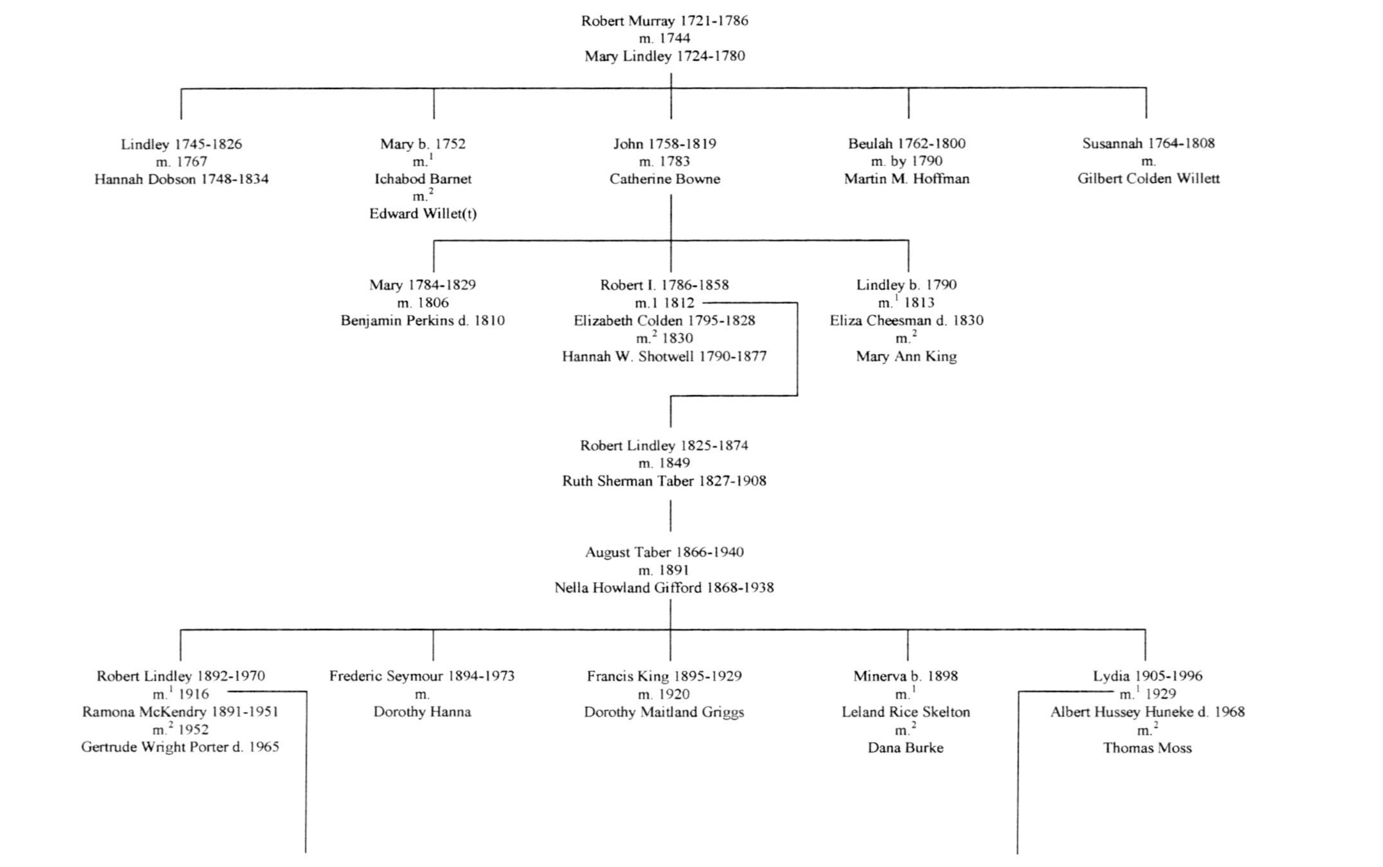

Robert Murray 1721-1786
m. 1744
Mary Lindley 1724-1780
Lindley 1745-1826
m. 1767
Hannah Dobson 1748-1834
Mary b. 1752
m.1
Ichabod Barnet
m.2
Edward Willet(t)
John 1758-1819
m. 1783
Catherine Bowne
Beulah 1762-1800
m. by 1790
Martin M. Hoffman
Susannah 1764-1808
m.
Gilbert Colden Willett
Mary 1784-1829
m. 1806
Benjamin Perkins d. 1810
Robert I. 1786-1858
m.1 1812
Elizabeth Colden 1795-1828
m.2 1830
Hannah W. Shotwell 1790-1877
Lindley b. 1790
m.1 1813
Eliza Cheesman d. 1830
m.2
Mary Ann King
Robert Lindley 1825-1874
m. 1849
Ruth Sherman Taber 1827-1908
August Taber 1866-1940
m. 1891
Nella Howland Gifford 1868-1938
Robert Lindley 1892-1970
m.1 1916
Ramona McKendry 1891-1951
m.2 1952
Gertrude Wright Porter d. 1965
Frederic Seymour 1894-1973
m.
Dorothy Hanna
Francis King 1895-1929
m. 1920
Dorothy Maitland Griggs
Minerva b. 1898
m.1
Leland Rice Skelton
m.2
Dana Burke
Lydia 1905-1996
m.1 1929
Albert Hussey Huneke d. 1968
m.2
Thomas Moss

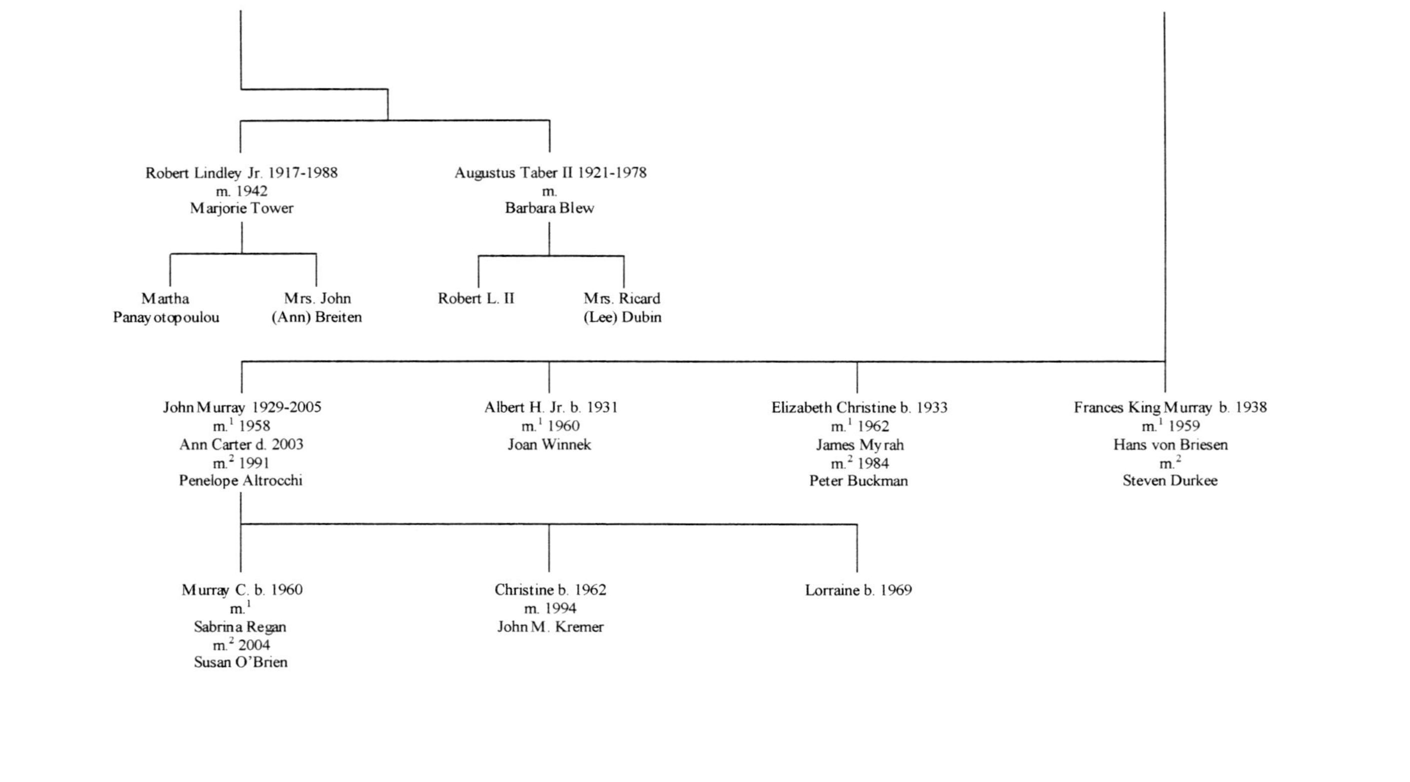

Robert Lindley Jr. 1917-1988
m. 1942
Marjorie Tower
Augustus Taber II 1921-1978
m.
Barbara Blew
Martha Panayotopoulou
Mrs. John (Ann) Breiten
Robert L. II
Mrs. Ricard (Lee) Dubin
John Murray 1929-2005
m.1 1958
Ann Carter d. 2003
m.2 1991
Penelope Altrocchi
Albert H. Jr. b. 1931
m.1 1960
Joan Winnek
Elizabeth Christine b. 1933
m.1 1962
James Myrah
m.2 1984
Peter Buckman
Frances King Murray b. 1938
m.1 1959
Hans von Briesen
m.2
Steven Durkee
Murray C. b. 1960
m.1
Sabrina Regan
m.2 2004
Susan O'Brien
Christine b. 1962
m. 1994
John M. Kremer
Lorraine b. 1969

The Murray men: Lindley, Frederic, Augustus, and Francis.
(Courtesy Chrissie Kremer)

7
Robert Lindley "Lin" Murray at Stanford

Robert Lindley Murray, like his paternal grandfather (and namesake) who had curly blond hair, blue eyes, and a Quaker passion for social justice, was born in San Francisco on November 3, 1892. As he was the first of five siblings, his drive to excel both athletically and intellectually was no doubt encouraged by his father Augustus. "Lin" Murray graduated from the fledgling Palo Alto High School already knowing what he wanted to do, as he was fascinated by chemistry.

Along with four of his five siblings and several nephews and nieces, he attended Stanford, where Augustus taught the classics, earning Phi Beta Kappa honors in 1913 with a major in chemistry. He earned a master's degree in chemical engineering in 1914. At the same time Lin Murray became a superb six-foot-two athlete at 155 pounds.

Initially trained by his father, Lin Murray played tennis as a Stanford freshman in 1909 and also competed in middle distance running under Dr. E. W. Moulton as coach. Lin Murray ran the mile for Stanford in the 1912 and 1913 Stanford-Cal meets. On April 20, 1912, on the Stanford oval, Murray finished third, close on the heels of the favored Wood of California, while Bill Fletcher of Stanford, who finally passed Wood on the back stretch, took first in the event; Fletcher's time of 4:28.4 set a new intercollegiate record for the mile.[1] On April 19, 1913, on the California oval, Murray again annexed third in the mile event. P. R. Wilson of Stanford finished first and Wood of California second again. "Wilson's ... winning time was almost two seconds [4:26.6] better than the intercollegiate record made last year by Bill Fletcher" with Murray only ten yards behind Wilson at the finish.[2] The world record time for the mile in 1913 was 4:14.4.[3] It was at that meet that Lin Murray's younger brother Feg '16, finished second and third to Herb Whitted '16, in the high and low hurdles, respectively. The time for the high sticks was announced at 15.2, a Pacific intercollegiate record, with three watches indicating 15 flat, while 25.2 was the figure in the low hurdles.[4] In open competition on March 21, 1914, Lin Murray set the Pacific Coast record for the half-mile (880 yards), winning the race in 1:57.2. The referee recorded that the runner was far ahead of the field of contestants.[5] Lin Murray then left the track and field events to his younger brothers Feg and Francis.

As early as 1892, Stanford and the University of California, Berkeley, began the first intercollegiate team versus team matches in the country; Cal won the majority of those clashes. In April of 1909 the formidable Long brothers from UC, Melville and Herbert, won the intercollegiate contest 3–0. Mel Long defeated E. Jordan, 6–4, 6–3, while H. Long defeated A. J. Gowan, 6–3, 6–3. The Longs easily won the doubles contest, 6–2, 6–1.[6] At the U.S. Championships that year on center court, in the fourth-round, five-set match between Mel Long and Maurice McLoughlin, "Eastern society witnessed a fast-paced game unlike anything played up to that time."[7]

Lindley Murray, obviously having played pre-college tennis, made an impact at Stanford in the fall of his 1909 freshman year. He was a finalist in one tournament and won another. Murray lost to H. S. Morgan, class of '12, in a Tennis Club handicap tournament with seventy-five entrants, 4–6, 6–3, 6–3, and at Thanksgiving won the Thiele Cup tournament (with an entry list of sixty-four) over H. L. Loud in three deuce sets, 5–7, 9–7, 6–4. The *Stanford Quad* said that "Murray shows excellent form and style, and promises to develop into a strong man."[8]

In 1910, Lin Murray's inaugural year on Stanford's tennis team, Stanford and California played five matches, three singles and two doubles, instead of two singles and one doubles match, which could be accomplished using only two players. California won all five matches on the California courts on April 15 and 16. Powell (UC) demolished H. Mann '10 (captain), 6–2, 6–0; Melville Long (UC) beat H. S. Morgan '12, 6–1, 6–3; and at third singles Herbert Long (UC) defeated R. L. Murray '13, 6–4. In first doubles the Long brothers won from Mann and Morgan while Trees and Rogers (UC) defeated Murray and G. L. Shaul '13, 5–7, 6–2, 6–2, 6–2.[9–10]

The 1912 Stanford tennis team earned its first victory over California since 1907. "After four fast tryout tournaments, Captain R. L. Murray, '13, H. S. Morgan, '12, V. A. Sheldon, '15, and W. Hutchinson, '15, were chosen to represent Stanford."[11] On April 5–6, 1912, the Stanford Indians eked out a 3–2 win by taking all three singles. In the first match Sheldon easily disposed of Harry Rogers, 6–0, 6–3. Sheldon's reach, coupled with his powerful drives, were too much for H. Rogers. In the second match, Frees and Breeden of California found the corners and beat Hutchinson and Sheldon, 6–2, 6–1, 6–3. The match between Captain Murray and Charles Rogers was the closest and most spectacular of the tournament. After losing the first set, 6–4, Murray settled down, got his serve in fine working order, and won the final two sets, 10–8, 7–5. Morgan won his match with Frees, while in the fifth and final match the Rogers brothers defeated Murray and Morgan, representing the first Stanford doubles team, 2–6, 6–2, 6–3, 4–6, 6–2.[12–14]

In 1913, one of the longest droughts in Stanford athletic history began as California handed the Indians thirteen straight defeats in their annual tennis meetings, despite the fact that Murray captured the 1913 Pacific Coast intercollegiate singles title and the doubles title paired with J. S. Hutchinson in late April at the Ojai Valley tournament. Murray beat Newell of USC, 7–5, 3–6, 12–10, while Murray and Hutchinson beat Herlihy and Montgomery of Occidental, 6–2, 6–1.[15–16] Stanford men also captured the 1914 and 1915 Pacific Coast intercollegiate singles titles: Herbert Hahn in 1914 and H. Van Dyke Johns in 1915.

The winning 1912 Stanford tennis team. From the left H. S. Morgan, V. A. Sheldon, Captain R. L. Murray, and W. Hutchinson. (From the 1912 *Stanford Quad*)

Cal defeated Stanford, 4–1, in 1913. Senior Lin Murray captured the only win for Stanford from Willis E. Davis in a three-set match.[17] Davis would make his mark later that year as a finalist to Tom Bundy in the Southern California singles. Bundy and Maury McLoughlin were national doubles champions and would repeat in 1913 and 1914.

Murray also had a good year in the 1913 fall tournaments at Stanford. He won the Regent Cup handicap tournament over Herbert L. Hahn '16 and the interclub singles, again over Hahn. "In the finals of the doubles Murray and Chapman, Kappa Alpha, defeated Hahn and Sloss of Encina after a hard-fought five-set match."[18] Murray easily won the interclass singles giving him the university singles championship for the year. His only glitch was in the annual Thanksgiving tournament for the Thiele Trophy. Hahn, having a slight handicapping advantage (owe 15½), defeated Murray (owe 40½) in a five-set final.[19]

Unable to compete in 1914 because he had already played four years, Murray coached the 1914 squad. The tryouts for the team consisted of five tournaments won, respectively, by K. B. Uhls '16; H. L. Hahn '16, J. S. Hutchinson '16, L. Sloss '15 (captain), and F. S. Pratt '13. In a round robin to determine singles places, Hahn came in first, Sloss second, and Uhls third. The two doubles teams were chosen by the coaching committee, which consisted of Sloss, Murray, and Hahn. Sloss and Hahn played first while Pratt and Hutchinson played second. The match with UC resulted in a clean sweep for California, although four of the matches were close, as shown in the California Tennis chapter.[20]

The Stanford drought also included the year 1921 when Phil Neer, as a junior, broke the stranglehold Ivy League schools had on the national intercollegiate singles championship, becoming the first player from a Western university to win that title. A year later he and Jim Davies won the NCAA doubles title, the first non–Ivy League players to do so.[21]

Writing in 1919, Phil Neer said: "Not since the days when 'Lin' Murray with his famous serve and Herbert Hahn with his terrific drive won paths to international repute on Stanford's tennis courts has interest in the outdoor sport attained the position which it now occupies in student activities." With that introduction, Neer's article applauded the efforts of Dr. A. D. Browne, head of the men's department of physical training, for raising money to build three new tennis courts. In the past, "through the lack of proper facilities, the Cardinal men have been forced to play their matches against California on the Berkeley courts," thereby giving the Bruins home advantage.[22]

Lin Murray's name first entered the lawn tennis record books in 1911 at the end of his sophomore year at Stanford. In the Pacific States championship at Santa Cruz, the eighteen-year-old Murray paired with Stanford teammate J. Hutchinson in the junior doubles tournament, losing in the final to Clyde Curley and Bill Johnston, 6–2, 2–6, 10–8, 6–1. Bill Johnston doubled by beating R. Greenberg in the junior singles.[23]

At the time Murray won the 1913 Pacific Coast intercollegiate singles title and the doubles title paired with J. Hutchinson at Ojai, Bill Johnston beat John Strachan, 6–4, 6–8, 6–2, in the singles event of the Ojai Valley Open championship.[24] The California State championship took place on the courts of the Claremont Country Club in Oakland beginning on September 6. In the sixth and final round Bill Johnston beat Lin Murray, 6–4, 5–7, 6–4, 6–4.[25] Two years younger than Murray, Bill Johnston would be one of Murray's biggest hurdles in years to come.

The key players from Northern California just prior to and during Murray's career were Clarence Griffin, Herbert and Melville Long, Charles Foley, Carl Gardner, George Janes, Maurice McLoughlin, Bob Strachan and his younger brother John, Elia Fottrell, Willis Davis, Bill Johnston, H. Van Dyke Johns, and Roland Roberts, most of whom had been trained at the aggressive and well-organized Golden Gate Club. The Southern California players of note were Alphonzo Bell, Thomas Bundy, Trowbridge Hendrick, Simpson Sinsabaugh, and Ward Dawson.

After graduating from Stanford in 1914, Murray exploded on the Eastern circuit that summer, mowing down the former 1911 U.S. intercollegiate champion from Harvard and the current New England intercollegiate champion, as well as winning several Eastern tournaments and earning a national ranking of no. 4.

He thus continued in the footsteps of Maurice McLoughlin, Melville Long, and Bill Johnston. McLoughlin, Johnston, and Murray would each win the U.S. Championship twice between 1912 and 1919 interrupted in 1914 and 1916 by *Titanic* survivor Dick Williams, who defeated McLoughlin and Johnston in those respective finals.

An astute *New York Times* tennis reporter noted a little over a month after Murray's 1914 eastern invasion that tennis was not his primary interest. Although he trained assiduously before he went east, Murray had not been part of the Golden Gate Tennis Club and was a Phi Beta Kappa chemical engineer. He took a job with the Pacific Coast Borax Company in Oakland, California, had no 1915 national ranking, transferred to the company's Bayonne, New Jersey, plant in October of that year, and exploded onto the 1916 circuit, again ranking fourth nationally.

What is truly amazing is that he had no intention of playing in either the 1917 or 1918 U.S. Championships and literally had to be dragged away from his job. Yet he won both those championships, the 1918 title over Bill Tilden in the final with only eight days' hard practice, including one tournament before the nationals. It usually takes players weeks—if not months—of practice and tournament play to develop sufficient confidence and expertise, but Murray, basically starting from scratch, continually improved during that short period, match by match, like a computerized machine, peaked when it counted, and, by his own admission, beat Tilden at the latter's own backcourt game on that day.

After again achieving a no. 4 ranking in 1919, Murray largely retired from the circuit and devoted himself to his job with the same dedication and enthusiasm, reaching the pinnacle in business as well, becoming president and CEO of Hooker Electrochemical in Niagara Falls, New York. The following is the story of this remarkable individual.

8
The 1914 Eastern Invasion

On January 20, 1914, Lin Murray was named Stanford's tennis coach for the coming season. He was a veteran of four intercollegiate tournaments in addition to getting his letter in track. At the time he was ranked among the five best tennis players in California. In early 1914 a plan was afoot "to send a tennis team east as soon as college closes to compete with some of the large Eastern universities." However, "[f]inancial difficulties are the source of the present uncertainty."[1] The "financial difficulties" were apparently resolved, though, for after graduation in May, Lin Murray, 1913 Pacific Coast intercollegiate champion, and his Stanford teammate Herbert L. Hahn, 1914 Pacific Coast intercollegiate champion, started east to play as many matches as possible with the leading colleges of the East including Harvard and Yale.

Amherst had won the New England intercollegiate championship, held on the dirt courts of the Longwood Cricket Club, May 18–22. Among the schools competing were Amherst, Bowdoin, Dartmouth, MIT, Trinity, Tufts, Wesleyan, and Williams. The final round was all Amherst. Fenimore Cady beat L. Shumway, 4–6, 5–7, 6–2, 6–4, 6–3.[2] Against Harvard on May 27, Lin Murray defeated E. H. Whitney, 1911 intercollegiate champion, 6–4, 3–6, 6–3, while Herbert Hahn defeated Watson Washburn, 6–0, 8–6. The Californians lost to Washburn and J. J. Armstrong in doubles, 6–2, 6–4.[3] On May 28 Murray and Hahn played the two Amherst finalists. Murray demolished Fenimore Cady, 6–0, 6–2, while Hahn defeated Shumway, 6–4, 6–4, and the Stanford pair won the doubles final 6–3, 6–1, 6–2.[4]

Their success soon attracted attention, and they received many invitations to play in the leading tournaments of the East—particularly Murray, who played a brilliant game with that dash that belonged to all the leading players of the Pacific Coast. The young left-handed Californian made his Eastern debut at the first invitation tennis tournament held June 6–8 by the Sleepy Hollow Country Club on clay courts. Lin Murray won the singles event after defeating, in this order and, remarkably, on the same day, Fred Alexander, 6–2, 6–3; Karl Behr, 4–6, 6–2, 6–2; and in the final W. Merrill Hall, 6–2, 4–6, 6–2, a truly wonderful exhibition of tennis tactics and stamina. In the doubles event Murray and Hahn defeated S. C. Millett and H. A. Plummer, 6–2, 6–2, and F. B. Alexander and B. S. Prentice by default, and then lost to Dean Mathey and Watson Washburn in the final round, 6–4, 6–2.[5]

Lin Murray next won the New England championship on June 13 on the courts of the Hartford Golf Club, defeating the titleholder Alrick H. Man Jr. of Long Island in the challenge round, 6–1, 6–1, 6–2.[6] Along the way Murray beat Peasley, 6–0, 6–1; Hyde, 6–0, 6–2; Lawton, 6–1, 6–2; Cushing, 6–0, 7–5; and Cole in the final, 6–2, 6–1, 6–2. Murray also won the doubles title with Hahn over Burgwin and Richards, 6–1, 7–5, 6–1.[7]

Murray and Hahn entered the Metropolitan championship in the first tournament held on the new grounds of the West Side Tennis Club at Forest Hills, Long Island, June 13–20. The former champion and Harvard captain, Watson M. Washburn, was defeated by Murray in the quarters, 4–6, 6–1, 6–3. (Hahn had lost to Washburn, 6–3, 6–4, in the previous round.) In the final Murray defeated Frederik B. Alexander, three-time winner of the title, in five hard-fought sets, 6–8, 7–5, 7–5, 2–6, 6–4. The *New York Times* reported on June 21, 1914,

> Murray is a left-handed player, and serves a difficult ball, like many of the Californians. His cross-court shots baffled his opponent, but his ground strokes are weak. The first three sets of the match went to deuce and vantage, with Murray leading, 2 sets to 1. Alexander played a plucky game, and repeatedly baffled Murray with the brilliancy of his play. The veteran captured the first set, 8–6, and made a good start in the second, but as the contest progressed the Westerner improved and carried the attack into the West Sider's territory. Alexander led in the set, 5 to 4,

> when Murray ran three straight games and made the sets 1–all. In the third set the pair again played evenly up to the eleventh game, when Murray forced the pass and won out.
>
> The long rest after the third set helped Alexander, as he played a much stronger game in the fourth set, sweeping the younger off his feet. It was the most one-sided set of the match, and Alexander won 6–2. For a time it appeared as though Alexander would pull through. After losing the first game he captured the next three, and headed strong for the finish, but Murray once more rallied and carried the score to 4 all. This was Alexander's last chance, as the Californian finished the match in whirlwind style.[8]

Spalding's Lawn Tennis Annual said: "In the final Alexander brought into use all of his wonderful craftiness and all of his old speed and daring. At times, and they were frequent, he made phenomenal shots, and his court covering and brilliance were remarkable. Murray was up against the struggle of his life, and won because he refused to give up and because he tried for everything. He covered miles of court, and served like a whirlwind. At times he drove like Alexander, who sent the ball over the net so fast it could scarcely be seen."[9]

On his way to the final Murray beat G. H. Bartholomew, 6–0, 6–0; G. A. L. Dionne, 6–4, 6–1; Dean Mathey, 6–2, 6–4; Watson M. Washburn, 4–6, 6–1, 6–3; and in the semi-finals George M. Church, 6–2, 7–5. In the doubles event Hahn and Murray lost to Church and Mathey in the quarters, 6–2, 6–3, the latter pair defeating Pell and Behr in the semis, 6–2, 3–6, 7–5, and Shafer and Smith in the final round, 6–3, 7–9, 6–4, 12–10.[10]

Murray became recognized nationally and attracted the attention of the International Committee, which cast its eye toward the defense of the Davis Cup. The committee said they would find considerable difficulty selecting a team owing to the many candidates "and it is not improbable that the defending team will be composed entirely of California players."[11]

Murray was to compete next in the Middle States lawn tennis tournament at South Orange, New Jersey, but defaulted to Theodore R. Pell in the first round because of a sprained shoulder, an injury he had sustained the previous Saturday in that five-setter against Alexander at the Metropolitan championship.[12]

The ninth annual Delaware State championship took place on the turf courts of the Wilmington Country Club the week of June 29. Lin Murray defeated Joseph J. Armstrong in the final round, 6–2, 7–5, 6–3, but he lost the challenge round to George M. Church of Princeton, whom he had beaten in the Metropolitan semis, in a hard-fought four-set match, 6–3, 5–7, 6–3, 6–4. With a bye in the first round Murray beat in succession E. du Pont, 6–0, 6–2; F. W. Paul, 6–0, 6–1; S. Thayer, 6–2, 6–1; and A. D. Thayer, 6–2, 6–1. Murray's Stanford colleague H. L. Hahn won three rounds before losing to W. F. Johnson (U.S. no. 7), 6–4, 8–6, in the fourth. Armstrong then beat Johnson, 6–4, 9–7, in the semis.[13]

Bill Tilden's older brother Herbert had paired with A. D. Thayer Jr. to win the Delaware State doubles title in 1913 over Princetonians George M. Church and A. M. Kidder, 1–6, 8–6, 6–4, 8–6, in the final round and F. C. Inman and A. Holmes, 4–6, 6–3, 6–3, 6–3, in the challenge round. In singles Thayer beat Tilden in the semifinals, 6–2, 6–3. Church beat Thayer in the final round, 6–3, 4–6, 6–4, 7–5, and Dean Mathey in the challenge round, 6–4, 1–6, 6–3, 8–6.[14] In their 1914 defense they lost to W. F. Johnson and J. J. Armstrong, 6–0, 11–9, 6–2.[15]

The July 5 issue of the *Times* produced a feature doting on Murray's three successive tournament wins—particularly his remarkable stamina in disposing of three "topnotchers" in one day to win the Sleepy Hollow and his five-setter with Fred Alexander in the Metropolitan final. After losing two of the first three deuce sets, Alexander easily won the fourth at 6–2 and was leading 3–1 in the fifth, when the young Californian rallied to win the set and title at 6–4, showing his character, a determination to stay the course. The writer then called attention to his good looks and affable demeanor, which made him very popular, particularly with the young ladies in the audience. Referring to Lin Murray as another young tennis prodigy from California, the writer noted:

> No tennis season is complete nowadays unless California sends on some dashing youngster to capture the fancy of tennis fans. Five years ago came McLoughlin and Melville Long, then Bundy, then, last year, Johnston and Strachan, both of whom won places in the First Ten....
>
> And now comes Lindley Murray, blonde-haired, tall and straight, upstanding, confident—as vigorous a young animal as you could find anywhere in these United States; twenty years old and just graduated from Leland Stanford.

> They are all young, these tennis wonders that come out of the Far West. If California sent on to the East a player who was old enough to vote it would cause a decided shock. There must be some State law compelling them to go forth before they reach manhood, or not at all.
>
> And how this latest one does swat the ball! He is a left-hander, which seems, somehow, to give an impression of force to his play. When he serves he winds up like an eccentric baseball pitcher, and the ball leaves his racket with lightning speed; and, what is more to the point, it usually leaves in the right direction. He tears up to the net after serving, ready to deal the ball another murderous blow if his opponent succeeds in returning it.[16]

Referring to his tournament debut at Sleepy Hollow, June 6–8, and the Metropolitan, June 13–20, the *Times* reporter wrote:

> For did he not beat F. B. Alexander, Karl Behr, and Merrill Hall, all topnotchers, in a single afternoon? They stepped up, one after the other, in the Sleepy Hollow tournament, and took their medicine. And did he not win the classic Metropolitan, winning a second time from Alexander in a thrilling five-set match? He did, and now the Davis Cup Committee … has told him to hold himself in readiness to try for a place on the team that is to defend the cup against the nations of the world this Summer.
>
> About that Sleepy Hollow tournament where the boy took the scalps of the Eastern topnotchers: He had been heard of before that. The other Californians, McLoughlin and the rest, had brought tales of his prowess, but he was practically an unknown quantity here in the East. The chance that he might beat the veterans would have been sniffed at six or seven years ago, before California came to be famed as a producer of crack tennis players. The succession of winners from "out there," however, had generated a mighty respect for California tennis talent, so Murray was the object of much speculation. At that, neither the players nor the spectators were prepared for what happened. One singles match in a day is enough for

an able-bodied man. Often tournament players protest at being asked to play two. But three matches, with really first-class players—that is work not for a man but for a steam engine.

When Murray took Behr [Alexander] into camp, to the surprise of the crowd, the lookers-on thought that either he would not play again that day, or else would lose to a fresh, untired opponent. Straightaway he won from Alexander [Behr]. But not yet was he exhausted; in fact, he seemed only to be getting under way. He made it known to the Tournament Committee that he was willing to play again if it so desired. It did so desire, and he took on Merrill Hall—and beat him, too.

After winning here he went to Connecticut and annexed one of the leading New England titles. After that came the Metropolitan, on the courts of the West Side Club at Forest Hills, the first big event of the tennis year. In succession Dean Mathey, Watson M. Washburn, and George M. Church, all high-ranking players, went down before the newcomer, and he came through to face F. B. Alexander in the finals.

This was one of the most impressive contrasts ever staged on a tennis court. On one side of the net Murray, all fire and activity and vigor, bubbling over with animal spirits; on the other Alexander, almost twice the Californian's age, suave, easy moving, the personification of correct tennis form. From start to finish the battle was between youthful force and endurance, combined with remarkable natural skill, and the finished science of a veteran. And finished science had to "take the count."

Rarely has a closer contest been seen. The match ran to five sets, and every set was close except the fourth, which Alexander won with rather impressive ease. With such ease, indeed, that it looked as if he had saved the best that was in him to squelch the youngster at the end. In the fifth set, however, the boy came back strong. The advantage veered from side to side—there were times when the gain or loss of one point seemed likely to turn the scale—but finally Murray won in a magnificent final spurt. Every one

> of the fifty-odd games in the match had been marked by play of the most brilliant character, and the winning of the final point was the signal for a demonstration such as the West Side Club had never seen before.[17]

On his audience appeal and personality the writer lauded:

> Already Murray has qualified as a gallery favorite of the most pronounced kind. He is a good-looking boy, with a complexion that would serve perfectly as an advertisement for a health food, and a frank, laughing face that fairly radiates good humor. When he swings his brawny left arm in a wide circle and the ball goes shooting beyond his opponent's reach, exclamations of joy ripple along the sidelines and there is ecstatic clapping of hands.
>
> Young girls are always plentiful in the crowd at a tennis tournament, and their eyes follow the Californian's movements with an admiration that is almost doting. One of them, after his recent triumph in the finals of the Metropolitan, ran out on the court and kissed him. But do not be alarmed; that particular girl was his sister, who had just come East on a vacation with the rest of the family. The other girls around the court did not venture such emphatic approval, but they applauded with an enthusiasm that made Murray's rosy cheeks rosier than ever.[18]

Calling Murray "the wonder of the hour in tennisdom," the *Times* was quick to mention that "As in every other phase of human activity, proficiency in tennis is a relative term." The astute reporter then pointed out that Murray had yet to be tested by Maury McLoughlin, Dick Williams, Wallace Johnson, Bill Clothier, or Nat Niles, the top five for 1912, not to mention current no. 4, Bill Johnston. The *Times* correctly prophesied that Murray wouldn't beat McLoughlin or Williams, at least not at that stage in his career, and gave reasons why. "First," the observer explains, is "his service":

> His first service is very hard, and he is surprisingly successful in getting it in. But it has nothing of the "break"

> that makes McLoughlin's so difficult. Murray's ball has a curve of a rather old-fashioned kind. A first-class player can return it consistently, while many of the best men in the country can do almost nothing with McLoughlin's service. Murray's second service is not to be compared with McLoughlin's.
>
> Again, in following his service to the net Murray suffers in the comparison. His ball travels with such speed and bounds so straight that he can't get close to the net before the return is made; the return is apt to catch him in a bad position. McLoughlin's service, fast as it is, has such an exaggerated twist and bounds so high and in such unexpected directions that when the ball comes back—if it comes back at all—he is in an excellent position to finish the point.
>
> On the forehand ground stroke the Leland Stanford man fares better in the comparison. This is his strongest point; he puts great force behind the ball, and sends it close to the sidelines and fairly deep. On his backhand he is weaker than McLoughlin, and McLoughlin is considered weaker there than anywhere else. In fact, the backhand ground stroke is accounted the weak spot, relatively, in the play of all the Californians. Murray's arm does not travel in a graceful sweep—as Alexander's does, for example—when he takes a ball on his backhand; it is a kind of shove, or punch.
>
> Overhead and in volleying Murray is not nearly so effective as McLoughlin.[19]

In a nutshell, the writer was saying that Murray's first serve was hard and accurate, accounting for a high percentage in, but his "break" wasn't as effective as that of McLoughlin thus Murray would get caught at the service line or no-man's-land on the best players' returns. Although his forehand ground stroke was good, his backhand was a rather awkward shove, which Tilden later described as a "poke."

> Of course, it must not be forgotten that Murray has had nothing like the experience of the champion. Many of the same defects that he exhibits were noticed in McLoughlin

> when the latter first came East. Perhaps the younger man may overcome them, just as McLoughlin has done.
>
> Murray does not impress the spectator as having the ease and grace of the champion. He seems to be working very hard when he plays, and his feet hit the ground with heavy thuds. McLoughlin, on the other hand, seems to have his muscles moving harmoniously; he is quicker on his feet, despite the fact that Murray has won fame as a sprinter.
>
> "He will be a lot better"—that is what everybody was saying about Murray at Forest Hills during the Metropolitan.[20]

Then the sportswriter goes on to pose an interesting question as to Murray's commitment:

> Undoubtedly he will be better if he wants to devote time and study to tennis. But does he want to? Some of his friends say not.
>
> Young Murray enjoys playing mightily. He is having a "huge" time this Summer, spending his vacation on a round of the tournaments. But he is not wrapped up in tennis—as so many of the cracks are, if the truth be told. He is a Phi Beta Kappa man, he did well in his classes at Leland Stanford, and his ideas are other than frivolous; he has no particular ambition to make tennis a career.[21]

Thus the reporter hits the nail on the head. Commenting to a California friend at Forest Hills, Murray exclaimed, "These people make a lot of a fellow's playing tennis—they certainly do seem to take it seriously!"

> Murray's father is said to have suggested to him, early in the year, that after graduation he take a few months' vacation before settling down to work. Whereupon the student started to practice. That was back in the Winter, and during the Spring he spent as much time on the courts as he could spare. His successes this Summer are the result.

> Unlike most of the California tennis cracks, Murray has not had careful training at the hands of an expert. They have a sort of tennis school out there, and that is one of the explanations of the quality of tennis talent they turn out. But Murray is not one of those who has had the benefit of this tennis education. In fact, for a long time he was a track athlete, and it was comparatively a short time ago that he tackled tennis with any enthusiasm. He is just a natural-born player.[22]

On July 26 the *Ohio State Journal* wrote a shorter version of the laudatory article published in the July 5 issue of the *Times.*

> [U]p to a few weeks ago, there weren't a dozen ... "bracketed" players in the East who even knew his name. They do now. R. Lindley Murray, the boy wonder from California, has taken the measure of nearly every one of them—Mathey, Church, Washburn, Touchard, Alexander, Behr, Hall—topnotchers all.
>
> He's the talk of tennisdom.... Murray has had none of the experience or the years of careful training which the great Eastern players have enjoyed. He's just a natural-born player, with a cannon ball serve like McLoughlin's, a smash that is wickedness itself, a faculty for covering court like a seven-league booter, an inhuman reach and stamina galore. He has taught himself.[23]

What was all the more amazing was what the writer reported next: Murray had only been playing tennis for four years, beginning as a freshman at Stanford.

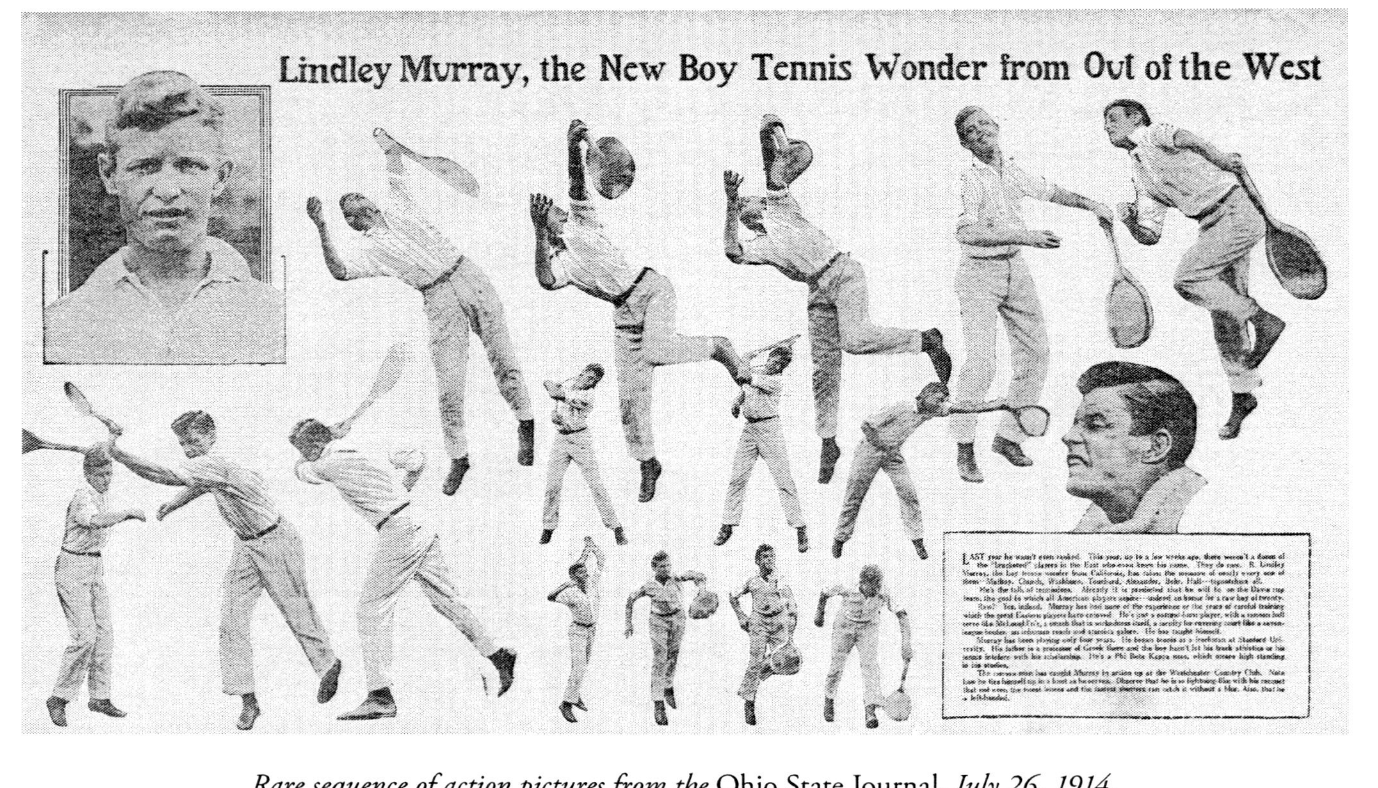

Lindley Murray, the New Boy Tennis Wonder from Out of the West

LAST year he wasn't even ranked. This year, up to a few weeks ago, there weren't a dozen of the "bracketed" players in the East who even knew his name. They do now. R. Lindley Murray, the boy tennis wonder from California, has taken the measure of nearly every one of them—Mathey, Church, Washburn, Touchard, Alexander, Behr, Hall—topnotchers all.

He's the talk of tennisdom. Already it is predicted that he will be on the Davis cup team, the goal to which all American players aspire—indeed an honor for a raw boy of twenty.

Raw? Yes, indeed. Murray has had none of the experience or the years of careful training which the great Eastern players have enjoyed. He's just a natural-born player, with a cannon ball serve like McLoughlin's, a smash that is wickedness itself, a faculty for covering court like a seven-league booter, an inhuman reach and stamina galore. He has taught himself.

Murray has been playing only four years. He began tennis as a freshman at Stanford University. His father is a professor of Greek there and the boy hasn't let his track athletics or his tennis interfere with his scholarship. He's a Phi Beta Kappa man, which means high standing in his studies.

The camera man has caught Murray in action up at the Westchester Country Club. Note how he ties himself up in a knot as he serves. Observe that he is so lightning-like with his racquet that not even the finest lenses and the fastest shutters can catch it without a blur. Also, that he is left-handed.

Rare sequence of action pictures from the Ohio State Journal, *July 26, 1914, after Lin Murray's successful string of victories on the Eastern circuit.*

The annual invitation grass court tournament of the Country Club of Westchester, New York, was next played beginning July 6. This tourney was definitely high-class with several top tenners, including Dick Williams (no. 2), Bill Johnston (no. 4), Theodore Pell (no. 5), Nat Niles (no. 6), Wallace Johnson (no. 7), Gus Touchard (no. 8), George Gardner (no. 9), Karl Behr (no. 3 for 1914), George Church (no. 7 for 1914), Watson Washburn (no. 9 for 1914), Ray Little (no. 8 for 1912), and Bill Larned (by then past his prime, tied with R. D. Sears and Bill Tilden with seven U.S. singles titles; Larned was in the U.S. top ten nineteen times in twenty years, 1892–1911). Bill Johnston beat Murray in the quarters, 7–5, 11–9, while Hahn had lost to Karl Behr in the previous round. Williams beat Johnston in the final, 2–6, 9–7, 6–4. Murray paired with Williams in the doubles, but they lost in the semis to Church and Dean Mathey, 4–6, 6–4, 6–4.[24]

The annual Seabright invitation tournament held the week of July 13 at the Seabright Lawn Tennis and Cricket Club near Rumson, New Jersey, was made more notable by the fact that it was one of the preliminary tryouts from which the Davis Cup defending team was to be chosen. Dick Williams, ranked second, came through a field of thirty-two famous contestants, challenging and defeating Pell, holder of the Achilles cup, after a five-set battle. The event was played during one of the hottest spells of the year. Two of the leading players were overcome by the heat on July 16 and were compelled to withdraw. George Gardner was so exhausted that he defaulted to Gus Touchard after each player had won one set and with the score 5–5 in the third.

After splitting the first two sets in his quarterfinal with Dick Williams of Philadelphia and with a commanding 5–3 lead in the third and deciding set, Murray showed excessive fatigue in the ninth game. Many of the spectators thought he was saving himself for his own service in the tenth, but the Philadelphian broke through. Murray was hardly able to keep on his feet and at 5–5 staggered to the referee's seat, where he rested his head between his hands. Robert Wrenn, George Adee, and Henry Slocum quickly reached the exhausted player, advising him to default the match. For a time Murray declined but was finally prevailed upon to quit. Assisted by Mr. Wrenn, he walked to the clubhouse amid the cheers of the spectators. While inside, Murray fainted, but he had recovered and was feeling no ill effects by the time a physician arrived. The score reported was, 6–4, 4–6, 5–5, default.[25–26]

The winner of the Longwood championship held at the historic Longwood Cricket Club, July 20–28, was practically a foregone conclusion.

The national champion, Maurice McLoughlin, was among the entrants, and his path to victory was never seriously threatened. "McLoughlin came through the 'all-comers' without losing a set, although apparently somewhat forced by Dabney, who put up a splendid fight, and by his fellow Californian, the youthful Murray, in one of the most sensational matches ever played at Longwood."

The Longwood tourney featured the star-studded cast of Maurice McLoughlin (no. 1), Dick Williams (no. 2), William Clothier (no. 3), William Johnston (no. 4), Nat Niles (no. 6), Wallace Johnson (no. 7), George Gardner (no. 9), Karl Behr (1914 no. 3), Fred Alexander (1914 no. 8), Watson Washburn (1914 no. 9), and Elia Fottrell (1914 no. 10)—seven top tenners and four top tenners for the coming year.

McLoughlin romped through the tournament, beating in succession W. D. Bourne, 6–0, 6–1; Nat Niles, 6–3, 6–4, 6–2; Tom Bundy, 6–0, 6–0, 6–1; A. S. Dabney, 6–3, 6–3, 7–5; and Dick Williams in a semifinal, 6–3, 6–3, 6–4. In the other half Lin Murray beat in succession J. Wheelwright, 6–2, 6–2; Russell Dana, 6–1, 6–3, 6–1; F. C. Inman, 6–4, 6–3, 6–2; Elia Fottrell, 9–7, 7–5, 4–6, 8–6; and Wallace Johnson in a semifinal, 8–6, 6–3, 7–5. As Williams played and beat Clothier in the second round, Murray had an easier run since this was well before seedings were initiated in 1922. In the final round McLoughlin beat Murray, 6–3, 6–3, 9–7, and then the previous year's winner Bill Johnston, 6–4, 6–4, 6–1, in the challenge round.[27]

Murray's next stop was the New York State championship held on the grass courts of the Crescent Athletic Club at Bay Ridge, Brooklyn, from July 29 to August 8. Upsets and reversals were frequent during the competition and an American marathon record was set by Hoffman Nickerson and E. R. McCormick in their fourth-round singles match, the former running the score up to 19–17 in their second set, thus eclipsing all previous long-distance tournament records.

Murray was in the opposite half of the draw from national champion Maurice McLoughlin and disposed of Bill Johnston, by default; Palmer, 6–1, 6–2; Anderson, 6–1, 6–0; and Graves, 6–4, 6–1. In the quarterfinals Alexander beat Chambers, 8–6, 7–5; Murray beat McCormick, 6–2, 6–4; Inman beat Bundy, 6–1, 6–4; and McLoughlin beat Wayne, by default. *Spalding's 1915 Guide* reported:

> McLoughlin, showing very brilliant form disposed of Inman in three sets in the semi-final match, but the other

> semi-final proved to be the best contest of the tournament. It was a meeting between Murray and Alexander, who had met twice before during the season and in both instances Murray was declared the victor. This last match at once resolved itself into a contest of furious speed and brilliancy. Murray had the speed, the dash, and the stamina, while Alexander had the head and tennis strokes.
>
> Murray won the first set by breaking through the veteran's service, and pulled out the second after being behind at 5–3. He lost the third after Alexander had point set on him eight times. The Californian played well in the fourth set and ran into a lead of 5–2, only to be caught again by Alexander in a wonderful spurt at 5–all. An extra kick to his serve enabled Murray to run out the set at 8–6 and with it the match.[28]

In the match, as recorded by the *New York Times*,

> Murray faced the hardest task since his Eastern invasion in disposing of Frederick B. Alexander, the former internationalist, 8–6, 8–6, 8–10, 8–6. The latter match resolved itself into a contest between youth and experience, and the [former] won out after the best battle witnessed in this year's championship tournament.
>
> Alexander played a brilliant game against his youthful opponent, and it was only the vitality of the latter that brought about the result. The veteran used all the tricks of the court, of which he is a past master. He kept Murray busy chasing the erratic bounding of the ball at all points of the court, but the Californian made a number of almost impossible gets and received his full share of luck. During the match sixty games were played and the men were on the court three hours. The aggressiveness of the play of both men can be estimated by the fact that at the end of the third set the turf was so badly cut up that a change of court was suggested but declined.
>
> One interesting feature of the match was the number of times each man won his opponent's service. This was particularly the case in the deuce games, when on several

> occasions the players were within a point of winning the set. The stubborn defense of Alexander and his ability to play the stinging service of Murray earned for him rounds of applause from the big gallery, and but for a tumble in the fourth set, when he was within two points of the set, the result might have been different. In running after a comparatively easy shot he slipped and fell as the ball bounded out of court.[29]

McLoughlin started the final match with wonderful speed, while Murray was a bit nervous and off his game. McLoughlin ran off the first four games before Murray took the fifth, his only game of the set. The second and third sets found a great improvement in Murray's play, especially in serving. McLoughlin found the twisting ball very difficult to handle but took the serve just often enough to keep comfortably in the lead at all times.[30] The *New York Times* of August 20 said, "McLoughlin disposed of the rangy youth from Palo Alto in straight sets, 6–1, 6–3, 6–4, thereby winning back the title which he held in 1911 and 1912."[31]

Robert Lindley Murray climaxed a spectacular inaugural Eastern tennis vacation by winning the annual invitation of the Meadowbrook Club at Southampton played during the week of August 17. With some stars of past years among the entries, the tourney offered a high-class list and was full of sensational upsets such as the quarterfinal defeats of Bill Johnston (no. 4) by Watson Washburn, Elia Fottrell by Alfred Dabney, and Wallace Johnson (no. 7) by George Gardner (no. 9). Murray defeated Watson M. Washburn in the final round, 6–2, 7–5, 6–4. Along the way Murray beat Clarence Hobart, 6–2, 6–3; Peaslee, 6–2, 6–3; Parker, 6–0, 6–3; Harte, 6–1, 6–2; and Gardner, 6–4, 6–4.[32] The *New York Times* of August 22 reported:

> [Richard] Harte [of Philadelphia] had been playing strong in the early rounds, defeating Lyle E. Mahan and Robert LeRoy. Murray complained of being over-trained recently, and had not been showing his usual dash and speed on the court. Therefore when they faced each other on the championship court speculation was rife as to the outcome. Murray soon set all doubts at rest, however, and mowed down his young opponent in straight sets at 6–1, 6–2.

> The Californian rushed to the net to nip off Harte's forehand drives and rained placement shots to all corners of the court. Harte quickly discovered that the swift drives he had been able to use held no terrors for the Californian. Many of the Philadelphian's drives were taken at the half volley by Murray, who sent them back in the form of cross-court shots that piled up the points. The Pacific Coast youth's sensational overhead smashes thrilled the spectators, while his deep forehand drives caused Harte to keep on the jump every minute of the time.
>
> Watson M. Washburn fought his way into the final bracket by defeating his fellow-student [Alfred S. Dabney] at 6–4, 6–1. As against William Johnston of California yesterday, Washburn's low drives scored many points by passing Dabney on both sides of the court.[33]

Because Johnston was renowned for his topspin forehand drive, which he hit shoulder high with a Western grip, he would have been more vulnerable to low balls. Taking a low ball on the forehand with his grip, he came up under the ball, applying topspin.

Elon Hooker, president of Hooker Electrochemical in Niagara Falls and Murray's subsequent employer, played doubles at Southampton with H. H. Stebbins, losing in the first round to F. W. Paul Jr. and Dr. J. O. Downey, 4–6, 6–1, 7–5. The national champions McLoughlin and Bundy captured the doubles title from the famous stars Bill Larned and Australian Norman Brookes, 7–5, 6–2.[34]

The thirty-fourth national championship was the last to be staged at the Newport Casino. The world's leading player, Maurice Evans McLoughlin, was regarded as the certain winner but was beaten in straight sets by his international teammate, Richard Norris Williams II, 6–3, 8–6, 10–8. *Wright & Ditson's 1915 Guide* said, "The Cambridge lad and Harvard captain became the 'super' player, rising to dizzying heights of skill and defeating his many-time conqueror on merit. It is fair to say that McLoughlin, splendidly as he played in that match, was not the same player who had triumphed over Brookes and Wilding."[35] Although the United States lost the Davis Cup challenge round to Australasia by a score of 3–2, August 13–15, at the West Side Tennis Club, "the Comet" McLoughlin defeated both Norman Brookes in a record opening set of 17–15 and then Tony Wilding.

The match to McLoughlin at the U.S. Championships was an anticlimax to his real task of the season, and he showed the effects of a mental and psychological letdown. However, none of this should detract from Williams's performance, for on that day his game was near perfect.[36]

The entry list was strong and contained a powerful California contingent including Elia Fottrell, Clarence Griffin, William Johnston, R. Lindley Murray, and of course the California Comet. Bill Johnston lost to Williams in the second round, Murray lost to Karl Behr in the fourth round, and Griffin lost to McLoughlin in the quarters, while Fottrell reached the semis, where he lost to Williams. *Wright & Ditson's 1915 Guide* said, "Behr … was forced to five wonderful sets by Murray in one of the most thrilling matches of the event."[37] The score in that contest was 3–6, 6–2, 7–5, 3–6, 8–6. In a battle between *Titanic* alumni, Dick Williams defeated Karl Behr in the quarters, 6–2, 6–2, 7–5, only a few blocks from the Atlantic Ocean from which they were rescued.

When the 1914 U.S. rankings were calculated and posted in the *Times* on December 19, 1914, Maurice E. McLoughlin was no. 1; R. Norris Williams II, no. 2; Karl H. Behr, no. 3; R. Lindley Murray, no. 4; and William M. Clothier, no. 5. This was the first time in the history of the U.S. Championships that the national champion had not been given top honors. The reason for the committee's decision was that "the phenomenal victories of McLoughlin over Norman E. Brookes and Anthony F. Wilding in the memorable [Davis Cup] matches at Forest Hills last August overbalanced Williams's victory at Newport, especially as Williams followed by losing to George M. Church in the inter-collegiates."[38]

During his 1914 Eastern invasion, Murray defeated the New England intercollegiate champion, won Sleepy Hollow, New England, Metropolitan, Southampton, and Delaware State, but lost the challenge round, and was a finalist to McLoughlin at New York State and Longwood. Murray had lost to George Church, William Johnston, Dick Williams, Maurice McLoughlin (2), and Karl Behr. He had defeated Tallant, Alexander (3), Behr, Hall (2), Man, Mathey, Washburn (2), Johnson (3), Church, Armstrong, Fottrell, Inman, Gardner, Harte, McCormick, and Hobart.

Murray returned home to Palo Alto in the fall and played in the California State championship at the Claremont Country Club in Oakland beginning October 24. Murray beat Leon Strauss, 6–2, 6–4, in the second round but defaulted to Roland Roberts in the third. John R. Strachan had a superb tourney, defeating William Johnston in the quarters, 6–4, 6–2;

Clarence Griffin in the semis, 6–4, 6–2; and C. B. Detrick in the final, 6–1, 6–1, 6–3.[39]

In summing up the 1914 tennis season, *Spalding's Annual* said:

> The early spring season started off in the East by an invasion of two young Pacific Coast players—R. Lindley Murray and Herbert Hahn—two heretofore unknown men East of the Rockies, and both college boys. In the dual meets with the two representative best players in the different Eastern universities, they swept all before them, capping the climax when they defeated the strong Harvard team, composed of Watson F. Washburn and Edward H. Whitney. In singles, Murray quickly rounded into form and showed one of the strongest games that any Western man has ever played on Eastern courts in his first season.
>
> In his first tournament, the Sleepy Hollow Invitation, Murray defeated consecutively, in one day, Frederick B. Alexander, Karl Behr and William [Walter] M. Hall, a feat which the experts and authorities of the game would have declared even impossible for the great McLoughlin himself to do.
>
> Later he won the Metropolitan Championship at the West Side Tennis Club in New York City, defeating Washburn and Church in the earlier rounds, and then Alexander in a hard five-set match in the finals. These two tournaments naturally placed him in a position to be considered seriously for the next International team.[40]

Tennis writers everywhere paid tribute to the "brilliant young Californian." The *Boston Transcript's* expert said of him: "He played the spectacular smashing type of game with which McLoughlin first electrified eastern galleries. His service was terrific, he covered a prodigious amount of territory, often going far out of court to return seemingly impossible drives, and smashed with such force as to threaten the destruction of bats and balls."[41]

9
The 1915 Season

Lin Murray remained on the Pacific Coast for most of the 1915 season. He had taken a position with the Pacific Coast Borax Company in Oakland, California, as an "agricultural chemist," probably late in 1914 as he was assistant head chemist at the time of publication of *Spalding's 1915 Annual*, which would have been available shortly after the February 5, 1915, USNLTA annual meeting.[1] (This was the company that established and aggressively developed the famous *20 Mule Team Borax* trademark.) He had written that he would not be a competitor in the U.S. Championships at its new location, the West Side Tennis Club in Forest Hills.

Murray played in the Panama–Pacific Exposition games, held on the asphalt courts of San Francisco during the second week of July, which pitted the top Eastern players against those from the West. Playing for the Eastern states were R. Norris Williams II, national champion; George M. Church, 1912 and 1914 Princeton intercollegiate titleholder; Watson M. Washburn, 1913 Harvard intercollegiate doubles champion; and Dean Mathey, 1910 and 1911 Princeton intercollegiate doubles champion. The Pacific Coast lineup included Maurice E. McLoughlin, rated as the greatest player in the world; John R. Strachan; William M. Johnston or "Little Bill," who was to win the 1915 national title and go on to become a tennis legend; and R. Lindley Murray, 1913 Pacific Coast intercollegiate singles and doubles champion.[2]

It was in the *Niagara Falls Gazette*'s reporting of the San Francisco tournament that R. Lindley Murray's name first came to light in that paper, on July 9, 1915, in an article entitled "Eastern Tennis Stars Invade

West."[3] The tournament resulted in a clean sweep for the Pacific Coast players, both in the tournament itself and in the team matches. The Eastern team found the unfamiliar hard courts and high winds very little to their liking. Washburn lost on July 12, while Clarence J. Griffin, who held the Coast doubles championship with Bill Johnston, disposed of Church, 6–1, 6–1, and Strachan beat Mathey, 6–4, 6–2, on July 13. Williams progressed by defeating Murray, 8–6, 7–9, 9–7. The *New York Times* of July 14 wrote, "Champion Williams had one of the hardest matches of his career with Lindley Murray, the Stanford star, who was the sensation in the East last season."[4–5]

Williams was the only Eastern player to reach the tournament quarterfinals, the match-ups being Williams versus Griffin; McLoughlin versus Willis Davis, a local player who attended the University of Pennsylvania; William Johnston versus R. J. Greenberg; and Mel Long versus John Strachan.[6] On July 14 Clarence Griffin, holder of the U.S. Clay Court doubles title with Johnny Strachan, defeated the national champion Dick Williams in three sets, 6–3, 5–7, 6–1. The *Times* noted: "It was evident to those who watched the match that Williams was perceptibly weakened by his hard match on Tuesday afternoon with Lindley Murray. In the last set the Easterner made a sorry showing, taking but one game from the San Franciscan. His service was poor and his usual agility in the back court went pretty badly at critical moments."[7]

Lin Murray played the California State championship tournament at Oakland, September 2–9. There he lost in the final round to Willis Davis of the University of California in five sets, 3–6, 6–3, 6–4, 3–6, 6–3.[8] For 1915 Murray was ranked fifth on the Pacific Coast behind William M. Johnston, John R. Strachan, Clarence J. Griffin, and Willis E. Davis.[9]

Murray's Stanford teammate and 1914 East Coast traveling companion, Herbert Hahn, had a great season in California. Hahn was a finalist for the intercollegiate singles title in April at the Ojai Valley championship, losing to Stanford teammate H. Van Dyke Johns, 6–0, 5–7, 6–1. The Stanford pair won the intercollegiate doubles title over Morrow and Little of the University of Southern California, 6–0, 7–5.[10] On the courts of the California Lawn Tennis Club during the week following October 30, Hahn won the Pacific States championship despite the fact that among the contestants were the new national champion, William M. Johnston, Clarence J. Griffin, H. Van Dyke Johns, and seventeen-year-old Roland Roberts, the Southern California champion. In the semis Johns beat Johnston, 4–6, 6–4, 6–3, 3–6, 7–5, while Hahn beat Griffin, 4–6, 6–4,

4–6, 6–2, 6–3. In the final round Hahn beat Johns, 6–1, 6–4, 3–6, 6–1. Hahn paired with Allan Barber in doubles and lost in the final round to the national doubles champions Johnston and Griffin.[11]

In the East Elon Hooker, president of Hooker Electrochemical in Niagara Falls played in the National Clay Court championship at the Pittsburgh Athletic Association beginning on June 26. Hooker easily won his second round match over Chall Stehley, 6–0, 6–1, before losing to Lawrence Curtis in the third round by the same score. Lin Murray's future friend, nineteen-year-old Jack Castle of Buffalo (see profile in part III), played that 1915 tournament, defeating in succession W. P. Snyder, 6–2, 6–2; Dornberger, 6–3, 6–2; A. H. Wright, 6–3, 6–3; Sunstein, 6–0, 6–1; and Fred C. Inman (ranked no. 24 for 1915), 8–6, 4–6, 6–4, before losing to Watson M. Washburn (no. 9) in the quarters, 6–1, 6–0. Other quarterfinalists were George Church, Charles Garland, national champion Richard Williams, Dean Mathey, Nat Niles, and William McEllroy.[12] For 1915 Jack Castle was ranked no. 42 and Bill Tilden no. 70, while Lin Murray didn't make the top one hundred, since no Pacific Coast player was ranked who had not played throughout the Eastern circuit in three or more sanctioned events, as requested by the executive committee of the Pacific States Lawn Tennis Association.[13]

Elon Hooker also played the Southampton invitation, which began August 23, just before the nationals; he won the first round in two deuce sets but was beaten handily by Harold Throckmorton in the second.[14] This was the final Eastern tournament won by Lin Murray in 1914 during his spectacular run.

At the 1915 Delaware State championship, won by Lin Murray in 1914, Bill Tilden and his older brother Herbert played the week of June 21, Herbert having won the doubles there the previous year. Herbert lost in the third round while Bill lost in the quarters to L. C. Wister, 4–6, 10–8, 6–4.[15] Less than three months later Herbert M. Tilden died of pneumonia on September 22, 1915, at the age of twenty-nine.[16] *Wright & Ditson's 1916 Guide* paid tribute saying, "America lost one player of more than average ability last year in the death of Herbert M. Tilden one of Philadelphia's leading experts. He died of pneumonia September 22. Mr. Tilden was born in Germantown, November 3, 1886, received his education at the Germantown Academy and the University of Pennsylvania, and at the time of his decease was holder of the Pennsylvania and Delaware State tiles in Doubles. His loss is deeply felt."[17]

The *Guide* also paid tribute to Anthony F. Wilding of the Australasian 1914 Davis Cup championship team, winner of four successive Wimbledon singles titles from 1910 to 1913 and three doubles titles. He was killed in action at La Bassée in Northern France on May 10, 1915, in the Great War. Wilding was only thirty-one and still at the zenith of his power as a player. He volunteered early and at the time of his death was a captain in the Armoured Car Section of the Naval Air Service.[18]

Five Californians played in the U.S. Championships at the West Side Tennis Club in Forest Hills—Maurice E. McLoughlin, Thomas C. Bundy, William M. Johnston, Clarence J. Griffin, and Ward Dawson. The notable Pacific Coast absentees included Elia Fottrell, R. Lindley Murray, and John R. Strachan. Johnston defeated Williams in the semis, 5–7, 6–4, 5–7, 6–2, 6–2, and McLoughlin in the final, 1–6, 6–0, 7–5, 10–8. For 1915 William Johnston was no. 1; Dick Williams, no. 2; Maurice McLoughlin, no. 3; Karl Behr, no. 4; and Theodore Pell, no. 5.

Lin Murray's first job after graduating from Stanford in 1914 was as a draftsman at a California sugar refinery.[19] Murray then took a position with the Pacific Coast Borax Company in Oakland as indicated above, but transferred to Bayonne, New Jersey. As reported by the *New York Times* on October 28, 1915, Murray "is now a chemist in the Bayonne, N. J., works of the Pacific Coast Borax Company. The young California player will do his playing as a member of the West Side Tennis Club at Forest Hills, although he will probably not join the club until next Spring. He has been here for the past few weeks, but has not appeared on the tennis courts. Very few persons knew that the Palo Alto youngster had finished his course in the Leland Stanford University and had made his home in the East."[20]

10
The 1916 U.S. Indoor Championship

Lin Murray made his 1916 debut in Brooklyn. On February 6, the *New York Times* reported:

> Karl H. Behr and Theodore R. Pell, holders of the Middle States doubles championship, were defeated in an exhibition indoor tennis match yesterday afternoon on the courts of the Heights Casino in Brooklyn by R. Lindley Murray, the sensational California player, and Harry McNeal, the Heights Casino professional. Behr and Pell were outplayed almost throughout and showed in their work the lack of practice.
>
> It was the play of Murray that was astonishing. Having had little time to bring his game to a keen edge, he still played with a dash that was too much for the veterans. Murray and McNeal won at 7–5, 6–3, 6–1, which shows the decreasing efficiency of the Middle States champions as the match neared its close.
>
> Murray had a lightning-fast service that was particularly effective on the board courts. There was some "top" to the ball, and this, combined with the terrific force, made the service hard to return.
>
> The third set was one-sided, the champions getting only one game. It was really the brilliancy of Murray that counted most heavily against Pell and Behr. His drives were hard, and many of the points were the result of his

> careful placing. His ground stroke, too, was particularly effective, and those who saw the match predicted that Murray, who is entered for the indoor championships at the Seventh Regiment, would be one of the most formidable contestants no matter what other stars of the tennis world might enter.[1]

The National Indoor tennis championship started February 12, 1916, at the Seventh Regiment Armory in Manhattan. In his first day of play, Murray captured a trio of matches. In the morning he defeated G. Carleton Shafer, 6–3, 6–3; he next won over Carleton Y. Smith, one of the well–known Southern players, 6–4, 6–1. Unable to play every day because of his job in New Jersey, the tournament committee permitted Murray to play his third match that first day, probably much to the chagrin of his opponent, King Smith, who had recently won the armory's singles championship. Smith also was outplayed by the Californian, losing 6–2, 6–3.

It was anticipated that Murray's contest with Shafer would be hard-fought. Shafer did not quite play up to his form, whereas Murray played almost flawlessly. His overhead game was remarkable, and not once during the two sets did he make an overhead error. Murray's fast twist service, with which he scored a number of aces, kept Shafer well back of the baseline. With Shafer so deep, Murray hit tantalizing drop volleys, and when Shafer did return the ball, Murray lobbed over his head. The Californian placed accurately, and time and again drew Shafer out of position and then passed him cleanly. In Murray's second match, Carleton Smith led him 4-0 in the first set before Murray ran out twelve of the next thirteen games.

Two Western New Yorkers also played the event, and one of the tournament surprises was the defeat of Alfred S. Dabney (no. 32) by G. O. Wagner of Buffalo, 6–3, 6–3. In the first round Dabney defeated C. M. Amerman, 6–4, 6–1, while Wagner beat Merle Johnson, 6–1, 6–3.[2] E. H. Hooker lost in the first round to F. M. Loughman in three sets, 5–7, 6–3, 6–4.

Four days later, the *New York Times* reported, "R. Lindley Murray gave another demonstration of his brilliant tennis play on the hard courts of the Seventh Regiment Armory yesterday afternoon when he triumphed without difficulty over Dr. A. W. Waite, the senior metropolitan indoor champion, in the fourth round of the national indoor singles championship." After winning the first game on serve, Waite was thereafter virtually helpless.

"Murray's driving was terrific whether with forehand or backhand, and he was equally good with either. There was a lot of top to the ball and it broke sharply over the net and bounded low. Waite had trouble even to make the return, without seeking to place it, and he seldom passed Murray." Murray won, 6–2, 6–0, to reach the semis while Watson M. Washburn (no. 8) won the right to play Murray by defeating G. A. Walker Jr., 6–4, 6–0.[3]

Wylie C. Grant and Alrick H. Man Jr., advanced to the other semifinal.[4] Murray scored an easy victory over Washburn, 6–1, 6–1, while Man eliminated Grant, five-time holder of the indoor title and twice runner-up, 7–5, 6–3. Washburn proved to be no match for his speedy Western rival, his slow and methodical game being ineffective against the terrific speed of Murray.[5] The *New York Times* said on February 23:

> R. Lindley Murray, the remarkable California player, defeated Alrick H. Man, Jr. in the singles event in straight sets, 6–2, 6–2, 9–7.... When Murray first came East in 1914, his first championship was won at the expense of Man. In the challenge round of the New England championship, the Californian was the victor and it was a strange coincidence that the final round of the first national tournament this year should find these two pitted against each other. Due to his former experience Man was accustomed in some degree to the fast play of the Californian. He adopted a different plan of campaign than did the previous opponents of Murray. Instead of taking the bullet service far back of the baseline, he stood close in and shot the Westerner's serve back at him with almost its initial velocity. His driving copied Murray's and he was clever in placing, getting many of his points after drawing the Californian out of position and then passing him by cross courting or lightning shots down the lines.[6]

Murray was erratic in the first part of the third set and, down 4–1, played more consistently to eke out a close victory after Man was within a point of set. Despite his easy conquest of the indoor title, the *Times* said: "There was nothing graceful about Murray's stroking, but at all times he was wonderfully effective."[7] Now that Murray was living and working in Bayonne, it was expected his playing would be confined to a few of the larger tournaments. Commenting on Murray's indoor victory at the armory, a February 28 *Times* article reported:

> Murray won, though he had not had full opportunity for practice. It was another demonstration of the effectiveness of the Californian type of tennis. Murray showed himself a master in the fine points of the game, as well as in tremendous driving and serving power. It should be remembered also that he was playing under unaccustomed conditions, the indoor game with its uncertain light being comparatively new to him. But whether the light was good or bad—and it was more often bad—his ability in nowise suffered.[8]

After finally winning a national title, Murray again lost to Dick Williams of Harvard, 1913 and 1915 intercollegiate champion and 1914 national amateur tennis champion, at the opening of the new indoor tennis courts of the Buffalo Tennis and Squash Club on February 26. The score was 6–2, 6–3. Murray and Dean Mathey of Princeton, 1910 and 1911 intercollegiate doubles champion, lost in the doubles to Williams and Harry Johnson of Boston by 3–6, 6–3, 6–2.[9]

Miss Molla Bjurstedt, a Norwegian living in Brooklyn, won the March 11 women's indoor singles event at the Heights Casino in Brooklyn over Mrs. Frederick Schmitz, 6–2, 6–2. She then teamed with R. Lindley Murray to play mixed doubles against Miss Alberta Weber and Harry McNeil. Bjurstedt and Murray won, 6–2, 6–4.

> Murray was at his best, apparently being unaffected by the slower playing surface of the Casino, as compared with the boards at the Seventh Regiment Armory. His service was so speedy that it gave McNeil trouble, owing in part to the narrow confines of the court. Murray decreased the speed of his service to Miss Weber, but McNeil showed little leniency in this respect toward Miss Bjurstedt.
>
> The match really turned on the playing of McNeil and Murray, and the Californian showed to the better advantage. Repeatedly he drove the ball at McNeil so fast that the latter could make only a feeble effort at a return.

> Miss Weber showed a powerful forehand drive comparing favorably with that of Miss Bjurstedt, and she succeeded in keeping it well in bounds. How effective Murray's serve was may be gathered from the fact that it was not broken through until the sixth game of the second set, and then it was because the indoor champion threw away points by errors.[10]

On April 22, Alberta Weber and Harry McNeil got a measure of revenge over Molla Bjurstedt and Lin Murray in an exhibition tennis match at the Heights Casino in straight sets, 8–6, 6–2.[11]

R. Lindley Murray made his debut in Eastern tennis two years ago by winning the first annual invitation tournament of the Sleepy Hollow Country Club at Scarborough on clay courts. He returned to the scene in May 1916 to oust Robert LeRoy (no. 16) in the second round, 8–6, 6–4. In each set LeRoy led at 4–2 only to have the Californian bring the score even. When coming from behind, Murray had an uncanny way of mixing pace. After a blazing drive he would chop the ball just over the net with LeRoy waiting in the back court.[12] Harold Throckmorton (no. 18) defeated Murray, 6–3, 6–3, in the third round by playing a forcing game, chasing down everything, and in the rallies successfully outguessing his more experienced rival. In the afternoon Throckmorton played another Californian in the semis, Willis E. Davis; Davis had defeated Murray in five sets at the 1915 California State championships. This was Davis's first Eastern tournament, and he upheld the honor of the Golden Gate by annihilating Throckmorton, 6–3, 6–2, 6–0.[13] In the final Davis defeated George M. Church (no. 9), 6–2, 6–2, 2–6, 5–7, 6–2.[14]

Bypassing the Metropolitan tournament the week of June 10 due to job commitments, Murray next played in the Nassau Country Club invitational, which began on July 1. In the quarterfinals Theodore Pell defeated Watson Washburn, 7–5, 8–10, 6–1; Nat Niles defeated S. Howard Voshell, 5–7, 6–4, 6–3; and R. Lindley Murray defeated Harold Throckmorton, 6–3, 6–3, thereby avenging his loss to Throckmorton by the same score at Sleepy Hollow. It was quite a different Murray on the Nassau courts. In the previous encounter Murray plainly showed that he was far from his capable form. Conditions at Glen Cove on grass were more to his liking, which allowed Murray to show his best game.[15] In the last quarterfinal, former Princetonian Dean Mathey outplayed one of the most brilliant—and temperamental—experts of the courts, Karl H. Behr (no. 4). In the semifinals Mathey defeated Pell (no. 5), 13–11, 6–8, 9–7, while Murray easily defeated Niles (no. 6). Murray won the singles event final over Mathey (no. 17), 6–2, 7–5, 10–8. "Though he was the victor in straight sets," Murray had to rise to his greatest heights to vanquish the persistent and formidable Mathey, who had "never played better tennis in his career than in" this "tournament against men of the highest rank."[16]

In an exhibition tennis match on July 22 at the Crescent Athletic Cub in Bay Ridge, Karl H. Behr and R. Lindley Murray defeated the national doubles champions from Northern California, William M. Johnston and Clarence J. Griffin, 8–6, 6–1, 4–6, 3–6, 6–4. The matchup was national singles champion Johnston's first appearance in the East that year, and despite the inclement weather, there were nearly one thousand persons gathered at the Bay Ridge courts.[17]

California's tennis prestige suffered a severe setback on August 4 and 5 on the courts of the West Side Tennis Club when the Easterners won an overwhelming and unexpected victory by a score of 6–1 in a series consisting of five singles and two doubles. Former national champion Dick Williams of Philadelphia defeated national champion Bill Johnston in five hard sets, 3–6, 6–3, 8–6, 4–6, 9–7. In two other matches George M. Church defeated veteran Clarence J. Griffin, 6–3, 6–1, 6–4, while Karl H. Behr overcame Willis E. Davis, 6–0, 3–6, 6–1, 6–1, a surprisingly one-sided count, considering that Davis was the national clay court champion.

A fourth Eastern victory, however, must be qualified. Watson M. Washburn defeated R. Lindley Murray, but the conquest came as the result of a default in the fifth set. Although the Californian won the first two sets, his play showed a lack of the aggressiveness for which he was noted. In the third set Murray showed signs of weakening, and in the fourth it was apparent that something was wrong.

It became known later that Murray had had no sleep the night before the match, owing to illness in his family. Early in the morning Murray sent word to the Tennis Committee asking to postpone his match; if that was not feasible, he said, he would default. He was prevailed upon to come to Forest Hills, stormed through the first two sets as if he wanted to quickly conclude the match, but fatigue left Murray playing the fourth set and part of the fifth purely on nerve. Washburn won the match at 1–6, 3–6, 6–4, 6–1, 2–2, default. "In the fourth set Murray almost collapsed on the court. He persisted in playing, but in the fifth set his weakness was so evident that several of those in charge of the tournament drew him to one side and tried to induce him to leave the court. Dr. Barringer, Robert D. Wrenn, the referee of the tournament, and W. S. Campbell found their efforts unavailing, and it was not until Clarence J. Griffin of the California team talked to Murray that he consented to default the match."[18]

One week later Murray played in the final of the Seabright, New Jersey, invitational at the expense of the plucky Japanese player, Ichiya Kumagae. "It required three sets for the Californian to … defeat … his rival in a match that held many moments of keen excitement." George M. Church (no. 9) of Tenafly, New Jersey, advanced by defeating Willis E. Davis, 6–4, 6–4.[19] The 1912 and 1914 Princeton intercollegiate champion defeated Murray in the final, 6–4, 6–2, 6–4.[20]

Two days later, on August 13, 1916, in the final round of the Crescent Athletic Club open tournament at Bay Ridge, Murray again was compelled to summon his entire tennis prowess to win in straight sets against Ichiya Kumagae, 8–6, 6–4, 7–5. The New York State champion made Murray play his fastest pace throughout, and there never was a moment when the national indoor champion could take matters easy. Kumagae covered the court in catlike fashion and with remarkable agility. Save for Kumagae's wonderful gets, which were as frequent as they were spectacular, Murray would have won much more easily.[21]

In the national championships at Forest Hills, Murray in succession defeated A. Dabney, default; E. Thomas, 6–3, 6–2, 6–2; R. Stevens, 6–1, 6–0, 6–0; and Karl Behr (no. 4) in the fourth round, 6–4, 6–3, 3–6, 9–7. Behr had defeated Murray in the 1914 fourth round, 8–6 in the fifth set. Murray eliminated George Church (no. 9), who had absorbed more of the California game at the net than any of the other Eastern players, in the quarters after losing the first two sets, 3–6, 4–6, 6–2, 6–4, 6–4. The September 20 *Gazette* said of this match:

> The tall blonde youth from Palo Alto, California, is hailed as a wonder in the larger tennis circles of the East. True it was that he had displayed erratic form, but the desperate battle which he waged against Church in the national championships at Forest Hills, L. I., was a revelation to the tremendous crowd which had expected that he would be eliminated in this match.

> Never before had the East witnessed such an exhibition of nerve, gameness and endurance which the California southpaw demonstrated in this match. Church had won the first two sets and Murray's defeat appeared almost certain. Awkward, though he was, grim determination spurred him on and he finally emerged victorious when his slashing drives and perfect physical condition had beaten Church to a frazzle.[22]

The subsequently famous William T. Tilden wrote in 1921 to "Never allow a 3 out of 5-set match to go to the fifth set if it is possible to win in less; but never give up a match until the last point is played, even if you are two sets and five games down." Continuing, he said a "regrettable incident occurred in the famous match between R. L. Murray of California and George M. Church of New York in the fourth [fifth] round of the American National Championships in 1916."

> George Church, then at the crest of his wonderful game, had won the first two sets and was leading Murray in the third, when the famous Californian started a sensational rally. Murray, with his terrific speed, merry smile, and genial personality, has always been a popular figure with the public, and when he began his seemingly hopeless fight, the crowd cheered him wildly. He broke through Church's service and drew even amid a terrific din. Church, always a very high-strung, nervous player, showed that the crowd's partiality was getting on his nerves. The gallery noticed it, and became more partisan than ever. The spirit of mob rule took hold, and for once they lost all sense of sportsmanship. They clapped errors as they rained from Church's racquet; the great game collapsed under the terrific strain, and Church's last chance was gone. Murray won largely as he wanted, in the last two sets. No one regretted the incident more than Murray himself, for no finer sportsman steps upon the court than this player, yet there was nothing that could be done. It was a case of external conditions influencing the psychology of one man so greatly that it cost him a victory that was his in justice.[23]

In anticipation of two of the sharpest battles of the tournament, some twelve thousand fans journeyed to Forest Hills, taxing to the fullest the seating capacity of the stands. Even the windbreak at the end, which only provided standing room, was filled; subsequently, seats were arranged beneath it to accommodate the overflow, while outside the gate many others were clamoring for admission at one dollar a person. R. (Dick) Norris Williams of Philadelphia, who won the championship in 1914, and Clarence J. Griffin of San Francisco, played first, Williams winning, 6–3, 6–3, 6–3.

Just after the conclusion of their match Colonel Theodore Roosevelt appeared on the clubhouse porch and applause rippled across the stands. Johnston and several other players were introduced to him, and in the spirit of the tennis atmosphere, Roosevelt said, "I was President … and Ambassador Jusserand was Vice President. Any one who defeated either Jusserand or myself was, under the rules, forever barred from membership [to the Tennis Cabinet]."[24]

R. Lindley Murray then played William M. Johnston of San Francisco, the previous years' winner, in the semis, losing 6–2, 6–3, 6–1. "The Coast star loosened the full fury of his game against Murray and the brother-Californian, who is among the acknowledged leaders in tennis, was beaten back, baffled and chastened. Twice this season Johnston has met with defeat, and for the most part his play has been only passing fair. But yesterday, under the knowledge that Murray must be crushed, he raised his game to the pinnacle."[25]

> Against Church [Murray's] chief asset had been service and a lightning fast delivery that almost defied return, but the slim little fellow from the Coast who faced him on the other side of the net was not to be frightened by any such play. With service nullified, Murray was brought to a realization of the forces which go to make up the well-rounded play of a champion, and the enforced tutelage at the hands of Johnston was not at all to his liking.
>
> Johnston's skill was balanced to a nicety. He drove and volleyed and half-volleyed with an accuracy that was amazing, but more than all this was the cool, collected way in which he did his playing. There was nothing impetuous, little of the so-called Californian game. His greatest advance toward the net was when he came to the

> forecourt and, once ensconced there, he finished off the points quickly. Murray, on the other hand, tried to play right over the barrier, but he was many times beaten back by a well-directed lob or a passing stroke by Johnston and, having found the strength of his rival, he held, thereafter, due respect for the perilous path to the net.
>
> Johnston's forehand was a thing of terror to Murray. It was burned across with such dazzling speed that the Palo Alto star could offer scarcely any defense. One of the prettiest shots in the champion's repertoire was the forehand across courting stroke off the ground, which frequently passed Murray.[26]

It took five sets, but Williams brought the national title east again by defeating Johnston, 4–6, 6–4, 0–6, 6–2, 6–4. Leading 3–0 in the fifth, Johnston tired and was unable to fight off the rally staged by Williams.[27]

At year's end R. Lindley Murray duplicated his 1914 national ranking at no. 4 behind Dick Williams, William Johnston, and George Church, and his home was given as Niagara Falls, New York. He won the National Indoor, Nassau, Crescent, and reached the national semifinals. In tournaments Murray defeated Church, Behr, Kumagae (2), Niles, Washburn, Mathey, Man (2), Throckmorton, Tilden, Stevens, Voshell, Hunter, LeRoy, Rand, Mikami, Shafer, and others. He lost to Johnston, Church, Throckmorton, and Washburn.

Lin Murray charging the net with determination after serving.
(Courtesy International Tennis Hall of Fame)

11
Hooker Electrochemical Company

Born in Rochester, New York, on November 23, 1869, Elon Huntington Hooker (1869–1938) was the third of eight children born to Susan Pamela Huntington and Horace B. Hooker. The Huntingtons and Hookers were originally old New England families, whose ancestors included the Reverend Thomas Hooker, founder of Hartford, Connecticut, two colonial governors of Connecticut, and the first mayor of New York.[1]

Elon received a bachelor's degree in 1891 from the University of Rochester, where he was not necessarily a good student. He then worked a year with Emil Kuichling, a Rochester city engineer. Kuichling had a significant influence on Elon, who was determined to become a civil engineer. In the fall of 1892, he entered Cornell University and finished four years of undergraduate training in two, graduating in June of 1894 with a BS in civil engineering. Elon subsequently earned his PhD in hydraulic engineering at Cornell in 1896.[2]

In 1899 Elon was appointed deputy superintendent of public works for the State of New York by then-governor Theodore Roosevelt. This position opened to Elon political, business, and social contacts with many people of great influence and wealth, who would later prove valuable in business.[3]

While in Rome during 1895, Elon met Blanche Ferry, the girl he would later marry in January 1901 in her father Dexter Ferry's Detroit home. In July of 1901, a friend of the Ferry family, impressed with Elon's ability and personality, made him vice president of the Development Company of America. The company's function was to locate potentially profitable but undercapitalized enterprises and to supply the needed backing and management to put them on a paying basis. This accomplished, subsidiary companies were then formed to continue the businesses under the control of the parent company.[4]

Elon Hooker was apparently so confident in his ability that he launched his own firm in January 1903, the Development and Funding Company.[5] He canvassed wealthy people willing to invest in long-term profitable projects and within three weeks raised sixty thousand dollars with two hundred thousand dollars more in subscriptions.[6]

Over 250 projects were examined by the company before Elon became interested in manufacturing bleaching powder and caustic soda using the Townsend electrolytic process. By passing an electric current through brine (saltwater), chlorine, caustic soda, and hydrogen are formed. Chlorine is formed at the anode, while caustic and hydrogen are formed at the cathode:[7]

$$2NaCl + 2H_2O + \text{electricity} = 2NaOH + Cl_2 + H_2$$

(salt + water + electricity) = (caustic soda + chlorine + hydrogen)

The chlorine is then passed over lime (CaO) or calcium hydroxide [$Ca(OH)_2$] to form bleaching powder [calcium hypochlorite: $Ca(ClO)_2$]. Although the electrolytic principle had been demonstrated as early as 1807, the process was not commercially viable until the development of the electric dynamo in the late 1800s.

In November of 1903 the Townsend process was brought to Elon's attention. Elon agreed to have the "caustic soda proposition looked into." John K. Jessup, a chemical salesman and Elon's uncle, went to Washington to see the small experimental cell in action. Meanwhile, Elon arranged for his older brother, Albert Huntington Hooker (1865–1936), then chief chemist for a Chicago paint company, to also go to Washington.[8] At the time, Albert was one of the country's few trained chemists.[9]

On the basis of favorable reports submitted by Jessup and A. H. Hooker, Elon acquired an option on the Townsend process.[10] Within a few weeks, Jessup and Horace Willard Hooker (1876–1937), Elon's youngest brother, had located a plant site in a former boiler house rented from the Edison Electric Illuminating Company in Brooklyn. This experimental plant is where the Townsend cell was first tested in the summer of 1904.[11]

The initial tests were discouraging due to chlorine leakage and graphite anode corrosion. At the time the cells had been operating with unsaturated brine. Chemist Clinton P. Townsend, co-inventor of the cell with Elmer

A. Sperry, was retained by Elon as a consultant. Townsend felt that they must constantly circulate a maximum amount of salt through the cells. In late July 1904, the cell was rebuilt and ran with higher efficiencies than ever before with only moderate anode wear.[12]

With only sixteen thousand dollars, Elon quickly raised the necessary funds for a manufacturing facility. The process required power, salt, and water. What could have been more ideal than Niagara Falls, New York, only a few hundred yards from the largest fresh water supply in the world, flowing from four of the five Great Lakes, and within sixty miles of the largest salt mine in the Western Hemisphere. With the power of the falls itself to generate electricity, Niagara Falls was to become one of the greatest electrochemical centers of the world.[13]

The plot itself was a 6.75-acre orchard on the corner of Buffalo Avenue and Union Street, now Forty-seventh Street. Ground was broken May 5, 1905, and on January 9, 1906, the plant went into operation. By mid-June the Development and Funding Company was producing five tons of caustic soda and eleven tons of bleaching powder a day.[14]

In those early years disbursements exceeded sales, and the working conditions were horrendous. Work in the bleach chambers was highly disagreeable, as the irritating chlorine gas was piped from the cell house to the bleach building, where it passed from chamber to chamber over layers of slaked lime [$Ca(OH)_2$] spread on the floor. As gas "masks were not yet known," workers created their own protection—they carved wooden-framed goggles to protect their eyes and wrapped wet flannel around their faces, wrists, and ankles.[15] The company subsequently developed suitable protective equipment shortly before World War I.

Members of the bleach gang, who spread the lime and kept it fluffed up by raking, worked twelve-hour shifts, 365 days a year. The pay was fifteen cents an hour, and the turnover was tremendous. Despite these drawbacks, the board of directors decided to quadruple capacity to gain economies of scale. By early 1910 the output was twenty tons of caustic soda and forty-two tons of bleach per day. On November 6, 1909, the company set up its one and only subsidiary, the Hooker Electrochemical Company.[16]

Primitive firefighting equipment and frame construction made fires a constant menace. Small fires were almost unavoidable in the cell house. The cell cathode compartment was sealed with oil and flammable hydrogen, which was liberated at the cathode, seeped through the oil and escaped to the air, carrying with it fine oil particles, which were deposited on the wooden walls and ceilings. The cells were connected in series electrically, and when a cell was taken out of operation, a copper jumper bar was connected to the cells on either side. "When a cell was jumped, sparks flew" which "often set individual cells on fire."[17] On May 27, 1910, fire broke out in a cell house, quickly setting the oil-soaked timbers ablaze and spreading to other cell houses and buildings. The plant was completely destroyed.[18] The May 27 *Niagara Falls Gazette* headline read: "$300,000 Fire at Up-River Factory."

The smoke had hardly cleared before plans for reconstruction were underway. Elon Hooker sought new funds while Clarence W. Marsh, the chief engineer, began a new plant design.[19] Reconstruction began under Harry M. Hooker (1872–1949), one of Elon's younger brothers, who had been working as a contractor with his father in Rochester.[20] All four male Hooker siblings were now with the firm.

The new brick and steel plant was completed five months later, and the current turned on October 24, 1910.[21] By the spring of 1911, the plant was "earning substantial profits, about $20,000 a month or about eight times as it had earned during its entire first two years of operation."[22] In the early summer of 1911, Elon sailed for a holiday in Europe after turning over the acting presidency of both companies to John F. Bush, one of the early backers. On his return he again entered politics. Teddy Roosevelt ran in the 1912 election and named Elon national treasurer of his own one-time Bull Moose (Progressive) Party.[23] Sometime later Elon sought the Republican nomination as a candidate for governor of New York.[24]

When war broke out in Europe in early August 1914, Hooker was still producing only bleach and caustic soda. By the time the war ended in November 1918, Hooker was manufacturing fifteen new chemicals with chlorine bases. Prior to the war, Germany had held a monopoly on organic dyes, perfumes, and medicinals produced synthetically from coal tars.[25] The German chemical and dyestuffs cartel had suppressed competition throughout the world by underpricing.[26]

Shortly after the outbreak of the war, American supplies of coal tar products, particularly dyes, were practically exhausted.[27] Dozens of new chemical companies sprang up in 1915, while others expanded their facilities in an effort to furnish dyes and medicinals to textile firms and pharmaceutical houses. In 1915, Hooker Chemical built the first monochlorobenzene (C_6H_5Cl) plant in the country. This coal tar intermediate led to the manufacture of several other chemicals, including hydrochloric and picric acids. By the end of the war, Hooker was the largest monochlorobenzene plant in the world.[28]

In 1917 the plant foreman was a twenty-six-year-old chemical engineer from Norway, Bjarne Klaussen, who started with the company in 1916. As the story goes, that year Klaussen headed straight for Niagara Falls, then one of the world's leading chemical centers, where he walked the streets observing the people coming out of the chemical plants. "The people at Hooker," Klaussen recalled, "looked happier than any of the others and on that basis alone, I decided to try them."[29]

This was the situation at Hooker when R. Lindley Murray started. Murray had graduated from Stanford in California with a master's degree in chemical engineering in 1914. He came east to play tennis that year and first attracted Elon Hooker's attention with his skill on the tennis court. Lin Murray may first have met tennis aficionado and Hooker Electrochemical president Elon Hooker at Southampton in 1914. Elon was well respected by the USNLTA executive committee and attended many of their meetings. In September 1916 Murray started as a research chemical engineer with Hooker in Niagara Falls.

R. Lindley Murray shared responsibility for the success of the monochlorobenzene plant, where he assisted Bjarne Klaussen in the management of a Hooker-operated explosives plant for the government, becoming manager of research at the end of the year. Klaussen himself became superintendent, works manager, executive vice president, president, and director—and along the way, an enthusiastic tennis player.[30]

Murray was a research chemical engineer in 1916, assistant in running a Hooker-operated explosives plant for the government in 1918, manager of the research department in 1920, plant superintendent in 1921, chief engineer in 1932, director of development in 1937, vice president of development and research in 1941, and executive vice president in 1949; he became company president on January 17, 1951. He served continuously as chairman of the board from mid-1955 and chief executive officer as well until 1958. He retired from active management on November 1, 1959, after forty-three years with the company at age sixty-seven, a year after being elected to the National Lawn Tennis Hall of Fame. He had continued in active service beyond the company's normal retirement age by special request of the board of directors.

In addition to his tennis accomplishments, Murray earned recognition in the chemical industry. He received the Jacob F. Schoellkopf Medal of the Western New York Section of the American Chemical Society in 1949 for his engineering talent and his work in directing chemical research; was appointed to honorary membership in the American Institute of Chemists in 1953; and in 1956 was awarded the Chemical Industry Medal of the Society of Chemical Industry, American Section, for "conspicuous service to applied chemistry."

"The following year he also received the professional achievement award of the Western New York Section, American Institute of Chemical Engineers in recognition of his outstanding engineering and executive ability."[31] A new research laboratory on Grand Island was dedicated to Murray in the summer of 1959 in ceremonies attended by Governor Nelson A. Rockefeller. R. L. Murray was president of the Niagara Falls Country Club in 1942; his son, Augustus "Tad" Murray, became president in 1963.

While playing in an invitation tennis tournament in Greenwich, Connecticut, in 1916, Murray stayed in the Greenwich home of Elon Hooker. When Hooker learned that his tennis-playing houseguest was also a chemical engineer, he promptly offered him a job. But only two years out of college Murray was already doing well with the Pacific Coast Borax Company as assistant superintendent in Bayonne, New Jersey. He wasn't sure he should accept Mr. Hooker's offer because he was much interested in his present job and he was close to the major metropolitan tennis events. "I didn't say I'd take it," Murray recalled. "But Mr. Hooker was a stubborn man and didn't like to take no for an answer." But he thought it over from June until the end of August 1916, when he decided to cast his lot with Hooker Electrochemical.[32]

One wonders how Elon Hooker enticed Murray to come to Niagara Falls from Bayonne. Although Bayonne was no tourist attraction as Niagara Falls was at the time (the Niagara Reservation State Park, the first state park in the country, was commissioned in 1885), despite all the factories lining the banks both upstream and downstream of the reservation, it was closer to the metropolitan tennis activity.

Perhaps he used the line that the Niagara Frontier attracted the best players in the United States and Canada, which was true. The major Niagara Frontier tournaments were the International Lawn Tennis Open, held on the grass courts of the Queen's Royal Hotel at Niagara-on-the Lake around late August, and the Western New York championship (Great Lakes championship after 1911) at the Park Country Club of Buffalo, founded in 1903; the former tournament had its inception in 1887.

Elon could have mentioned some of the notable International winners over the years, for example, Malcolm Chase from Yale in 1894 (intercollegiate champion from 1893 to 1895); Juliette Atkinson in 1898

(1895 U.S. women's champion); Harold Hackett in 1900 (U.S. doubles finalist with Fred Alexander a record seven consecutive years beginning in 1905, winning from 1907 to 1910); Beals Wright from Boston in 1902 (1903 and 1908 U.S. champion); Alphonzo Bell from Los Angeles in 1904; and Irving Wright, brother of Beals, from 1905 to 1907.

May Sutton, fresh from her Wimbledon conquest, won in 1907 and honored Buffalonian Harry Kirkover by pairing with him in the mixed. In 1908 Nat Niles, 1908 Harvard intercollegiate champion, beat Wallace Johnson, 1909 Penn intercollegiate champion, while "Queen of the Boards" Marie Wagner beat Canadian champion Lois Moyes. And Nat Niles returned in 1909 and 1910 to win. May Sutton won again in 1909 but lost to national champion Hazel Hotchkiss in 1911.

Dick Williams from Harvard, possibly more partial to freshwater than saltwater only four months after his ordeal on the *Titanic*, won in 1912 as did national champion Mary Browne from California. In 1913 Clarence Griffin won the singles event and paired with his favorite partner Bill Johnston to win the doubles. Niagara Falls was a must stopover for the California players. Griffin was back in 1914 with Elia Fottrell. Griffin beat George Church, 1912 and 1914 Princeton intercollegiate champion.

Championship caliber tennis players also graced the Great Lakes tournament in Buffalo. May Sutton won in 1909 and again in 1911 over her sister Florence, keeping the hardware in the family. May again paired with Buffalonian Harry Kirkover to win the mixed event. Tom Bundy reined May in a little when the pair married in 1912.

12
The 1917 Patriotic Tournaments

In 1917 R. Lindley Murray spent most of the year at Hooker in Niagara Falls, and except for his play in "Patriotic" events, all local tournaments were put on hold while the United States joined its allies—Britain, France, and Russia—on April 6, 1917, to fight in World War I until Germany formally surrendered on November 11, 1918. The tournaments were patriotic affairs designed to raise money for the war effort.

War has often been called a game, and the call to arms in 1917 met no more immediate response than that among followers of athletic sports. Of the first ten in tennis, "Ichiya Kumagae, a Japanese, met the obligations of his citizenship. Richard N. Williams, 2d, was commissioned a lieutenant in artillery and later became a captain. William M. Johnston was an ensign in the navy. George M. Church was a captain in aviation. R. Lindley Murray was a chemist whose duties in producing explosives were so important that he had to remain a civilian. Clarence J. Griffin was a lieutenant in artillery, transferring later to aviation. Watson M. Washburn was a captain in artillery. Willis E. Davis was a lieutenant in aviation. Joseph J. Armstrong was an ensign and Dean Mathey was a lieutenant in artillery."[1]

Before the beginning of hostilities the delegates at the annual USNLTA meeting placed their organization at the disposal of the government. Some of the more important tasks with which the USNLTA was engaged included recruiting campaigns for the army in general, recruiting for the Ordnance Department, raising money for the Red Cross, helping to sell Liberty Bonds, helping to organize the Four Minute Men (a group of volunteer spokesmen for the government, who talked in movie theaters during the four minutes between reel changing, under direction of the Committee on Public Information), and putting into effect the plans of the War Department Commission on Training Camp Activities.[2]

In the meantime the USNLTA Executive Committee, with the approval of the national government, determined to keep the game going. Tennis thus jumped into the vanguard of American sport and many players, already overburdened by new responsibilities bred by the war, gave their services at the club, sectional, and national level. USNLTA President George Adee called upon the sport to raise one hundred thousand dollars to provide two ambulance sections, fully equipped and manned by tennis players for active service under the Red Cross.[3]

Historic events, from the national championship down—events which had been held for many years and the titles and trophies of which were coveted by every tennis player—were suspended and in their places were played Patriotic tournaments with only the advancement of the common cause at stake. No prizes were given since every cent raised was dedicated to the Red Cross. The clubs holding tournaments were also instructed not to inscribe names on challenge cups. Clubs were urged to charge entrance fees and gate receipts for all tournaments and to turn over the net profits to the Red Cross.[4–5] Clubs were also asked not to make a special effort to get players from other sections of the country to enter their tournaments but to strive rather for a large entry from their immediate locality and also to play all matches if possible after 3:30 p.m., thus permitting players to compete in tournaments without interfering with their day's work. In addition, the national rankings, dear to the heart of every tournament player, were abolished for 1917.[6]

The above regulations applied to the schedule of women's events, as well as the men's, but not to the junior and boys' events. The junior and boys' schedules (no one nineteen years old before October 1, 1917, was eligible to compete) would be played exactly as planned, including all championship events. And in the case of cessation of hostilities, all championships scheduled after that date would be played.[7]

With the war in Europe the British Championships were canceled between 1915 and 1918 and the Australian Championships from 1916 to 1918. The first national French tournament, begun in 1891, was open only to members of French clubs until 1924. Another tournament, the World Hard Court Championships held on clay courts in Saint Cloud, was played from 1912 to 1923 except the war years (1915 to 1919) and was open to international competitors.[8] World no. 1 New Zealander, Tony Wilding,

Wimbledon champion from 1910 to 1913 and Saint Cloud winner in 1913 and 1914, was killed in action in Northern France on May 10, 1915.[9]

When it became apparent early in the season that no large sum would be realized from the proceeds of their Patriotic events, the USNLTA officials decided to schedule a series of exhibition matches by some of the most prominent players in the country.[10] It was Karl H. Behr who thought of the idea and submitted the plan to President Adee, who immediately recognized its merit and began negotiations with the Red Cross. The recruitment circular sent out by G. Adee called for "a series of exhibition matches beginning about July 20 and continuing for six weeks" but was actually concluded September 29. A total of thirty exhibition sites were played with more than one day at half of the sites. The Western New York sites included Buffalo, Niagara Falls, and Rochester.[11]

The schedule conformed as far as possible to the dates and places of sanctioned tournaments. The players who agreed to give up their time to these matches included Bill Johnston and Mary K. Browne of California, Fred Alexander, Harold Throckmorton, Karl Behr, Molla Bjurstedt, R. Lindley Murray, Nat Niles, and S. Howard Voshell, in addition to some of the players now at the officers' training camps after August 12.[12] Another person who made a significant contribution was John Strachan of California.

Of the thirteen women and forty men who took part in the ambulance-fund drive, which was a severe physical and mental strain for a period of two months between July 20 and September 29, five players who traveled from coast to coast playing almost daily exhibition matches deserve special praise. National champion Molla Bjurstedt of New York and former champion Mary Browne of San Francisco played fifty-three and forty-nine matches respectively and faced each other twenty-seven times, twenty-two of them in three sets. The three men who bore the brunt of the work were Fred Alexander (fifty-five matches), Harold Throckmorton (forty-nine matches), and John Strachan (forty-six matches). Strachan took the place of William Johnston after the latter had competed in thirteen matches.[13–14]

"From that blistering day in July when Miss Browne stepped off a transcontinental train at Utica, N. Y., to [play] Miss Bjurstedt, to that day many weeks later when she had to leave St. Louis to hurry home on account of her mother's illness," the pair traveled six thousand miles and never failed to meet any request made of them.[15]

The same was true of the men who helped make the matches a success, particularly Fred Alexander, who managed the trip and brought it to a successful completion.[16] The other major participants and matches played included S. Howard Voshell (24 matches), Charles Garland (23), Karl Behr (21), R. Lindley Murray (14), Sam Hardy (11), and many others who played less frequently.[17]

"In the early winter of 1918 enough money had been received so that the Association could undertake the financing of the two [ambulance] sections, No. 603 and Company No. 8, which were undergoing their preliminary training at Allentown. After money had been set aside to furnish the ambulances for these units there was still a balance in the fund."[18]

In a Patriotic Great Lakes tournament at Buffalo, Lin Murray achieved two notable victories in the first day's play on July 2, 1917. Murray vanquished J. P. Merrill in two love sets and then beat Eric Hedstrom of Buffalo, 6–2, 6–3. One of the Buffalo papers noted that "R. Lindley Murray and Eric Hedstrom added a dash of ginger to the rather monotonous business of the early elimination. Hedstrom was beaten, as it was expected he would be, but he put up a game against the former indoor champion that was the envy of many of the less brilliant players. Possibly it was the concession of defeat that helped Hedstrom's game. A player with an admitted chance might have been unnerved by the knowledge of the man who stood across the net from him. But several times the Buffalo Country club youth caught his experienced senior napping and by deft backhand work scored his point and won from the gallery the only applause of the afternoon."[19]

Murray next beat Lynn in two love sets and, paired with Miss MacDonald, triumphed over Miss Cutler and Pooley of Buffalo, 6–3, 6–1.[20] In the semifinals Murray defeated R. J. Oster, Cleveland's best representative, 6–0, 6–2, 6–4, while Chuck Garland, the Pittsburgh "crack," defeated Harold Hodge, former Western New York champion, in three straight sets. In the mixed doubles, Murray and Miss MacDonald beat Moore and Miss Yates, 6–0, 6–2. In the men's doubles Murray and Bartlett of Niagara Falls downed Pooley and Bowen, 6–2, 6–2.[21]

On Friday Murray and Miss MacDonald defeated Miss Bjurstedt and Hendrick, 4–6, 6–3, 8–6, in the mixed semis but only finished two and a part of the third set at the Park Club. On Saturday afternoon Murray won the Great Lakes championship from Garland, 9–7, 6–1, 6–4, followed by finishing the mixed semifinal and then defeating Miss Best and Garland Saturday night in the mixed final on the indoor courts of the Buffalo Tennis and Squash Club, 6–2, 4–6, 10–8, all in a day's work.[22]

The tournament was the most successful of any for several years and raised $750 for the Red Cross.[23] Regarding the men's final, the *Gazette* said this:

> Garland and Murray justified the expectation of a good match. While the former Californian was clearly the better man in all departments of the game and never allowed his opponent to gain a real threatening advantage, Garland did most of the leading. Murray seemed to relax when out of danger and spurt when he thought he had to.
>
> Garland opened by playing the net. His ability to pass the big lefthander from this position and his use of a [drop volley] over the net that died as it hit the ground were the best points of his game.
>
> Murray mastered to some extent his opponents attack in the second set and drove him from the net. Then Garland masterfully played on Murray's back hand. The younger man's service has not the nasty deceptivity of his older opponent, neither was it as steady but Garland for a while scored many points by playing the corner in service and drawing Murray out of position for an angle shot to the other court. This attack was shortlived. Murray uncorked a bottle on the court covery for which he is famous. Lunging from side to side he used his top spin and volley and half-volley on Garland's angle lobs in a manner that was almost uncanny. From one side of the court to the other seemed only a step for the rangy Westerner.
>
> In one of these zigzagging journeys, an incident brought out one of Murray's sporting qualities that overshadowed his brilliant play. Garland had dragged his sandy-haired opponent across the courts until interest was at a high pitch. Murray returned a lob into the net with such speed that it passed through. Without waiting for the referee's decision, Murray motioned to him that it had been low, although most of the gallery and probably the judge thought it had passed fairly over the webbing.[24]

After a rest of ten days Murray entered the Utica two-day, round-robin tourney, held July 20–21, where the cream of U.S. tennis talent was entered for the benefit of the Red Cross. Among those entered were William M. Johnston, 1915 national singles champion and twice national doubles champion; Frederik B. Alexander, four times national doubles champion; Harold A. Throckmorton, national junior singles champion; Samuel T.

Hardy; Charles S. Garland, future national intercollegiate champion; George Wightman, Boston; George M. Church, 1912 and 1914 national intercollegiate champion; Irving C. Wright, 1915 national mixed doubles finalist; Molla Bjurstedt, national singles and doubles champion; and Mary K. Browne, former three-time national singles, doubles, and mixed doubles champion.[25]

Lindley Murray won three singles matches: Harold Throckmorton, 1–6, 6–3, 6–1; George Church, 7–5, 7–5; and Bill Johnston, 6–2, 4–6, 9–7. In the doubles event Johnston and Murray defeated Wright and Wightman, 6–4, 4–6, 6–4, but lost to Alexander and Throckmorton, 6–4, 5–7, 6–1. Church and Garland won the round-robin doubles competition by virtue of a default by Johnston and Murray. The former team had two wins to their credit.[26–27]

On July 29 Murray played a mixed doubles match in Greenwich, Connecticut, before some three thousand spectators. Murray teamed with Mary Browne to defeat Molla Bjurstedt and George Church, 14–12, 6–3. As recorded by the *New York Times*:

> Mixed doubles tennis of a quality rarely seen in this country was witnessed by some 3,000 spectators at the Field Club of Greenwich yesterday when Miss Mary Browne of Los Angeles, the versatile Californian exponent of the game, and Robert Lindley Murray defeated an equally notable team composed of Miss Molla Bjurstedt and George M. Church. The score of the match was 14–12, 6–3, and the first set took rank among the remarkable long doubles encounters. It was the opinion of several yesterday that this was the longest set ever played in mixed doubles between such formidable contestants.
>
> It would have been hard to pick two rival teams of greater prominence. Miss Browne was three times holder of the women's national championship, while Miss Bjurstedt is the present titleholder. Of the men, Church was placed third in the national ranking of a year ago, being superseded only by Richard Norris Williams, 2d, and William M. Johnston. Murray, who possesses a harder service than almost any other player, was fourth. Sometimes such a gathering of stars fails to reveal the

> quality of game which is expected, but yesterday the match glittered with exceptional efforts.[28]

The USNLTA advanced the date of the National Patriotic tournament at Forest Hills from August 30 to August 20 and eliminated the Newport invitation tournament because it was realized that the success of the Patriotic tournament depended on getting the best talent.[29] The date of the event was scheduled to coincide with the week of furlough granted the officers who had just finished training at Plattsburgh so that the first magnitude tennis stars might compete (the first camps closed August 12 and the second camps opened August 27).

The entry list was kept small at sixty-four because of the necessity of finishing within the week but contained enough players of national and international fame to assure an excellent tourney.[30] Among those expected to compete were Dick Williams, holder of the national singles title, Clarence J. Griffin, Watson M. Washburn, Willis E. Davis, and Dean Mathey. Others who might take part were Frederik B. Alexander, William M. Johnston, former national champion, Karl H. Behr, and R. Lindley Murray.[31]

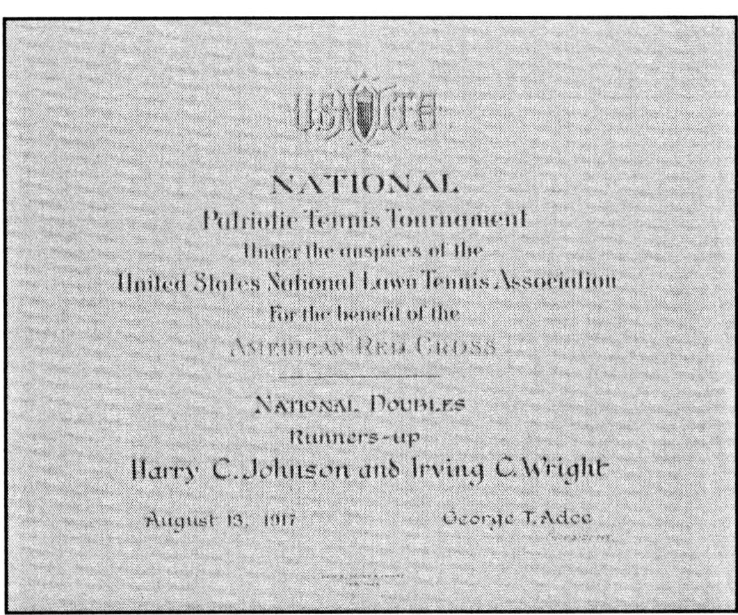

USNLTA

NATIONAL

Patriotic Tennis Tournament

Under the auspices of the

United States National Lawn Tennis Association

For the benefit of the

American Red Cross

National Doubles

Runners-up

Harry C. Johnson and Irving C. Wright

August 13, 1917 George T. Adee

Engraved certificates were given at the 1917 Patriotic tournaments instead of prizes.
(From *Wright & Ditson's 1918 Guide*, p. 91)

The July 19 issue of the *Gazette* reported: "Murray has not decided whether he will compete … at Forest Hills, L. I., on August 20. He will probably await the results of the federal draft. His serial number is 644. Murray, however, is married and has a bouncing youngster. He will probably be exempt."[32] Lin Murray was also exempt by reason of employment in an occupation essential to the war effort. He was engaged in the manufacture of chemicals, specifically picric acid, used for high explosives on a big contract with the French government.

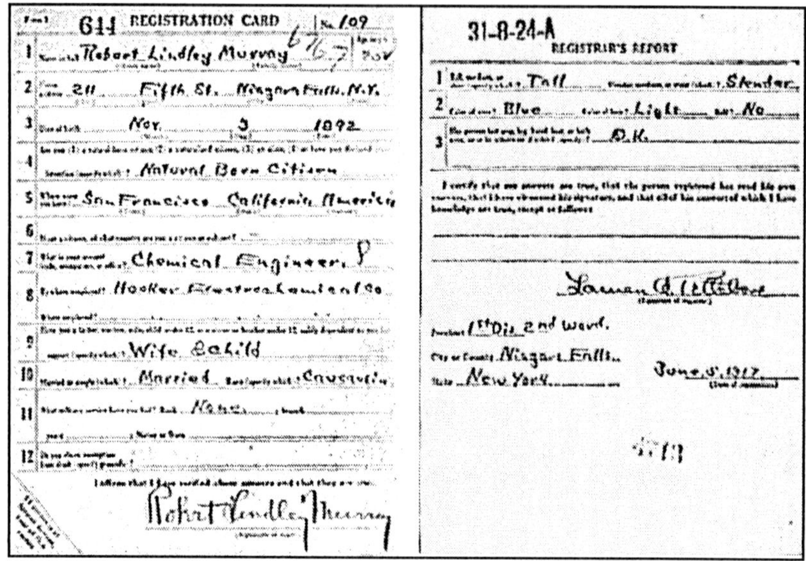
644 REGISTRATION CARD No. 109

1 Robert Lindley Murray 27
2 211 Fifth St. Niagara Falls, N.Y.
3 Nov. 3 1892
4 Natural Born Citizen
5 San Francisco California America
6
7 Chemical Engineer
8 Hooker Electrochemical Co.
9 Wife & child
10 Married Caucasian
11 None
12

Robert Lindley Murray

31-8-24-A
REGISTRAR'S REPORT

1 Tall Slender
2 Blue Light No
3 O.K.

1st Dis 2nd ward.
Niagara Falls
New York
June 5, 1917

Robert Lindley Murray's draft registration card, dated June 8, 1917.

Murray had no intention of entering the 1917 championships, billed as a "Patriotic" tournament, a World War I substitute for the national championship to raise money for the Red Cross. Hooker Electrochemical president Elon Hooker, USNLTA president George T. Adee, and Julian Myrick persuaded him that it was the right thing to do, and he had an explosive tourney. In the third round Murray triumphed over the hard-hitting Bill Tilden of Philadelphia in a contest that was carried to four sets with the score, 3–6, 6–4, 6–3, 6–3.[33] In the quarters, Murray won a tough five-set match from Craig Biddle of Philadelphia, 4–6, 6–1, 6–4, 4–6, 6–2.[34] Murray made his way to the final by defeating John Strachan of San Francisco in a sparkling four-set match at 4–6, 6–3, 6–3, 6–1.[35] As reported in the August 26 issue of the *New York Times*, "Robert Lindley Murray of Niagara Falls, became the 'Pretender' for the national singles crown yesterday afternoon when he defeated Nathaniel W. Niles of Boston in the final round of the national patriotic tournament at the West Side Tennis Club at Forest Hills in a spectacular four-set match with the score 5–7, 8–6, 6–3, 6–3."[36] After Bob Wrenn and Beals Wright, Lin Murray became the third left-handed U.S. champ. The *Gazette's* subtitle on August 27 was, "Superior Speed and Remarkable Endurance of Local Champion Eliminates Niles in Four Sets." The *Gazette* continued:

> The tennis world pays homage to a new champion. He is none other than Robert Lindley Murray, who has been most instrumental in placing Niagara Falls on the tennis map. Murray was crowned international tennis king at Forest Hills, L. I., Saturday afternoon after he had vanquished Nat Niles of Boston, in the finals of the National singles patriotic tourney. It was the local champ's dazzling speed, remarkable endurance and unlimited energy, which forced Niles to succumb to the same fate as Tilden, Biddle and Strachan experienced during the past week.
>
> For the fourth consecutive time, Murray made a bad beginning by losing the first set. In the first stages of the match, his service was poor as usual, but once the tall southpaw hit his stride, no one could stop him. He constantly increased his speed and smashing tactics and Niles slowly, but surely wilted under the strain. When Murray emerged victorious, 4000 spectators cheered him to the echo. He lost the first set, 5–7, but won the remaining sets, 8–6, 6–3, 6–3.[37]

It was significant that none of the entrants who had been devoting their summer to military training came through to the final. That was due to the tremendous amount of preparation and practice required by even a player of the highest skill before he can do his best in serious match play, and these players had not had the opportunity to do so. National champion Dick Williams lost in the semis while other 1916 top tenners—Clarence Griffin (no. 6), Watson Washburn (no. 7), and Dean Mathey (no. 10)—lost in earlier rounds. The 1916 national doubles champions, Fred Alexander and Harold Throckmorton, repeated in 1917 earlier; but in the singles

Alexander was beaten by Craig Biddle, and Throckmorton was beaten in the quarters by Williams.[38]

However, the play of 1904 champion Holcombe Ward, a veteran who had been out of competition for years, as well as Bill Tilden, Craig Biddle, and the youthful John Strachan from San Francisco was excellent. Since all of Murray's opponents played above their normal ability he had a fight on his hands in every round.[39] "In winning, Murray played a game about on a par with his play of 1916," reported *Wright & Ditson's 1918 Guide*, "smashing, dashing, almost irresistible when he was consistently successful in getting to the net, and backed up by unfaltering courage when things seemed to be going against him.... Although losing in the ultimate round, when he was beaten by the shear desperation of the winner's attack, Niles played the most perfect tennis of his career." The *Guide* continued: "His [Niles's] strokes came off with the perfection of a well-oiled machine, and were executed with rare judgment and plenty of pace but he shot his bolt early and when the second set had ended there was little doubt of the final outcome."[40]

At the risk of being somewhat redundant Lin Murray wrote for the USLTA 1931 Golden Jubilee:

> I had to play in succession Westfall, Tilden, Craig Biddle, Johnny Strachan and then finally Nat Niles. Bill Tilden had not yet reached the summit of his game and I was able to come out on top only after a bitter struggle. Craig Biddle gave me even more of a battle and it took me five hard sets to subdue him. I shall never forget the game fight he put up. I didn't want any more tennis on that day. Next, I had to meet Johnny Strachan whom I had never been able to beat on the Pacific Coast and who had my goat if any player had. I am not at all sure that I should have beaten him on this occasion if it had not been for a thunderstorm which approached and put him quite off his game. I do believe, however, that I could always give him a better run on grass than on hard courts.
>
> I had played "Nat" Niles only once before opposing him in the final, that being in practice, and he had beaten me. So I went into our match with no feeling of over-confidence, and thoroughly convinced that I was going

to have my hands full. Niles played an all-around game, having beautiful ground strokes, a severe serve and at the same time being deadly at the net. More than all this I feared his generalship and strategy, which at that time was excelled by few.

My strong points if any were a vicious serve, a quick dash to the net and the ability to volley quite decisively anything that came anywhere near me. My overhead smash was also strong and I could cover miles of court, getting to any shot that came over the net, albeit at the expense of tremendous energy. Due to my athletic training at Stanford University, particularly as a runner, I was always in good condition and had considerable endurance, otherwise I should never have been able to stand the exceedingly strenuous kind of game I used to play. As it was, a hard match always took a tremendous toll of me. I could, however, go at top speed through a five-set match unless the day was particularly humid, which would always affect me, I think, more than many of the other players.

I succeeded in beating Nat Niles 5–7, 8–6, 6–3, 6–3, plenty of indication that the match was close and hard fought. I remember well that, try as I would, I could not get into the full swing of my game those first two sets. This was due to the fact that my opponent was driving beautifully, particularly low, fast ones to my backhand. In addition, he was lobbing so accurately and deeply that, try as I would, I could not bring off my kills. Nat led me one set to love and 6–5 in the second set which was mighty close to being two sets down. But about that time my game began to get going. Up until that time I had just been missing and while desperately dashing all over the court my shots would end in just hitting the net or just going out. From the twelfth game of the second set, on for the rest of the match, things began to go right, and at the end I felt as if I was playing as well as I knew how. Under the circumstances the tournament was really a fine success and very well attended.[41]

United Press staff correspondent H. C. Hamilton likened Murray to "the California Comet" Maurice McLoughlin, the first male tennis singles champion from the Pacific Coast. He was in five straight U.S. singles finals starting in 1911, winning in 1912 and 1913. Hamilton said that "Murray … showed an enthusiastic crowd at Forest Hills that he was about the nearest approach to McLoughlin the tennis fans have ever seen."

> At the net game, where McLoughlin himself was rated a star, it may be said that Murray has no equal. He is the embodiment of grace at the net. McLoughlin's range of play at this point made it possible for him to serve, dash to the net and finish off his points from there. It was always believed there never would be another tennis player who could meet him at that game, but it is doubtful if the Comet would have shown better at this particular style of play than did Murray in the recent tournament.
>
> McLoughlin was also good at back court play, a point that Murray has neglected so long that it was difficult for him to perfect the low, stinging volleys just over the net and at the feet of an opponent. He finally mastered it, however, and surprised his audience when he met Nathaniel W. Niles at this game and beat him at it.
>
> Niles is a survivor of the old English method of play, personified in a number of internationalists who have played on American courts. He depended wholly on an ability to accurately send his return shots over, relying on Murray or any other opponent to finally smash a drive into the net or out of bounds. It was through this style of play that he was able to down Williams, but found a new style in Murray, who alternated an excellent back court game with a dashing return from the net, and a passing point from the latter position when the opportunity presented itself.[42]

The "Pretender" title was given to Murray for his tournament victory since a championship event was taboo that season because of the war. As a result, Richard Norris Williams of Boston was still the titleholder and no change was made in the rankings. "In after years those who glance through the list of champions as published in the official guide will find Murray's name placed opposite the year 1917, with an asterisk to call attention to the footnote saying that he won the patriotic singles tournament, which was that year, because of war conditions, substituted for the national championship."[43] If that was in any way a stigma, it would be erased the following year.

Champion Robert Lindley Murray.
(From *American Lawn Tennis*, September 15, 1918, p. 241)

After Murray's 1917 win, the front page of the "Sporting Section" of the *Niagara Falls Gazette* was largely devoted to Lin Murray's triumph including an action illustration. On the evening of August 27, 1917, the "new national tennis king" was honored at a big banquet arranged by officials of the Hooker Electrochemical Company at the Hotel Imperial in Niagara Falls. H. M. Hooker was toastmaster at the affair, and a variety of speakers touted Murray's qualities as husband and father, scientist, producer, sport, good fellow, and public idol, as the tennis champ squirmed in his chair.[44]

Practically every speaker alluded to the fact that Murray had been instrumental in bringing a Patriotic tournament to Niagara Falls on Labor Day. Showing his leadership skills and popularity, he induced Molla Bjurstedt, Mary Browne, Harold Throckmorton, John Strachan, and Chuck Garland to come. (Molla Bjurstedt won both the national women's singles title and the doubles title paired with Eleonora Sears while Harold Throckmorton won the doubles with thirty-seven-year-old Frederik Alexander, another Hall of Famer.)

The tournament's goal was to raise one thousand dollars as the city's share toward the hundred-thousand-dollar fund to be raised by the USNLTA for the maintenance of two ambulance units in France. As the house-to-house canvas of the city was in progress a small army of workmen were preparing the Quay Street clay courts of the Niagara Falls Tennis Club by brushing and rolling, followed by placing a tarpaulin over the surface to protect it from rain. All the adjoining streets were roped off, and every inch of space was utilized in providing seats for the mammoth crowd expected. Bleachers were erected, and chairs were placed on every available inch of space. Automobiles could be parked in the alley between Jefferson Avenue and Quay Streets.[45–46]

In speaking of this exhibition match, President Adee of the USNLTA said: "It should be borne in mind that neither the club, nor the association nor the players receive a penny from these matches, all of the proceeds being devoted to the ambulance fund. This point is emphasized merely so the public can realize the splendid service the players and club are rendering by their co-operation in making these matches possible."[47]

Furthermore, the *Gazette* reported that "John R. Strachan, the California tennis wizard, whose spectacular play in many patriotic tournaments on eastern courts, ... will receive his ... long awaited opportunity to regain the laurels he lost" at Forest Hills.[48] Murray agreed to meet his formidable rival only in his home town and their match would be first on the docket. Strachan's supporters attributed his defeat at Forest Hills to his natural fear of lightning. Their semifinal was the only match played on the exhibition courts during the day and in the last three sets rain interfered with the contestants, which was said to have caused Strachan to slacken his speed.[49]

This schedule the players agreed to is analogous to a professional tour, except that the receipts were for the war effort. On Tuesday, August 28, the players were in Rochester, and the strain was telling. The match between Mary K. Browne, the Pacific Coast star, and Molla Bjurstedt was shortened to one set because of Miss Bjurstedt's illness. Miss Browne won, 8–6. In singles Charles Garland, junior champion, defeated Marshal Allen of Seattle, 6–4, 6–1, while in men's doubles Murray and Strachan defeated Alexander and Throckmorton, 6–4, 6–3. The players left that night for another ambulance-fund tournament at Cleveland before heading back to Buffalo and Niagara Falls.[50]

On Labor Day, September 3, the tennis fans of Niagara Falls were treated to men's singles, women's singles, men's doubles, and mixed doubles by some of the greatest players in the country. Every seat was occupied before two o'clock, and the crowd waited twenty minutes before Murray and Strachan appeared and Harry Kirkover of Buffalo (who had played mixed doubles with May Sutton a decade earlier) mounted his elevated pedestal. John Strachan defeated Murray, 11–9, 6–3, after Murray had downed him in three sets in Buffalo on Saturday. One spectator attributed Murray's defeat to the fact that he had labored all morning in assisting to put the court in shape. In any case Strachan was in great form. All over the court Strachan employed fast drives and a wonderful backhand, which nullified Murray's slashing drives and a well-placed lob when Murray came to the net. In men's doubles Murray and Strachan conquered Alexander and Throckmorton, 6–3, 2–6, 9–7.[51]

The September 4 issue of the *Niagara Falls Gazette* said, "A well-liked favorite was Miss Browne, former national woman champion [1912–14], who went to the Sargent School at Cambridge until she found there was not enough tennis in the course of study to suit her. Her stature and energy are in inverse ratio and her whole appearance stands out in sharp contrast to her Norwegian rival of thick hair of copper and arm banded with muscles. Slapping her hip with her racquet about every time a disappointing shot bobs up is an amusing Browne mannerism." Mary K. Browne and Molla Bjurstedt played only one set, the former winning 6–1. In mixed doubles, Throckmorton and Browne won over Murray and Bjurstedt by 6–1.[52]

Now that Murray had reached the pinnacle of U.S. tennis, despite the asterisk of "pretender," he was given the appellation "Meteor" in the press and compared more and more to "the California Comet" Maurice McLoughlin because of his powerful service, spectacular volleys, overhead smashes, and affable personality. The volley was not new to the game, but it had not nearly been the finishing stroke that Red Mac made it.

Before the U.S. Championships Murray had given evidence earlier in the season that he was playing in better form than ever before. The Californian had rounded out his game appreciably since 1914, when he first astounded the East by his spectacular style of play and earned a national ranking of no. 4. In those days "Murray was the embodiment of Pacific Coast tennis, as exemplified first by the great McLoughlin." It was a case of terrific service and then crowding the net, followed by smashing or volleying. "It was sensational tennis to watch, but it entailed a tremendous waste of physical energy, and when pitted against" the games of Johnston or Williams, it could not prevail.[53]

"But since then the Californian," now New Yorker, "has curbed his wild and undirected speed and has brought to his aid a repertoire of ground strokes that, while not of the soundness possessed by some others among the top notchers, nevertheless are sufficient to help him out of tight situations and bolster up his net attack. Murray can now afford to wait in the back of his court until an opening presents itself and then rush to the net to finish off his points. His volleying has also undergone a marked change for the better. Some of his low volleys … at Forest Hills were remarkably sharp and decisive, and these did their part in encompassing the downfall of Niles. The Californian is still prone to expend too much energy in going after almost unreasonable shots, but even here he has put a check on himself, with the result that he can survive the rigors of a hard five-set match far better than … before."[54]

13
The 1918 U.S. Championships

Now primarily devoted to government contract work at Hooker and family life, Lin Murray had little time for what some called frivolous pursuits. He undoubtedly practiced at tennis and trained but didn't take time off for tournament play. The first evidence of competitive play was at the 1918 Great Lakes championship held on the ten clay courts of the Park Club of Buffalo beginning on July 8. Arthur J. Vesey of Montreal won the tournament over A. V. Duncan of Los Angeles. Vesey paired with T. C. Fulton to win the doubles over A. V. Duncan and T. W. Hendrick, a local Buffalo star, in five slashing sets. On the ladies' side national champion Molla Bjurstedt returned to capture her third successive title at Buffalo over Eleonora Sears and paired with Miss Sears to win the doubles.[1] Eleonora Sears was a remarkable woman in her own right and is profiled in part III. She was the daughter of Fred Sears, one of the first to play tennis in the United States with James Dwight at Nahant in 1874, and the niece of Richard Dudley "Dick" Sears who won the first seven U.S. Championships.

Lin Murray, now working on a dangerous picric acid facility at Hooker for the government, found time to play three exhibition matches at the Great Lakes championships. Murray was defeated by Bill Tilden, 7–5, 6–1, 6–4, while Molla Bjurstedt and Murray won over semifinalists Florence Ballin and Tilden, 10–8, 6–4. T. C. Fulton of Seattle, 1911 Idaho State champion,[2] teamed with Murray to defeat Tilden and Arthur Vesey, 6–4, 6–3.[3]

The *New York Times* said on July 24 that, "It is certain now that Robert Lindley Murray, the highest ranking tennis player in the country at the present time, will not play in the national tennis championship at Forest Hills, the latter part of next month. Edwin Fullier Torrey, Secretary of the United States National Lawn Tennis Association, was talking the matter over with Murray a few days ago and the former Pacific Coast star, who is now a chemical engineer connected with a plant in Niagara Falls, which manufactures war products, said that it would be useless to argue the subject of competing in the nationals as his views of what it was right for him to do were firmly fixed and that there was no chance of his playing for the title."[4]

In addition, *American Lawn Tennis* said that Murray "had resolved, two weeks before the meeting began, that he would not compete."[5]

In 1918 the USNLTA decided to resume the national championship, partly to "carry-on" and partly to raise money for the war commission on training camp activities, but Lin Murray was absolutely obstinate about competing. Murray didn't agree with the decision but fully appreciated the spirit that prompted it. The plant in which he was working had entered into a contract with the U.S. government to make picric acid, a highly explosive material used in shrapnel. During the spring and early summer the company had built a plant to manufacture the material and by August was in full production but not without serious problems.[6]

None of them had ever made this most hazardous of explosives, and they were extremely behind on production. More important, several men had died from poisoning.[7] The synthesis required adding nitric acid to a mixture of phenol and concentrated sulfuric acid, which produced poisonous nitrogen dioxide gas.[8]

Murray had not played tournament tennis all summer, and when the USNLTA finally decided to hold the U.S. Championships, Hooker president Elon Hooker came to Niagara Falls expressly to get Lin Murray to break away for the tournament. According to Murray, they battled day and night for five days, with Hooker saying he would not leave until Murray had agreed to play. On the final night Murray walked over to where Elon was staying and found him sitting alone on the lawn. It was then that Murray's direct chief and one of his closest friends, probably Bjarne Klaussen, became involved. He had backed Lindley up from the beginning and at that point said he would resign if Murray was forced to play against his wishes.[9]

That was the proverbial straw that released Murray from his adamant stand. Murray later revealed, "He was manager of our big plant and all of the hundreds of employees were dependent upon him. In addition his work was far too important to our country, so there was nothing else to do but give in."[10]

It had taken five days for Murray to consent to play. The championship was only eight days away, and he hadn't played for months. Elon Hooker now rushed Murray to his farm in the middle of New York State where awaiting them was Harry McNeil, the tennis pro at the Heights Casino in Brooklyn. The pair went at it for two days—before breakfast, after breakfast, and most of the afternoon—trying to whip the "Meteor" into shape. Then came the dash to Southampton, Long Island, where the Meadow Club was holding its invitational, which was to be the only play on grass before the U.S. Championships. While at Southampton Mr. Elon Hooker became seriously ill and was rushed to a private hospital in New York.[11]

When Bill Tilden vanquished Murray in the semis, 6–3, 6–3, after overcoming a 3–1 first-set deficit, the nationals were only three days away. In the other semi Theodore R. Pell defeated Walter T. Hayes, 6–2, 7–5. The *Times* said that "Murray was far from being in condition to withstand the driving attack that Tilden kept up through two sets. Murray was not 50 per cent as strong as he was two years ago, or even last year. Many of his shots so characteristic of his play were faulty. There was not one time during the contest when he succeeded in getting a half volley shot over the net, and he was weak on the low full volley."[12] The *Gazette* said of this match that "Murray's lack of competitive practice showed very plainly and probably accounted for his defeat. He has been busily engaged in war work all summer and has had little or no time to keep in form, while Tilden has been playing the greater part of the season."[13] The *Times* continued: "[W]ith Pell as his partner, Murray was beginning to find himself." But the pair fell to Hayes and Ralph H. Burdick of Chicago in the semifinals, 7–5, 2–6, 6–4.[14]

William T. Tilden II, undefeated that season, beat Pell of New York in the final, 6–4, 6–2, 6–4, with a minimum expenditure of effort. The newly crowned national doubles champions, Tilden and Vincent Richards, defeated Hayes and Burdick after five spirited sets, 6–4, 1–6, 6–3, 5–7, 6–4.[15]

Sandwiched between tennis players Ichiya Kumagae and R. Lindley Murray from left to right are (2) Julian S. Myrick, West Side Tennis Club president 1915–17 and USLTA president 1920–22; (3) Dr. Joseph E. Raycroft of Chicago; (4) Walter Camp, sportswriter and football coach known as "Father of American Football"; and (5) Edwin F. Torrey, secretary of the USNLTA.
(From *Wright & Ditson's 1919 Guide*, p. 41)

The premier tennis event of the country, the thirty-seventh national singles championship, began on the turf of the West Side Tennis Club on August 26. The upper half of the draw included Murray, Craig Biddle, S. Howard Voshell, Vincent Richards, Elliott Binzen, Nathaniel W. Niles, Frederik B. Alexander, Ralph H. Burdick, Harold A. Throckmorton, and Theodore R. Pell. In the lower half were Alex Graven, Fred C, Anderson, Beals C. Wright, Ichiya Kumagae, William A. Horrell, Conrad B. Doyle, William T. Tilden, Walter T. Hayes, and Walter Merrill Hall.[16]

From somewhere in France, on the eve of the championship, a cheery greeting to the tennis players was sent by Lieutenant R. N. Williams II, the 1916 champion, who was serving in the artillery. His cablegram to Julian S. Myrick, vice president of the USNLTA said, "Best luck for national. Wish I could be with you. Remember me to all."[17]

The 1918 tournament was being played for the benefit of the War and Navy Department Commissions on Training Camp Activities. Train service on the Long Island Railroad from Pennsylvania Station at Thirty-third Street and Seventh Avenue to Forest Hills, and return was arranged with a plethora of schedules.[18] As the championship started, Elon Hooker's condition became still graver, and although Murray saw him every day at first, he subsequently reached such an acute condition that Murray wasn't permitted in.[19]

In a first-round struggle Harold A. Throckmorton, once known as the "schoolboy wonder" of Elizabeth, New Jersey, won a record eighty-two-game contest against Brooklyn youth Harold L. Taylor. The score was 6–8, 6–2, 11–9, 7–9, 13–11, eclipsing the eighty-game record set way back in 1888. (See appendix for tiebreak origins.) Throckmorton, a sergeant in the Coast Artillery, remarked to one of the linesmen after the fourth set, "Life in the army is a perfect cinch compared to a tennis match like this." Murray easily outclassed his first opponent, Jack Dudley, 6–0, 6–0, 6–1.[20]

Only two days later, four players were in the quarterfinals (fifth round): Craig Biddle, S. Howard Voshell, Bill Tilden, and Walter Merrill Hall. Murray made his way through the third round with a decisive victory over Theodore R. Pell, fellow Howland heir noted for his backhand play, in straight sets, allowing his opponent only two games in the match—both of those in the first set. Bill Tilden, who had yet to be defeated that season, won a decisive fourth round match over Conrad B. Doyle of Washington. Two of the best matches of the day went to five sets in which the eventual winners lost the first two sets. In a third round match Frederik B. Alexander defeated Harold A. Throckmorton, 2–6, 3–6, 7–5, 6–0, 6–3. In the fourth round S. Howard Voshell, the national indoor champion, was also on the verge of defeat to the heady, sixteen-year-old Vincent Richards but rallied to win the match at 5–7, 4–6, 6–0, 6–2, 7–5.[21]

Thunderstorms seriously interfered with play on August 29; only three complete matches were finished during the afternoon. Both Murray and Tilden had narrow escapes with two veteran New Yorkers, Frederik B. Alexander and Walter Merrill Hall, respectively.[22] The *New York Times* reported on August 30:

> Playing with a skill that betokened the pinnacle of his game, Robert Lindley Murray of Niagara Falls won salvos of applause from the spectators at the national singles tennis championship at the West Side Tennis Club at Forest Hills yesterday afternoon when he defeated Frederick B. Alexander in a gloriously contested match of five sets with the score 6–8, 8–6, 6–0, 4–6, 6–0. No contest of the tournament has brought out such high flights of tennis. Brilliant shots flashed from the racquets of one or the other of the rival contenders with such frequency that the onlookers were kept at the highest pitch of excitement. Any doubt that there may have been of Murray's ability to gain high place in the tournament, if not victory itself, was dispelled by his triumph over Alexander, one of the most finished racquet wielders in the country.[23]

With Alexander serving at 6–5 in the second set, Murray won the next three games to avoid going down two sets. On the final point of the fourth set, Alexander's drive struck some two or three inches below the top of the net and climbed over.[24] Murray confessed he always had a terrible time beating his old rival and friend Fred Alexander.[25]

Other fourth-round winners were Lyle E. Mahan and Nathaniel W. Niles, the previous year's runner-up to Lin Murray. In the quarterfinals, S. Howard Voshell defeated Craig Biddle, 6–2, 6–3, 9–7, while Walter Merrill Hall was leading Bill Tilden, 6–3, 1–6, 7–5, 3–2; the next game was at deuce, with Tilden serving, when the storm drove them to the clubhouse.

The three remaining quarterfinals were completed the following day, August 30. In picking up his match, down two sets to one, serving at 2–3 and deuce, Tilden tied the set at 3–3. But Hall swept through the next two games, breaking Tilden in the second to make the score 5–3. Serving for the match at 30–15, Hall played a kill to the corner that Tilden chased down well beyond the baseline. In sheer desperation he tossed up a lob, which barely managed to fall on Hall's side of the net. It was a sitter, but to the amazement of the spectators and to the consternation of Hall himself, he missed the ball completely. He had lost sight of it momentarily in the glare of sunlight. Instead of serving at double match point the score was deuce, and the Middles States champion's psyche was shattered. Tilden took the forth set by running off four straight games, and Hall was able to win only one game in the fifth. The final score was 3–6, 6–1, 5–7, 7–5, 6–1. Murray defeated the famous Boston baseliner, Nathaniel W. Niles, in four sets at 7–5, 6–4, 2–6, 7–5.[26] In the last quarterfinal match Japanese player, Ichiya Kumagae, defeated Lyle E. Mahan, 4–6, 6–3, 6–0, 6–1.

The semifinal pairings were then set—Murray versus Voshell and Tilden versus Kumagae. Murray defeated Voshell in straight sets, 6–4, 6–3, 8–6, while Tilden smothered the no. 5 U.S. player Kumagae in less than forty-five minutes, 6–2, 6–2, 6–0.[27–28] As expected, the final pitted Robert Lindley Murray of Niagara Falls against William T. Tilden II of Philadelphia. When Murray beat Howard Voshell in the semifinals he felt that he was almost at the top of his game.[29]

R. L. Murray and W. T. Tilden shake hands and smile just before going on the court for the match that decided the 1918 U.S. Championship.
(From *American Lawn Tennis*, September 1, 1918, p. 216)

On the morning of the final match, Murray received word that Mr. Hooker wanted to see him. Lin Murray recalled:

> I found him flat on his back in bed, scarcely able to speak above a whisper. But I doubt if any college football team on the eve of a big game ever received a more inspiring talking to. At least that is the way I thought about it. I always was in the habit of talking myself into fighting shape before I went into important matches, but on the occasion of my final match with Tilden I had keyed myself into almost a state of frenzy. This always helped my game immeasurably and I really believe I relied on it

> to a very great extent. When I finally walked out on the championship court and saw, up on the top balcony of the club house, a figure lying on a cot attended by a doctor and a nurse and realized that Mr. Hooker had done the impossible and in some way gotten himself out to Forest Hills, I made up my mind that I was going to win that match if it was the last one I ever played.[30]

This had all the elements of "Win one for the Gipper." Tuesday, the day of the final, was just about perfect: sunny but not warm, with an air stirring and the best light. There was the usual pleasant formality, the officials being in place when the two six-foot-two tennis titans, Murray and Tilden, stepped from the clubhouse porch and walked over to the court in the center of the enclosure. Murray won the toss and elected to serve. E. C. Conlin was in the chair, and F. B. Alexander was foot fault judge. The linesmen included M. S. Hager, S. W. Merrihew, editor of *American Lawn Tennis*, W. D. Bourne, M. S. Charlock, H. A. Throckmorton, R. D. Richey, Harold Swain, R. A. Johnson, and A. L. Hoskins.

The *New York Times*' September 4 issue reported it this way:

> Robert Lindley Murray of Niagara Falls, one of the finest sportsmen and most proficient racquet wielders who ever came forth from the Golden Gate, was crowned yesterday as the national singles tennis champion when he defeated William T. Tilden, 2d, of Philadelphia in the final round of the tournament at the West Side Tennis Club at Forest Hills, with the score 6–3, 6–1, 7–5. Probably there has seldom, if ever, been a case in the long history of the championship when a player so little coveted the title as did Murray this season. A month ago it was his firm intention not to play in the event, and he was shaken from his resolve only because he was impressed with the motives which induced the tennis officials to provide funds for the soldiers and sailors in this manner.
>
> Even when Murray did consent to play there was hardly a possibility that he would be able to go through the tournament. He had had no practice, being engaged in war work, he had more serious things to interest him than tennis. It has been the history of championship tennis that

> a player must prepare during an entire season before he could even hope to stand forth prominently in a national singles event. How much the worthy successor to Maurice E. McLoughlin, William M. Johnston, Richard Norris Williams, 2d, the champion of 1916, accomplished in the short space of time allotted to him is indicated by his victory yesterday, an accomplishment as amazing as it is gratifying to a host of Murray's admirers.[31]

The local paper subtitle read, "Local Tennis Star Furnishes Surprise of Season, Defeating Opponent in Three Straight Sets." The *Gazette* continued:

> [T]he California meteor brought to a close the first national tennis championship tournament since 1916 and the only one of the year in the tennis world by decisively defeating his opponent in fifty-five minutes of court battle, which proved conclusively that Murray is the ranking American player of the season.
>
> Following in the footsteps of Maurice E. McLaughlin who won in 1912 and 1913 and William M. Johnston, the title holder of 1915 Murray showed the same well-rounded game and the same calm confidence in his racquet ability that marked the play of his predecessors from the far coast. Notwithstanding the fact that Murray had not played serious tournament tennis until about ten days ago, his progress through the present tournament stamps him as a tennis star of extraordinary ability.
>
> Favored by many experts to reach the final round, it was the consensus of opinion that Tilden, owing to his improvement and greater tournament practice this year, would prove Murray's master in the struggle for premier tennis honors. The Californian playing from the Niagara Falls, N. Y. Tennis club, however, even in the short space of time allotted to him for practice, had attained court skill and strategy that proved bewildering to Tilden.[32]

In all fairness to Tilden it must be noted that he played that match with a huge boil on the Achilles tendon of his right ankle[33] and he was still almost two years away from developing an offensive backhand. But southpaw Murray's slice serve pulled Tilden wide on the ad court to his weak backhand. Murray later said:

> The final score was 6–3, 6–1, 7–5 in my favor and I am quite certain that it represented the best tennis I have ever played either before or since. I shall always believe that it was my usually weak forehand and backhand drive which actually won that match for me. For some unknown reason I believed that I could match Bill at the back-court game at least on that day and I had determined to try it at least to a certain extent. I do not believe I have ever approached the ground strokes which I had during that match. In addition, my serve was at its best. My total of twelve service aces in three sets was fairly high but even when aces were not scored outright I had Bill reaching for everything. This was a great help, and when I found that I could swap drives with him and then very frequently finish off with a net attack, I obtained renewed confidence. Tilden had the misfortune to have an abscess on his heel which had broken that same day and although he gallantly refused to admit it, this undoubtedly affected his game to a considerable degree.[34]

"Instead of suffering a serious relapse for disobeying all orders and leaving the hospital to see this match, Mr. Hooker recovered very rapidly."[35] Born in 1869, Elon Hooker lived for another twenty years. Murray's results:

First round: J. Dudley, 6–0, 6–0, 6–1
Second round: Hugh Kelleher, w/o
Third round: Theodore Pell, 6–2, 6–0, 6–0
Fourth round: Fred Alexander, 6–8, 8–6, 6–0, 4–6, 6–0
Quarters: Nat Niles, 7–5, 6–4, 2–6, 7–5
Semis: Howard Voshell, 6–4, 6–3, 8–6
Final: William Tilden, 6–3, 6–1, 7–5

Murray finally and deservedly received the place of honor in the ranking of players for the 1918 season. The top ten were (in order, beginning with the top-ranked player): R. Lindley Murray, William Tilden II, Fred Alexander, Wallace Hall, Walter Hayes, Nat Niles, Ichiya Kumagae, Chuck Garland, Howard Voshell, and Theodore Pell.

Two conspicuous absences in the tournament were Dick Williams of Boston, 1916 defending champion, who was in France with the army, and Bill Johnston of San Francisco, winner of the 1915 tournament and runner-up to Williams in a five-set match in 1916. Johnston was doing his duty by serving in the navy.

The ⅝-inch gold tennis ball pendant given Lin Murray for his 1918 U.S. title. On the front is inscribed "U·S·N·L·T·A National Championship Singles," across the bottom "R. Lindley Murray," and on the back "1918." (Courtesy Chrissie Kremer)

14
Family, Exhibitions, and Local Events

After winning the national indoor title in February 1916, Murray appeared in Buffalo. There was then a short gap in his tennis career—and with good reason. He felt that this was a good time to return to Palo Alto to marry his Stanford sweetheart Ramona McKendry. They were married on May 9, 1916. Born March 4, 1891, Ramona was almost two years older than Lin. Before Murray was even living in Niagara Falls, an article appeared in the June 17, 1916, issue of the *Niagara Falls Gazette.*

> When Robert Lindley Murray of California won the national indoor tennis championship in the Seventh Regiment Armory in New York City early in the year he was so far above all the others that his form caused the critics to favor him as a contender for the outdoor title this year. Murray, however, took part in an outdoor tournament at Sleepy Hollow Country Club at Scarborough-on-Hudson, N. Y., a short time ago and played so indifferently that a number of the so-called sharps found it necessary to revise their former estimate of his powers.
>
> There are several followers of the course game who believe that Murray has one game indoors and another outdoors. This is entirely wrong. In practice Murray is a dangerous man on either the board floor or turf or dirt courts. The whole truth of the matter is that he had not played much tennis between the time that he won

> the indoor championship and his appearance at Sleepy Hollow. Added to this was the fact that he had been married only a short time before and was in that blissful state that makes a man view the whole world through rose-colored spectacles even up to that point where he does not care if the other fellow defeats him and even takes his money and his socks, providing he can retain his bride and his happiness.[1]

Lin Murray left Bayonne for Niagara Falls on September 5—but not before saying goodbye to a number of his friends at Forest Hills—"and remarked as he left that he hoped to be able to play in some of the tournaments in this section next year."[2] A *Gazette* sportswriter interviewed him on Thursday, September 7, only two days after his arrival in Niagara Falls.

> Niagara Falls is to be honored with the presence of a real champion. Only yesterday came the surprising but welcome news that R. Lindley Murray, the sensational California tennis star, formerly of Bayonne, N. J., is to locate in this city. Murray holds a responsible position at the Hooker plant. The prominence of the Westerner can be deduced from the fact that he holds the National Indoor Tennis championship and is rated as fourth in the national standing of wielders of the racquet. Until this time the city has never been able to secure renown from the exploits of a champion but with Murray obtaining affixed abode here, it should not be long before the "old burg" comes into its own.
>
> The writer was accorded the pleasure of an interview with the tennis luminary and contrary to expectation found him to be a mere youth [he was 23], imbued with "pep" and vigor and at the same time as modest and gentlemanly an athlete as could be discovered in the realms of sportdom. "Although we have been here only two days, (for Murray has already signed up for life) we are delighted with the surroundings and once we have determined on a permanent home, we will consider ourselves as regular Falls people. It is certainly a relief to escape the wiles of

> gay old New York and enjoy a little rest." The tall youth told of his many experiences in the far West and Gotham and never lost his favorite smile.[3]

Murray lived in a two-story home with his wife at 211 Fifth Street from 1916 to 1921. The house, also occupied by Clifton S. Tuttle, was an excellent example of a two-story Prairie-style residence with a low-pitched, hipped roof and broad, overhanging eaves with brick and stucco walls; it was one of the few examples of that style in the city. It was three homes north of Jefferson Avenue and an excellent location for Murray, being only two blocks from the Niagara Falls Tennis Club on Quay Street.

Lin Murray and his wife Ramona.
(Courtesy Chrissie Kremer)

In the "City of Niagara Falls Intensive Level Resources Survey" completed by Clinton Brown Company Architecture in March 2005, the

211 Fifth Street home was considered for historic preservation. Fifth Street was a short north-south street between Jefferson Avenue (now Rainbow Boulevard) to the south and Erie Avenue. In their 2002 compact with the state the Seneca Indian Nation was promised about fifty acres of downtown land on which to build a casino in exchange for a share of the slot-machine profits. Seneca Niagara Casino opened in 2002, and the twenty-six-story hotel opened in March 2006. In a letter dated December 1, 2005, New York State gave the Seneca Indian Nation additional land around its casino when the Empire Sate Development Corporation (ESDC) exercised its power of eminent domain, despite objections from businesses and homeowners.[4] As a result all the homes on Fifth Street were leveled.

Lindley and Ramona's home at 211 Fifth Street in Niagara Falls.
(Courtesy Niagara Falls Public Library)

While living in that house, Lin Murray and Ramona had two sons—Robert Lindley Murray Jr., born April 24, 1917, and Augustus Taber Murray II, born October 29, 1921. In 1921 Murray moved to Center Street in Lewiston and then in 1947 to a beautiful stone home set far back on Mountain View Drive, overlooking the escarpment, only three houses from the Niagara Falls Country Club, where he spent much of his leisure time.

Lin Murray had a tennis court in the backyard of his Center Street home. Dr. Doug Murray, son of Lin's brother Francis, recalls being there in the 1930s. "If I pestered him long enough he'd give me a lesson now and then when I was visiting. These sessions usually ended with him whistling an invisibly fast serve by me with the exclamation that 'that used to be the fastest serve in the country.'" Doug also affectionately recalls that Lin possessed "a big smile and a big whoop of a laugh, sort of resembling Ralph Bellamy."[5]

539 Mountain View Drive, Lewiston Heights.

Ramona died on June 23, 1951, at age sixty, from hemorrhage and shock during an operation and was cremated at Forest Lawn. R. Lindley Murray died on January 17, 1970 of a stroke after a two-year illness. He lived at 539 Mountain View Drive, Lewiston Heights, before entering St. Mary's Manor on Sixth Street between Ferry and Walnut in Niagara Falls, and is buried in Riverdale Cemetery.[6]

Robert Lindley Murray is buried at Riverdale Cemetery in Lewiston, New York, along with his wife Ramona McKendry and his youngest son, Tad.

Robert L. Murray Jr., attended DeVeaux Academy, Niagara Falls, from 1931 to 1935, and in 1939 he graduated from Stanford University, his parents' alma mater, where his paternal grandfather had taught the classics for forty years. He was elected to Phi Beta Kappa at Stanford and continued his study of classical languages at Harvard University before serving in the U.S. Army from 1942 to 1946. He taught at the Southfield School, Shreveport, Louisiana, for two years before joining the faculty of Colgate University, where he was a colleague of the late J. Curtiss Austin. In 1953 he was awarded his MA in classical philology from Harvard University, and in 1964 he received his PhD from Cornell University. Following in his paternal grandfather's footsteps, Murray taught Greek and Latin at Colgate from 1948 until his retirement in 1985, moving up the ranks from instructor to full professor. He served as chairman of the Department of Classics, Slavic, and Oriental Languages, and led study groups to Italy and Greece. Dr. Murray taught core courses, as well as Greek drama and history. He said, "Classics is the liberal arts subject. We do everything—philosophy, drama, literature, history—it's a microcosm." Teaching and his relationships with students were everything to him. "What a life!" he said. "All my energies go into preparation for the classroom."

R. L. Murray Jr., married the former Marjorie Tower on November 21, 1942, in Niagara Falls, New York. Living on Brookview Drive, in Hamilton, New York, Murray was a member of St. Thomas Episcopal Church, Hamilton, and at one time served as a Village Trustee in Hamilton. Murray died Friday, April 1, 1988, at Crouse Irving Memorial Hospital, Syracuse, following a long illness. He was survived by his wife, Marjorie; two daughters, Martha Panayotopoulou of Athens, Greece, and Mrs. John (Ann) Breiten of Redwood City, California; and four grandchildren, Natasha and Constantine Panayotopoulou of Athens and Rebecca and Elizabeth Breiten of Redwood City. Burial was in Colgate Cemetery, Hamilton, New York.[7]

Augustus Taber (Tad) Murray, named after his paternal grandfather, attended Niagara Falls High School from 1935 to 1937, where he played on the golf team along with Bob Kay who shot a sixty-eight in a league match at Hyde Park in Niagara Falls. This was two strokes above the links record established by his professional father two days before. Tad won the Western New York Boys' Championship at the Grover Cleveland course in Buffalo. He also won a mixed doubles badminton tourney paired with Barbara Templeton. After his sophomore year he transferred to Phillips

Academy in Andover, Massachusetts, graduating in 1939. Tad attended Princeton University, where he won the Eastern intercollegiate badminton championship and then graduated in 1943 with a BA in economics. He served in the U.S. Army in World War II as an intelligence officer, worked in sales at Carborundum from 1947 to 1968, and also worked for the New York Stock Exchange at the Hornblower-Weeks-Hemphill-Noyes and Company in Buffalo before joining E. F. Hutton and Company in Niagara Falls.

His extracurricular activities were prodigious. He was a member of the United Way of Niagara, the Buffalo District Golf Association of Western New York, the City Club of Buffalo, the Old Fort Niagara Association, the Niagara Club, the Princeton Club of Western New York, and the Niagara Falls Rotary Club. He was chairman of the Niagara Falls Sharks hockey team and the Bond Club of Buffalo, 1963 president of the Niagara Falls Country Club, one of the founders of the Porter Cup (a prestigious amateur golf tournament inaugurated in 1959), the Buffalo-Niagara Sales Marketing Association, and director and treasurer of the Amateur Hockey Association of Western New York.

Tad Murray, fifty-seven, living at 539 Mountain View Drive, the home of his parents, died of colon cancer on June 24, 1978, in Memorial Medical Center, predeceasing his wife, Barbara Blew Murray, and leaving a son, Robert L. Murray II of Lewiston, and a daughter, Mrs. Ricard (Lee) Dubin of Seabury, Massachusetts.[8]

1936 Niagara Falls High School Golf Team. From left to right: Coach Parsons, Bob Lawler, Bob Kay, Tad Murray, Fred Oldfield, and Walter Puto.
(From the 1937 Niagara Falls High School yearbook, the *Niagarian*, p. 85)

1919

R. Lindley Murray was rated first and Tilden second for the 1918 season by the ranking committee. Murray continued playing—largely exhibitions and local events—but not with the commitment of a player dedicated to making tennis his career, for he was already committed to less "frivolous" pursuits, as the 1914 *Times* reporter so aptly recognized. Murray was a dedicated employee, first and foremost, with a young son and wife to care for. His competitive spirit was in the business of chemical engineer and manager. He had done his part in tennis for the war effort, and there would be no future in professional tennis anyway. (In 1926 promoter C. C. "Cash and Carry" Pyle changed this by recruiting centerpiece Suzanne Lenglen, Mary Browne, Vinnie Richards, Howard Kinsey, Harvey Snodgrass, and Paul Feret for the first professional tennis tour, which traveled throughout the United States and Canada.)[1–2] Murray would play in the U.S. Championships for the last time in 1919.

His first event of the season was an interclub match between the Heights Casino in Brooklyn and the Buffalo Tennis Club on the latter's indoor courts. Fred Alexander defeated Murray, 7–5, 4–6, 6–4.[3] In doubles, Alexander and Harold Taylor, the national junior champion, defeated Murray and Hendrick, 6–1, 7–9, 6–3. Murray, though, now had local players to practice with, including T. W. Hendrick and Harold Hodge, both of whom had twice been holders of the Buffalo City championship title, and Eric Hedstrom, and Jack Castle who would relocate to Buffalo that year.[4–5]

In May at the West Side Tennis Club exhibition matches, Walter Merrill Hall and S. Howard Voshell defeated R. Lindley Murray and Harold Throckmorton in straight sets, 6–2, 6–3, 7–5.[6] In another invitational exhibition tournament, Clarence Griffin and Willis Davis defeated Murray and Leonard Beekman, 10–8, 4–6, 8–6.[7]

The July 2 *Gazette* reported that Lindley Murray had been selected to captain the Eastern Team at Cincinnati the following week. Bill Tilden would play no. 1; Lin Murray, no. 2; Ichiya Kumagae, no 3; Howard Voschell, no. 4; Wallace Johnson, no. 5; and Vincent Richards, no. 6. The pairings in doubles were Tilden and Richards, Voschell and Johnson, Murray and Kumagae. Bill Johnston would captain the West.[8]

In the East versus West tournament held in Cincinnati in July, six singles and three doubles matches were to be played. Murray, now playing for the East, defeated veteran Samuel Hardy on July 12 in five quick sets, 6–2, 6–3, 1–6, 2–6, 6–1. Instead of running away with the match, as was his style in 1918, Murray faltered for two sets before relentlessly driving the tiring Hardy.[9] As reported by the *Gazette*, Murray "seemed to have the match at his mercy in the first two sets, his hard drives proving too much for Hardy." However, Hardy improved as the match progressed while Murray lost considerable speed. Hardy easily won the third and fourth sets, and it looked as though Murray was going down to defeat, "but with the sets standing two and two, he came back to his old form in the final and caught Hardy weakening."[10] Murray paired with Ichiya Kumagae to beat Ralph Burdick and A. L. Green Jr. (West), 7–9, 6–4, 6–1, 6–2.[11]

Lin Murray brought Ichiya Kumagae to Niagara Falls to play an exhibition at the Quay Street courts on Monday, July 14. Murray easily won the match 6–0, 6–2. At the beginning of the second set, Kumagae "smashed short snappy drives to the sides of the court and many times caught Murray off his guard. However, after winning three straight games Murray's speed and stamina began to assert itself and Kumagae, tired after last week's strenuous play at Cincinnati and a long train ride began to tire, while his opponent, who towered high above him, smashed the ball across the net with but few returns." In a doubles match Kumagae and Taylor of New York defeated Murray and Hedstrom of Buffalo, 4–6, 6–2, 6–3.[12]

At the Great Lakes championship in Buffalo, which began on July 14, Bill Tilden beat Buffalonian T. W. Hendrick in one semifinal, while Ichiya Kumagae, obviously fully recovered, beat Lin Murray in the other, 6–2, 5–7, 6–1, 6–1. The five-foot-three Kumagae beat Tilden in the final, 6–2, 10–8, 8–6, and A. J. Vesey more easily in the challenge round. Kumagae paired with H. Taylor to beat Murray and Buffalonian Eric Hedstrom, 7–5, 6–2, 6–4, for the doubles title. En route to the semis Hendrick easily beat San Franciscan H. V. D. Johns, 1915 Pacific Coast intercollegiate titlist, 6–1, 6–2; A. J. Vesey, 3–6, 6–1, 6–2; and George Reindell, 9–7, 6–2.[13] Jack Castle, having recently settled in Buffalo, lost to Walter Wesbrook of Detroit, 1919 and 1920 Big Ten singles titlist for the University of Michigan[14] in the third round by a score of 6–3, 6–4 and paired with F. O. Wilson to beat Bill Tilden and Gerald Emerson, 1–6, 7–5, 6–3, in the quarters while Murray and Hedstrom beat Castle and Wilson in the semis, 6–2, 4–6, 6–3.[15]

A little later that July in Greenwich, Connecticut, Murray defeated F. G. Inman, 6–0, 6–2, and then Theodore Pell, 9–7, 6–4.[16–17] Because of a rainstorm, the tournament was postponed for almost a month to mid-August.

After Murray's win over Kumagae in Cleveland in five spectacular sets on Saturday, July 26, 4–6, 6–2, 7–5, 0–6, 7–5, after Kumagae led 5–2 in the fifth, Murray's father and two brothers, Fred and Frank, visited Niagara Falls. Fred, a national hurdles champion who would win a bronze medal at the 1920 Olympics, and Frank, at nearly six feet five, was one of the best football players in the Far West. In accordance with popular demand, Lindley and his dad played a special match with Fred and Frank at the Niagara Falls Country Club (NFCC) courts on Sunday, July 27.[18]

On August 7 at the Newport Casino, Rhode Island, Kumagae got a measure of revenge in the fourth round over Murray, by defeating the national champion in one of the fastest five-set matches ever staged at the Casino, 3–6, 7–5, 3–6, 8–6, 6–3. Murray had played Niles in the morning, and it was apparent after the afternoon match was over that he was completely worn out.

> The lithe, speedy champ of the "land of the rising sun" played with deadly accuracy and his placing of shots throughout the sets held the crowd spellbound with tense excitement. The American champ played a wonderful game, particularly so in view of the fact that his match with Niles in the morning was a "sizzler."[19]

Speaking of the Kumagae match, Murray acknowledged that he was not in shape for two hard matches:

> I never felt so "all in" in my life as I did after the matches with Niles ... and Kumagae, both of which were played the same day. I did not know until that morning that I was obliged to meet Kumagae also, but I hopped to it and did the best I could. We started to play at 11 o'clock in the morning and did not finish until nearly dark. After it was all over I hit the feathers and slept for over fourteen hours.[20]

After Newport, Murray brought New Yorker Harry McNeil back to Niagara Falls with him to play on the grass court at Niagara-on-the-Lake, August 14 and 15, as a tune up for the national championships.[21] As reported by J. O. Sanders to the *Gazette*:

> The chief features of the match were the bewildering serve, smashing drives of Murray and the remarkable pickups of McNeil.
>
> Without question Murray has one of the speediest and puzzling serves that has been witnessed on any court in the country for many years.[22]

Back at Greenwich Murray won over Kumagae by default and Willis Davis, 6–3, 8–6. In men's doubles, Murray and Dean Mathey beat Willis Davis and Julian Myrick, USLTA president from 1920 to 1922, by a score of 6–2, 7–5, and Maurice McLoughlin and Thomas Bundy, 6–4, 6–2, but lost in the final round to Karl Behr and Theodore Pell, 6–8, 7–5, 6–2. In mixed, Murray and Eleanor Goss won from Marie Wagner and Dick Williams, 7–5, 4–6, 6–2.[23–24]

The stage was now set for the nationals at Forest Hills. In the first round Murray overwhelmed Dr. William Rosenbaum in straight sets.[25] Murray then disposed of Dean Mathey, the former Princetonian from Cranford, New Jersey, 6–2, 6–4, 10–8.[26] In the third round Murray defeated Lucien Williams from Chicago in straight sets, 6–2, 6–2, 6–2. Murray had made his way to the quarterfinals where he again succumbed to the eventual champion, Bill Johnston, in a bitterly contested four-set battle, 5–7, 6–1, 6–2, 6–4.[27–28] At year-end, Murray was ranked fourth behind Johnston, Tilden, and Kumagae.

Although Murray played some exemplary tennis in the future, this was largely at exhibitions and local tourneys, as he confined himself to his employment at Hooker until his retirement in 1959 at age sixty-seven after forty-three years of service.

As Murray's International Tennis Hall of Fame write-up states: "He had a brief, bright run in the U.S. Championships." Murray played the most tournament tennis when he first came east in 1914. Once his chemical engineering career began, he became a dedicated employee and at Niagara Falls put his energies into raising a family and making Hooker Electrochemical a prominent growth company, where he spent the remainder of his long working career.

Murray didn't go out of his way to play doubles, although his game was ideally suited for it, particularly as a left-handed serve and volleyer. Despite his apparent lack of interest in even participating in the two national championships he did win, he nevertheless trained assiduously for each occasion. He never beat McLoughlin when they played in 1914. Red Mac peaked that year and lost to his younger compatriot Bill Johnston in the 1915 final. In 1916, after winning the first set in the fourth round, George Church easily won the next three. The two players peaked at different times, however, as in the following round Murray defeated Church in the aforementioned spectacular five-setter.

Murray's 1917 and 1918 national championship wins during those war years have been asterisked by some because the top players, particularly Johnston who was serving in the navy, didn't participate. Dick Williams lost in the 1917 semis to Nat Niles but was far from his best, having returned from the army to defend his 1916 title. Murray was crushed by Bill Johnston in the 1916 semis and again in 1919 after Murray had gamely won the first set of the quarters. Although Murray defeated Bill Tilden four times, Tilden didn't become famous until after he emerged from the East Providence indoor court in 1920 at age twenty-seven as the superstar of the tennis world. Tilden, Johnston, and Williams dominated Davis Cup play between 1920 and 1926.

Regarding the 1919 Johnston match, the *Times* sportswriter said Johnston had never lost to Murray (in important matches). Full of confidence, he played a game he had seldom equaled; his forehand drive had far more speed, his service was steady and aggressive, and his volleys were accurately angled. Continuing, the writer analyzed Murray's style of play:

> Murray put up a game battle, but his physical strength was unequal to the demands he made upon it. He won the opening set through sheer grit, hanging on desperately and serving his head off to keep in the game, while Johnston coolly bombarded him with every shot in his repertoire. Murray's style is exhausting, for every service requires his full power, and at every volley he comes off the ground, jarring his whole system as he lands on one or both feet. He works harder than any other man on the courts for the results he attains, and consequently he is practically certain to succumb to exhaustion if an opponent can carry him beyond three hard sets.[29]

After Bill Tilden had for the first time captured a major singles championship, and in fact both the Wimbledon and U.S. titles in 1920, he published *The Art of Lawn Tennis*. Directly under his name on the title page, printed in a smaller font was "Champion of the World." The first printing was on October 14, 1920. In his book Tilden took the liberty of discussing the personality and play of some "famous players." Of Maurice McLoughlin, he said it was the "wonderful dynamic personality … the dazzling smile and vibrant force of the red-haired Californian … that swept crowds off their feet.… R. L. Murray has much of M'Loughlin's [*sic*] fire, but not the spontaneity that won the hearts of the crowd."[30]

Lin Murray was called the new California Comet by Tilden. Regarding Murray's game Tilden said:

> His service is of the same cyclonic character as M'Loughlin.… He hits a fast cannon-ball delivery of great speed and an American twist of extreme twist. His ground strokes are not good, and he rushes the net at every

> opportunity. His forehand drive is very fast, excessively topped, and exceedingly erratic. His backhand is a "poke." His footwork is very poor on both shots. He volleys very well, shooting deep to the base-line and very accurately. His shoulder-high volleys are marvelous. His overhead is remarkable for its severity and accuracy. He seldom misses an overhead ball.
>
> Murray is a terrifically hard worker, and tires himself out very rapidly by prodigious effort. He is a hard fighter and a hard man to beat. He works at an enormous pace throughout the match.
>
> He is large, spare, rangy, with dynamic energy, and a wonderful personality that holds the gallery. His smile is famous, while his sense of humor never deserts him. A sportsman to his finger-tips, there is no more popular figure in American tennis than Murray. His is not a great game. It is a case of a great athlete making a second-class game first class, by shear power of personality and fighting ability. He is really a second M'Loughlin [*sic*] in his game, his speed, and his personal charm.[31]

Tennis writers said Murray played the game with determination and zest. His strong points were his ability to deliver both services deep and well-placed, at top speed with spin, his skill in accurately finishing overheads and volleys with great force, his excellent conditioning and court coverage, as well as his great reach, unusual agility, courage, and perseverance. Defects in his ground strokes "were compensated for by attention to detail, hours of practice, and a doggedness on the court in retrieving practically every shot his opponents hit at him."[32] Murray was thus forced to take the net on drives not sufficiently deep, depending on his quickness and anticipation to intercept the return. This worked against most players but against the likes of giant-killer Bill Johnston or Dick Williams, who on a good day hit accurately, deeply, and close to the lines, was enervating for Murray in a long match despite rigorous training and prodigious effort.

Whether or not Murray read those assessments of his game, he was well aware of the fact that he had never beaten Johnston, Williams, or Tilden at their best. So what he did, partly by promoting tennis in Niagara Falls and partly by demonstrating that he still possessed championship caliber tennis skills, induced Johnston, Tilden, and other American (and several foreign) champions to play at Niagara Falls or the Niagara Falls Country Club (NFCC) in Lewiston Heights or at other exhibition venues between 1920 and 1926.

1920

As part of the twenty-fifth anniversary reunion of the University Club of Niagara Falls, R. Lindley Murray played Ichiya Kumagae, the famous Japanese tennis star, on the Quay Street courts on Saturday, June 12, 1920.[1]

At the National Clay Court tennis championships in Chicago on July 14, Lin Murray went through five rounds, the first two by default. In the third, Murray played a Chicagoan, Lou Hayes, and won, 6–1, 6–3. In the fourth, Murray defeated Harry Grinstead of Louisville, Kentucky, 6–1, 6–2. In the fifth round, Murray was confronted with the Western intercollegiate champion, Walter Wesbrook, again easily winning 6–1, 6–2.[2] Playing the best tennis of his career, Alex Squair, Western champion in 1915, defeated Murray in the quarters by 0–6, 6–4, 6–4.[3] The ultimate tournament winner was Roland Roberts of San Francisco, who defeated Vincent Richards of Yonkers, New York, 6–3, 6–1, 6–3. As with most Californians, Roberts's service and drives, which he followed to the net, made the difference.[4]

On October 3 in Bethlehem, Pennsylvania, before a gallery of two thousand persons on the courts of the Northampton Country Club, Lin Murray defeated Bill Tilden, 6–2, 6–3. Paired with Stanley Pearson of Philadelphia, Eastern Pennsylvania champion, Murray defeated Tilden and Carl Fischer, University of Pennsylvania champion, 3–6, 6–3, 7–5.[5] "Lindley Murray was in rare form and exhibited the best brand of tennis he has shown in some time. His terrific service, for which he is noted, had 'Big Bill' guessing and fans who saw the match said they had not seen Murray in such perfect form for some time."[6]

1921

On July 8, 1921, Lin Murray of Niagara Falls won the New York State tennis championship on the Park Club courts in Buffalo by defeating Kirk Reid, Ohio State champion, 7–5, 5–7, 6–1, 6–1. In the semis, Murray defeated Buffalo champion Jack Castle, 6–2, 5–7, 4–0. The effort made by

Castle in the second set exhausted him for the third. Reid won his way to the finals by defeating Phil Neer of California,[1] 1921 U.S. intercollegiate champion. In doubles, Samuel Hardy, captain of the U.S. Davis Cup team, and Carl Fisher of Philadelphia, were defeated in the semis by Wallace Bates and Edmund Levy of Stanford University, 4–6, 6–2, 6–1, 7–5.[2]

Cliff Marsh, a youngster who would later figure prominently in Western New York tennis, won the Buffalo Tennis Center junior championship, which began on August 8, over Wilson, 6–3, 6–2, 6–4.[3]

At the Queens Royal Hotel courts in Niagara-on-the-Lake, Ontario, on August 13, Lin Murray defeated Clifford B. Herd of Chicago, 7–5, 8–6, 6–3, to take the International Lawn Tennis championship.[4] On his way to the final, Murray defeated M. W. Duthie of Toronto, 6–0, 6–0; Willis M. Fulton of Cleveland, 6–4, 7–5; E. A Purkiss of Toronto, 6–2, 6–2; and Cleveland's Walter Wesbrook, Ohio State champion, 6–3, 6–1. Murray then paired with Clifton Herd to win the doubles championship over Frank Anderson of New York, national indoor champion, and Walter Wesbrook in a thrilling four-set match, 9–7, 6–4, 8–10, 6–3. Four Niagara Falls players were in the tournament: F. H. Dunnington, Charles Brackett, Myron Watrous, and Andrew Grabau. Dunnington and Brackett won their first-round matches. Watrous and Grabau paired and won their first-round doubles match.

1922

In the Middle States Indoor tennis tourney early April in Philadelphia, Bill Tilden of Philadelphia defeated Lawrence Rice of Boston, 4–6, 6–0, 12–10, in one semifinal, while Vincent Richards of Yonkers defeated Lin Murray in the other, 6–4, 4–6, 7–5. In their second match of the day, twenty-three-year-old Richards defeated Tilden in the finals, 2–6, 6–1, 6–4. Richards teamed with Wallace Johnson of Philadelphia, national runner-up, to defeat Tilden and Sandy Wiener of Philadelphia in the doubles semifinal, 6–2, 2–6, 6–4. Richards gained his second title when, paired with Johnson, beat Lawrence Rice and Arnold Jones of Providence, 6–3, 6–4.[1] Arnold Jones, the 1919 U.S. boys' champion, was the youngster with whom Bill Tilden practiced during the winter of 1919 and 1920 to perfect his backhand.

To open the tennis season at the NFCC on Sunday, June 4, Murray played Jack Castle, Buffalo champion and one of the best players in Western New York. Murray won the exhibition, 6–2, 6–3, 6–2.[2]

In another exhibition match at the NFCC, held on Sunday, July 2, Murray defeated Kirk Reid, Cleveland and Ohio State champion, 6–3, 10–12, 6–2. Notably, Murray said the second set was the hardest he had ever played.[3]

The National Clay Court tourney for women and the Great Lakes championship for men were held concurrently at the Park Club in Buffalo early July. Seventeen-year-old Helen Hooker of Greenwich, Connecticut, a niece of Albert H. Hooker Sr., Elon's older brother, defeated Kate Gardner and advanced to the semis by defeating Ruth King, 6–0, 6–3, where she lost to Leslie Bancroft of Brookline, Massachusetts, 6–1, 6–2.[4] Helen teamed with Mrs. Harry Bickle of Toronto to gain the finals of the women's doubles, losing to Mrs. Frank H. Godfrey and Bancroft, 3–6, 7–5, 6–1. Bickle went on to defeat Bancroft, 3–6, 6–1, 7–5, to clinch the Women's National Clay Court championship, becoming the first Canadian woman to win the title.

Helen Hooker would be sandwiched between subsequent world champions Helen Wills and Helen Jacobs in the USTA Girls' National championships. Wills won in 1921 and 1922, Hooker in 1923, and Jacobs in 1924 and 1925. Hooker teamed with Wills to win the girls' 18 doubles event in 1922 and with Elizabeth Hilleary for the 1923 title, which they won by a score of 6–0, 6–0. Hooker defeated Hilleary, 6–1, 6–0, in the 1923 singles final. Helen reached the quarterfinals of the 1923 U.S. women's singles event, losing to Molla Bjurstedt-Mallory, who in turn lost to Helen Wills after beating her in 1922. This was the beginning of Wills's run to legendary status. The USLTA Ranking Committee placed Helen Hooker at no. 10 for 1923.

In the Great Lakes championship, Lin Murray had little difficulty in defeating R. D. Hausauer of Buffalo, 6–0, 6–1. Murray played R. D. Johnson in one semi, while Kirk Reid of Cleveland played Dick Talley.[5] Murray of Niagara Falls "showed superb form and amazing speed … in defeating Ray Johnson of Pittsburgh … in three straight sets, 6–3, 6–2, 6–2," while Kirk Reid easily defeated Talley, a New York University player, 6–1, 6–2, 6–3.[6] "Following a bad start, the Falls player's game was phenomenal, Murray showing the same form and amazing speed which carried him to the National championships in 1917 and 1918." The scores against Kirk Reid were, 1–6, 6–1, 6–2, 6–4. Following the singles, Murray and Gerald Emerson of Columbia University defeated Reid and Henry Wick of Cleveland in the finals of the Great Lakes doubles in five hard sets, 6–4, 2–6, 10–8, 3–6, 6–2.[7–8]

The July 15 issue of the *Gazette* noted Murray would not defend his New York State title at Syracuse the following week for business reasons.[9]

Murray did win from Charles Garland, Pittsburgh star, in an exhibition match in Cleveland on July 23, before the finals of the National Inter-City doubles. The scores were 6–1, 6–4, 2–6. In another exhibition match, Kirk Reid of Cleveland defeated William McElroy of Pittsburgh, 6–4, 6–3, 6–2.[10]

In an Inter-City tennis match at the Park Club in Buffalo, held on August 4 and 5, Murray played with the Buffalo team in matches with Toledo, Detroit, and Cleveland. Six singles and three doubles were played; the semifinal matches were held on Friday, August 4, and the finals on Saturday. Buffalo played Detroit, and Cleveland played Toledo. Lin Murray easily defeated Ira Reindel, 6–0, 6–1, but, playing with Dan Talley, lost to the Reindel brothers, 6–2, 5–7, 6–4. The Buffalo winners were Murray, Jack Castle, Chet Gale, and Dunbar Hausauer. Buffalo won one of three doubles putting out Detroit 5–4, while Cleveland defeated Toledo 7–1.[11]

It seems surprising, based on the close win over Detroit and Cleveland's easy win over Toledo, that Buffalo would come out on top. In fact, Buffalo won all nine matches:

R. Lindley Murray, Buffalo, defeated Harold Bartel, Cleveland, 6–0, 6–1.
Jack Castle, Buffalo, defeated Johnny Virden, Cleveland, 6–2, 6–2.
John Gowans, Buffalo, defeated Leonard Keith, Cleveland, 6–4, 6–2.
Chet Gale, Buffalo, defeated Ralph Oster, Cleveland, 6–2, 6–0.
Cliff Marsh, Buffalo, defeated Val Ely, Cleveland, 7–5, 6–2.
Dunbar Hausauer, Buffalo, defeated Paul Westenhaver, Cleveland, 6–3, 3–6, 7–5.
Murray and Castle defeated Bartel and Wick, 6–1, 6–2.
Gowans and Gale defeated Virden and Oster, 6–4, 6–0.
Klinck and Hausauer defeated Ely and Keith, 7–5, 6–3.[12]

R. Lindley Murray invited Charles Garland, Pittsburgh star and 1920 Wimbledon doubles champion with R. Norris Williams, to play on the Quay Street courts on Sunday, August 13. Also invited were Jack Castle and Eric Hedstrom of Buffalo for a subsequent doubles match. Garland and Hedstrom had played together on the Yale University team.[13] Murray defeated Garland in a close three-set match, 8–6, 5–7, 6–3, as a crowd of over one thousand watched. The *Gazette* reported that all through the match Garland worked with the coolness of a cucumber and the steadiness of a machine. Murray was not up to form initially and missed several critical shots. Murray played better in the third but not up to the form he had showed against Harold Bartel, Cleveland City champion, last weekend. It being so late, only one doubles set was played. Castle and Murray defeated Hedstrom and Garland, 9–7. "Hedstrom and Garland led nearly all the way and were within a point of set no less than five times before Castle and Murray finally pulled it out of the fire."[14]

At Niagara-on-the-Lake, Ontario, on Saturday, August 26, Lin Murray again won the International Lawn Tennis singles title by defeating Armand Bruneau of Brooklyn, 6–2, 6–2, 6–2. Murray played fast and loose, as was his style, "and kept Bruneau zigzagging back and forth," causing Bruneau to net thirty-five balls compared to Murray's fifteen. In the morning Murray won his semifinal against Johnny Virden of Cleveland, 6–2, 6–2. The presentation of prizes to the winners was made Saturday evening at the dance in the Queens Royal Hotel. Colonel Bickford, a Buffalo-resident and former officer in the Canadian army, made the presentations. Murray received a bronze trophy and also a new Dayton steel racquet, which was offered to the winner of the open singles event by the *Niagara Falls Gazette.* This was the racket designed and manufactured by Bill Larned, seven-time U.S. singles champion.

Mrs. Harry Bickle of Toronto, Canadian women's champion and U.S. national clay court champion, was an easy winner in all her matches. She defeated Miss E. McDonald of Toronto in the women's singles final, 6–2, 6–2.[15–16] It was she who had teamed with Helen Hooker in the Women's National Clay Court doubles.

R. L. Murray played another exhibition match on Sunday, September 17, at the NFCC, this time against Australian Davis Cup player James O. Anderson, who had lost to both Bill Johnston and Bill Tilden in the Davis Cup challenge round earlier in the month. Anderson would go on to win the Australian championships in 1924 and 1925. Murray had not been up against the top players, especially in the last two years, and Anderson would be good preparation for Bill Johnston the following week. A gallery of over four hundred fans watched Murray breeze through the first set, only to falter in the second and third and lose a tight fourth. The scores were 0–6, 6–2, 6–3, 10–8. "[T]all of stature with a wonderful physique,... Anderson covered the court with the ease of a perfect machine. His sense of direction was also uncanny and he seemed always to be in position to play [the] ball. Murray, on the other hand, played his usual spectacular, dashing game, one moment being deep on the court and the next flashing to the barrier for a terrific smash or reaching sideways, almost on all fours, for a lightning return." Murray had a 4–1 lead in the final set only to see Anderson come back with three games for a 4–4 tie. Murray held serve and was up double set point 15–40 on Anderson's serve. Anderson scored first with an ace and then with a winning placement to bring the game to deuce. Murray again was within point of set at 7–6, but Anderson closed out the tiring American.[17]

As early as July 25, the *Gazette* reported William M. "Little Bill" Johnston would be in town after the U.S. Nationals to play an exhibition match with Murray. Johnston was national champion in 1915 and 1919 but had lost to "Big Bill" Tilden for the past three years. In an interview, Murray "stated he believes that Johnston is without a doubt the best player in the world today. He is admitted by all to be one of the fastest men who ever stepped on a court." Temporary bleachers were constructed for the immense crowd, as delegations were expected from Buffalo, Jamestown, Rochester, Toronto, St. Catharines, and Niagara Falls, Ontario. The match on Sunday, September 24, was open to the public free of charge. A special Gray Bus was scheduled to leave the Gorge office at two o'clock for the 3:30 p.m. match and would return after the game. The edge favored Johnston, as Murray had only defeated him once, in the New York State championships at Utica in 1916, while Johnston defeated Murray in the 1916 national semis and in the 1919 national quarterfinals, where he went on to beat Tilden in the final.[18] "With a chill, raw wind, cutting players and spectators to the bone, William M. Johnston of California, with a wonderful exhibition of super tennis, defeated R. Lindley Murray of this city.... The scores were 6–4, 1–6, 6–3, 2–6, 7–5."[19]

Murray had scouted out the Johnston-Tilden final at the national championships in Philadelphia at the Germantown Cricket Club on Saturday, September 16, in which Tilden defeated Johnston, 4–6, 3–6, 6–2, 6–3, 6–4. Murray was right on the firing line, as it were "in Johnston's corner," and had a great chance to watch the "little wonder" in action. As Murray told it that Sunday afternoon to an interested group of spectators in the Country Club locker room while he was getting ready for his match with J. O. Anderson, "Tilden won because he was a big man and had the physical strength which Johnston lacked to go through a grueling five set match."[20]

"Murray was with Johnston during the ten minute intermission between the third and fourth sets, and he stated it was plain to see that Johnston was very tired," whereas Tilden seemed fresh in comparison. "When asked whether he thought the best player won, Murray" stated: "No, I wouldn't put it that way. Because I believe that Johnston has a little on Tilden, but Big Bill deserves all the credit in the world. He knew Johnston, and feared him, and so, playing hard all the time, he just wore down the Californian, and then, in the third set, struck when the proper time came." Murray continued, "I have seen all the nationals of recent years, which were touted as the greatest tennis ever played, but Saturday's battle between the 'two Bills' was, in my mind, the greatest exhibition of super tennis the world has ever seen."[21] By virtue of having beaten Gerald L. Paterson of Australia, holder of the so-called world's championship (that is, Wimbledon), in the semifinals, Tilden could justly lay claim to the highest pinnacle in tennis after defeating William Johnston in three consecutive U.S. Championships.

Johnston had beaten Tilden in 1919 but lost to the resurrected champion in 1920 and 1921. The twelve thousand fans, though they were Tilden's townsmen, were happy for Johnston's sake after he won the first set and swept through the second. "On a table off to one side of the court, in full view of all, glistened the national championship cup," wrote Allison Danzig. Johnston had won it in 1915 and 1919 and Tilden in 1920 and 1921. All the little man with the blazing forehand needed was one more set to lift the cup to his lips, and it would be his for all time. And then Tilden let loose with all his wizardry to win the cup for the third time as "a grim, stricken little player, worn to the point of exhaustion, wan and pale, made his way through a lane of worshipping admirers," oblivious to all, even his wife, who hurried to console him.[22]

Duplicating Tilden's feat of coming back from two sets down, Murray extracted a measure of revenge the following day in Toronto when he played unbeatable tennis to defeat Johnston in a terrific five-set match before a gallery of nearly a thousand people. The scores were 5–7, 2–6, 14–12, 6–0, 6–2. As the score testifies, the long third set was critical as the "Falls player covered the court like a demon, time after time returning shots that were classed as absolutely impossible." After that Murray was at the peak of his game and played unbeatable tennis. "He was master of the situation at every moment, and although Johnston was also playing the best tennis at his command, he was simply outclassed by Murray."[23]

1923

According to the May 16, 1923, issue of the *Gazette*, "Sunday will be the greatest tennis day in the history of Niagara Falls. William Tilden, 2d, world's champion, and his partner, Sandy Wiener, will play R. Lindley Murray of this city, former national champion and Eric Hedstrom of Buffalo in the doubles at the Niagara Falls Country Club. Tilden will oppose Murray in the singles. Conceded by tennis experts to be the greatest player who has ever held the title, having won all his international matches, Tilden has met and defeated all comers for the past three years."[1] Tilden played doubles with fourteen-year-old Sandy Wiener in the Philadelphia championship on May 28, 1922, but they lost in the semifinals.[2]

It was necessary to erect temporary grandstands along the west side and on the veranda of the NFCC. A small fee of twenty-cents was charged to non-club members, and a staff of experienced linesmen was secured. "Tilden's style of play has not been handicapped by the loss of his finger, and experts claim that he is as perfect as ever."[3] In 1922 Tilden's middle finger on his playing hand had become infected and was subsequently amputated. But he simply modified his grip and continued to play at the same level at which he had played before the accident.

Tilden won the singles exhibition match from Murray on Sunday, May 20, 6–3, 6–4, 6–4, while Tilden and Sandy Wiener won two straight sets from Murray and Eric Hedstrom of Buffalo, 6–4, 6–4.[4]

In exhibition tennis at the official opening of the Ottawa Tennis and Bowling Club, on June 4, Bill Tilden and Lindley Murray played three sets, the former winning 3–6, 6–4, 6–1. In doubles Murray teamed with Samuel Hardy to defeat Tilden and Willard Crocker, Ontario champion, 4–6, 6–2, 6–3.[5] Samuel Hardy of Chicago won the 1917 Chicago Patriotic tournament[6] and reached the doubles final of the 1920 U.S. Indoor championships at the Seventh Regiment Armory. He played with S. Howard Voshell to defeat Wylie C. Grant and G. Carlton Shafer, 7–5, 6–4,[7] losing in the final to Bill Tilden and Vincent Richards. Sam Hardy was 1920–21 Davis Cup captain. The International Tennis Hall of Fame annually presents the Samuel Hardy Award to a USTA volunteer in recognition of long and outstanding service to the sport of tennis.[8]

Beginning June 20, Murray, three-time winner of the Great Lakes championship, one of which was decided as "no championship" play, would again represent Niagara Falls in the tournament held on the Park Club courts in Buffalo. "Should Mr. Murray win the tournament this season the bowl will be his permanently."[9] World champion "Big Bill" Tilden was in the singles and paired with youngster Sandy Wiener in the doubles, while Murray was paired with Jack Castle, Buffalo City champion.[10]

The list of entries was quite impressive, headed by Bill Tilden, the world champion; Nat Niles, runner-up to Murray in the 1917 nationals; Manuel Alonso, former Spanish champion; Sandy Weiner, Tilden's protégé; Donald Strachan, Roy Coffin, G. B. Pfingst, all of Philadelphia; Canadian champion Willard Crocker and his doubles partner Jack Wright; Lin Murray, Ed Bartlett, and William Ross of Niagara Falls; Sam Hardy and William Rosenbaum of New York; Franklin P. Ferguson of Brooklyn; Henry C. Wick and Charles O. Benton of Cleveland; and Roy Johnson and Charles Garland of Pittsburgh. The Buffalo players included city champion Jack Castle, John Gowans, Clifford Marsh, L. L. Hanlon, L. L. Leigh, D. and R. Hausauer, C. W. Pooley, N. L. Danforth, P. V. Bowen, Walter Misner, David Jackson, and others.[11]

Murray won by default in the first round and the next two matches easily. He downed his second-round opponent R. S. Bennett of Buffalo, 6–0, 6–0, and his third round opponent Fred Myers of Buffalo, 6–0, 6–1. Jack Castle reached the third round, while Clifford Marsh was extended in the first round by William Ross of Niagara Falls, 7–5, 7–5.[12]

Tilden easily reached the semifinals by beating Henderson, 6–0, 6–2; Corson, 6–0, 6–0; and Gowans, 6–2, 6–0. Jack Castle defeated Dunbar Hausauer, 6–4, 6–0, and Jack Wright, Canadian doubles champion from Montreal, 6–2, 8–6. Murray defeated Willard Crocker, Canadian champion from Toronto, 6–1, 6–2, and Clifford Marsh, 1923 Western New York junior champion, 6–1, 6–2. Alonso defeated R. Hausauer, 6–2, 6–0, and G. B. Pfingst, 6–1, 6–1.[13]

The semifinal matchups were Bill Tilden versus Jack Castle and Lin Murray versus Manuel Alonso, Spanish Davis Cup player. Murray succumbed to the heat during the furious attack of Alonso, 6–4, 6–2, default, while Tilden easily defeated Castle, losing but one game. In the final round Tilden defeated Alonso, 7–5, 6–3, 6–3.

To reach the doubles semifinals Tilden and Weiner defeated Gowans and Hausauer, 3–6, 6–4, 6–1; Murray and Castle defeated Wright and Crocker, 6–3, 6–1; Hardy and Wick defeated Coffin and Pfingst, 6–3, 6–2; and Alonso and Garland defeated Bartlett and Torrey, 6–3, 6–1.[14] Tilden and Weiner beat Murray and Castle by default, while Alonso and Garland beat Hardy and Wick, 8–6, 6–3, 2–6, 6–2. In the final Tilden and Weiner disposed of Alonso and Garland by a score of 6–1, 6–1, 7–5.[15]

In 1923 the International Lawn Tennis tourney was played on the three new courts at the Clifton Hotel in Niagara Falls, Ontario. Many fine players represented big cities: Willard Crocker of Montreal, the second-best Canadian player; Clifford Marsh, youthful Lafayette High School star; Harold Taylor of New York; Hutchison, a Californian representing Cleveland; Harold Bartel, Cleveland City champion; and players from Boston, Pittsburgh, Ottawa, and Toronto.[16]

Herbert Bowman of New York City, the current New York State champion, and the previous year's New York, New Jersey, and Maryland titleholder, defeated Clifford Marsh in the quarters, 6–2, 6–1, and Walter Wesbrook, Western champion from Detroit, in the semis, 6–3, 6–4, 6–3.[17] In the other half, Lin Murray defeated C. C. Morin of Hamilton in the quarters and George Lott of Chicago, the sixteen-year-old national junior clay court and Chicago champion, in the semis. The scores were 6–3, 8–6, 6–4. After playing those three hard sets against Lott in the morning, Murray won a tough five-setter from Bowman, 6–2, 4–6, 6–2, 3–6, 6–3. As recorded by the *Gazette* on August 13:

> Playing almost frantically in the last three sets, battling against the terrible combination of the New York state champion and endurance, and thrusting every ounce of strength into each and every stroke in the fifth, and deciding set, R. Lindley Murray of this city won a glorious victory over Herbert Bowman of New York city in the finals of the open singles and feature event of the International Tennis tournament on the Clifton hotel courts Saturday afternoon. It was a memorable match in which the International singles champion again defended his title most gallantly after a strenuous tilt a few hours before when George Lott, the national junior clay court champion, pressed the local player hard to oust him from the running. Murray's win in the afternoon will go down in the annals of history as one of the hardest and most gamely fought court battles anywhere.[18]

In one doubles semifinal Walter Wesbrook and George Lott defeated P. Westenhaver of Cleveland and Herbert Bowman, 6–1, 8–6, while Lin Murray and Cliff Marsh disposed of E. Teschereau and C. Gordon Spanner of Toronto, 6–3, 6–4. Playing the doubles final after eight sets of singles, Murray didn't have enough left in the late afternoon to support Cliff Marsh as the pair lost to Lott and Wesbrook, 6–2, 6–3.

In the Buffalo championship at the Park Club beginning September 3, Jack Castle defeated Clifford Marsh in the final round, 6–4, 6–4, 5–7, 6–0, and paired with Marsh to beat Gowans and Kelly in the doubles.[19]

1924

The competition for the 1924 Great Lakes title began on June 16 on the Park Club courts in Buffalo and was won by William T. Tilden over Alex H. Chapin Jr. of Springfield, Massachusetts, New England champion, 3–6, 7–5, 6–1 4–6, 8–6.[1] Tilden had beaten Gerald Emerson of Columbia University and Summit, New Jersey, runner-up to Carl Fischer in the 1923 intercollegiates,[2] 6–2, 6–0, 7–5, in one semifinal, while Chapin beat seventeen-year-old George Lott of Chicago, national junior champion, in the other, 10–8, 6–8, 4–6, 6–1, 6–2.[3] Lott was subsequently touted "as being one of the greatest tennis players of all time."[4] He won the U.S. men's doubles title five times, the mixed three times, the French men's doubles once, the Wimbledon men's doubles twice, and the mixed once. He was inducted into the National Tennis Hall of Fame in 1964.

Murray didn't play the singles event, but two Buffalonians reached the quarters; the young Clifford B. Marsh Jr. put up an outstanding match against Gerald Emerson, losing 5–7, 10–8, 8–6, while Jack Castle lost to Alex Chapin.[5]

Lindley Murray and Sam Hardy of New York won the Great Lakes doubles title over Alex Chapin and Gerald Emerson in four sets, 6–2, 7–5, 1–6, 6–2. Murray and Hardy defeated Beals C. Wright of New York and Jack Castle, Buffalo City champion, in a quarterfinal match, and George Lott and Cliff Marsh in the semis. In the other semi Chapin and Emerson beat Bill Tilden and his protégé Sandy Weiner.[6]

At the National Lawn Tennis doubles event on the courts of the Longwood Cricket Club in Brookline, Massachusetts, Bill Johnston and Clarence Griffin, both of San Francisco and former national doubles champions in 1915, '16, and '20, defeated Lin Murray and Nat Niles of Boston, 6–4, 6–3, 6–2, in an early round match.[7]

Lindley Murray again used his marketing skills to attract two of the French "Four Musketeers," Jean Borotra and Jacques Brugnon, to play an exhibition match at the NFCC on Sunday, September 15. The year 1924 was essentially the start of French domination in international tennis.

Brugnon or "Toto" was the eldest of France's celebrated Four Musketeers, who won the Davis Cup in 1927 from the United States and kept it for six years. He preceded the other three—Jean Borotra, Henri Cochet, Rene Lacoste—as an internationalist, playing first on the Cup team in 1921. A master at doubles, he won Wimbledon four times, was runner-up three times, and won the French five times, the Australian once, and the French mixed twice for a total of twelve major titles.[8]

Jean Borotra, known as "the Bounding Basque" won five Grand Slam singles titles in the French, Australian, and British championships, having already won the 1924 French and British championships before appearing that year in the United States. Borotra was in his element on the fast board courts of the Seventh Regiment Armory, where he won the U.S. Indoor championship four times. With Brugnon, he won the British doubles twice, the French twice, and the Australian once. He stood out with a dramatic, aggressive style of play, having limitless energy, and always wearing a blue beret.[9] Both Borotra and Brugnon became Hall of Famers in 1976.

Before a crowd of one thousand at the NFCC on Sunday, September 15, the French stars Jean Borotra and Jacques Brugnon bested Lin Murray and Cliff Marsh, Buffalo City champion, 5–7, 6–4, 6–3. "The feature of Borotra's and Brugnon's playing was their work at the net. They were slightly outplayed by Murray and Marsh in the back court. Both Borotra and Brugnon dazzled fans and players with their serve."[10]

1925

Manuel Alonso, Spanish tennis champion, played Lindley Murray in the singles event at the NFCC and then some doubles on Sunday, June 7. On June 5 the *Gazette* promoted this march by saying, "Alonso is the most dashing and popular player in the game today.… He also is one of two players who have defeated World's Champion Tilden in tournaments during the last three years. His game is one of the most beautiful to watch of any of the present day players and his striking personality and fine sportsmanship make him the most popular player in the game today."[1] Growing up on clay courts, Alonso would say of American tennis: "It is the speed that amazes me in America. I mean speed not only on the ball but speed of the players and their constant aggressiveness."[2]

As the first Spanish male tennis star of international stature, Manuel Alonso "made his country's best showing at Wimbledon and the U.S. Championships before Manolo Santana won them in 1966 and 1965, respectively. He beat Zenzo Shimizu in a terrific battle, 3–6, 7–5, 3–6, 6–4, 8–6, to reach the Wimbledon … final of 1921, where he lost to Babe Norton, 5–7, 4–6, 7–5, 6–3, 6–3." During the period from 1919 to 1925, when Bill Tilden and Bill Johnston were battling for the U.S. title, Alonso was a quarterfinalist in 1922, '23, '25, and '27 and was ranked in both the world and U.S. top ten in 1925, '26, and '27. He was elected to the International Tennis Hall of Fame in 1977.[3]

With about a thousand fans on hand at the NFCC, Alonso and Murray split sets. Murray won the first 9–7, and Alonso took the second, 6–1. In doubles play, Jack Castle and Murray defeated Alonso and Eric Hedstrom in two out of three sets, 4–6, 6–4, 6–4. The feature of Alonso's play was his backcourt game and his wicked serve, which kept Murray busy returning the ball. In the morning Murray took Alonso through both the Power Company and Hooker Electrochemical's plants, and all the players had luncheon at the country club.[4]

The 1925 Great Lakes tennis tournament was again held in Buffalo on the Park Club courts. Martin Tressel (see profile in part III) of Niagara Falls, city champion of Niagara Falls and 1923 Buffalo Municipal champion, lost to but extended Kirk Reid, Ohio tennis champion from Cleveland, 6–3, 8–6, in a preliminary round.

In the first round George O'Connell of Chicago beat Howard Kelly, 6–2, 6–2; Louis Schaefer beat Karl Hausauer, 6–2, 6–2; Charles Whiting beat Ike Edmands of Niagara Falls, 6–3, 6–2; Jack Castle beat Jim Tranter, 6–2, 6–1; Bryan Doherty of Toronto beat Weyland, 6–2, 6–1; Kirk Reid of Cleveland beat Ralph Byron, 6–2, 6–3; Nelson Dreyfus beat Don Tranter, 6–2, 6–2; Vinton Vernon beat Leo Kronman by default; Don Kent beat Crandall of Westfield, 6–3, 6–3.[5] Jack Castle, Leo Kronman, and Louis Schaefer are in the Buffalo Tennis Hall of Fame.

In the singles final on Saturday, June 13, Kirk Reid defeated Jack Castle in four sets, 6–2, 6–2, 3–6, 6–3. Reid played a conservative game and from the beginning tried to tire his opponent with driving crosscourts, while outclassing Castle at the net. Murray didn't play the singles event but teamed with Castle to win the doubles final over Kirk Reid and Henry Wick, both of Cleveland, 6–4, 6–4, 6–4. On their way to the finals Castle and Murray beat four players from Buffalo: Schaefer and Tettlebach, 6–0, 6–0, and Pooley and Kelly.[6–7]

1926

On the opening day program of the Evershed Tennis Club in Niagara Falls, on Sunday, June 6, Lin Murray played and defeated Martin Tressel in straight sets, 6–3, 6–2, 6–4. While Murray was far from peak form, he nevertheless produced sizzling returns and good ground coverage. "It was interesting to observe the expressions of some of the onlookers especially the younger fans who had not seen tennis like this played before," reported the *Gazette.* This was the club's second year, and Murray pronounced the courts very good and predicted a successful season. With seven new members that year the membership grew to fifty and approached the limit of sixty.[1]

Murray again persuaded the Spanish champion Manuel Alonso to play an exhibition match at the NFCC. Before a large gallery on Sunday, July 25, Murray defeated Alonso, 6–2, 9–7. Murray took the first set easily, Alonso finding his cutting serves very difficult to handle. Alonso improved in the second set, extending the former champion throughout. The *Gazette* described the scene: "In this set Alonso showed splendid delivery and sped from one side of the court to the other with the agility of a panther. He fought valiantly for points and made the local star show flashes of his old national championship form to save the set. The fans were liberal with applause at every brilliant play and spurred the contestants on to greater things." In a doubles exhibition Murray paired with Jack Castle to defeat Alonso and Lewis of Toronto in two deuce sets, 6–4, 8–6. Alonso had victories over "Big Bill" Tilden and was the fifth-ranking player in the United States at the time.[2]

Summary of Exhibition Matches and Post-1918 Tournaments

Exhibitions

1917 On the Quay Street courts on Labor Day, September 3, John Strachan of San Francisco defeated R. Lindley Murray, 11–9, 6–3, after Murray had downed him in three sets in Buffalo on Saturday. In men's doubles Murray and Strachan conquered Frederik Alexander and Harold Throckmorton, 6–3, 2–6, 9–7. Mary K. Browne and Molla Bjurstedt played only one set, the former winning 6–1. In mixed doubles, Throckmorton and Browne won over Murray and Bjurstedt by 6–1.

1919 Lindley Murray defeated Ichiya Kumagae on Monday, July 14, on the Quay Street courts, 6–0, 6–2. Kumagae and Harold Taylor of

New York defeated Murray and Eric Hedstrom of Buffalo, 4–6, 6–2, 6–3.

Lin Murray played Harry McNeil on the grass court at Niagara-on-the-Lake, August 14 and 15 as a tune up for the national championships.

1920 As part of the twenty-fifth anniversary reunion of the University Club in Niagara Falls, Lin Murray played Ichiya Kumagae on the Quay Street courts on June 12.

On October 3 in Bethlehem, Pennsylvania, at the Northampton Country Club, Lin Murray defeated Bill Tilden, 6–2, 6–3. Paired with Stanley Pearson of Philadelphia, Eastern Pennsylvania champion, Murray defeated Tilden and Carl Fischer, University of Pennsylvania champion, 3–6, 6–3, 7–5.

1922 Lin Murray defeated Jack Castle, Buffalo champion, 6–2, 6–3, 6–2, at the Niagara Falls Country Club (NFCC), on June 4.

On July 2 Lin Murray defeated Kirk Reid, Cleveland and Ohio State champion, 6–3, 10–12, 6–2, at the NFCC.

On July 23 Lin Murray played three sets in Cleveland with Charles Garland, Pittsburgh star. Murray won two of three sets, 6–1, 6–4, 2–6.

Lin Murray invited Charles Garland, 1920 Wimbledon doubles champion with Dick Williams, to play on the Quay Street courts on Sunday, August 13. Also invited were Jack Castle and Eric Hedstrom of Buffalo for a subsequent doubles match. Murray defeated Garland, 8–6, 5–7, 6–3. Castle and Murray defeated Hedstrom and Garland, 9–7.

Lin Murray played Australian Davis Cup player James O. Anderson on September 17 at the NFCC. Anderson won, 0–6, 6–2, 6–3, 10–8.

Bill Johnston of California defeated Lin Murray, 6–4, 1–6, 6–3, 2–6, 7–5, September 24 at the NFCC. Murray then defeated Johnston in Toronto the following day, 5–7, 2–6, 14–12, 6–0, 6–2.

1923 On May 20 at the NFCC, Bill Tilden defeated Lin Murray, 6–3, 6–4, 6–4, while Tilden and Sandy Wiener beat Murray and Eric Hedstrom of Buffalo, 6–4, 6–4.

At the official opening of the Ottawa Tennis and Bowling Club on June 4, Bill Tilden beat Lin Murray, 3–6, 6–4, 6–1. In doubles

Murray teamed with Samuel Hardy to defeat Tilden and Willard Crocker, Ontario champion, 4–6, 6–2, 6–3.

1924 Jean Borotra and Jacques Brugnon bested Lin Murray and Cliff Marsh, Buffalo City champion, 5–7, 6–4, 6–3, at the NFCC on September 15.

1925 On June 7 at the NFCC, Lin Murray and Manuel Alonso, Spanish champion, split sets. Murray won the first, 9–7, and Alonso won the second, 6–1. In doubles Jack Castle and Murray defeated Alonso and Eric Hedstrom, 4–6, 6–4, 6–4.

1926 On the opening day program of the Evershed Tennis Club in Niagara Falls on June 6, Lin Murray defeated Martin Tressel, 6–3, 6–2, 6–4.

At the NFCC on July 25, Lin Murray defeated Manuel Alonso, Spanish champion, 6–2, 9–7. Murray teamed with Jack Castle to defeat Alonso and Lewis of Toronto, 6–4, 8–6.

Tournaments

1919 Interclub match between the Heights Casino in Brooklyn and the Buffalo Tennis Club on the latter's indoor courts: Fred Alexander defeated Lin Murray, 7–5, 4–6, 6–4. Alexander and Harold Taylor, the national junior champion, defeated Murray and T. W. Hendrick, 6–1, 7–9, 6–3.

East versus West tournament in Cincinnati on July 12: Lin Murray defeated Samuel Hardy, 6–2, 6–3, 1–6, 2–6, 6–1.

Great Lakes championship in July: Ichiya Kumagae beat Lin Murray in a semifinal, 6–2, 5–7, 6–1, 6–1. Kumagae and Harold Taylor beat Murray and Buffalonian Eric Hedstrom for the doubles title, 7–5, 6–2, 6–4.

Cleveland on July 26: Lin Murray beat Ichiya Kumagae, 4–6, 6–2, 7–5, 0–6, 7–5, after Kumagae led 5–2 in the fifth.

Newport Casino on August 7: Ichiya Kumagae beat Lin Murray in the fourth round, 3–6, 7–5, 3–6, 8–6, 6–3.

Greenwich, Connecticut, mid-August: Karl Behr and Theodore Pell defeated Lin Murray and Dean Mathey in the finals, 6–8, 7–5, 6–2, after Murray and Mathey had beaten Maurice McLoughlin and Thomas Bundy, 6–4, 6–2. In the mixed finals, Murray and Eleanor Goss won from Marie Wagner and Dick Williams, 7–5, 4–6, 6–2.

Nationals at Forest Hills: Bill Johnston beat Lin Murray in the quaterfinals, 5–7, 6–1, 6–2, 6–4.

1920 National Clay Court tennis championships in Chicago, beginning July 14: Alex Squair, Western champion in 1915, defeated Lin Murray in the quarters, 0–6, 6–4, 6–4. The champion was Roland Roberts of San Francisco, who defeated Vincent Richards of Yonkers, New York, 6–3, 6–1, 6–3.

1921 New York State tennis championship at the Park Club in Buffalo, July 8: Lin Murray of Niagara Falls defeated Kirk Reid, Ohio State champion, 7–5, 5–7, 6–1, 6–1.

International Lawn Tennis championship in Niagara-on-the-Lake, August 13: Lin Murray defeated Clifford Herd of Chicago, 7–5, 8–6, 6–3.

1922 Middle States Indoor tennis tourney in Philadelphia, early April: Vincent Richards of Yonkers defeated Lin Murray in a semifinal, 6–4, 4–6, 7–5.

Great Lakes championships at the Park Club, beginning July 3: Lin Murray defeated Kirk Reid of Cleveland, 1–6, 6–1, 6–2, 6–4. Murray and Gerald Emerson of Columbia University defeated Reid and Henry Wick of Cleveland in the doubles finals, 6–4, 2–6, 10–8, 3–6, 6–2.

Inter-City tennis match at the Park Club, August 4–5: Buffalo defeated Detroit and then Cleveland. Lin Murray, ranked no. 1, won both singles matches with the loss of but one game each.

International Lawn Tennis championship in Niagara-on-the-Lake, August 26: Lin Murray defeated Armand Bruneau of Brooklyn, 6–2, 6–2, 6–2.

1923 Great Lakes championships at the Park Club, beginning June 20: Manuel Alonso, Spanish Davis Cup player, defeated Lin Murray in the semis, 6–2, 6–2, default. Bill Tilden defeated Jack Castle in the semis and Alonso in the final, 7–5, 6–3, 6–3.

International Lawn Tennis championship at the Clifton Hotel in Niagara Falls, Ontario, early August: Lin Murray defeated Herbert Bowman, 6–2, 4–6, 6–2, 3–6, 6–3.

1924 Great Lakes championships at the Park Club, beginning June 16: Lin Murray and Sam Hardy of New York beat Alex Chapin and Gerald Emerson, 6–2, 7–5, 1–6, 6–2.

15
Niagara Falls, Frontier, and Industrial Tennis

Note: This chapter lacks some specific references because it has been condensed and extracted from a book self-published by the author in 2009 entitled Niagara Falls & Frontier Tennis: Flannels & Petticoats to Shorts & Skirts: A History From 1892. *The majority of the information in that book came from* Niagara Falls Gazette *microfilm at the Niagara Falls Public Library, Earl W. Brydges Building, in Niagara Falls, New York, in addition to the other sources listed.*

Not many local people know that the Niagara Frontier attracted the best players in the United States and Canada in the late nineteenth century and the first quarter of the twentieth century. The International Lawn Tennis Open tournament, held on the grass courts of the Queen's Royal Hotel at Niagara-on-the-Lake mid- to late August, was a great warm-up for the U.S. Championships. After holding the Canadian Championships in Toronto from 1890 to 1893 and in Ottawa in 1894, the Canadian Lawn Tennis Association decided that the next tournament would be held at Niagara-on-the-Lake, commencing Tuesday, July 9, on the grounds of the Queen's Royal Hotel. The winner of the 1890 tournament was E. E. Tanner of the Buffalo Lawn Tennis Club.

The other big tournaments were held at the Park Country Club of Buffalo, founded in 1903 near Delaware Park. The clubhouse was located on Elmwood Avenue just north of the present Historical Society at Nottingham. In 1909 the land bordering on Elmwood, on which the clubhouse and tennis courts were located, was sold to developers. As a result, the club leased and purchased additional land and arranged for the clubhouse building to be moved on rollers along Nottingham to the corner of Nottingham and Lincoln Parkway. The club also leased additional land to the north as far as Amherst Street and laid out several new holes and ten clay tennis courts, hailed as the best in the state.

The tennis courts were in constant use from May to October with tournaments scheduled almost every weekend during the summer. The Great Lakes championship was decided there annually as well as other major tournaments intermittently such as the U.S. Clay Court, the New York State championship, the Western New York tennis tournament, and inter-city tennis matches (with players from Buffalo, Cleveland, Detroit, and Toledo). In addition, the Park Club was a member of the Niagara Tennis League, which included the Buffalo Canoe Club of Point Abino, the Claremont Club of Buffalo, the Niagara Falls Tennis Club, the Lockport Town and Country Club, and the Buffalo Valley Country Club of Elma. World-famous stars played on the Park Club courts. The 1926 season attracted Bill Tilden; Helen Wills; Jean Borotra, French champion; and Manuel Alonso, Spanish Davis Cup team captain.[1]

At the 1894 International tournament, Miss Hollister of Buffalo teamed with Malcom G. Chace, 1893–95 U.S. intercollegiate champion of Yale, to defeat R. W. P. Matthews and Maude Osborne, men's and women's Canadian singles champions for 1894. *Wright & Ditson's Lawn Tennis Guide for 1899* said:

> The writer remembers, and it is not so very long ago, either, when the advent of tennis week at Niagara caused him and his colleagues the most exquisite agony. You may think this is a gaudy pipe-dream but it is not. It is the nakedest kind of truth. Niagara was an undiscovered country then, from a tennis point of view, and the problem of enticing experts into its shady glades was one compared to which the administration of the Philippines is an idle jest.
>
> However, the bold policy of announcing, weeks before the event, in every newspaper from Baffin's Bay to Patagonia, that everybody who was anybody would be on hand for sure at the biggest tennis tournament on earth, had its effect at last, and it got to be so that that shower bouquet of stars, Bob Wrenn, Billy Larned, Eddie Fischer,

> Leo Ware, Mack Whitman, George Sheldon, etc., were scared to stay away. Yes, those were busy times and for a while it looked as though it were possible, after all, to fool all the people all the time.
>
> Then when the public began to scratch its head and think for itself, it was too late, the toboggan had started and Niagara-on-the-Lake had asserted its right to a front seat among the playgrounds of two nations.[2]

In July of 1900, Malcolm Whitman (U.S. no. 1) annexed for the second time the Canadian title at Niagara-on-the-Lake. Just after Whitman beat Bill Larned (U.S. no. 3) in the challenge round in five sets, a young lady inquired of the secretary of the Canadian Lawn Tennis Association (CLTA) on the piazza of the Queen's Royal, "And if that nice Mr. Whitman wins once more he keeps the big Cup for good, doesn't he?" After the official grudgingly said yes, the young lady replied, "Can't you fix it so that he wins for sure next year?"[3] Perhaps it was an innocent jab at the Canadians on their own turf. Even George Wright was there—presumably to see his son Beals play, but really because he could not stay away.

Many other notable players came that year to visit Niagara Falls. When the inaugural British Davis Cup team arrived at New York in 1900, the first thing Arthur W. Gore, Ernest D. Black, and H. Roper Barrett did was take the train to Buffalo and then to Niagara Falls where they "saw the wonderful Falls, crossed over to Canada, and subsequently went beneath them."[4]

Some fifteen miles north was the scenic village Niagara-on-the-Lake where the Niagara River empties into Lake Ontario. Originally site of the Neutral Indian village called Onghiara (also Ongiaahra, Ongiara, Onguiaahra, Ouinagarah, and numerous other variations, pronounced "Nee-ah-gah-rah" by the Iroquois Nation), thought to be the only word left of the Neutral Indians' language, meaning "neck of land" (between the lakes) or "the strait," the name sounded like "Niagara" to the frontiersmen who first heard it. The town was settled at the close of the American Revolution by Loyalists coming to Upper Canada. In 1792, Newark, as the town was named by Governor Simcoe, became the first capital of the newly created colony of Upper Canada. The town was burned down during the War of 1812 with the exception of the stone powder magazine of Fort George directly across the Niagara River from Fort Niagara in Youngstown, New York. Today the village is noted for the Shaw Festival with its three theaters, Fort George and the Historical Society museum, and the many specialty shops along Queen Street.

Many top American players that year came to see one of the world's great natural wonders and play the tournaments. In addition to Larned, Whitman, and Beals Wright were Harold Hackett, Bill Clothier, Ray Little, Eddie Fischer, and Fred Alexander, as well as Kreigh Collins and Louis Waidner from Chicago, and Sam and Sumner Hardy from San Francisco.[5]

The Queen's Royal also hosted the Niagara International, beginning August 22, in which Hackett of Yale beat Fischer of New York in the final, losing to Ray Little (holder and 1900 U.S. no. 10) in the championship round. Hackett, future Hall of Famer, won four U.S. doubles titles with Fred Alexander from 1907 to 1910. Miss Wimar of Washington beat Miss Parker of Chicago, 9–7, 3–6, 6–3, 6–2, for the ladies' title in one of those early best of five set matches. The Hardy brothers handily won the doubles over Chicagoans Collins and Waidner before assaulting the U.S. Championships.[6]

The International tournament had its inception in 1887, the same year the U.S. Women's singles championship was established. Peter A. Porter Jr. of Niagara Falls, an 1898 International handicap finalist, won the individual championship of the 1900 International Tennis League over George Peterson of St. Catharines in three 6–3 sets.[7]

The International Tennis League was organized in May 1899 and was originally composed of the clubs of Buffalo and Niagara Falls, New York, and St. Catharines and Merriton, Ontario. A series of home and away games between the clubs was played during the summer of 1899, which resulted in a victory for the Niagara Falls Club. A like series of matches was played during the 1900 season, the result being a tie between Buffalo and Niagara Falls. By mutual consent the tie was played off, and Buffalo won the championship by a score of 7–5. The annual tournament for the individual championship of the league was held at Niagara-on-the-Lake in conjunction with the International tournament and was won both years by Mr. Peter A. Porter Jr. of Niagara Falls, New York.[8–9]

The September 18, 1900, issue of the *Niagara Falls Gazette* surmised, "It must be somewhat humiliating for Buffalo with her host of tennis friends to have Porter walk off with the championship every time he cares to."[10] One might wonder whether that particular comment had anything to do with the fact that Porter owned the *Gazette*. Porter was the grandson of the famous Peter Buell Porter, who, together with his brother Augustus, purchased 401 acres of land immediately about and above the falls in 1805 and, by means of a float, purchased Goat Island and the islands adjacent thereto lying "immediately above and adjoining the Great Falls" on November 16, 1816. The Porters virtually owned the American Falls and almost one-third of the Canadian Falls once the boundary line was established. In 1885, New York State purchased the property and made it Niagara Reservation State Park.

Two Buffalo players made an impact in the Canadian and International championships: Howard Bissell and Harry D. Kirkover. Bissell and Kirkover played in the 1904 Canadian open singles; Bissell lost in the first round to Hunt, finalist, while Kirkover won his preliminary round, but lost in the first round to Glassco. Bissell was a finalist in the men's handicap losing to Paterson of Toronto; he won the consolation singles over Lewis of Yale, 6–1, 6–2.

In the 1904 International open singles, Holt beat Bissell, 6–2, 6–4 while Kirkover beat McDonnell, 7–5, 6–4. After a second round default Kirkover lost to Edward Dewhurst, ranked ninth in the United States in 1906, by a score of 6–1, 5–7, 6–0, in the quarters. Kirkover again beat McDonnell in the men's handicap final.

In the 1906 Canadian open singles, Kirkover lost to Irving Wright, 1906 U.S. no. 10 (and brother of Beals Wright, 1906 U.S. no. 3), in the semifinals, 6–4, 6–1. He paired with Wright to reach the doubles final and also the handicap singles final. In the 1906 International tournament in August, Kirkover paired with Dewhurst, losing in the finals to Wright and Johnson, 6–2, 9–7, 6–1. Kirkover beat Boys in the handicap final.

Buffalo and Toronto faced each other at Niagara-on-the-Lake on July 2, 1907; and even though Buffalo came out on the short end, Kirkover, McLaughlin, and Carroll went the distance in singles, and Carroll and Kirkover won their doubles. Howard Bissell had wrested the Buffalo City championship from Harry Kirkover on the preceding Saturday. In the 1907 International mixed doubles, Kirkover had the honor of playing with world-champion May Sutton, fresh from her Wimbledon conquest, but they lost in three sets to eventual winners Edith Rotch (1913 U.S. no. 8) and Nat Niles (1908 U.S. no. 8). Both Bissell and Kirkover won their preliminary and first round matches before bowing out in the quarters.

In the 1908 International singles Kirkover won four rounds before losing to Nat Niles in the semis, 6–4, 6–2. In the 1910 Western New York championship, five Buffalo players got through two rounds—Hinds (Niagara Falls), Spaulding, Wilhelm, Kirkover, and Bissell. Spaulding went on to win two more rounds before losing to Nat Niles in the semis, 6–1, 6–2. Kirkover and Bissell reached the doubles semifinals, while Kirkover was a mixed doubles finalist with Edith Rotch.

Nat Niles, 1908 intercollegiate champion from Harvard, won the 1909 International men's singles. Niles was ranked in the U.S. top ten from 1908 to 1913 and was ranked fourth in 1909. May Sutton, who won the U.S. title in 1904 and Wimbledon in 1905 and 1907, won the women's singles title. Beals Wright and Ray Little were doubles champions. Wright was in the U.S. top ten from 1899 to 1908 and in 1910, ranked first in 1905, and won the U.S. singles title in 1905 and 1908. Ray Little won the intercollegiate tennis title for Princeton in 1900, was ranked in the U.S. top ten eleven times between 1900 and 1912, and played on the U.S. Davis Cup team. Both Sutton and Wright became Hall of Famers.[11–13]

Harry Kirkover's 1907 International mixed doubles loss with May Sutton apparently didn't displease the lady champion, as the two paired again to win the 1911 mixed doubles championship at the Onondaga Country Club in Syracuse, held September 11 to 13. They defeated Miss Sutton's sister, Florence, and A. H. Lewis of Syracuse in the finals, 9–7, 3–6, 7–5. The pair returned to the Park Club in Buffalo on October 2 to capture the Western New York mixed doubles against Florence Sutton and F. H. Harris. Harris was a singles finalist to C. O. Benton of Cleveland, and they paired to win the doubles. F. H. Harris of Dartmouth College won the 1911 Ohio State singles championship.

In 1912 Harry Kirkover teamed with 1908 U.S. champion Beals Wright, losing in the finals to Gus Touchard (1912 U.S. no. 10) and Dick Williams (1912 U.S. no. 2), 2–6, 6–4, 7–5, 7–5, in the Great Lakes championship.

Richard (Dick) Norris Williams, the *Titanic* survivor, won the 1912 International singles and doubles tournaments. He subsequently won the 1914 and 1916 U.S. singles titles.

William "Little Bill" Johnston from San Francisco played in the 1913 International tournament, winning the men's doubles and mixed doubles. At year's end he was ranked fourth and subsequently won the 1915 and 1919 U.S. singles titles, defeating Maurice McLoughlin in 1915 and Bill Tilden in 1919.

In the 1913 Great Lakes championship T. W. Hendrick of Buffalo lost to R. Chauncey Seaver of Boston in the singles final, while Hendrick and A. T. Spaulding of Buffalo defeated Seaver and Hodge, 6–0, 2–6, 6–0, 5–7, 6–2, in the doubles final. Niagara Falls held an open tournament in 1915 in which Hendrick, a native of California, who won the Buffalo City championship in 1913 and was runner-up to Harold Hodge, now of Chicago, in the same event in 1914, defeated Edwin Bartlett of Niagara Falls, 6–1, 6–2, 6–3, in the singles final. Hendrick and Spaulding easily defeated fellow Buffalonians, Enoch and Sill, 6–0, 6–0, 6–3, in the doubles final.

Harry Kirkover had another banner doubles year in the 1914 Great Lakes tournament by teaming with Canadian and U.S. stars. He paired with Robert Baird of Toronto to win the doubles over Clarence Griffin and William Swift. Griffin won the 1914 U.S. Clay Court singles tournament, the 1913 U.S. Clay Court doubles championship with John Strachan, and the 1915 and 1916 national doubles titles with Bill Johnston. Kirkover also paired with Mary K. Browne, U.S. singles, doubles, and mixed champion from 1912 to 1914, losing in the mixed finals to Edith Rotch, U.S. no. 8, and Robert Baird, Canadian open tennis doubles champion in 1911, '13, and '14 with T. Y. Sherwell.

In 1912 the first annual tournament of the Western New York Tennis league was held at the Park Club. Wilhelm and Charles Pooley of the Park Club won the Western New York league singles title in 1912 and 1913 respectively and paired to win the doubles in 1912. In 1914 Richard Smith of the Park Club won the singles title while Walter Misner and Dr. Bott of Elma won the doubles title. Niagara Falls won the team title in 1913. The Falls players who deserved recognition in the second decade of the twentieth century include Edwin Bartlett, E. P. Hinds, William Ross, and Daniel W. Stubblefield, all of whom were city champions.

Tennis Club Development in Niagara Falls

The first tennis club in Niagara Falls was organized in May of 1892 as the City Tennis Club. The club started with a membership of sixteen and two or three courts.[1] In May of 1897 lawn tennis was in full swing at the Niagara Falls Club on Buffalo Avenue.[2]

In the 1898 season the Niagara Falls Club had defeated both the Buffalo Tennis Club and the Country Club. It was announced on May 29, 1899, that "a team of eight men, picked from both institutions, and representing all the best players in Buffalo, will play here in a final match tomorrow, Decoration Day."[3]

Without giving results, the June 1, 1899, issue of the *Gazette* reported "Tennis Match was a Tie. Each Team Won Six Events in the Game

Monday on the Buffalo Avenue Court." The party then adjourned to the Cataract House, where they enjoyed a good dinner. After dinner the party boarded Mr. Hope's tallyho "Niagara" and had a very pleasant drive. Today post-event activities would likely be a meal of salad, spaghetti, and beer at the local pub. A meeting was also held during which an International Tennis League was formed, consisting of clubs from Buffalo and Niagara Falls, New York, and St. Catharines and Merriton, Ontario.[4]

A match was arranged for June 17, 1899, in the International Tennis League between the Buffalo Tennis Club and the Niagara Falls Tennis Club on the latter's home courts. As reported on June 19, 1899, the Niagara Falls team easily defeated the Buffalo players. "The Falls players won all three of the doubles and each club won three singles."[5] Both teams dined at the International Hotel afterward; this was still a game for the affluent.

In August of 1900, the Niagara Falls Club was victorious over the Twin City Tennis Club of Tonawanda in an International Tennis League match. "Porter and McLaughlin have not been beaten in doubles this year. They recently won the open doubles at the Buffalo Tournament from Bissell and Lewis," the *Gazette* reported.[6]

On June 17, 1900, the Niagara Falls Country Club (NFCC) opened a clubhouse on Pine Avenue and Packard Road not far from what is now occupied by the Niacet Corporation. On April 22, 1901, it was announced that the "Niagara Falls Country Club has taken in the Niagara Falls Tennis Club and the Tennis Club has turned over all its effects." For "those wishing to become members the Country Club has reduced the initiation fee for one week to $10. It has been $15 and after May 1st it will be increased to $25."[7]

On May 10, 1901, the charter of the NFCC was accepted by the New York Secretary of State, formally establishing the founding date.[8] The nine-hole golf course, the city's first, was laid out in what is now Hyde Park, but it wasn't until 1906 that tennis courts were constructed.

At about that time the Echota Tennis Club, which claimed to be the oldest in the city, was organized near Buffalo Avenue and Sugar Street (now Hyde Park Boulevard). In 1909 the YMCA Tennis Club, not yet having their own courts, used the two courts of the Niagara Falls Power Company for a doubles tournament and that same year played a match against the Echota Tennis Club.

Also in 1909 the Riverside Tennis Club at Buffalo Avenue and Sixth Street held the first city championships on two grass courts while the

Francis Cup handicap tournament for club members competed for a trophy donated by Mr. Henry A. Francis in 1908. L. E. Saunders won the 1908 Francis Cup, and Edwin R. Bartlett won the 1909 city title. In 1912 the Riverside Tennis Club changed its name to the Niagara Falls Tennis Club and moved to Buffalo Avenue between Third and Fourth Streets, where it had two clay courts. In 1916 the Niagara Falls Tennis Club had two clay courts at Jefferson Avenue and Quay Street. Lin Murray carefully chose his residence at 211 Fifth Street, off Jefferson, about two blocks from the courts.

The NFCC was growing faster than the clubhouse and grounds could accommodate; so on October 15, 1914, the new home of the NFCC was opened west of its former location and just east of St. Joseph Cemetery at what is now 3920 Pine Avenue. The colonial clubhouse, which still stands today, was some distance north of the boulevard. On the first floor there was a large assembly room, which was also used as a dining room or ballroom. A dining porch afforded accommodations for at least a dozen, and another large porch on the east faced the golf links. A large bowling green was also to the east, and four tennis courts were to the south.[9]

One day in the summer of 1916 two prominent members of the NFCC, Paul Schoellkopf and Frank A. Dudley, a local attorney, were playing on the club course near Pine Avenue. Schoellkopf observed that the course was not very challenging. Dudley agreed, and a few days later an option had been taken on the Evans's Estate land in Lewiston Heights. Schoellkopf, Dudley, and Alfred W. Gray, one of Dudley's law partners, formed the Lewiston Heights Company. On May 10, 1919, the new home of the NFCC formally opened its doors. Two tennis courts were constructed between the clubhouse and Lewiston Road.

Under the headline "Tennis Revival," the *Gazette* noted on August 16, 1916:

> This has been a great year for devotees of tennis. Some of the most sensational matches witnessed here in years have been played on the courts of the University Club during the past two weeks. The racket handlers have banded together and erected excellent courts in every section of the city. Nurses at the Memorial Hospital may be seen daily, flitting about the courts of the institution, where they derive their chief recreation. No less than ten sets of

> courts have been laid out this summer, a fact which proves that the game is rapidly developing in this locality.

The January 2, 1922, issue of the *New York Times* included a listing of the Western New York men's singles rankings, which gave one the flavor of Niagara Frontier tennis:

1. R. Lindley Murray, Niagara Falls
2. Jack Castle, Buffalo
3. John Gowans, Buffalo
4. Eric Hedstrom, Buffalo
5. Dunbar Hausauer, Buffalo
6. Charles Pooley, Buffalo
7. Walter Misner, Buffalo
8. Charles Whiting, Buffalo
9. Myron Watrous, Niagara Falls
10. James Gheen, Niagara Falls[10]

In the first annual Country Club tennis tournament played September 2–4, 1922, "E. R. Bartlett won the men's singles title, by trimming an old time opponent, Bill Ross, in a grueling three set match, 2–6, 6–3, 7–5." In an exhibition handicap match after the men's finals, R. Lindley Murray defeated Edwin Bartlett, 6–2, 7–7.[11] The Echota Tennis Club began an inter-club rivalry with the South Avenue Club in 1923.

The new tennis court of the International Institute at Portage Road and Welch Avenue, which was made possible by a group of East Side businessmen as the first step in providing recreational facilities for that locality, was formally opened on Tuesday, June 18, 1929, with an exciting tennis match in which Martin Tressel and Charles Brackett defeated Ned Stafford and Harry Keating, 6–3, 6–8, 6–4.[12]

Hyde Park was formally dedicated that same year on Saturday, September 7. The dedication included an inter-city tennis match between Buffalo and Niagara Falls stars on one of its ten asphalt courts. Representing Buffalo were Leo Kronman and Lou Schaefer. The pair defeated Eddie D'Anna and Herb Peck, 6–4, and Tressel and Stafford, 6–3, 6–4.[13] (Tressel had beaten Peck in three sets for the city championship that same afternoon.)

In 1930 the Niagara Falls Tennis Club relocated to Pine Avenue east of Hyde Park to the site of the NFCC and was officially opened with a round-robin on Saturday afternoon, June 28. The colonial clubhouse built by the NFCC in 1914 still stands today behind the Holy Cross Orthodox Monastery at 3920 Pine Avenue just east of St. Joseph Cemetery. The six new clay courts were installed by the M. R. Lane Corporation of Philadelphia, which also engineered the Forest Hills and Merion Cricket Club courts. The clubhouse presented an excellent and convenient background for the players, and the membership was about one hundred forty.[14]

On August 4, 1932, four new tennis courts opened in Hyde Park, making a total of fourteen. On May 24, 1941, the six new clay tennis courts that had recently opened to the public in Hyde Park were officially dedicated. Bob Niehousen (1937 Big Ten singles champion and 1936 finalist from Ohio State) and Gordie Robinson (former University of North Carolina tennis star and 1939 Canadian Davis Cup player) squared off against Cliff Marsh (former eastern intercollegiate finalist and more recently one of the ranking players in Buffalo) and Perry Bliss (the stylist from Chicago). R. Lindley Murray, Niagara Falls's contribution to big-time tennis, who captured the national singles title in 1917 and 1918, refereed this match.[15]

The new Hyde Park clay courts, the eligibility of municipal city singles and doubles winners to compete in the National Public Parks championships, the loss of young men and women to World War II, and possibly other factors led to the financial failure of the Niagara Falls Tennis Club. It became the Juniaga Tennis Club when the Niagara Falls Power Company bought its 1.74 acres in 1943, but there were no reports of any activity there. The Holy Cross Orthodox Monastery purchased the property from the Power Authority in 1970.

Niagara Falls City Championships

The first city tennis tournaments started in 1909 at what was then the Riverside Tennis Club at the corner of Buffalo Avenue and Sixth Street "open to all gentlemen players residing in Niagara Falls," suggesting that tennis was still a sport for the affluent. Women weren't recorded as playing locally until 1916, when "[n]urses at the Memorial Hospital [could] be seen daily, flitting about the courts of the institution." The exception was at the locally prestigious International Lawn Tennis Open tournament at Niagara-on-the-Lake, held in late August, which in 1909 was in its twenty-third year. That tourney attracted the best men and women players in the

United States and Canada. The other major regional championship was the Great Lakes tournament held at the Park Club in Buffalo in July.

The Riverside Tennis Club had two grass courts and in 1912 moved down the street to Buffalo Avenue between Third and Fourth Streets and became the Niagara Falls Tennis Club with two clay courts. Charlie Brackett played in the first championship, and although he never won the title, he was still playing Industrial League tennis in 1940. In the twenty-first city championships in 1929, Brackett made a respectable showing in the semifinals against Martin Tressel, losing by 6–2, 6–3, 6–4.

The top players from 1909 to 1915 were Edwin Bartlett of Hooker Electrochemical, E. Percival Hinds, the Irishman William Ross, and Daniel W. Stubblefield, a Southerner noted for his twist service and lobbing. Bartlett was vice president of the Niagara Tennis League in which various Western New York clubs competed.

In addition to the city championships in 1915, an open tourney was held and won by T. W. Hendrick of Buffalo who was a native Californian. He had been runner-up in the Great Lakes tourney and was 1913 Buffalo champion. Since two Buffalo teams competed in the doubles final, Niagara Falls didn't again incorporate an open tournament until 1939.

Also in 1915 the tourney was held on the four clay courts of the Niagara Falls Country Club, which was then at "the Boulevard east of Sugar Street," or east of Hyde Park and St. Joseph Cemetery. The Niagara Falls Tennis Club would later relocate there in 1930, but the club was probably constructing the two clay courts on Quay Street that would be used between 1916 and 1929.

In 1916 R. Lindley Murray, 1916 national indoor titleholder, came to Niagara Falls on September 5 as a chemical engineer for Hooker. He had previously worked for the Pacific Coast Borax Company in Bayonne, New Jersey, but was recruited by tennis enthusiast extraordinaire Elon Hooker, president of the firm. Despite the fact that the September 20, 1916, issue of the *Gazette* said that Hinds, Ross, Ritter, "Red" Meyers, Bartlett, and others, were capable of giving the champion a hard battle in the eighth annual city championship, Murray pulverized C. L. Follmer in the finals of the tourney, 6–0, 6–1, 6–0.

In 1924 Martin Tressel came to town as an engineer with the Aluminum Company of America, formerly the Pittsburgh Reduction Company, which sat on top of the gorge downstream of the falls. Tressel had graduated from Massachusetts Tech (MIT) in 1924 where, as captain of the tennis team, he had captured the New England intercollegiate doubles title and dominated city tennis from 1924 through 1930, except in 1927 when he didn't enter the event.

In 1925 Tressel paired with Vinton Vernon from Cleveland, second only to Kirk Reid, Ohio State champion, to win the city doubles against R. L. Murray and A. M. Hamann of Niagara Electrochemical Corporation. The singles final between Tressel and Vernon was probably the best competitive tennis the city had seen except perhaps for the many exhibition matches Murray had played on the Quay Street courts and at the Niagara Falls Country Club in Lewiston Heights between 1917 and 1926 against the best American and international stars. Tressel would later become USTA president from 1965 to 1966.

That year the entry list was so great that some of the preliminary matches were played at the Echota Club and the South Avenue Club courts. The following year an association of tennis clubs was formed to run off the various tournaments.

In 1927 the "Four Horsemen" of Niagara Falls—Herb Peck, Eddie D'Anna, Harry Keating, and Ned Stafford—first appeared in the city tourney. Harry Keating defeated Herb Peck in the singles final, while Keating and Frank Williamson, Keating's high school doubles partner, won the doubles. Eddie D'Anna was a doubles finalist in 1929, and Ned Stafford and Harry Keating won the doubles event in 1930, the first of the pair's four consecutive doubles titles. D'Anna won the New York State interscholastic singles title in 1926, while Stafford and Keating won the New York State interscholastic doubles title in 1929. Herb Peck, originally from Wisconsin, was about four and a half years older than Stafford and probably attended high school in Buffalo as he was a protégé of Jack Castle.

The Morrill Cup, which was simply the Niagara Falls Tennis Club's play for men's tennis supremacy, began in 1929. Prior to the Morrill Cup was the H. A. Francis Cup, a handicap tourney for club members that began in 1908, which became the Minor Cup after 1927.

In 1930 additional diversity was thrown into the mix with junior boys' and girls' tourneys and a women's singles event. In 1931 mixed doubles made its first entry.

In 1932 the Department of Recreation, in conjunction with the Niagara Falls Tennis Club, held a men's and women's tourney at Hyde Park, which had opened in 1929 with ten asphalt courts. The winner of each category was given a free membership to the tennis club. The city championships began opening up the geographical boundaries to Southern Ontario, as well as to Lewiston and Youngstown.

In 1931 Martin Tressel left the area when the Aluminum Company of America plant closed; he relocated to their headquarters in Pittsburgh. When he returned to the city in 1936 as assistant superintendent of the reopened Aluminum Company of America, he found that the local players had improved considerably. Ned Stafford beat him easily in the Morrill Cup semifinals while Bob Baker defeated him in the city quarterfinals.

In 1933 another young man from across the river, Gordon Robinson, province of Ontario junior champion, began to make his presence felt. In 1934 he overwhelmed Henley Sklarsky, 1933 city champion, in the Morrill Cup final, winning by a score of 6–2, 6–0, 6–2. Robinson teamed with Sklarsky to win the city doubles title that year and in 1935 the singles and doubles event, again with Sklarsky.

In 1937 the city championships became open to just about anyone who was willing to make the trip. Buffalo, the Tonawandas, and Southern Ontario sent their best. Despite the strong outside competition, Ned Stafford had become a serious force and won the title three straight years, from 1937 to 1939, while Herb Peck at age thirty-five won the title in 1940.

The city tennis tournament of 1938 became the City Open tennis tournament in 1939, the City Muny tennis tournament in 1940, and the Cataract City Open or the "tournament of champions" in 1941. Starting in 1940 all tournaments were contested at Hyde Park, the six new clay courts being officially opened on May 24, 1941. The 1941 tourney included such outside stars as Jerry Goldsman, Norm Millard, Chet Fyderek, Lloyd Tack, Gus Franczyk, and Fred Wurster. Gordon Robinson of Stamford, Ontario, who in 1939 ranked fifth in Canada and was a Canadian Davis Cup player, blew off Jerry Goldsman of Buffalo, 6–2, 6–1 in the final.

With the construction of these six new clay courts, coupled with the official U.S. entry into World War II after Pearl Harbor, the Niagara Falls Tennis Club ran into financial difficulties and became the Juniaga Tennis Club in 1943 with no further reports of any activity there. What had been the Niagara Falls Tennis Club just east of Hyde Park became the Niagara Falls Municipal Tennis Club at Hyde Park, and George Rushton in 1941 was responsible for several tournaments there. The winners of the Muny singles and doubles events were also eligible to compete in the annual National Public Parks championships.

After 1941 the open tournaments were abandoned until 1946, although club and city championships were held. The 1946 Buffalonians included

Irv Brent, Bill Duke, Norm Millard, Roger Taylor, Gus Franczyk, Bob Kamprath, Chet Fyderek, and Bob Mack. In the semifinals, former top-ranked Niagara Falls High and Niagara University player George Rushton ousted Roger Taylor in a brilliant five-set semifinal match. After losing the first two sets and being down 5–4 and 40–30 in the fifth, Rushton staged a comeback to win. He followed this up with another fifth set comeback against Stafford in the finals down double match point. Gus Franczyk and Chet Fyderek of Buffalo won the doubles title.

In 1947 Ned Stafford, now aged thirty-eight, defeated Irv Brent in the singles final in straight sets. In 1948 Ed Lindsay of Buffalo won the singles title over George Rushton, while Bob Baker and Rushton copped first place in doubles over Stafford and Robinson. Two Buffalo players reached the singles final in 1949. Irv Brent defeated Ed Lindsay. In 1950 Baker defeated Stafford in the singles while Baker and Rushton won their fourth straight doubles title, this time over Jack Castle and Norm Millard. Jack Castle was a perennial Buffalo champion since moving there in 1919, and despite being in his fifty-fourth year, he and Cliff Marsh were legendary Queen City stars. Both Castle and Marsh were nationally ranked.

There was a great camaraderie, sense of fairness, and competitive spirit among these players, as demonstrated, for example, in the 1936 doubles final. Henley Sklarsky and Martin Tressel defeated Herb Peck and Eddie D'Anna, 6–4, 6–1, 6–2. However, prior to the staging of this match, in a gesture of good sportsmanship, all four finalists agreed that the winning team should play Ned Stafford and Harry Keating in a title match. They were forced to withdraw from play and defaulted by the tournament committee on a technicality. Sklarsky and Tressel put their newly won title at stake, and Stafford and Keating defeated them, 6–1, 6–4, 2–6, 6–1.

Another example came during the quarterfinals of the 1937 men's doubles club championship. Irv Dooher and Bernie Staneslow had split sets with Peck and D'Anna, 8–6, 6–8, when darkness set in and they decided to replay the entire match the following evening, August 20. They demonstrated that their match was no fluke by holding the seeded stars even again at 6–0, 6–8, 8–8, before darkness again halted the struggle just as it had the previous evening. In order to decide the match, a coin was flipped in the locker room. And as if fate were hinting that the match was a draw in all respects, the coin landed in a crack on the floor, and the match was still a draw. Herb Peck called heads on the next flip which landed heads up on the edge of a bench, only to slide off and turn tails up on the floor, giving the match to underdogs Dooher and Staneslow. Despite the coin toss D'Anna and Peck played Dooher and Staneslow a third time, the former winning 6–2, 6–2 to reach the semifinals.

The 1943 city championship final match between Ned Stafford and Herb Peck started out with Ned playing almost errorless tennis. He took the first set 6–2 and piled up a commanding 4–1 lead in the second before Peck sharpened up his shots and began to dust the lines for five games in a row and set. The third set saw Peck continue to angle and place his steady chops and drives, keeping Stafford continually on the defensive until Peck had the third set at 6–2 and a 2–1 lead in sets.

After the intermission Stafford jumped to an early lead, but Peck came back to even the count and go ahead 5–3. Winning either of the next two games would have given Peck the match, but Stafford evened up the score at 5–5. At that point both players were showing unmistakable signs of weariness, but Peck went out in front again at 6–5. Stafford staved off defeat by capitalizing on his severe service, and tied it up again at 6–6. Again Peck took the odd game, and again Stafford tied it up until the score stood at 9–9.

Both players seemed very tired, but Stafford seemed to have a little more in reserve. Summoning what little energy he had left, Stafford managed to take the next two games and the set at 11–9. At the start of the fifth set, Peck advanced to the referee's stand and said he was too exhausted to continue. Stafford attempted to persuade Peck to rest for a time and then continue—but to no avail. The match was awarded to Stafford after the two veterans had played at a strenuous clip for well over three hours. Stafford won by 6–2, 4–6, 2–6, 11–9, default.

The population of Buffalo, notwithstanding the suburbs of Kenmore and the Tonawandas, etc., as opposed to Niagara Falls, is given in the following table in thousands. The number in parentheses is the U.S. population urban ranking. Between 1900 and 1930 the population of Niagara Falls increased by a factor of almost four.

Year	Buffalo	Niagara Falls
1900	352 (8)	19
1910	424 (10)	30
1920	507 (11)	51
1930	573 (13)	75
1940	576 (14)	78
1950	580 (15)	91

It is noteworthy that Niagara Falls could be competitive with the Buffalo players for most of these five decades despite a population difference ranging from 19:1 to 6:1. Niagara Falls had developed a tennis contingent that could compete with the best regional players for over two decades, but it consisted always of the same players—Martin Tressel, Harry Keating, Herb Peck, Ned Stafford, Henley Sklarsky, Gordon Robinson, Eddie D'Anna, Bob Baker, and George Rushton. Despite their attempts, it must be said (with no disrespect) that the next generation of players didn't develop to the same extent. By 1946 Ned Stafford and others had relocated to the Badminton and Tennis Club in Niagara Falls, Ontario, a thriving organization. As voiced by sportswriter Mike Quinlan on September 20, 1946, "local devotees are anxious to restore the game to all its former popularity and the veterans, who still are winning tournaments, are striving mightily to interest the growing youngsters in the game."

Harry Keating, an excellent badminton player who, along with Bobby Williams, twenty-three-year-old Niagara Falls Country Club star, was rated the second U.S. doubles team by the National Badminton Association. Ned was the only one of the group to keep his game at a high level all his life. In fact, Ned kept getting better with age, relatively speaking, winning the Canadian lawn tennis 45s and the U.S. lawn tennis doubles 70s with Joseph Lipshutz.

Niagara Falls Industrial Tennis League

A central industrial athletic association meeting took place in the Niagara Falls YMCA on April 3, 1919, as representatives of fifteen industrial plants assembled for a conference under the guidance of Industrial Director Peake. Athletic leaders were enthusiastic about "obtaining a field of operations for their teams under the supervision of a central body, of fostering a more cooperative spirit and amicably settling minor difficulties among teams and of enlarging the scope of industrial athletics." The article continued, "Following the organization of the association tonight, officers will be elected and committees appointed." One of the possible officers mentioned was R. Lindley Murray.[1]

Sports were huge in Niagara Falls and on the Niagara Frontier in 1919. Industrial sports included baseball, basketball, bowling, soccer, and volleyball. Baseball alone was the biggest draw with a twilight industrial league, junior city league, high school league (which included the Collegiate Institute in Ontario), inter-city and inter-club (semi-pro), and factory league (semi-pro). Union Carbide had an inter-department baseball league. The girls had club and industrial basketball. Inter-city basketball was played at the Main Street Armory court. There was an inter-city bowling league, and Hooker won the 1919 Industrial Bowling League championship. The Niagara Falls Wanderers was one of the Frontier League soccer teams, and Bethlehem Steel's soccer team from Buffalo won the national championship. Boxing was also on the menu, and the Arena A. C. Boxing Club staged bouts at the Queen Street Arena in Niagara Falls, Ontario.

Burr H. Ritter of Hooker Electrochemical wrote a letter, dated June 5, 1919, to Niagara Falls City Chairman W. E. Mack outlining the tennis league's formation. On June 9 all plants were contacted, and by Saturday, June 14, the very first Industrial Tennis League doubles matches were played, formally opening the newly constructed "Y" courts, a fact colorfully disclosed on June 13: "Garbed in white 32 players, representing sixteen of the city's largest industries will move about on attractive courts throughout the city in the first competitive doubles matches."[2]

The time was ripe for taking tennis, a sport that started in the late nineteenth century at country clubs for the affluent and well-positioned, out of the dark ages and making it a sport for the public parks players locally. World War I had just ended and more than two million soldiers came home. Getting the plants involved in tennis in no small measure accelerated the popularity of the sport in Niagara Falls and vicinity and also led to several outgrowths—the Church Tennis League in 1919, the Girls' Industrial Tennis League in 1920, to which R. Lindley Murray gave a short talk, and the local inter-club competition in 1923.

Tennis had been well organized in Niagara Falls since before 1909 when the first city championships were held at the Riverside Tennis Club, which subsequently became the Niagara Falls Tennis Club. At that time there were at least two other clubs in the city—the Echota Tennis Club, the Niagara Falls Country Club, and possibly the South Avenue Tennis Club, Echota claiming to be the oldest. The *Gazette* reported on June 7, 1919: "Six courts, constructed under the supervision of the local 'Y' on the city hall site at Main Street and Cedar Avenue will be ready by the end of next week and will likely be used by the new league. Several plants may also be used." The plants having at least one tennis court were Union Carbide, Shredded Wheat, Power House (two courts), National Carbon, Graphite (two), Mathieson, and possibly others. Also "[t]here are about five (5) sets of courts in the city which would be available for playing purposes"[3]—the "Y" courts, the Twelfth Street court, the Portage Road and Ferry Avenue court, the DeVeaux Academy courts (probably three), and the Seventh Street court.

The Industrial League plans were ambitious at first. In 1919 matches were played on Wednesdays and Saturdays on a variety of courts in a round-robin format. In addition to the doubles round-robin, there was a doubles elimination which determined supremacy as well as a singles tourney. The doubles elimination passed out of the records after 1923 when it was won by R. L. Murray and A. L. Watson of Hooker and the last singles final was recorded in 1920, the league's second year. In the first doubles elimination Norman Duffett and Charles Brackett of Union Carbide won, and Brackett won the singles event. Charles Brackett played in the first city championships in 1909 and was pulled out of retirement to play in the Industrial League competition in 1940.

On August 22, 1919, the *Gazette* disclosed that league members had applied for admission into the National Lawn Tennis Association, and several tennis enthusiasts had asked Lindley Murray about how the league was progressing when he was last in New York City.

By 1920 Hooker had one or two courts, and in 1921 National Graphite was constructing two courts, providing a total of twelve for league play. In 1922 the Niagara Falls Tennis Club offered its courts, and in 1923 Spirella had one and Carborundum, two.

In 1924 the Niagara Falls, Echota, and South Avenue clubs offered their courts for league play. Additional courts included U.S. Light and Heat, Carborundum (Eleventh and Walnut), Niagara Wall Paper (Third and Pine), Spirella, Union Carbide, Norton Company (Chippawa, Ontario), Power Company, Hooker (Union Street), Kimberly Clark (Wisconsin Club), American Cyanamid (Niagara Falls, Ontario), and Graphite (Portage Road).

In 1922 two divisions were established with the winners of each playing for the title, but these divisions were discontinued the following and subsequent years. A new ruling permitted smaller plants to combine that year. The R. Lindley Murray trophy, first mentioned in 1922, was probably offered to the doubles tournament winner, either round-robin or elimination, from the beginning. The cup had to be won three times to ensure permanent possession at which time it was replaced by a new one.

In 1923 the R. Lindley Murray trophy was presented to the first-place team, and permanent trophies were also given for the first two places. That year winners Murray and Watson each received a twelve-dollar racket while runners-up Foster and Sayford were given a fifteen-dollar gift certificate to Rae's Sporting Goods store in Niagara Falls.

In 1929 the league was given permission to use two courts at the newly constructed Hyde Park complex on Tuesdays and Fridays for completion of the schedule. In 1927 Aluminum-Magnesium retired the R. Lindley Murray Cup, and in 1929, prizes were awarded to the first three places. There was also a consolation prize of five dollars awarded to the last-place team. As announced on June 4, 1929, the player rule was interpreted as meaning that no combination of the same two players could participate in more than 50 percent of the games played and that no one player could participate in more than 75 percent of the games played.

The R. Lindley Murray Cup.

In 1930, matches were played Tuesdays and Fridays on a variety of courts—Hyde Park, Echota, Hooker, etc.—as well as at the newly constructed Niagara Falls Tennis Club with six clay courts at 4000 Pine Avenue just east of Hyde Park.

In 1933 a colorful array of fourteen entries representing professional, fraternal, retail sales, manufacturing, and other industrial units were eligible for Industrial Tennis League play. Seven matches were scheduled for each Tuesday and Friday evening with play held on two Carborundum courts, two at the Echota Tennis Club, one at Hyde Park, and two on the Hooker court, the first match at 5:30 p.m. and the second at 6:30. The play was so hotly contested for first place that five teams were entered into a round-robin playoff. YMCA came in first, but three teams were tied with two wins and two defeats each, requiring another playoff.

In 1935 Lindley Murray recruited Dr. Eugene McCauliff from Yonkers, New York, ranked seventeenth nationally, to play for Hooker, giving them an undefeated season.

In 1937 the Industrial Tennis League used the Hyde Park courts exclusively with play on Tuesday and Thursday evenings as it still does to this day. That year the R&H DuPont team won the R. Lindley Murray trophy for the third time thereby securing permanent possession. The cup was not subsequently mentioned. The next three years, from 1938 to 1940, Niacet won the league championship and was awarded permanent possession of the Francis Optical cup.

In 1938 Niacet defeated Carborundum in the playoff for first place. Unfortunately that was the closest the company would get to winning the league during the period from 1919 to 1952, even though Carborundum was represented every year. That was also the year Frank Bauer first played for Carbo, with whom I practiced in 1966 and many years thereafter. Other familiar names from the 1960s and 1970s were Russ Previte (Oldbury), Les Nassoiy (Kimberly), and Joe Granieri (Hooker), who made their Industrial League debuts in 1935, '42, and '45, respectively.

In 1939, Hyde Park courts numbers five through ten were used at 6:15 p.m., and the singles championship was given its proper due and recorded for the most part round by round through 1952. Bob Baker defeated Herb Peck in that inaugural reactivation in a four-set final. The Niagara Falls Industrial Tennis League continued unabated, even to the present day, playing Tuesdays and Thursdays on courts numbers one through six for the most part at 6:15 p.m.

The Women's Industrial Tennis League first became prominent in 1940, the Carbo girls winning it. It was dormant in 1941 and revived between 1942 and 1949. The women played primarily on Monday evenings at Hyde Park. The outstanding team in 1942 was R&H Electrochemical, with such luminaries as Rita Jane Niger, Lorraine Puto, Dagfried Holm-Hansen, Muriel Pitman, and Lena Lavery, while Carborundum won again in 1948–49 with the Paluck sisters—Irene, Sophie, and Victoria.

Season-ending banquets were the rule from 1941 on, although they may not have been advertised earlier. Lindley Murray was guest speaker in

1945; Jack Castle, noted Buffalo tennis champion from 1919 to 1926, in 1947; and Norman (Norm) Millard, veteran tennis player and Kensington High School coach, in 1950. Millard lauded the Hyde Park courts and had high praise for the fine brand of tennis played there. One seasoned veteran, while finding no fault with the past and modestly refraining from mentioning the present, did look with alarm to the future: "The veterans still are winning every year in local tournaments." There were no promising youngsters coming on.

It was the end of an era. The same players had been winning since 1924: Martin Tressel, Harry Keating, Henley Sklarsky, Ned Stafford, Gordon Robinson, Eddie D'Anna, Herb Peck, Bob Baker, and George Rushton.

16
Lin Murray, the Industrialist

Although his last U.S. Championship was in 1919, Lin Murray played mostly local exhibitions and tournaments and relegated what little leisure time he had to golf. He generally shot in the low eighties and, with a handicap around twelve, won a few tournaments. His younger son Augustus "Tad" Murray, his paternal grandfather's namesake, was more inclined to pursue his father's interest in sports, particularly badminton and golf, while R. L. Murray Jr. pursued his paternal grandfather's passion for the classics and became a full professor and chairman of the Department of Classics at Colgate University.

The *Gazette* wrote of fifteen-year-old Tad, a sophomore at Niagara Falls High School: "[He] is a natural athlete and enjoys playing when the going is the toughest. During the winter months he devotes most of his time out of school to badminton, with the best in the district."[1]

On Saturday, June 12, 1937, the Niagara Falls High School golf team won the team and individual titles in the second annual invitation Western New York interscholastic golf tournament on the Hyde Park links. Among about seventy golfers, representing fourteen district high schools, Bob Kay and Tad Murray, both sophomores at the Falls school, tied for the individual title as each turned in brilliant rounds of seventy-three, just two over par.[2] Bob Kay was the son of Hyde Park professional Wendell Kay and ten years later would break the course record with a sixty-four.[3] In 1952, as a thirty-two-year-old pro in West Hartford, Connecticut, Kay won the Shair Line Open over such notables as National Open champion

Julius Boros and Jimmy Demaret with a six-under-par 101 for the twenty-seven-hole competition.[4]

A month later, Lin Murray and his son Tad captured first place in the father-and-son golf event at the Niagara Falls Country Club (NFCC) producing a round of seventy-seven with a handicap of eight, net sixty-nine. Murray Sr. drove off the odd numbered tees and Tad the even, and each played alternate shots.[5]

Later in the season, Dwane Tower Jr. and Tad Murray qualified for a thirty-six-hole final match in the annual junior golf tournament at the NFCC. In the semifinals Tower carded a seventy-one, while Murray scored a seventy-three.[6] The fifteen-year-old Tad Murray won the thirty-six-hole playoff, three up at the end of the morning round and clinched the match in the afternoon.[7]

In July of 1940 Lin Murray managed to tie for first-place honors in a NFCC golf tourney with a thirteen handicap,[8] while later in the season he carried off top honors in the golf competition again at the NFCC, as he won both the Saturday and Sunday sweepstakes in A class and then teamed with H. M. Hooker, R. E. Wilkin, and H. B. Young to tie for top prize in the best foursome competition.[9]

In September of 1945 Tad captured the regular NFCC Labor Day contest, which ran over three days, by playing very steadily for his three rounds with seventy-one, seventy-one, and seventy-five.[10]

Lin Murray's colleague and Industrial League tennis player, Edwin R. Bartlett, employed in 1907, chairman of the board of Hooker Electrochemical Company's Foreman's Association, as well as Burr H. Ritter, works chemist, employed 1913, and former Forman's Association president, retired from the association on October 1, 1950 under the company's retirement plan.[11] As chairman of the Committee on Industrial Tennis, Ritter got the Niagara Falls Industrial Tennis League going with a letter to the Industrial Athletic Council dated June 5, 1919.[12]

On January 17, 1951, Edwin Bartlett was elected to the office of chairman of the board of directors of Hooker, and Lin Murray, who had been serving as executive vice president, was elected to the office of president of the firm.

When Bartlett came to Hooker, then known as the Development and Funding Company, in 1907, his first job was that of timekeeper of the firm. "Since that time he had held a number of positions including purchasing agent, assistant superintendent, superintendent, and works manager. In 1924, Mr. Bartlett was made a vice president of the company and served in that capacity until 1941 when he was elected to the office of executive vice president. He became president in 1945."[13]

Murray became superintendent in 1921, chief engineer in 1932, director of development in 1937, vice president of development and research in 1941, and executive vice president in 1949. He "has been active in American Chemical society, American Institute of Chemical Engineering, Society of the Chemical Industry, Electrochemical society, and since 1943 has been a member of the panel of arbiters of the American Arbitration association."[14] Murray served "on the board of directors of several other companies" and in community affairs served on various committees of the Community Chest of Niagara Falls, YMCA, hospitals, and other fundraising drives. Many patents were issued in his name, and he was frequently called upon to speak before technical societies.[15-16] "He was special investigator for the Chemical Warfare Service for three years and in 1945, just before the end of World War II, he was sent to Germany by the U.S. Government to survey the facilities and processes of German plants which manufactured military chemicals."[17]

Lin Murray with his nephew and best fan, John Murray Huneke, around 1947 in Inglewood, California. A senior at Inglewood High School, John was chosen for Boys' State as a student leader representative and flown to Sacramento to learn about the state's government.
(Courtesy Chrissie Kremer)

As a result of his extensive writing on the chlorine and alkali industry, his work in this field won him the Schoellkopf Medal of the Western New York Section of the American Chemical Society (ACS) in May 1949.[18] (The Schoellkopf Medal is the oldest local section award in the nation and was named in honor of chemical industry entrepreneur Jacob F. Schoellkopf, founder of National Aniline Works. It is, in part, a testimony of achievement in chemical technology on the Niagara Frontier.) Frank J. Tone, president of the Carborundum Company in Niagara Falls and father of the actor Franchot Tone, was the first recipient of the medal, which was formally presented to him on September 2, 1931 for his work "on the production and commercial properties of silicon carbide [SiC], the production of pure metallic silicon, and the industrial application of electrochemistry."[19]

On February 4, 1953, Lin Murray was presented the second-highest award of the American Institute of Chemists (AIC)—that is, honorary membership—by the National Council of the American Institute of Chemists at a meeting of the Niagara Chapter at Hotel Niagara attended by seventy high-ranking chemists. Honorary membership is bestowed by the AIC on persons of distinction and accomplishment who, by their work, advance chemistry as a profession. The citation read:

> Outstanding leader in research and development in the chemical industry who was devoted to skillful and sympathetic human relations with his professional associates, particularly in the line of training and guidance of younger men who, with him, have made outstanding contributions to the chemical industry.

Murray was the forty-sixth recipient of the award since its inception in 1924. Honorary membership is second in esteem only to the gold medal, which is awarded "to a person who has exemplified the highest traits as a chemical scientist and an exemplary citizen."[20–21]

An outgrowth of the AIC is the American Institute of Chemists Foundation (AICF), which annually awards "outstanding seniors, post-baccalaureate and post-doctoral students majoring in chemistry, chemical engineering or biochemistry." The first such award was made in 1985.

The Murray brothers, Feg and Lindley, in Carmel, California, around 1953.
(Courtesy Chrissie Kremer)

It was on January 14, 1955, as the company's fiftieth anniversary dawned, that Lin Murray, as president of Hooker, tied together one of the Niagara Frontier's biggest industrial mergers of all time (which was consolidated with Hooker on April 29). Rated for some time as one of the fastest-growing chemical companies in the country, Hooker under Murray's leadership purchased the Durez Plastics and Chemicals Company of North Tonawanda in a merger deal worth over $50 million. Investors who stayed with Hooker did well for themselves. The merger not only was the biggest industrial marriage on the Niagara Frontier in many years, but it kept one of the largest area companies under local control. A modest investment of one thousand dollars in Hooker in 1935 was worth fifty-four thousand dollars, including dividend returns, twenty years later.[22] Murray, with high praise, attributed much of the success of the Durez merger to his number-one assistant, executive vice president Bjarne Klaussen, a native Norwegian who had been closely associated with Murray ever since the pair joined the company in 1916.[23]

Hooker Electrochemical has had a reputation for its liberal viewpoint toward management-labor relations. Murray's philosophy was to break down the dividing line between management and labor by the face-to-face communication of vital news alerts. Immediately following the meeting in which Durez directors agreed to merge Durez into Hooker, Murray rushed to a phone and asked his executive vice president to call a meeting of supervisors, department heads, and union executives so as to notify Hooker's employees before merger news reached the media. His efforts and those of his associates obviously paid off, as Hooker has never had a work stoppage—a pretty good record for a company with three big plants, nearly 2,400 employees, and fifty years of operation. Hooker and Murray were also famous for the attention given to building up a strong second team of young men trained to take over top responsibility in five to fifteen years.[24]

Murray, the sixty-two-year-old "friendly, tasteful, personable president of Hooker Electrochemical Co., which celebrates its 50th anniversary in Niagara Falls this year, has always attached more importance to people than statistics," reported Tom Hewitt, *Gazette* staff writer, on March 19, 1955. "More than anything else, Hooker owes its success to its 'loyal employees,'" said the chief executive. "Our employees have always taken an active interest in the company's growth and development," he said, and "have been willing to maintain costs at reasonable levels." The "white-haired but youthful appearing Hooker president has always played an important part in setting the company's buoyant, confident spirit" and "still seems to be as enthusiastic and immersed in his job as a young man just starting out on a career."[25]

Under Murray's leadership, rapid adjustments were possible through "mobility of management" and the "management development program." Since most of the top executives were all together on Buffalo Avenue, they could get together on a moment's notice to reach decisions that helped cut through the red tape that frequently slowed action in other corporations.

The management development program was designed to bring along younger executives by giving them a taste of handling greater responsibilities on a trial basis for a limited time and allowing them to sit in on top-management discussions and participate frequently at meetings of the board of directors. The program has given Hooker "management depth" with top officials in their middle and late thirties and early forties. Murray was conscious of Hooker's responsibility of insuring the future by making provisions in the present for capable leadership in later years.

Murray explained Hooker's success this way: Hooker's stock, which has appreciated more than fifty-three times in the twenty years since 1935, is "high because people want to buy it," Murray said simply. In recent years Hooker has "been willing to disclose helpful information to" security analysts "as long as it doesn't disclose information which hurts us competitively and is not in the best interest of our stockholders. Apparently, these people are recommending our stock," he continued. "They say they have confidence in our management, and they seem to like the way we do business," he added. "They're impressed with our labor relations."[26]

Murray would be the first to disclaim credit, but it is significant that Hooker started to grow after he took over the duties of chief engineer and director of research and development in 1932, emphasizing product diversification. Chlorine, caustic soda, and hydrogen, the original bread and butter products of the company, were used in developing new "processed" chemicals, thereby increasing the list to over one hundred chemicals sold principally as intermediates to firms that turn out consumer products.

Murray credited his three predecessors—Elon Hooker, the founder; Harry Hooker, Elon's brother, who became president in 1938; and Edwin Bartlett, who took the reins in 1945 and was chairman in 1955—who were all strong believers in building good human relations and extensive research as well as in good public and financial relations.[27]

Robert Lindley Murray, president of Hooker Electrochemical Co. in 1955, with the trophy he won at the Meadow Club invitation tournament in Southampton, Long Island, August 1914.
(*Buffalo Evening News Magazine*, March 19, 1955)

On June 22, 1955, Murray was elected chairman of the board, succeeding Edwin Bartlett who resigned as board chairman to become chairman of the company's newly created finance committee. Executive vice president Bjarne Klaussen was elected company president. Bartlett, who would continue as a member of the board, stated that there would be no change in the executive responsibilities. He said, "Mr. Murray will continue to be the company's chief executive officer," and explained "that the board of directors had requested both Mr. Murray and Mr. Klaussen to remain in the active service of the company for a period of two years beyond their normal retirement dates in 1957."[28]

Bjarne Klaussen rose through Hooker's ranks in a manner similar to that of Murray. Born in Kristiansand, Norway in 1891, he graduated from the University of Oslo as a chemical engineer in 1916. Klaussen came to Hooker that year as a research chemist, and except for the three-year period in which he was manager of technical sales service, most of his positions had been in the production side of the business. He became Niagara Falls works manager in 1941, a director in 1942, vice president in charge of production also in 1942, and executive vice president in 1951, when Murray became president.

His principle hobby, modern painting, has won Klaussen many prizes. Although he became an American citizen in 1926, Klaussen has been Royal Norwegian vice-consul for many years and was awarded the honorary decoration of the Knight's Cross, First Class, of the Royal Order of Saint Oslo, conferred by King Haakon of Norway in 1954.[29]

On October 6, 1955, the proposed consolidation of Hooker Electrochemical Company and Niagara Alkali Company was approved by the boards of the two Niagara Falls firms.[30] The thirty-four-million-dollar stock transaction joined the two chemical manufacturing concerns, which had been friendly neighbors and competitors on Buffalo Avenue for more than half a century. At the beginning of 1955 Hooker's net worth stood at approximately $40 million. Acquisition of Durez increased this 40 percent to $56 million, and the addition of Niagara Alkali's estimated $10 million net worth raised Hooker's net worth to approximately $66 million, making the company 65 percent bigger than it had been a year before.[31]

As chairman of the Hooker Electrochemical Company board, Murray received the 1956 Chemical Industry Medal of the American Section of the Society of the Chemical Industry in ceremonies at the Waldorf-Astoria Hotel in Manhattan, on April 27, before a gathering of more than six hundred leaders of the chemical industry. Among the more than forty persons from Niagara Falls and area were Mayor Calvin L. Keller and State Senator Earl W. Brydges, after whom the present Niagara Falls library is named. Brydges also played in the Industrial Tennis League. Mayor Keller presented to Lin Murray a key to the city of Niagara Falls in brief City Hall ceremonies on April 24.[32–33]

The medalist Lin Murray was introduced by Edwin Bartlett, and the chemical industry's most prestigious honor was presented by Dr. Clifford F. Rassweiler, vice chairman of the board of Johns-Manville Corporation. Presiding at the award meeting was Raymond Stevens, chairman of the American Section and president of Arthur D. Little, Inc., of Cambridge, Massachusetts. Lin Murray was the twenty-third recipient of the Chemical Industry Medal, first presented in 1933 and bestowed annually in recognition of "conspicuous service to applied chemistry" in America. Murray was "recognized for research, engineering, production and administration in the electrochemical industry and for his important contributions to the development of this industry."

In his acceptance address, "The Care and Feeding of a Growth Company," Lin Murray defined a growth company and likened management's position and responsibilities in a growth company to those of a conductor who leads a large and complex orchestra and must keep all the varied and intricate instruments in the symphony in "near-perfect balance and harmony."

At the podium Murray defined a growth company as "one which has grown at a faster rate than the average of all companies and gives every evidence of continuing to do so." Using Hooker as an example, he "said that whereas the Dow-Jones industrial average increased about 240 per cent in the last 20 years, Hooker stock increased nearly 6,000 per cent and sales rose from about 4½ million dollars to over 90 million dollars in the same period." Continuing, Murray indicated that

> growth begins ... with the day-by-day decisions that result in quality products, which are efficiently produced and fairly priced. To achieve these ends management is somewhat in the position of a conductor who leads a large, enormously complicated symphony. Among the instruments in the industrial orchestra are sales, engineering and production; research, accounting and purchasing; general development, legal work and patent work; and industrial relations, financial relations, and public relations. These, and many more must be meshed into one harmonious whole—although they often seem to play conflicting tunes. All these instruments must be kept in proper tune if the industrial orchestra is even to function. And a growth company even more—a near-perfect balance and harmony.
>
> Achieving this harmony is management's principle function. If it succeeds it does so by meeting decisively a deluge of day-in-and-day-out problems. It can meet these problems only by performing exceptionally well under what Lydia Strong, in an article in the Management Review, has called 'The Ordeal of Executive Decisions.' As Miss Strong pointed out, 'The first group Dante met in the Inferno were the wretched souls of those who could not make up their minds. They lived without blame and without praise. Heaven cast them out and hell would not

> receive them.' The management of a growth company may have its wretched souls, but not because they are indecisive. You may be certain they are earning a welcome either in heaven or in hell.[34]

The remainder of Murray's acceptance speech is included in the appendix.

As noted on January 7, 1956, in the *Gazette*: "For the sixth consecutive year Hooker Electrochemical Co. was certified as 'Excellently Managed' by the American Institute of Management."[35]

To broaden Hooker's basic product line, Hooker officials announced merger negotiations with another Niagara Falls plant in July of 1956, Oldbury Electrochemical Company, adjacent to Hooker's plant. Oldbury's principal products were phosphorus, phosphorus derivatives, chlorates and perchlorates, and oxalic acid, none of which were produced by Hooker. With Hooker common stock at forty-nine dollars, the value of the proposed merger was approximately $22 million.[36]

As early as January 21, 1956, plans for building a six- to eight-million-dollar research center on Grand Island, which splits the Niagara River just south and upriver of Niagara Falls, were reported. The multimillion dollar research center was welcomed by the Grand Island Planning Board as a tax boon for the rapidly growing town with an estimated population of six thousand and a total assessed valuation over $8 million.[37] The projected Hooker research center was the second major commercial development for the island. The first was a two-million-dollar shopping center on a fourteen-acre tract of land at the intersection of Baseline Road and Grand Island Boulevard (then Express Highway) to begin construction in the summer.[38–39]

At the Buffalo Launch Club on February 28, Donald Taylor, manager of general development for Hooker, and Dr. J. H. Bruun, research director, addressed the Grand Island Chamber of Commerce.[40] They said the contemplated research center would resemble a college campus devoted exclusively to research and excluding any manufacturing operations on a 130-acre tract of land between Long Road and Buckhorn Island State Park.[41] With no industrial zoning at that time, town officials prepared a special ordnance permitting the construction of research facilities and setting forth regulations governing their operation.[42]

After nearly three years the Hooker Chemical Corporation completed its new $3.8 million (well below the initial estimate) research center on Long Road, which was designed so that it could be more than doubled in size when required in the years ahead. Each of Hooker's laboratory groups moved to the facility on a predetermined schedule. Maintenance and storeroom personnel were the first to cross the North Grand Island Bridge, followed by Hooker's library valued at two hundred thousand dollars.[43]

By January 25, 1959, a number of researchers were already at work in their spacious laboratories including Dr. Emil Geering and Dr. Edward Elon, the former moving to a home on West River Parkway, within walking distance of the facility.[44]

The move was proceeding slightly ahead of schedule, according to officials, who estimated it would be completed the week of January 25. The new center on a sixty-one-acre site located between the New York State Thruway and the West River Parkway and adjacent to Buckhorn Island State Park provided space for two hundred research workers in a sixty-nine-thousand-square-foot building. The dedication and formal opening was planned for May when the weather would be more temperate and the landscaping well advanced.[45]

To R. Lindley Murray's surprise, the Hooker research center was dedicated to him on June 2, 1959, in ceremonies attended by R. Wolcott Hooker, senior vice president, Thomas E. Moffitt, president and chief executive officer, and Nelson A. Rockefeller, governor of New York State.[46]

Unveiling of the plaque dedicating the Hooker Chemical Corporation's research center to R. Lindley Murray. From the left are R. Wolcott Hooker, Gov. Nelson A. Rockefeller, Murray, and Thomas E. Moffitt.
(Gazette Photo)

The dedication was kept a secret from Murray and most of the audience members. At the last moment, Moffitt introduced Murray, and the two Hooker officials and Governor Rockefeller joined in unveiling a bronze plaque dedicating the center to Murray. The plaque reads:

Hooker Research Center
Dedicated in Honor of
Robert Lindley Murray
Board Chairman and Past President

In appreciation of his devoted service,
inspired vision, and untiring efforts
since 1916 for the enduring benefit of

Hooker Chemical Corporation
June 2, 1959

Rockefeller then spoke on the dependence of state economic growth on expanded research. He pointed out that "the Niagara Frontier is second only to metropolitan New York City in industrial importance" and that "our state has a vital stake in the future of this area. Research is a key to our future, the means through which we progress toward a better world, whether in industry, or science or education. Research is a continuing necessity for an expanding economy and for expanding job opportunity in New York State." The new center "shows what business can do to expand the state's research facilities."[47]

Lindley Murray retired from active participation in the company's management on December 15, 1959, but would retain the title of chairman until the next annual directors' meeting on March 9, 1960. At sixty-seven he had continued in active service two years beyond the company's normal retirement age at the request of the board after more than forty-three years of continuous service.[48]

Hall of Fame

The National Tennis Hall of Fame and Tennis Museum headed by James Van Alen, president, and William J. Clothier, chairman, announced on August 9, 1958 that Maud Barger-Wallach, Molla Bjurstedt-Mallory, William M. Johnston, and R. Lindley Murray, all U.S. singles champions, had been elected to the Tennis Hall of Fame. Mrs. Barger-Wallach had won the women's championship in 1908 and was runner-up in 1906 and 1909.[1]

The four inductees were selected on their playing records through the year 1919, although Molla and Bill's tennis careers continued well beyond and both became legendary. Bill Johnston died in 1946 at the age of fifty-one, and Mrs. Barger-Wallach died in 1954 at the age of eighty-three. Molla was on vacation in San Francisco, so Lin Murray, accompanied by his son Tad (and probably by Murray's other son, Robert Jr., and their wives) was the only inductee present at the enshrinement ceremonies on Saturday, August 16, the day of the semifinals of the annual Newport Casino invitation tournament.[2–3]

The tournament was strictly an Australian affair in which Mal Anderson defeated Ashley Cooper, 6–4, 7–5, 7–5, to retain the Casino Cup. Cooper and Neale Fraser beat the just-turned-twenty-year-old Rod Laver and Bob Mark for the doubles honors. In the semis, Anderson won from Alex Olmedo, while Cooper easily defeated Fraser, who was runner-up to Cooper at Wimbledon in four sets.[4]

Five years later Jimmy Van Alen invited Murray to attend the enshrinement ceremonies at Newport.[5] Following his wife Ramona's death in June 1951, Lin remarried in September 1952. He apparently had an affinity for older and elegant women, as he married Mrs. Gertrude Wright Porter. Born in Buffalo to Mr. and Mrs. A. J. Wright, she came to Niagara Falls in 1903 after graduating from the Rosemary Hall School for girls in Greenwich, Connecticut, as the wife of Augustus Granger Porter, one of Niagara Falls's most highly esteemed citizens.[6]

Mr. Porter, born June 23, 1878, in the Porter family's ancestral home at 117 Buffalo Avenue, was the great grandson of Judge Augustus Porter, the first white settler of Niagara Falls. He was educated at Niagara Falls public schools, DeVeaux, Nichols in Buffalo, King's School in Stamford, Connecticut, and Harvard University, from which he graduated in 1900. He was manager of the A. J. Wright & Company brokerage office, which became Goodbody & Company, with offices in the United Office building in Niagara Falls. Mr. Porter died August 3, 1950, at age seventy-four after leaving his duties at Goodbody only about two weeks before his death. He and his wife had two daughters and one son.[7]

In a handwritten letter from his home, which he called Murray Hill, Lin Murray wrote to Jimmy Van Alen that he could not attend the 1963 enshrinement ceremony, as his wife had just returned from the hospital after breaking her hip and to "please give my best to some of my old tennis friends particularly and especially to Mike Myrick."[8]

Lindley Murray's wife died April 1, 1965, in Memorial Hospital at age seventy-nine. She had been in ill health with Parkinson's disease for some time and was buried in Oakwood Cemetery.[9] A year later Tad and his wife moved in with his father. That year, 1966, Van Alen again invited Lin Murray to the enshrinement ceremonies, ostensibly to work with Van Alen on the National Tennis Hall of Fame. Tad wrote back that his father was on a six-week freighter cruise in the South Pacific and would be in Hong Kong on August 20, the date of the event. Tad's footnote said: "Nice going with your scoring system—looks like it's here to stay now!"[10] Tad was referring to the 1965 sudden death tiebreak implemented for the first time at the 1970 U.S. Open. The death knell of the advantage set scoring system was the 1969 first round Wimbledon match when Pancho Gonzales beat Charlie Passarell, 22–24, 1–6, 16–14, 6–3, 11–9, in a contest which lasted more than five hours over two days.[11]

After Molla received her notice of induction, she replied on July 16 to Henry Heffernan, Tennis Hall of Fame secretary-treasurer, that she would be in San Francisco on vacation during the August 16 ceremony.[12] Subsequent to that reply Molla received an invitation to attend her formal induction and certificate of enshrinement presentation at the Park Avenue home of Julian S. Myrick, chairman of the National Tennis Hall of Fame and Tennis Museum. The great champion, so unflappable on a tennis court, was devastated that she might have to make an acceptance speech and wrote Heffernan on July 22 to ask Julian Myrick to "make a little speech for me" because "years and years ago he used to speak for me when I was tongue-tied in front of a lot of people."[13] She adamantly wrote nine days later that she couldn't attend a New York ceremony saying, "I told you I am shy and it is true a few years ago they dragged me in front of a microphone to congratulate Miss Connolly I sat and watched win, and completely forgot her name. So please let Mr. Myrick accept and give my thanks."[14]

Molla had a bit of a temper and disliked being pried by reporters. While awaiting her turn at the 1916 National Clay Court tournament at the Lakewood Club in Cleveland, Molla slipped quietly into the press stand with her ladylike supply of cigarettes and crocheting. While watching Willis Davis mow down Charles Garland, the wonder woman nonchalantly lit a cigarette and began her needlework. As an intrepid scribe queried about her smoking and breathing, Molla retorted:

> It's my affair if I choose to smoke. Other women smoke. Nothing is thought of it in Europe. But I do not wish to be interviewed. Neither will I pose for photographs on the courts. If the newspaper boys want pictures of me while in action I have no objection.
>
> I always hate to visit strange cities because I dislike meeting people who continually try to pry into my affairs. Am I different than other girls just because I play tennis?[15]

Regarding her defensive remarks quoted above, Robert (Bob) Kelleher, president of the USLTA from 1967 to 1968 and a ball boy during her era, once said, "She looked and acted tough when she was on the court hitting tennis balls. She walked around in a manner that said you'd better look out or she'd deck you. She was an indomitable scrambler and runner. She was a fighter."[16]

Apparently the November 20 ceremony went well, as William Clothier, 1956 Tennis Hall of Fame inductee and its first president, and Molla stayed on for dinner. The trustees attending the presentation were tennis players Hugh Kelleher, William Talbert, Watson Washburn, Clothier, and sportswriter Allison Danzig.[17] Molla died the following year while on a visit to the land of her birth, Norway, at age seventy-five.

Bill Johnston, one of the most durable champions who had as much fight as anyone and many times came off the court dripping with perspiration and weighing five to eight pounds below his usual 120 to 125 pounds, died of tuberculosis in 1946 at the early age of fifty-one. Bill was given a memorial dinner on January 30, 1959, at the Olympic Club in San Francisco. Julian S. Myrick, Chairman of the National Tennis Hall of Fame, made the enshrinement presentation. Part of what he said follows:

> When I received the letter from Mr. Moffet inviting me to be present at this memorial dinner in honor of the late William M. Johnston and his enshrinement into the National Tennis Hall of Fame, I decided to accept, especially since Irene [Bill's wife] and he wanted me here. I also wanted to pay tribute to other persons and events of California that have meant so much to the game of lawn tennis.
>
> I have known all the champions from the first, Dick Sears, on a first name basis. To me Bill Johnston is the ideal of a real champion, not only a great player but a fine character and sportsman. From the time he started out here as a junior in 1909 until he retired in 1927 he played the part of a champion.
>
> After having established his ability out here he was sent to represent you in 1913. I well remember being in Longwood that year when he electrified everyone by defeating William J. Clothier. From then on until 1927 he was ranked in the first ten.
>
> His record in our championships and Davis Cup play are second to none. I could bring back many memories but one I always remember is when he won his first championship in 1915. I was walking off the court with him and asked if he would like anything done. He said he would like a telegram sent to his mother and gave me her

> address. It was sent. Then he went to join the navy from my home in 1917.[18]

After discussing Irene's donation of Bill's trophies and mementos, his interest in the junior development program, and his Davis Cup record, Myrick then reflected on California tennis.

> We turn now to the great influence you have had out here since 1900. Under the leadership of Sumner Hardy and others, the boys developed by Dr. Marvin in Golden Gate Park—what an influence they and their successors have had upon the game, both in this country and the world.
>
> The first players from California were ranked in 1909—Maurice McLoughlin and Melville H. Long. From then on a steady procession coming on each year of both men and women. I wish I could name them all but they are all a part of this great record. Certainly McLoughlin and Johnston stand out as does Hazel Wightman, May Bundy, Mary Browne and Helen Wills Rourk. All one has to do is study the record of our championships, Davis Cup and Wightman Cup competitions to see what a great contribution California has made under the stimulating leadership of Sumner Hardy and the teaching of Dr. Marvin. We can all take pride in what they accomplished and honor their memory.

Epilogue

R. Lindley Murray, the first of five siblings, was born November 3, 1892, in San Francisco, California, to Augustus Taber Murray and Nellie Howland Gifford. Augustus graduated from Haverford College in 1885 and received his doctorate from Johns Hopkins University in 1890. In 1892 he joined Stanford's Department of Classics, where, except for two absences, he served for forty years. In 1928 he became President Herbert Hoover's religious advisor for five years. At Haverford, Augustus was tennis champion, fullback on the varsity eleven, and a member of the baseball team. He subsequently trained his eldest son, Lindley.

Lindley graduated from Stanford in 1913 with a degree in chemistry and Phi Beta Kappa honors and received a chemical engineering master's degree in 1914. Murray played on the varsity tennis team for four years, being captain in his junior and senior years; as a member of the track team, he held the Pacific Coast record for the half-mile in 1914 with a time of 1:57.2. He was a big-serving, six-foot-two, blond, left-handed, 155-pound tennis player. As 1913 Pacific Coast intercollegiate champion and one of the five best tennis players in California, Lin Murray went east after his graduation in 1914 with Stanford teammate Herbert Hahn. Murray disposed of the 1911 intercollegiate champion E. H. Whitney of Harvard and demolished the New England intercollegiate champion Fenimore Cady of Amherst.

Murray then made his Eastern tournament debut by winning a number of tournaments: (1) the Sleepy Hollow Invitation over Fred Alexander, Karl Behr, and W. Merrill Hall in the final, all on the same day; (2) the New England championships over F. W. Cole in the final and Alrick Man in the challenge round, in addition to the doubles with Herbert Hahn; (3) the Metropolitan championships over George Church in the semis and Fred Alexander in the final, 6–8, 7–5, 7–5, 2–6, 6–4; and (4) the Southampton Invitation over Watson Washburn, 6–2, 7–5, 6–4, Washburn having defeated U.S. no. 4 Bill Johnston in the quarters. Murray was a finalist in the New York State championships to Maurice McLoughlin, the 1912 and 1913 national titleholder. In the U.S. Championships at Newport, Murray lost to Karl Behr in the fourth round in five grueling sets, 3–6, 6–2, 7–5, 3–6, 8–6. At year's end Murray was ranked fourth nationally behind Maurice McLoughlin, Dick Williams, and Karl Behr.

In late 1915 Murray transferred from the Pacific Coast Borax Company in Oakland, California, to their Bayonne, New Jersey, works as a chemist and didn't compete in the nationals. He started the 1916 season off with a bang by capturing a trio of matches in his first day of play at the National Indoor tennis championships in the Seventh Regiment Armory. Murray scored an easy victory over Watson Washburn in the semis and then defeated Alrick Man in the singles final in straight sets, 6–2, 6–2, 9–7. Man eliminated Wylie Grant, five-time holder of the indoor title, in the other semifinal. In March, Molla Bjurstedt teamed with Murray at the Heights Casino in Brooklyn to win the mixed doubles event over Alberta Weber and Harry McNeil. Bypassing the Metropolitan tournament due to job commitments, Murray next played in the Nassau Country Club invitational where he won the singles final by defeating Dean Mathey, 6–2, 7–5, 10–8. In an exhibition tennis match July 22 at the Crescent Athletic Cub in Bay Ridge, Karl Behr and Lin Murray defeated the national doubles champions from Northern California, Bill Johnston and Clarence Griffin, 8–6, 6–1, 4–6, 3–6, 6–4.

Murray reached the final of the Seabright, New Jersey, invitational, where he lost to George Church of Tenafly, New Jersey. The former Princeton intercollegiate champion won 6–4, 6–2, 6–4. Two days later, on August 13, 1916, in the final round of the Crescent A. C. open tournament at Bay Ridge, Murray barely defeated Japanese champion, Ichiya Kumagae, 8–6, 6–4, 7–5.

In the National Championships, Murray defeated Karl Behr in the fourth round, 6–4, 6–3, 3–6, 9–7, and then eliminated George Church in the quarters after losing the first two sets, 3–6, 4–6, 6–2, 6–4, 6–4, avenging his loss at Seabright. Murray then played Bill Johnston of San Francisco, last year's winner, in the semis, losing 6–2, 6–3, 6–1. At year's end Murray was again ranked fourth, behind Dick Williams, Bill Johnston, and George Church.

In the 1917 Patriotic Great Lakes tournament in Buffalo, Murray teamed with Miss MacDonald to defeat Molla Bjurstedt and T. W. Hendrick, 4–6, 6–3, 8–6, in the mixed semis on Friday, but they only finished part of the third set because of darkness. Saturday afternoon Murray won the Great Lakes championship from Charles Garland, 9–7, 6–1, 6–4, followed by finishing the mixed semifinal and then defeating Miss Best and Garland on Saturday night in the mixed final on the indoor courts of the Buffalo Tennis and Squash Club, 6–2, 4–6, 10–8—all in a day's work.

Murray entered the Utica two-day round-robin tourney of ten of the leading players in July. He won three matches: Harold Throckmorton, 1–6, 6–3, 6–1; George Church, 7–5, 7–5; and Bill Johnston, 1915 national champion, 6–2, 4–6, 9–7. One week later Murray teamed with Mary Browne (Browne won the U.S. singles, doubles, and mixed doubles three consecutive years, from 1912 to 1914, and was runner-up to Molla Bjurstedt in the 1921 U.S. Championships) at the Field Club of Greenwich, Connecticut, to defeat Bjurstedt and Church, 14–12, 6–3.

Lin Murray caught the eye of Elon Hooker, president of Hooker Electrochemical Company in Niagara Falls, an influential USNLTA committee member, and a player of sorts, as both Hooker and Murray competed in the 1914 Southampton Invitation. When Hooker learned that his tennis-playing houseguest in a 1916 Greenwich, Connecticut, tournament was also a chemical engineer, he promptly offered him a job.

In September of 1916, Murray was working at Hooker Electrochemical as a research chemical engineer.

Working on explosives production during World War I, Murray had no intention of entering the 1917 U.S. Championships; billed as a "Patriotic" tournament, the event was a World War I substitute for the national championship to raise money for the Red Cross. His employer, Elon Hooker, talked Murray into entering, and he had an explosive tourney. In the third round Murray triumphed over the hard-hitting Bill Tilden of Philadelphia in a contest that was carried to four sets, 3–6, 6–4, 6–3, 6–3. In the quarters, he won a tough five-set match from Craig Biddle of Philadelphia, 4–6, 6–1, 6–4, 4–6, 6–2. Murray made his way to the final by defeating John Strachan of San Francisco, 4–6, 6–3, 6–3, 6–1, and became the "pretender" for the national singles crown when he defeated Nat Niles of Boston in the final round at the West Side Tennis Club at Forest Hills in a spectacular four-set match, 5–7, 8–6, 6–3, 6–3. His win at the nationals did not affect the rankings. If there was in any way a stigma attached, it was erased the following year.

Murray had resolved, two weeks before the 1918 U.S. Championships began, that he would not compete. After a five-day struggle with Hooker President Elon Hooker, who came to Niagara Falls expressly to get Lindley to break away for the tournament, he finally consented. Having played no tournament tennis all summer and with the Championships only eight days away, he trained assiduously. In a warm-up tournament at Southampton in August, Bill Tilden vanquished him in the semis, 6–3, 6–3. The *New York Times* said, "Murray was not 50 per cent as strong as he was two years ago, or even last year." He was a quick study, though, as in the doubles, with Pell as his partner, Lindley was beginning to find himself.

The thirty-seventh national singles championship began on the turf of the West Side Tennis Club on August 26. Murray was in the upper half of the draw, while Bill Tilden, who had yet to be defeated during the 1918 season, was in the lower half. Murray made his way through the third round with a decisive victory over Theodore Pell in straight sets, while Bill Tilden also won decisively over Conrad Doyle of Washington. In the fourth round Murray defeated Fred Alexander in a gloriously contested match of five sets, 6–8, 8–6, 6–0, 4–6, 6–0. In the quarterfinals Murray defeated the famous Boston baseliner, Nat Niles, in four sets, 7–5, 6–4, 2–6, 7–5.

The semifinal pairings were then set: Murray versus Voshell and Tilden versus Kumagae. Murray defeated Voshell in straight sets, 6–4, 6–3, 8–6, while Tilden smothered Kumagae, 6–2, 6–2, 6–0, setting the stage for the final between Murray and Tilden. Tuesday, the day of the final, was just about perfect: sunny but not warm, with an air stirring and the best light. There was the usual pleasant formality; the officials were in place when Murray and Tilden stepped from the clubhouse porch and walked over to the court in the center of the enclosure. Murray won the toss and elected to serve. The *New York Times* reported the following day that "Robert Lindley Murray of Niagara Falls, one of the finest sportsmen and most proficient racquet wielders who ever came forth from the Golden Gate, was crowned yesterday as the national singles tennis champion when he defeated William T. Tilden, 2d, of Philadelphia in the final round of the tournament at the West Side Tennis Club at Forest Hills, with the score 6–3, 6–1, 7–5." At year's end Murray was ranked first, followed by Tilden, Fred Alexander, Wallace Hall, Walter Hayes, and Nat Niles.

Although Murray played in the 1919 U.S. Championships, where he succumbed to the eventual champion, the indefatigable giant-killer Bill Johnston, in a bitterly contested four-set battle, 5–7, 6–1, 6–2, 6–4, he largely confined himself to exhibitions and local tourneys. Locally, Murray won the Great Lakes singles and mixed doubles titles in 1917, the singles and men's doubles titles in 1920 and 1922, and the men's doubles title in 1924, the year Bill Tilden won the singles event. Murray also won the New York State title in 1921 and the International singles event from 1921 to 1923, as well as the men's doubles event in 1920 and 1921.

On May 9, 1916, Lin Murray married Ramona McKendry from Stanford. The couple lived in a two-story home at 211 Fifth Street from 1916 to 1921, only two blocks from the Niagara Falls Tennis Club on Quay Street. While living in that house, Lin Murray and Ramona had two sons: Robert Lindley Murray Jr. and Augustus Taber Murray II, both of whom had outstanding careers outside tennis.

Murray the promoter, demonstrating his leadership skills and popularity, induced many top national and international players to come to Niagara Falls for exhibition matches. On Labor Day 1917, Murray, John Strachan, Fred Alexander, Harold Throckmorton, Mary Browne, and Molla Bjurstedt played singles, doubles, and mixed doubles matches on the Quay Street courts to raise money for the ambulance fund in France. From 1919 to 1926 Murray played singles and doubles exhibitions in Niagara Falls or at the Niagara Falls Country Club with Ichiya Kumagae, the transplanted Japanese champion, ranked as high as no. 3 nationally (1919); Kirk Reid, Ohio State champion; Charles Garland, 1920 Wimbledon doubles champion with Dick Williams; Australian Davis Cup player James Anderson; Bill Johnston; Bill Tilden; French champions Jean Borotra and Jacques Brugnon; Spanish champion Manuel Alonso; and many others. Buffalo champions Eric Hedstrom, Jack Castle, and Cliff Marsh also often participated.

Lin Murray was instrumental in organizing the Niagara Falls Industrial Tennis League in 1919. That first year sixteen teams competed, and the league hasn't missed a beat in ninety-two years. Murray was responsible for the growth of tennis in the city for the next three decades as advisor, promoter, referee, and speaker. The Quay Street courts were built under his direction, and in 1933 there were over thirteen thousand registered players on the city courts in a city having a population of about seventy-five thousand. Murray influenced players like Herb Peck, Harry Keating, Ned Stafford, Henley Sklarsky, Gordon Robinson, Eddie D'Anna, Bob Baker, and George Rushton.

Murray the chemical engineer was plant superintendent at Hooker Electrochemical within a few years. He was chief engineer in 1932, director of development in 1937, vice president of development and research in 1941, executive vice president in 1949, and company president January 17, 1951. He served continuously as chairman of the board beginning mid-1955 and was chief executive officer as well until 1958. He retired from active management on November 1, 1959, after forty-three years with the company at age sixty-seven, a year after being elected to the National Tennis Hall of Fame. He had continued in active service beyond the company's normal retirement age by special request of the board of directors.

Murray received the Jacob F. Schoellkopf Medal of the Western New York Section of the American Chemical Society in 1949; was appointed to honorary membership in the American Institute of Chemists in 1953 and in 1956 was awarded the Chemical Industry Medal of the Society of Chemical Industry, American Section, for "conspicuous service to applied chemistry."

The following year he received the professional achievement award of the Western New York Section, American Institute of Chemical Engineers in recognition of his outstanding engineering and executive ability. A new research laboratory on Grand Island was dedicated to Murray the summer of 1959 in ceremonies attended by Governor Nelson A. Rockefeller. Lin Murray was president of the Niagara Falls Country Club in 1942 while his son, Tad Murray, was president in 1963.

R. Lindley Murray won three national singles titles: 1916 U.S. Indoor and 1917 and 1918 U.S. Championships at Forest Hills. He defeated the immortal Bill Tilden four times. He was ranked first in the United States in 1918 and fourth in 1914, '16, and '19. Murray was the first tennis player to be inducted into the Stanford Athletic Hall of Fame (1914). He was also named to the USTA Northern California Hall of Fame (Elmer Griffin, original founder and president), the Intercollegiate Tennis Association (ITA) Men's Hall of Fame in 1992 (inaugural year: 1983), and the most prestigious International Tennis Hall of Fame in 1958 (inaugural year: 1955) along with Molla Bjurstedt-Mallory and Bill Johnston. Murray died on January 17, 1970, in Lewiston Heights, New York.

Part III: Players During Murray's Era

Frederik Beasley Alexander*

Born August 14, 1880, in Seabright, New Jersey, Fred Alexander, a Princeton man, won the U.S. intercollegiate doubles title with Raymond Little in 1900 and the singles title in 1901. Alexander crushed Ross Burchard, 6–0, 6–2, 6–0, in the 1905 Metropolitan final. An excellent doubles player, he was a U.S. doubles finalist a record seven straight times paired with Harold Hackett, beginning in 1905 and winning from 1907 to 1910. In 1917, at thirty-seven, he won a fifth U.S. doubles title with nineteen-year-old Harold Throckmorton. He was also a finalist in 1900 with Raymond Little and in 1918 with Beals Wright, as well as a 1918 U.S. mixed doubles finalist with Molla Bjurstedt.[1]

Alexander also won six U.S. Indoor doubles championships: from 1906 to 1908 with his favorite partner Harold Hackett, in 1911 and 1912 with Theodore Pell, and in 1917 with Dr. W. Rosenbaum. At the Kings County Tennis Club in Brooklyn in May of 1908, Alexander put out in succession O. H. Hinck, G. F. Touchard, H. L. Westfall, H. J. Mollenhauer in the final, and I. C. Wright in the challenge round, and found time in the intervals of idleness to go through the doubles event—partnered with H. H. Hackett, of course—defeating E. P. Larned and C. F. Watson, 6–2, 6–2, 6–2, in the finals.[2]

As the first foreigner to win the Australian titles, Alexander beat Alf Dunlop in 1908 and paired with native Dunlop to take the doubles over Tony Wilding and Granville Sharp. In the 1908 Davis Cup challenge round against Australasia in Melbourne, Alexander lost to Norman Brookes in five sets and Tony Wilding in three while Beals Wright beat the two Australasians, Brookes at 12–10 in the fifth. The American pair lost the doubles in five and thus the Cup 3–2.[3]

Alexander was inducted into the National Tennis Hall of Fame in 1961 and died in Beverly Hills, California, on March 3, 1969.

*International Tennis Hall of Fame

Manuel Alonso*

Manuel Alonso, born November 12, 1895, was the first Spanish male tennis player of international stature. A dark-haired, five-foot-nine, 145-pound right-hander, Alonso was a Davis Cup team member in 1921, '24, '31, and '36. He made his country's best showing at Wimbledon and the U.S. Championships before Manolo Santana won them in 1966 and 1965, respectively. Alonso was a 1921 Wimbledon all-comers finalist defeating Algernon Kingscote (1919 Australian titlist) and Zenzo Shimizu, 3–6, 7–5, 3–6, 6–4, 8–6, before losing to Brian "Babe" Norton (runner-up to Bill Tilden in the challenge round), 5–7, 4–6, 7–5, 6–3, 6–3.[1–3]

A U.S. resident for several years during the 1920s, he was a U.S. Championships quarterfinalist four times. In 1922 he defeated in succession Robert LeRoy (1904 and 1906 U.S. intercollegiate champion and 1907 U.S. singles finalist to seven-time champion William Larned), S. Howard Voshell (1917 national indoor champion), and Watson Washburn (future Hall of Famer) before losing to Bill Johnston. In 1923 he defeated Jacques Brugnon, 6–3, 6–2, 3–6, 5–7, 6–4, before losing to Bill Tilden. In 1925 he again lost to Johnston and in 1927 defeated Washburn and John Van Ryn (future Hall of Famer) before losing to Rene Lacoste, 6–8, 6–4, 6–1, 6–2.[4]

Alonso was ranked in the U.S. top ten from 1925 to 1927, no. 2 in 1926. He was also in the World top ten those three years, no. 5 in 1927. He entered the International Tennis Hall of Fame in 1977 and died October 11, 1984.[5]

James Outram Anderson

Born September 17, 1894, in Sydney, New South Wales (NSW), Australia, James O. Anderson won the Victorian schoolboys' tennis championship in 1912 and became NSW champion in 1914. Anderson, 1919 NSW champion, was instrumental in helping Australia win the

1919 Davis Cup over Great Britain before Bill Tilden and Bill Johnston dominated for the next seven years. "Between 1919 and 1925 he played in fifteen Davis Cup ties."[1] His greatest achievement came in 1923 when he beat Wimbledon champion Bill Johnston, previously undefeated in the Davis Cup, in five sets. As a result, Anderson displaced fellow Aussie Gerald Paterson as no. 3 in the world behind Tilden and Johnston.

He is perhaps best known for his three wins at his home tournament, the Australian Championships. Anderson defeated Davis Cup teammate Gerald Patterson in five sets for the 1922 title, Bob Schlesinger in five for the 1924 title, and Patterson again in four for the 1925 title. In 1922 he paired with Wimbledon singles finalist Randolf Lycett to win the doubles over fellow Aussie Davis Cuppers, Gerald Patterson and Pat O'Hara Wood, 3–6, 7–9, 6–4, 6–3, 11–9.[2-3]

Karl Howell Behr*

Karl Howell Behr, born in New York City on May 30, 1885, was the brother of Max H. Behr, the well-known golfer, golf course architect, one of the greatest writers on golf of all time, and was the first editor of *Golf Illustrated.* Karl attended Yale University where in 1904 he won the intercollegiate doubles with G. Bodman and was admitted to the bar association in 1910. Behr made one of the better American showings at Wimbledon in 1907, reaching the fourth round where he gave the champ, Norman Brooks, a stiff fight, 6–4, 6–2, 2–6, 3–6, 6–1. He paired with Beals Wright to gain the doubles final, losing to Brooks and Tony Wilding, 6–4, 6–4, 6–2. Behr again paired with Wright to extract a measure of revenge by defeating Brookes and Wilding, 3–6, 12–10, 4–6, 6–4, 6–3, in a 3–2 losing effort to Australasia in the final round of the 1907 Davis Cup. He ranked in the U.S. top ten seven times, no. 3 in 1907.[1–2]

Behr had been in Europe on a business trip for his father's firm, Herman Behr & Company, when he learned that Helen Newsome, a friend of his sister, had booked passage on the RMS *Titanic.* Mrs. Beckwith, Helen's mother had been attempting to discourage the relationship between Helen and Karl, and had taken Miss Newsome on a European Grand Tour to separate them for a time. Behr seized the opportunity by inventing a business trip and booking passage on the *Titanic* to continue his courtship.

On the night of the wreck, Behr joined Helen, her mother and stepfather, Richard and Sally Beckwith, and another couple, Edwin and

Gertrude Kimball, on the starboard boat deck. Third Officer Herbert Pitman was in charge of loading lifeboat five. Gertrude Kimball asked J. Bruce Ismay, chairman of the White Star Line, if all of their group could enter the boat. Ismay replied, "Of course, madam, every one of you," the men to do the rowing. As a result Karl Behr and his companions were rescued in the second boat to leave the ship. After the rescue, several newspapers reported that Behr had proposed to Miss Newsome in the lifeboat.

While aboard the RMS *Carpathia* rescue ship, Behr and several other passengers, including Molly Brown, presented *Carpathia*'s captain, Arthur Rostron, with an inscribed silver cup for his efforts and gold medals for each of the ship's 320 crew members.

Despite her mother's objections, Behr married Helen Newsome in March 1913 at the Church of the Transfiguration in New York City. The couple had four children, and after Karl's death in 1949, Helen remarried one of his best friends and former tennis partners, Dean Mathey.[3–4]

Although nearly twenty-seven at the time of the disaster, Behr still had some good tennis left. He ranked in the U.S. top ten seven times between 1906 and 1915, no. 3 in 1907 and again in 1914, when he beat R. Lindley Murray, 3–6, 6–2, 7–5, 3–6, 8–6, to reach the quarters of the U.S. Championships at Newport. There he lost to eventual champ Dick Williams, 6–2, 6–2, 7–5, in a battle of *Titanic* alumni less than a mile from the unforgiving Atlantic Ocean. In 1906 at no. 11, he bounced the eight-time top-ranked and current no. 3 William Larned in the second round, 6–4, 6–4, 7–5, and fought past ninth-ranked Raymond Little, 2–6, 6–2, 6–8, 11–9, 6–4, to the final of the all-comers, where no. 4 Bill Clothier stopped him, 6–2, 6–4, 6–2. Clothier went on to easily defeat Beals Wright in the challenge round, 6–3, 6–0, 6–4.[5] One of Behr's most memorable wins was in the 1915 final of the Seabright, New Jersey, invitational. There he defeated Maurice McLoughlin, "the California Comet," rated as the world's best tennis player in straight sets, 8–6, 7–5, 7–5.[6]

Behr later went into banking. He was vice president of Dillon, Read & Company and sat on the board of the Fisk Rubber Company, the Goodyear Tire and Rubber Company, and the National Cash Register Company. At the time of his death, he was a director of the Interchemical Corporation, the Behr-Manning Corporation of Troy, New York, and the Witherbee Sherman Corporation. Behr died October 15, 1949, and was posthumously inducted into the National Tennis Hall of Fame in 1969.

Molla Bjurstedt-Mallory*

For a few brief moments in 1933 Johan Haanes led Norway to a 3–2 triumph over Sweden to win its first ever Nordisk Cup. After having defeated the no. 2 Swedish player and teaming with Ragnar Hagan to win the doubles, Haanes faced Ostberg, the star of the Swedish team with the series between the two Nordic nations tied at 2–2. At two sets apiece and 4–4 in the fifth, Haanes broke through Ostberg's service and fought on to victory.

In 1935 Hannes, with the help of a young Finn Smith, again brought the Nordisk Cup to Norway. Haanes, again after each team had won two matches, produced the decisive blow by outclassing Sweden's top player, Kalle Schroder, 8–6, 9–7, 6–2.[1]

No Norwegian players of note have reached international stature, but less than five decades later, the Swedish contingent, led by Bjorn Borg, Mats Wilander, and Stefan Edberg, started winning major titles and were dominant in 1980s Davis Cup play with three victories and four defeats. In 2009 Robin Soderling beat Rafael Nadal (world no. 1) at the French Open.

But back in 1894, when King Oscar II reigned over the dual monarchy of Sweden and Norway, the daughter of an army officer was born March 6 near Trondheim in Norway, destined to become national singles champion of Norway, win her country's first-ever Olympic tennis medal, and ultimately reign as the queen of American tennis—a strange aberration indeed.

Her name was Molla Bjurstedt. As a child her family moved to Oslo, and young Molla's tennis horizons broadened. She "began to develop a style which would mark her long and successful career: hard, steady, and aggressive play, powerful forehand stroke, deadly baseline shooting and skillful placements, and an uncanny talent for passing an opponent at the net."[2]

She won eight Norwegian singles championships and a bronze medal at the 1912 Stockholm Olympics. Molla lost to gold medalist Marguerite Broquedis of France in the semis, 6–3, 2–6, 6–4, by no means a walkover, and won her bronze medal match 6–2, 6–2.

Molla left for America in the fall of 1914 to visit her mother's cousin in Brooklyn. She liked the country so well she decided to stay, finding work as a masseuse.[3] After a few months she entered the 1915 National Indoor tennis championships unheralded. She breezed through to the final round where she upset defending champ Marie Wagner, 6–4, 6–4, to win the first of her five singles titles at that event—the other four to follow in 1916, '18, '21, and '22. She also won the Cincinnati title in 1915.

Bjurstedt was a fierce competitor, running with limitless endurance. Bob Kelleher, a former USLTA president and a ball boy during Molla's era, remembered Molla as "a nice lady," but added that "[s]he looked and acted tough when she was on the court hitting tennis balls. She walked around in a manner that said you'd better look out or she'd deck you. She was an indomitable scrambler and runner. She was a fighter."[4]

Interviewed by writer Emma Harrison around 1955, Molla sized up ladies' tennis by saying, "I don't think they have the stamina.... I think they pamper themselves too much. They don't seem to have any fun. You know, I think they go to bed at 9 o'clock. In my day we had fun. I went out dancing, even the night before a match." Molla advised players to hit the ball harder and have passing shots, like Maureen Connolly, and stop relying on net play. "You can beat anybody at the net with placements, hard hitting and passing shots. Put the ball where the other fellow ain't. Don't hit it back and wait for him to make an error.... There's something on a tennis ball called top spin and they haven't got it." She continued, "Louise Brough has it. I didn't know I had it until Bill Tilden told me. I said to Bill, 'Really I don't know very much about tennis.'"[5]

Molla was a player of the old school. She held that a woman could not sustain a volleying attack in a long match and relied on her baseline game, consisting of strong forehand attacks and a ceaseless defense that wore down her opponents. She took the ball on the rise and drove it from corner to corner to keep her rival on the constant run. Her quick service returns made her passing shots all the more effective.[6–7]

In her inaugural 1915 U.S. Championships final, Molla defeated three-time titlist, Hazel Hotchkiss-Wightman, 4–6, 6–2, 6–0. After the first set Wightman began to tire and could not get to the volleying position. Molla went on to win eight U.S. singles (a record for both men and women) and four consecutive women's singles titles (from 1915 to 1918), tied with Helen Jacobs (who won from 1932 to 1935) and Chris Evert (titleholder from 1975 to 1978).

Molla destroyed Louise Raymond in 1916, 6–0, 6–1; beat Marion Vanderhoef in 1917, 4–6, 6–0, 6–2; Eleanor Goss in 1918, 6–4, 6–3; Marion Zinderstein in 1920 as Mrs. Franklin Mallory, 6–3, 6–1; Mary K. Browne in 1921, 4–6, 6–4, 6–2; Helen Wills in 1922, 6–3, 6–1; and Elizabeth Ryan in 1926, 4–6, 6–4, 9–7. In the 1926 championship, she came back from 0–4 in the third set and saved a match point. Her win at age forty-two established her as the oldest singles champion in the event's history. "Never had a gallery at Forest Hills in the years of her triumphs cheered her on as it did in this remarkable rally."[8]

She was a finalist to Helen Wills in 1923 and 1924, and in fifteen years at the U.S. Championships her worst finish was as a quarterfinalist in 1927. She also won two women's doubles (1916 and 1917) and three mixed doubles (1917, '22, and '23). Molla also played on the Wightman Cup team from 1923 to '25 and in '27 and '28. The first Wightman Cup match took place as the christening event of the new Forest Hills permanent stadium and was confined to the United States and England.

One of the two most controversial defaults in women's tennis occurred in the 1921 U.S. Championships. In the second round at Forest Hills, August 16, 1921, Bjurstedt played the great Suzanne Lenglen from France in what was to become a very controversial episode for Lenglen. "In 1920 Suzanne won two Olympic gold medals at Antwerp and retained her Wimbledon singles crown with ease." She "triumphed at Wimbledon again in 1921 and, having won every set she had played during a two-year period, decided she was ready for a new challenge."[9] Suzanne wanted to play Molla, whom she had easily beaten at the World Hard Court Championships, 6–2, 6–3, that spring, for the U.S. title. While Suzanne was still en route across the Atlantic, the USLTA made the draw. Those were the days before seeding and Molla and Suzanne were on course to meet in the second round. Suzanne's first-round opponent, Eleanor Goss, withdrew, reportedly because of illness.

"Before the match, Bill Tilden advised Mallory to 'hit the cover off the ball.' Once the match began, Mallory 'attacked with a vengeance' and was ahead 2–0 (40–0) when Lenglen began to cough. Mallory won the first set 6–2 and was up 40–0 on Lenglen's serve in the first game of the second set when Lenglen began to weep and walked to the umpire's stand and informed the official that she was ill and could not continue. This match ranks among the most sensational dramas ever recorded on the tennis court. After the match, the USTA accused Lenglen of feigning illness."[10]

Lenglen avenged the loss by defeating Mallory, 6–2, 6–0, in twenty-six minutes before an adoring crowd of fourteen thousand in the 1922 Wimbledon final, still the fastest major match on record. Suzanne reportedly said to her opponent after the match, "Now, Mrs. Mallory, I have proved to you today what I could have done to you in New York last year," to which Molla reportedly replied, "Mlle. Lenglen, you have done to me today what I did to you in New York last year; you have beaten me."[11]

In defense of Lenglen, who had been coughing throughout the match, left the court to inform the umpire that she could not continue as she could not breathe. The European champion collapsed into a chair with a towel at her mouth and in a violent spasm of coughing, which caused the tears to roll down her face. She was quickly assisted to the clubhouse and shortly after to her private apartments in a nearby hotel. Her physician, Dr. R. B. Baringer of the New York hospital, said it was a recurrence of an attack of bronchitis, which she had had for several weeks.[12]

Two days after the match Mlle. Suzanne Lenglen expressed fear that Americans would regard her as a "poor sport." She was disgusted with herself for playing at all, declining the doctor's advice and her own better judgment. Lenglen had so looked forward to coming to America and making a good impression. She said "of course I show my feelings more than you calm Americans. My one ambition now is to meet Mrs. Mallory again."[13]

The second controversial default was that of Helen Wills-Moody to Helen Hull Jacobs in the 1933 U.S. final. Beaten for the first time since 1922 in American tennis championship competition (she lost to Molla Bjurstedt-Mallory in the 1922 final, 6–3, 6–1, and didn't participate in 1926, '30, or '32), Queen Helen the First's long reign at Forest Hills added a controversial and dramatic chapter as tennis fans and critics have long debated the extent that Mrs. Moody's ailments contributed to her downfall or whether she might have found sufficient reserve to finish after losing the first three games of the final set. The match score was recorded as 8–6, 3–6, 3–0 retired. The on-site reporter gave this account:

> Delayed exactly a week by rain, the championship final was a duel of invalids. Miss Jacobs, too, had been under a doctor's care throughout the tournament as a result of over-strain. But "Helen the Second" outplayed her rival in most of the critical exchanges and she was much the stronger of the two starting the third set, after an hour's hard play in which she pulled out the first set 8–6 and lost the second 3–6. For the first time in eight contests between the two California girls, Miss Jacobs played Mrs. Moody on even terms and clearly earned her laurels.

> Whether or not Mrs. Moody could have continued, she was obviously fast losing her physical resources, handicapped by wearing a brace to protect her injured back and a weakening right leg. Only Queen Helen herself knew how close she was to utter collapse. Her statement afterwards was that she simply could not continue because she felt "as if I were going to faint."
>
> At the time Mrs. Moody simply was going through the motions of playing tennis. She made no effort whatever to reach some of Miss Jacobs low-spinning shots.
>
> It could have added little or nothing to Miss Jacobs' victory for the match to be finished under the circumstances. Coupled with the physical strain was the fact that Mrs. Moody's usually steady and resourceful game has gone to pieces under her rivals pressure and brilliant stroking. Yet there were many "die-hards"—forgetting the criticism for permitting Ellsworth Vines to play until he collapsed at Paris—who felt apparently that Mrs. Moody should have played out the match at any cost—in other words "taken it."
>
> There were also some who saw in the outcome the possible finish of Mrs. Moody's championship career, at home as well as abroad.
>
> She is only 27 years old but she has been playing national championship tennis for a dozen years. The signs this season already pointed to the end of her long domination of the women's court.[14]

Miss Jacobs went on to win two more U.S. Championships (to make it four straight), while Mrs. Moody did not compete in any more U.S. Nationals. Moody did, however, win eight Wimbledon titles between 1927 and 1938, winning all that she participated in. She defeated Helen Hull Jacobs in the 1935 and 1938 finals, but that's another era and another story.

Molla Bjurstedt-Mallory was ranked in the world top ten from 1925 to 1927 (the first three years of those rankings) and in the U.S. top ten thirteen times between 1915 and 1928, no. 1 in 1915, '16, '18, '20, '21, '22, and '26. Her farewell to the U.S. Championships was as a forty-five-year-old semifinalist in 1929. Molla was inducted into the National Tennis

Hall of Fame in 1958 and died November 22, 1959 in Stockholm.[15] Molla was posthumously inducted into the U.S. Open Court of Champions, on September 7, 2008, along with Pete Sampras, a US Open and USTA Billie Jean King National Tennis Center attraction honoring the greatest singles champions in the history of the U.S. Championships/US Open.[16]

Mary Kendall Browne*

Born on June 3, 1891, in Ventura County, California, Mary K. Browne was a tennis champion, a notable golfer, and a writer. She came east in 1912 and captured three consecutive hat tricks at the U.S. Championships on the Philadelphia Cricket Club courts, winning the singles, doubles, and mixed doubles events in 1912, '13, and '14. The 1912 finals were all played on the same afternoon, June 15, much of it in a downpour, before tarp court coverings and rain delays. The grass was mushy, and her many period garments were soaked, adding considerable weight to her small five-foot-two frame.[1] Mary played eighty-two games beating Eleonora Sears, 6–4, 6–2, in singles; paired with Dorothy Green to win the doubles, 6–2, 5–7, 6–0; and partnered with Dick Williams, who only two months before had been fished out of the icy North Atlantic, to win the mixed, 6–4, 2–6, 11–9.

In 1913 and 1914 she repeated the hat trick but with a new mixed doubles partner, a University of Pennsylvania dropout named Bill Tilden, who didn't become really good for another half dozen years. The newspaper accounts implied that Mary carried him to victory.[2]

After 1914 Mary dropped out of big-time tennis for a few years. A February 1918 *Times* article said she had quit tennis for a banking career in Venice, California, but had played in Los Angeles for the Red Cross war effort.[3] Mary reappeared at the 1921 U.S Championships, now transferred to Forest Hills, where she battled reigning champion Molla Bjurstedt-Mallory to three sets, 4–6, 6–4, 6–2, in a losing effort. However, she won the women's doubles with her 1913 and 1914 partner, Louise R. Williams, and paired in the mixed with Bill Johnston at Chestnut Hill, Massachusetts, to defeat that year's singles titlists, Molla Mallory and Bill Tilden, 3-6, 6-4, 6-3.

She again disappeared from national competition until 1924. Mary faced a new rising star and defending champion in the semifinals. Helen "Wills squeezed out a 6–4, 4–6, 6–3 victory that left both women so exhausted that it was minutes before either had the strength to come to the net for the traditional handshake."[4] The next day Wills beat Molla Mallory, 6–1, 6–3, for the title and went on to dominate women's tennis for another fourteen years. Mary paired with Helen Wills to win the 1925 U.S. Women's doubles and with Elizabeth Ryan to win the 1926 Wimbledon Women's doubles. Between 1912 and 1926 she had won a total of thirteen majors—three singles, six women's doubles, and four mixed doubles. Contrary to Molla's baseline strategy, Mary was famous for attacking and volleying at net as often as possible.

Mary had taken up golf after 1914 and two weeks after losing to Wills, she entered the 1924 U.S. Women's Amateur golf tournament. She won her preliminary matches and played the legendary Glenda Collett Vare, future World Golf Hall of Famer, in the semis. As told by Glenda:

> The most sensational battle of my life took place with her [Mary] at the Rhode Island Country Club at Providence, when she as a comparative novice had advanced to the semifinal round of the National Woman's Championship to play against me. She did this by displaying the same courage and power under stress of competition that had made her several times winner of national tennis titles. Just two weeks before this match she had been runner-up to Helen Wills at Forest Hills.
>
> Our game that day at Providence was nip and tuck all the way. Crowds increased as we advanced. Every one was amazed to see such stamina and nerve in this player. Mary K. Browne, a tennis star, but surely not a golf light! At the eighteenth green we had halved the match. We must play an extra hole. On the nineteenth, Mary's drive sailed two hundred yards straight down the fairway. With victory apparently snatched away from me, I made a last valiant stand. My drive equaled hers for distance and position.
>
> The fight was on. It was anybody's match. Our second shots both pitched into traps. We played out, I going past the pin, she short. I putted first. My ball stopped three inches short of the cup. That meant I had three strokes. Mary was still to play her third.
>
> With her ball twenty feet from the hole, a breathless silence descended over the gallery. I stood by, trying to look becalmed, but feeling hot and cold all over. If Mary

> sunk that putt I was done for. Mary sunk that putt. And that is Mary K. Browne all over. She does what she has to do—at the right moment. She takes her courage by the hand and walks along with it to the last ditch. It never fails her.[5]

Glenna Collett Vare was known as the female Bobby Jones. The greatest female golfer of her day, she won five U.S. Championships, two Canadian, and one French in an era when there was no LPGA. In 1924 Collett won fifty-nine consecutive matches before losing to Mary Browne. Browne subsequently lost in the final to Dorothy Campbell Hurd.[6]

As the first American female professional tennis player, Mary joined promoter C. C. "Cash and Carry" Pyle's original 1926 troupe of touring pros including centerpiece Suzanne Lenglen, Vinnie Richards, Howard Kinsey, Harvey Snodgrass, and Paul Feret. During the winter of 1926 and 1927, at age thirty-five, she played one-night stands across North America against the invincible Lenglen, losing all thirty-eight matches.[7]

Mary was barred from amateur golf for three years after her professional tennis tour.[8] Immediately following the tour Mary wrote for the *Saturday Evening Post* and published *Top Flite Tennis*, a 128-page book in 1928.[9] After winning the Southern California women's golf championship, she settled in Cleveland, where she became part-owner in a ladies' exclusive sportswear shop. Mary won the Women's Ohio State Amateur Championship in 1931 and the Cleveland (CWGA) District Championship in 1931, '32, '34, and '35.[10–11]

From 1930 until 1951, Browne was a part-time tennis instructor at Lake Erie College in Painesville, Ohio, "except during World War II when she served with the American Red Cross in Australia and Italy." While at Lake Erie College, she was responsible for many outstanding tennis players coming to the college for exhibition matches and invitational tournaments. In addition to *Top Flite Tennis* published in 1928, Mary authored *Streamline Tennis* in 1940 and *Design for Tennis* in 1949. "Later she became a very successful and much sought after portrait painter, but she always continued to play the games at which she so excelled." After her very active tennis and golf career, she returned to California. Alice Marble, a California tennis player, twenty-two years Mary's junior, who won eighteen Grand Slam championships from 1936 through 1940, was with her when she shot a seventy-five on an admittedly easy golf course; however, Mary was then seventy-five years old![12–13]

In tennis Mary ranked no. 1 in the U.S. in 1913 and 1914, the first two years of the Women's top ten, returning to the select group at no.2 in 1921 and 1924 and no. 6 in 1925. In 1926 she was world no. 6, the USLTA declining her a high ranking because she had turned pro. Mary was elected to the National Tennis Hall of Fame in 1957. Kenneth-Smith from New York, "who had not seen Mary since their high school days together a half-century before, except to watch her play, telephoned her and asked if he could drive her up to Newport."[14] She was sixty-six and he about a year older. They stood together during the induction ceremony and, shortly afterward, stood together again for another ceremony—their marriage.[15]

In golf the Mary K. Browne Memorial tournament at Kirtland Country Club near Cleveland is a thirty-six-hole two-day low-net event open to sixty players with full handicap. The winner receives the Mary K. Browne trophy, the original donated by Browne in 1952. Mary entered the Greater Cleveland Sports Hall of Fame in 1977 and the Lake Erie College Athletic Hall of Fame in 1991.[16-17] She died on August 19, 1971 in Laguna Hills, California.[18]

Jack Castle

Jack Castle at five-foot-three and 115 pounds, the Buffalo Bantam with the big heart and big game, won his first tournament in 1911 at age fifteen in Pittsburgh, Pennsylvania. From 1914 to 1918 he had an undefeated record at Allegheny College in Meadville, Pennsylvania. In 1916 at age twenty he was ranked no. 42 nationally in singles by the USNLTA. In 1919 he came to Buffalo, following army service in World War I, and dominated the Western New York tennis scene until 1932. From 1919 to 1928 he won the Buffalo singles title seven times, including five wins in a row, and was runner-up to Cliff Marsh the other three years. He captured several city doubles crowns with Leo Kronman. In 1931 he was Muny singles champion and doubles champion with Kronman in 1930 and 1931 and from 1929 to 1931 won the Ohio State doubles with Cliff Marsh. Castle also won the National Clay Court mixed doubles tournament with Marie McDonald and the National Inter-City doubles title with Marsh. In 1931 he held a National Public Parks ranking of eighth in singles and sixth in doubles with Kronman.

Back when the Great Lakes tourney was held at the Park Club, Castle and his partner won a match and were told by the committee they would have to play another that evening. It seems Bill Tilden wanted to get the doubles out of the way so he could concentrate on his singles match the following day. In the course of play, Tilden kept a running commentary with the only spectator, Molla Bjurstedt-Mallory, the eight-time national singles champion. After winning the first set Tilden and his partner lost the next two. That was quite a shock to Tilden, who came back the following year to beat Castle in the semifinals.[1]

In the National Inter-City tournament in Cleveland around 1931, Castle was asked if he'd mind playing a preliminary match with a fifteen-year-old boy in shorts. As relayed by Castle: "That boy just didn't make any errors. I finally beat him, two tough 6–4 sets, by drawing him out of position and going to the net." That boy was Frankie Parker, who ranked in the U.S. top ten for seventeen straight years (from 1933 to 1949) and won the U.S. title in 1944 and 1945.[2]

Jack turned professional during the depression to earn money by playing, teaching, and umpiring between 1932 and 1947. He regained his amateur standing after World War II. In a 1934 pro tennis match in Chicago, Jack "won the longest and most bitterly contested match of the tournament from Ed Faulkner of Philadelphia, 6–1, 5–7, 7–5, 6–3. After Castle took the opening set, Faulkner came to the net and, driving steadily cross court, won the second. He had set point twice in the third set, once at 5–1, and again at 5–4, but Castle rallied to square it. The Buffalo player broke through Faulkner's service and won his own to take the set; Castle then won the last one with little difficulty."[3]

While refereeing in 1939 at the Broadway Auditorium in Buffalo, one of the pros, Bruce Barnes, had an attack of appendicitis, and Jack was called down to play two sets of singles with Dick Skeen (runner-up to Fred Perry in the 1941 Professional Tennis Championships). He then teamed up with Don Budge in doubles and afterward went on to referee the main exhibition matches.[4]

He also was a teacher, coach, umpire (both amateur and professional), sought-after speaker, published author of tennis articles, and co-founder of the Buffalo Racquet Club in 1954. From the late 1930s to early 1940s he umpired world pro matches at Memorial Auditorium for Jack Kramer, Bobby Riggs, Pancho Segura, Don Budge, and Bill Tilden. In 1952 the fifty-six-year-old grandfather won the Buffalo City doubles with his twenty-two-year-old partner, Bruce Heacock, over Irv Brent and Chet Fyderek, 6–2, 4–6, 6–2, 6–4. Jack won three more doubles titles that year: Canadian National Veterans in Toronto, Great Lakes Veterans in Erie,

Pennsylvania, and Park Club Member–Guest. Lou Schaefer, forty-seven, paired with Castle at Toronto and Erie.

An insurance agent, he served as president of the Buffalo Life Underwriters and established an independent agency in the 1940s. With his wife, Elizabeth, he raised four children: Jack Jr., with whom he played in several national father-and-son tournaments, Carol, Bill, and Allen.

Lindley Murray invited Castle to Niagara Falls for tennis exhibitions. In 1922 Murray played Castle in singles and paired with Castle in doubles against Charles Garland, Pittsburgh star and 1920 Wimbledon doubles champion with Dick Williams, and Buffalonian Eric Hedstrom, Garland's Yale teammate. In 1925 Castle and Murray squared off against Manuel Alonso, Spanish champion, and Hedstrom; in 1926 the pair played Manuel Alonso and Lewis of Toronto. In 1967 Castle died in Florida of a heart attack at the age of seventy following a round of golf.

George Myers Church

Possibly about two years younger than Lin Murray, George M. Church won the 1911 interscholastic title for Irving High School in New York. Following Dean Mathey's two consecutive intercollegiate doubles titles for Princeton in 1910 and 1911, Church, class of '15, won the 1912 and 1914 intercollegiate singles titles and the 1912 doubles title with classmate Winifred H. Mace.[1] Church won the 1913 Delaware State championship by defeating the 1912 winner, Dean Mathey, in four sets, 6–4, 1–6, 6–3, 8–6,[2] and successfully defended his Delaware State title in 1914 over Murray, 6–3, 5–7, 6–3, 6–4.[3] Church only won two games in his 1913 intercollegiate match with Dick Williams but wrested the 1914 intercollegiate championship from Williams, the titleholder and national champion, 8–6, 9–7, 4–6, 7–5. Less than a month earlier, Williams had defeated U.S. no. 1 Maurice McLoughlin for the national title. With only ten minutes' rest, Church returned to the courts and paired with A. M. Kidder to win a semifinal doubles match, 6–0, 6–3, 6–3, but then lost to Williams and Richard Harte in the final, 6–2, 6–2, 7–5.[4]

At the 1915 Clay Court championships in Pittsburgh, Dick Williams defeated Nat Niles of Boston, 6–4, 6–4, 6–2, in one semi, while George Church defeated Watson Washburn of the West Side Tennis Club, 7–5, 7–5, 6–2, in the other. Church overcame 3–1 and 5–2 deficits in the first two sets respectively to win.[5] The records show that Williams won the singles, while Church and Mathey won the doubles both in 1915 and 1916.

Church also won the 1916 National Clay Court mixed doubles title with Molla Bjurstedt.[6]

In the nationals Church reached the 1912 quarters where he was vanquished by Karl Behr, 6–2, 6–2, 6–0. Paired with Dean Mathey, Church won the 1914 U.S. all-comers doubles only to lose to Tom Bundy and Maurice McLoughlin. In 1916 he defeated U.S. no. 3 Maurice McLoughlin in the fourth round, 5–7, 6–1, 6–2, 6–3, but lost to Lin Murray in the quarters after winning the first two sets, 3–6, 4–6, 6–2, 6–4, 6–2. Church was ranked in the U.S. top ten three times—from 1914 to 1916—taking the no. 3 spot in 1916 ahead of Lin Murray. He was inducted into the 2003 ITA Men's Collegiate Hall of Fame.[7]

The first inter-city team competition for the George Myers Church Cup was held on the turf courts of the Merion Cricket Club in Haverford, Pennsylvania, June 7–8, 1918. This was a competition among players from Boston, New York, and Philadelphia, comprising six singles and three doubles matches.[8] The competition continued in that format, though it was not held between 1933 and 1945, and in 1946 the competing teams represented three USTA sectional associations: USTA Eastern, USTA Middle States, and USTA New England. In 1947 a fourth association (the USTA Mid-Atlantic) was admitted, and the competition has continued unabated since.[9]

William Jackson Clothier*

Born September 27, 1881, in Sharon Hill, Pennsylvania, William Clothier, a Harvard man, won the intercollegiate singles and doubles with E. W. Leonard in 1902 and won the U.S. singles four years later over Karl Behr in the final round, 6–2, 6–4, 6–2, and Beals Wright in the challenge round, 6–3, 6–0, 6–4. In a quarterfinal Clothier overcame triple match point (2–5, love–40) in the fifth against Fred Alexander by winning the last five games. The score was 8–6, 6–2, 4–6, 1–6, 7–5.

Clothier became a 1904 finalist to Holcomb Ward by defeating Bill Larned in five in the semis (there was no challenge round). In 1909 he defeated "the California Comet," Maury McLoughlin, in the final round, 7–5, 6–4, 9–11, 6–3, but lost to Larned in the challenge round, 6–1, 6–2, 5–7, 1–6, 6–1. He held a U.S. top-ten ranking for eleven years between 1901 and 1914, no. 1 in 1906 and no. 2 in 1904 and 1909. In 1905 Clothier beat two French champions—Max Decugis, 6–3, 6–4, 6–4, and Maurice Germot, 6–3, 5–7, 6–1, 6–3—in the first U.S. Davis Cup engagement abroad, a 5–0 semifinal victory at the Queen's Club in London. The U.S. blanked Australasia in the final without Clothier but lost in the challenge round to Great Britain 5–0. Both Larned and Clothier lost to Sidney Smith (Smith was All England Badminton champion in 1900. From 1897 to 1906 he was Welsh tennis champion and paired with Frank Riseley to win the 1902 and 1906 Wimbledon doubles titles. In 1905 and 1906 he was a member of the British Davis Cup team.)

Clothier, a powerful, aggressive six-foot-two, 170-pounder, caught the attention of distinguished British tennis authority A. Wallis Myers, who in 1908 published *The Complete Lawn Tennis Player*, a 333-page history of the game and its players. It was in the fourth round of the 1905 Wimbledon tournament that Bill led Tony Wilding, a six-foot-two, 185-pound right-handed New Zealander, 5–2 and 40–15, with two match points in the third on center court. Wilding went on to win the three-and-a-half-hour battle, 5–7, 1–6, 8–6, 7–5, 10–8. Myers wrote, "Both men were such splendid specimens of youth and vigor, such hard hitters, such gallant fighters." Wilding lost in the next round to Arthur Gore but would subsequently go on to win four consecutive Wimbledon titles from 1910 to 1913.

Bill was a 1912 U.S. mixed finalist with Eleonora Sears. He and his son, William Clothier II, won two U.S. Father and Son doubles titles in 1935 and 1936. Clothier was inducted into the 1956 National Tennis Hall of Fame[1–2] and the 1984 ITA Hall of Fame. He died in Philadelphia on September 4, 1962.

Willis E. Davis

Willis Davis's name first came to light in the 1913 California State championships. He partnered with Lin Murray, and the pair lost to Clarence Griffin and John Strachan in the quarters. Playing for the University of California, Berkeley, Davis beat the 1914 Pacific Coast intercollegiate champion Herbert Hahn of Stanford that same year. At the 1915 California State championships, the young San Franciscan beat Carl Gardner in the second round, Roland Roberts in the semis, and Lin Murray in the final. For 1915 Davis was ranked fourth on the Pacific Coast behind Bill Johnston, John Strachan, and Clarence Griffin.

Playing for the University of California from 1913 to 1914, Davis followed in the footsteps of Mel Long and entered the University of Pennsylvania in the fall of 1914.[1] In a 1915 *Times* article, Davis was compared to Maury McLoughlin and Lin Murray due to his breaking cannonball service, which he followed by close net coverage "with lightning-like volleys and ground strokes."[2]

Davis won the 1916 U.S. Clay Court title in Cleveland, following in the footsteps of fellow San Franciscans Mel Long (1910), John Strachan (1913), and Clarence Griffin (1914). He entered his first U.S. Championships that year losing to Watson Washburn in the fourth round. Davis paired with the multi-talented socialite Eleonora Sears to win the 1916 U.S. mixed doubles over Florence Balin and Bill Tilden propelling Davis to a no. 8 national ranking.

He next competed in 1919, losing to Dick Williams in the third round. Playing in the 1920 National doubles at Longwood, Davis and another San Franciscan, Roland Roberts, ran through Bill Clothier and Beals Wright, both former national singles champions; Watson Washburn and Dean Mathey in five sets; Dick Williams and Richard Harte; and Charles Garland and Bill Tilden, Wimbledon titlist, in the semis. In an all–San Francisco final, the pair was defeated by Clarence Griffin and Bill Johnston, the latter pair copping their third doubles title together. Davis achieved his highest U.S. ranking at no. 5 that year.

In 1921 Davis won the Meadow Club invitation tournament in Southampton, Long Island.[3] In the U.S. Championships he beat the national intercollegiate champion Phil Neer in the third round, Bill Clothier in the fourth, Robert Kinsey (1922 U.S. no. 6) in the quarters, before bowing to Bill Tilden in the semis. In 1922 Davis lost to 1920 Australian champion Pat O'Hara Wood in the third round and retired from active competition after losing in the first round in 1923. He was inducted into the USTA Northern California Hall of Fame.

Charles Stedman Garland*

Charles Garland, a five-foot-seven-and-a-half right-hander, was born October 29, 1898, in Pittsburgh.[1] He won the 1915 Yale section of the interscholastic championship for Edgemere High School in Pittsburgh over L. H. Wiley of Hartford High, 6–2, 6–4, 4–6, 6–3.[2] At Yale Garland won the 1919 intercollegiate singles title and the doubles event with K. N. Hawks. He came along at a tough time, when Bill Tilden was just starting to dominate tennis, but paired with former Harvard intercollegiate champion Dick Williams to win the 1920 Wimbledon doubles over Algernon Kingscote and James Parke, 4–6, 6–4, 7–5, 6–2, the first Americans to win the doubles at Wimbledon.

As early as 1915 he won the Indiana State singles and was a doubles finalist.[3] At the 1919 New York State championship in Utica in July, Ichiya Kumagae won the title for the third time—and thereby became permanent possessor of the Maurice McLoughlin Bowl—by beating Garland, 6–3, 6–1, 6–1. Garland paired with Clarence Griffin of San Francisco to capture the doubles over Fred Anderson Jr. and his brother Frank, 6–2, 7–5, 3–6, 6–3.[4]

At the 1919 Southampton tournament in August, Garland became the first winner of the challenge cup offered by the Meadow Club by defeating Willis Davis of California, 6–4, 6–3, 6–3, after Davis had eliminated world no. 5 Australian Norman Brookes the day before. Garland paired with Bill Tilden to win the doubles over Australians Randolph Lycett and R. V. Thomas, 7–5, 6–2, 6–4.[5]

Bill Tilden said Garland hit a well-placed slice service, a full swing forehand with slight topspin and deadly accuracy, and a backhand slightly sliced down the line and pulled flat crosscourt. His overhead was reliable and accurate but lacked aggressiveness; his high volleys were deep and fast, but his low volleys were weak and uncertain. He was the perfect stylist, the orthodox model for ground strokes. He anticipated wonderfully and covered a tremendous amount of court. Norman Brookes considered Garland one of the greatest ground stroke players in the world.[6]

Ranked three times in the U.S. top ten from 1918 to 1920, he was selected to the National Tennis Hall of Fame in 1969 as much for his service to the USTA as committeeman as for his playing. Garland later lived in Baltimore and died there on January 28, 1971.[7] In 1999 he was posthumously enshrined into the ITA Hall of Fame.

Clarence James "Peck" Griffin*

Clarence J. Griffin, a five-foot-seven right-hander, was born on January 19, 1888, in San Francisco and made his mark in doubles alongside fellow Californians Bill Johnston and John Strachan.[1] In 1913 California, Griffin paired with Strachan, losing in the finals to Bill Johnston and partner at the Coronado Country Club championship in February, the Pacific States championship in June, and the California State championship in September.[2–4]

Griffin won the 1913 National Clay Court doubles with John Strachan and reached the final of the 1913 U.S. men's doubles at Newport, again with Strachan, where they lost to Tom Bundy and Maurice McLoughlin, 6–4, 7–5, 6–1. Griffin won the 1914 U.S. Clay Court singles in a comeback beating of Elia Fottrell, 3–6, 6–8, 8–6, 6–0, 6–2. Griffin also won the 1913 International singles over E. H. Whitney, 9–7, 1–6, 6–2, 9–7, the latter having defeated Bill Johnston in the semis. Griffin and Johnston beat R. C. Seaver and Whitney in the doubles final.[5]

On September 19, 1915, Griffin won the Tri-State tennis singles at Cincinnati over W. S. McElroy of Pittsburgh in the challenge round, 6–4, 6–3, 6–3.[6]

Paired with Bill Johnston, Griffin thrice won the U.S. doubles title, each an all-California final: in 1915 over Maurice McLoughlin and Tom Bundy, in 1916 over McLoughlin and Ward Dawson, and in 1920 over Willis Davis and Roland Roberts. Griffin was ranked in the U.S. top ten three times: no. 7 in 1915 and no. 6 in 1916 and 1920. Clarence also had two outstanding tennis-playing younger brothers, Elmer and Mervyn (the father of the well-known entertainer Merv Griffin).

During the Great War, Griffin was a lieutenant in artillery, transferring later to aviation. He was inducted into the National Tennis Hall of Fame in 1970 and died in Santa Barbara, California, on March 28, 1973.[7]

Wallace F. Johnson

Wallace F. Johnson, a Haverford, Pennsylvania, native, excelled in four sports—football, baseball, basketball, and tennis. Prior to enrolling at Penn he won the 1907 National interscholastic tennis title for Haverford School.[1]

Johnson, class of 1911, played collegiate tennis at the University of Pennsylvania, where in 1909 he won the intercollegiate singles championship against Mel Long of the University of California in five tough sets and the doubles event with A. Thayer against Gardner and Sweetser of Harvard.[2] At the Cincinnati tournament, Johnson won the doubles title in 1910 and was a singles finalist in 1910 and 1911.[3] He won the 1914 Chevy Chase singles defeating Theodore Pell in the final, 2–6, 6–0, 0–6, 6–2, 6–2, and Charles Bull in the challenge round, 6–4, 6–4, 8–6.[4]

Johnson reached the singles final at the U.S. Championships in both 1912 and 1921, losing in 1912 to U.S. no. 2 Maurice McLoughlin in five sets and in 1921 to U.S. no. 1 Bill Tilden in three, the only year between

1919 and 1925 that Bill Johnston didn't make the final. Johnson was much more successful in mixed doubles. He paired with May Sayers to win the 1907 title and Hazel Hotchkiss-Wightman to win the 1909, '11, and '20 titles.

Johnson was part of the 1913 Davis Cup team, which won the Cup that year against England. While in England he won the Mid-Kent championship and was runner-up in the London County championship, bringing several trophies back with him.[5]

Johnson earned top-ten national rankings nine times from 1908 to 1924, a span of seventeen years, no. 3 in 1909 and 1912. Johnson coached the Quakers' men's tennis team from 1929 to 1959. He compiled a career 221–149–1 record as a head coach and led Penn to its only Eastern Intercollegiate Tennis Association championship in 1940. He also served as Penn's men's squash coach from 1924 to 1959.[6] In 1999 he was posthumously inducted into the ITA Hall of Fame and in 2008 into the USTA Middle States Hall of Fame.[7]

William M. Johnston*

"Little Bill" Johnston—at five foot eight and a half—will forever be linked with his Davis Cup compatriot and rival six-foot-two "Big Bill" Tilden. They beat the Australasians, Japanese, and French in the Davis Cup challenge round from 1920 to 1926, "a seven-year span of invincibility unequalled in those international team matches."[1] In fourteen challenge round ties during that period including two doubles with Tilden, he lost only one match, a five-setter against Aussie James O. Anderson in 1923, whom he had beaten in 1922.

Born November 2, 1894, in San Francisco, the son of Robert Johnston, a mechanic in an electric plant, and Margaret (Burns) Johnston, of Irish origin, the sandy-haired, freckled right-hander Johnston learned to play tennis on the asphalt courts of Golden Gate Park, preceded and aided by Davis Cup stars Mel Long and Maurice McLoughlin. His first tournament win was the 1910 Bay Counties junior singles.[2]

Johnston captured the 1912 California, Oregon, and Washington championships, defeating Mel Long in the last. In 1913 he graduated from Lowell High in San Francisco and won his first of ten Pacific Coast singles titles.[3] On his first trip east in 1913, the eighteen-year-old Johnston captured the Longwood Bowl over George Gardner, 6–2, 6–4, 6–4,[4] and the Empire State title at Bay Ridge over S. Howard Voshell, 6–4, 6–4,

4–6, 6–2.[5] He ranked fourth nationally in 1913 and dropped to sixth in 1914. In 1915 he won the national singles title, defeating Karl Behr, Peck Griffin, Dick Williams (who had defeated him in the 1913 and 1914 nationals), and his idol "the Comet" McLoughlin in the final, 1–6, 6–0, 7–5, 10–8.[6] In the 1916 nationals Johnston beat Lindley Murray in the semis but lost to Dick Williams in a brilliant final, 4–6, 6–4, 0–6, 6–2, 6–4.

Johnston was renowned for the power and deadliness of his topspin forehand drive, which he hit shoulder high with a Western grip and which was universally considered the best forehand of all time until the advent of Pancho Segura in the late 1940s with his two-handed forehand. Acute timing, quickness, and a sweeping backswing enabled him to pound his famous bullet-like forehand. A practically flat backhand hit with the same racket face, although less spectacular, proved more reliable. Johnston attacked continuously and followed severe, deep shots to the net, where he punched away smashes and volleys. His sliced serve was placed accurately but did not overwhelm opponents. A tenacious, persistent battler, he was also a modest, unassuming sportsman, greatly respected by opponents and spectators. Wearing the required-period flannels, Johnston many times came off the court dripping with perspiration and weighing five to eight pounds below his usual 120 to 125 pounds.[7–8]

During World War I, Johnston enlisted in the U.S. Navy, rose from ensign to lieutenant, and served mostly in the Pacific. He married Irene Norman of San Francisco in 1917 and had no children.[9]

In 1919 Johnston triumphed in the U.S. Championships, U.S. Clay Court, Longwood Bowl, Pacific Coast, and Northwestern singles and lost only two matches, both to Tilden.[10] In the U.S. Championships, he defeated Gerald Patterson, Lindley Murray, Wallace Johnson, and Bill Tilden, 6–4, 6–4, 6–3. Johnston was U.S. no. 1 and tied for world no. 1 with Gerald Patterson from Australia.

After 1919 Tilden dominated tennis. In the national championahips from 1920 to 1925, "Big Bill" conquered "Little Bill" all six times. Tilden defeated him in five finals, including three times in brilliant five-set classics. Only once, in 1921, did it fail to come off. That year the U.S. Nationals moved to the Germantown Cricket Club in Philadelphia, and many recognized a terrible inequity in the draw. It "was absurdly 'top heavy,' and Johnston had to battle ... Vinnie Richards in the third round [which he won in five sets after losing the first two] for the right to meet Tilden" in the fourth or round of sixteen.[11] Tilden prevailed in four sets and went on to rout Wallace Johnson in the final, 6–1, 6–3, 6–1. This was like having "Macbeth fight Macduff in Act II instead of Act V." The rules committee forthwith struck a telling blow against the anticlimax.[12]

The seeding was an unprecedented success in 1922. In Philadelphia, fourteen seeds reached the round of sixteen, the top eight all arrived as expected for their quarterfinals, the top four got to the semifinals, and the top two—Bill Tilden and Bill Johnston—met in the final.[13] This was the moment of truth since both players had twice won the cup and the winner of this match would retain it for all time. Johnston won the first two sets and could likely see his own confident and hopeful face reflected back to him from the glistening cup sitting on a table off to one side. Whether Tilden had been baiting Johnston is uncertain, but the former let loose with all his shot-making wizardry to win the last three sets and the cup. Lin Murray was in Johnston's corner, as it were, during the ten-minute intermission between the third and fourth sets and could see that Tilden seemed fresh in comparison to the tiring Johnston. Only eight days later, Murray would play an exhibition match with Johnston at the Niagara Falls Country Club.

Johnston ranked in the World top ten from 1919 to 1926 and in the U.S. top ten twelve times between 1913 and 1926, no. 1 in 1915 and 1919, and no. 2 in 1916 and from 1920 through 1925. In Davis Cup play, besides splitting two singles with James Anderson, Johnston defeated Gerald Patterson, Jean Borotra, and Rene Lacoste twice each and Andre Gobert, James Parke, Algy Kingscote, Norman Brookes, Zenzo Shimizu, Ichiya Kumagae, and John Hawkes once apiece.

Abroad in 1923, Johnston won the World Hard Court Championships (the precursor to the French Open on the clay courts of the Stade Francais in Saint-Cloud[14]) by beating Rene Lacoste and Jan Washer.[15] Then he conquered the All-England field by defeating Vinnie Richards in the fourth round, 6–4, 6–3, 7–5, Cecil Campbell in four in the quarters, Babe Norton in the semis, 6–4, 6–2, 6–4, and demolished Frank Hunter in the final, 6–0, 6–3, 6–1.

His end came in 1927 when he lost Davis Cup matches to Rene Lacoste and Henri Cochet. Lacoste finally beat Bill Tilden, and France took home the Cup the next six years. After defeating Frenchman Jacques Brugnon in the 1927 U.S. Championships quarters, Johnston lost to Lacoste in four in the semis, and Lacoste went on to defeat Tilden in the final.

Johnston won a total seven majors—the U.S. singles in 1916 and 1919, the U.S. doubles with Peck Griffin in 1915, '16, and '20, the U.S.

mixed with Mary K. Browne in 1921, and the Wimbledon singles in 1923. Following the 1927 season Johnston retired from competition. Despite his exemplary post–World War I record, his health had not been robust since he had served in the navy. He worked principally as an insurance broker and at his death in 1946 was president of a railroad equipment company. He was inducted into the National Tennis Hall of Fame in 1958.[16–17]

At the Olympic Country Club in San Francisco a memorial dinner was given for William M. Johnston on January 30, 1959. Julian S. Myrick, former USNLTA president and current National Tennis Hall of Fame chairman said:

> I have known all of the champions from the first, Dick Sears, on a first name basis. To me Bill Johnston is the ideal of a real champion, not only a great player but a fine character and sportsman. From the time he started out here as a junior in 1909 until he retired in 1927 he played the part of a champion.
>
> His record in our championships and Davis Cup play are second to none. I could bring back many memories but one I always remember is when he won his first championship in 1915. I was walking off the court with him and asked if he would like anything done. He said he would like a telegram sent to his mother and gave me her address. It was sent. Then he went to join the navy from my house in 1917. He had a fine war record.[18]

Ichiya Kumagae

Ichiya Kumagae's tennis career was quite astonishing. Born September 10, 1890, he was past twenty before he ever saw a tennis racket or ball and had never played the game until his freshman year at Keio University in Tokyo. He took up the game seriously in 1912 and seven months later (January 1913) played in his first tournament, the Far East championship in Manila. He was beaten but adapted well and forced eventual champion Bill Johnston to four sets. "I never learned so much tennis in my life as in that game," he later said.[1]

In 1915 Clarence Griffin and Ward Dawson of California took the boat ride to Manila, both falling to the superior play of Kumagae for the

1916 Championship of the Orient. Kumagae and Mikami were runners-up to Griffin and Dawson for the doubles title.[2]

Kumagae came to the United States in 1916 and within six months captured half a dozen championships. At the U.S. Championships, he lost in the second round to George Church, 6–3, 6–3, 6–1. Only two weeks before Kumagae had defeated then national champion Bill Johnston in a memorable five-set match in the Newport singles final.[3] He defeated Harold Taylor, 6–2, 6–3, 6–1, in the final round of the Metropolitan singles championship on the courts of the Crescent Athletic Club in 1918. [4] At the 1919 New York State championship in Utica in July, Kumagae won the title for the third time—and thereby became permanent possessor of the Maurice McLoughlin Bowl—by beating Charles Garland, 6–3, 6–1, 6–1. Kumagae also won in 1919 the Brooklyn, Great Lakes, Niagara International, Old Dominion, and Virginia State championships.

Kumagae didn't play in the 1917 nationals but reached the 1918 semis, where he lost to Bill Tilden in three and again lost to Tilden in the 1919 fourth round in five. He was ranked in the U.S. top ten five consecutive years (as a foreign citizen residing in the United States) from 1916 to 1921 (there were no rankings in 1917) and third in 1919, winning six tournaments that season. He weighed 134 pounds, was only five feet three, and his eyes were so poor he wore glasses at all times.

Commenting on Kumagae's game, Tilden said: "He came here to America in 1916, the possessor of a wonderful forehand drive and nothing else. Kumagae is left-handed, which made his peculiar shots all the harder to handle. He met with fair success during the year; his crowning triumph was his defeat of W. M. Johnston at Newport in five sets." In 1917 he returned to America to enter business in New York. He learned an American twist service, strengthened his backhand, and started coming to the net to volley, and commented Tilden, "his high volleying and overhead are now excellent."[5]

The 1920 season found Kumagae sweeping all before him when the American Davis Cup team comprising Charles Garland, Bill Johnston, Bill Tilden, and Dick Williams was in New Zealand. Tilden remarked, "Kumagae is still essentially a base-line player of marvelous accuracy of shot and speed of foot. His drive is a lethal weapon that spreads destruction among his opponents. His backhand is a severe 'poke,' none too accurate, but very deadly when it goes in. His service overhead and high volley are all severe and reliable. His low volley is the weak spot in an otherwise great game. Kumagae cannot handle a chop, and dislikes grass-court play, as the ball bounds too low for his peculiar 'loop' drive. He is one of the greatest hard-court players in the world, and one of the most dangerous opponents at any time on any surface."[6]

He won two silver medals at the 1920 Antwerp Olympics. He lost to South African Louis Raymond in the singles final, 5–7, 6–4, 7–5, 6–4, and, pairing with Seiichiro Kashio, lost to Oswald Turnbull and Maxwell Woosnam of Great Britain in the doubles final, 6–2, 5–7, 7–5, 7–5. Kumagae was Japan's first Davis Cup captain, including the runner-up finish to Bill Tilden and company in 1921, the Japanese team's first year of competition.[7]

Melville H. Long

Along with Maurice McLoughlin, Mel Long and his brother Herbert were among the first members of the Golden Gate Junior Tennis Club organized in the fall of 1904 in which stress was laid on an aggressive style of play. Mel and his brother Herbert were the 1904–5 Academic Athletic League (AAL) Tennis Boys doubles champions from Lowell High School.[1]

After the veteran Percy Murdock beat Mel Long in the 1906 California State semis by 7–5 in the third set, he was in no shape to contend with Mel's brother Herbert in the final. At the 1906 Pacific Coast championship, sixteen-year-old Mel Long won the title by beating in succession Nat Browne, brother of future Hall of Famer Mary K. Browne, Alphonzo Bell, Charles Foley, Tom Bundy in the final, and George Janes in the challenge round. He also won the junior title by defeating McLoughlin, Getz, and Batkin. He was a finalist to George Janes in the Bay Counties championship.

Mel won the 1907 California State championship over George Janes in the final and his brother in the challenge match. He also won the 1907 Southern California title, beating Carl Gardner in the quarters, Alphonzo Bell in the semis, and Simpson Sinsabaugh in the final without losing a set. He then outlasted Harold Braly in the challenge round, 7–5, 2–6, 4–6, 7–5, 14–12. Seven times Braly needed but one point for match but was too exhausted to capitalize. Maurice McLoughlin took away the Pacific Coast title from Long in the challenge round in five deuce sets. Mel paired with Carl Gardner to win the Bay Counties title over Clarence Griffin and R. Hunt in five hard sets. Long was ranked no. 2 on the Pacific Coast after McLoughlin that year.

At the annual 1908 Ojai Valley tournament Mel and his brother Herbert won the California intercollegiate title for the University of California, Berkeley, by beating Stanford in both the singles and doubles events. Herbert played tennis for UC from 1907 to 1910 while Mel played from 1908 to 1911. In the 1908 San Francisco semis Mel Long was forced to three sets by George Janes while his brother softened up Carl Gardner in a fifty-game, three-set match. Mel put the finishing touches on Gardner but succumbed to "Red Mac" McLoughlin in a five-set challenge match.

Eastern stars Irving Wright, Nat Niles, and Wallace Johnson found the pace faster than what they had been used to at the 1908 Pacific States championship. Long disposed of Niles in the second round, Johnson in the final, and McLoughlin the holder in the challenge round after dropping the first two sets, 8–10, 6–8, 6–4, 11–9, 6–0. Mel Long was ranked no. 1 by the PSLTA for 1908 over McLoughlin.

Tom Bundy, Mel Long, Maurice McLoughlin, and other Californians came east in 1909 to compete in the Eastern circuit. In the nationals the Comet defeated Long in the fourth round, 10–8 in the fifth set and reached the first of six U.S. finals. In that match on center court, "Eastern society witnessed a fast-paced, powerful game unlike anything played up to that time. Competitive tennis was generally a high society game reserved for the sons of the wealthy.... Modern tennis may be said to have been born that day at Newport."[2] McLoughlin said, we "there staged one of our good old five-set California battles so familiar to both of us—that a great majority of that colorful social gathering sat up for the first time in their chairs and began looking at tennis with a new interest."[3] At year's end Mel Long was ranked seventh, and in 1910 and 1911 he was ranked fifth.

Representing the University of California, Mel Long lost to Wallace Johnson of the University of Pennsylvania on September 13, 1909 in the intercollegiate lawn tennis tourney final in Haverford, Pennsylvania. The match went to five sets, the score being 6–4, 3–6, 5–7, 8–6, 6–4.[4]

Melville Long and Maurice McLoughlin were sent as sacrificial lambs to Sydney, Australia, to play the seasoned Norman Brookes and Tony Wilding in the 1909 Davis Cup challenge round as the two Bills, Clothier and Larned, who had earned the right to challenge for the trophy by beating the Brits in the final, found it impossible to make the trip to the Antipodes.[5] Australasia won 5–0, but the Americans gained valuable international experience, Long taking Brookes to three deuce sets. At the Omaha Field Club, Mel Long won the inaugural 1910 U.S. Clay Court singles title over Walter Merrill Hall with the loss of but two games in three sets.[6]

Mel Long began his medical studies at the University of Pennsylvania in 1911 returning to San Francisco as Dr. Long. He was later named to the USTA Northern California Tennis Hall of Fame.[7] Born on October 16, 1889, Mel Long died May 13, 1969, at age seventy-nine.[8–9]

Dean Mathey

Dean Mathey of Cranford, New Jersey, "first came to Princeton in 1907 to play in the University's annual interscholastic tennis tournament, which he won." In 1908 "he won the national interscholastic tennis championship [for Pingry School] at Newport" and entered Princeton that fall. Mathey, class of 1912, twice shared national intercollegiate doubles championships—in 1910 with a classmate Burnham Dell and in 1911 with another classmate Charles Butler—"and was captain of the University tennis team in his senior year."[1]

Mathey won the 1912 Delaware State championship over Wallace Johnson, 2–6, 6–2, 6–3, 2–6, 8–6.[2] In 1913 Mathey won the Nassau Country Club Invitation in Glen Cove, Long Island, over Labor Day. He defeated in succession Charles Bull, 6–0, 7–5; Theodore Pell, 6–0, 7–5; and Gus Touchard, 6–2, 6–2, 6–2,[3] avenging his loss to Touchard in the Middle States championship final at Orange, New Jersey, during the week of June 23. That score was 4–6, 6–2, 9–7, 3–6, 8–6.[4] While Lin Murray won the 1914 Metropolitan singles over Fred Alexander, Church and Mathey won the doubles over Shafer and Smith, 6–3, 7–9, 6–4, 12–10.[5] Paired with George Church, Mathey reached the 1914 national doubles final.

Mathey destroyed Robert Stoddart of Yonkers for the 1920 New York State title, 6–0, 6–2, 6–2. The *New York Times* reported, "Mathey … played almost flawless tennis yesterday, with everything contributing toward an absolutely irresistible attack. His greatest strength was at the net, where both his low volleys and his smashes were severe as well as accurate. He scarcely missed an overhead shot all through the match, and it was seldom that a single smash failed to put the ball away with complete finality."[6]

Mathey was much more than a tennis star. At Princeton he was elected to Phi Beta Kappa and graduated with honors. On graduation, Mathey started work as a bond salesman at fifteen dollars a week. He eventually became a partner of Dillon, Read and Company and gradually built up a sizeable fortune.[7] He was later chairman of the board of the Empire Trust Company and honorary chairman of the Bank of New York.[8] He came to live in an old Princeton farmhouse in 1927, where he gave luncheons for classmates and for university trustees and officers, and became one of the university's greatest benefactors. He was alumni trustee of Princeton from 1927 to 1931, charter trustee from 1931 to 1960, and trustee emeritus from 1960 until his death.[9]

Under Mathey's chairmanship of the finance committee from 1949 to 1960, and of its subcommittee on investments, the university's budget increased six times over and its investment pool doubled. His greatest love was the committee on grounds and buildings on which he served for thirty-four years and was chairman from 1942 to 1949. He had the greatest concern for the preservation of beauty and the human feel of the campus. Among his many gifts to the university were the Dean Samuel Winans wall, enclosing the rear garden of the John Maclean House, in memory of his father-in-law, and the Gertrude Winans Mathey faculty housing, in memory of his first wife. When his classmate Sanford B. White, 1911 first team all-America end, died in 1964, Mathey led the class of 1912 to provide in White's memory another pavilion.[10]

"Mathey College was dedicated on November 6, 1983 and named after Dean Mathey '12, one of the most devoted, energetic and generous supporters of the University in modern times. His association with Princeton covered a period of 65 years."[11] Mathey authored *Fifty Years of Wall Street* in 1966 and a book of Princeton reminiscences, *Men and Gothic Towns*, in 1967.[12]

Writing for *Fortune Magazine*, October 26, 1987, Christopher Knowlton said, "Dean Mathey's actions as chairman of Princeton University's investment committee twice helped Princeton's endowment: prior to the great Crash of 1929, when he moved the endowment from stocks into bonds; and midway through WWII, when he sold off 80% of the university's bonds and replaced them with common stock holdings," in each case an exquisitely timed maneuver.[13]

Along the lines of tennis philanthropy, Dean Mathey provided the land and built and developed the Pretty Brook Tennis Club in 1929, a racquet-sports-oriented club in Princeton, New Jersey. In addition to other amenities, the club today has five outdoor tennis courts, four of which are Har-Tru, one indoor tennis court, two squash courts, and two paddle tennis courts.[14]

He married Gertrude Winans on March 26, 1927; and the union produced three sons: Dean, Macdonald, and David.[15] Each of the boys became avid tennis players. Dean provided the first upset of the 1944 Eastern junior tennis tournament at Forest Hills by defeating the no. 2 seed Richard Savitt of Bayonne, 6–3, 6–2, advancing himself to the semis.[16] In 1951 Savitt won the Australian singles title, the Wimbledon singles championship, and was the top-ranked player on the United States Davis Cup team.[17] Dean and Macdonald won the 1943 USTA Interscholastic Boys' 18 doubles representing Country Day School, Princeton, and in 1944 and 1946 representing Deerfield School, Massachusetts. Dean also captured the 1945 title paired with F. Burton Smith. Macdonald Mathey paired with Sidney Schwartz to win the 1944 USTA National Boys' 16s doubles at Kalamazoo College.[18]

After the passing of his wife Gertrude on April 4, 1949, at the age of fifty-eight, Dean married Helen Newsom-Behr, the widow of his business colleague at Dillon, Read and Company, and tennis partner, Karl Behr, who also died in 1949. Both Mr. and Mrs. Behr were *Titanic* survivors. Helen died in Princeton in 1965 and Dean Mathey, born November 23, 1890, died April 1972.[19]

Maurice Evans McLoughlin*

Maurice Evans McLoughlin was born January 7, 1890, in Carson City, Nevada, the son of Harriet (Verril) McLoughlin and Irish-born George McLoughlin. George, a mason at the Carson City mint, was transferred to the Philadelphia mint in 1898 as superintendent of machinery and to the San Francisco mint in 1903.[1–2] Maurice graduated from Crocker Grammar and Lowell High School,[3] the oldest public high school west of the Mississippi.[4]

Maury began playing on the public asphalt courts of the Golden Gate Junior Tennis Club and subsequently joined the California Tennis Club, also in San Francisco. In 1907 McLoughlin won the San Francisco City championship and the Pacific States title over Mel Long the holder in five deuce sets and was ranked no. 1 on the Pacific Coast. In 1908 he beat Mel Long for the California State title and paired with George Janes to win the doubles.

Maurice qualified to enter the University of California in 1909 but elected to play tennis instead. He ventured east that year with fellow San Franciscans George Janes and Melville Long and electrified the U.S.

Championships by beating Mel Long in a good old California five-set, fourth-round center-court battle, Maury winning 10–8 in the fifth. He reached the final where U.S. no. 4 William Clothier exploited his ground stroke weaknesses in four sets.

Maury and Mel so impressed the Davis Cup Committee that they were sent to Australia to play the seasoned Norman Brookes and Tony Wilding in the challenge round as Bill Clothier and Bill Larned, who had beaten the Brits in the final, were unable to go. The United States lost 5–0, but Maury took Wilding to four sets and Long had three deuce sets with Brookes.

Because of his dynamic personality, dazzling smile, flock of red hair, and the vibrant force of his attack,[5] McLoughlin became affectionately known as Red, Red Mac, the California Comet, or simply the Comet. He took tennis from the aristocracy, converted the game from a defensive to an offensive one, and, through his power and personality, "opened the eyes of the public to tennis as a demanding game of speed, endurance and skill" with his powerful cannonball service, spectacular volleys, and overhead smashes. "The volley was not new to the game ... but it had not nearly been the finishing stroke that Red Mac made it."[6–7]

McLoughlin was the first male tennis champion from the Western United States, and as "the first champion from the public parks, he was the point man in the democratization of the game."[8] He was in five straight U.S. finals from 1911 to 1915, losing to Bill Larned in 1911, the last year of the challenge round, winning in 1912 against Wallace Johnson after losing the first two sets, and wining in 1913 against Dick Williams. He also won the U.S. doubles title three times with Tom Bundy, from 1912 to 1914, the last year the championships were held at Newport. He was ranked in the U.S. top ten seven straight years between 1909 and 1915, no. 1 from 1912 to 1914 and world no. 1 in 1914.

In his one venture to England in 1913 McLoughlin helped draw unprecedentedly large crowds to Wimbledon, where he won the all-comers over Aussie Stanley Doust, 6–3, 6–4, 7–5, the first American to be a finalist in the singles at Wimbledon. In the challenge round he lost to 1913 world no. 1 Tony Wilding, 8–6, 6–3, 10–8. In the 1913 Davis Cup the United States shutout Germany and Canada and split singles against Cup-holding Britain the first day. McLoughlin partnered with Harold Hackett to defeat Roper Barrett and Charles Dixon in five sets, 5–7, 6–1, 2–6, 7–5, 6–4, and he then defeated Dixon in singles, 8–6, 6–3, 6–2, to give the United States a 3–2 victory.[9]

McLoughlin reached his peak the next year in the Davis Cup final, even though the U.S. team lost. A crowd of fourteen thousand people from all over the world gathered each day at Forest Hills. The match between McLoughlin and Norman Brookes of Australasia "was a revelation to lawn tennis players, and their skill, headwork, change of pace—in fact, all round tennis—has never been equaled. The first set was not only a record breaker in the history of international matches, but also was probably the hardest played set, on both sides, that has ever been witnessed, both men exerting themselves to the utmost."[10] McLoughlin won, 17–15, 6–3, 6–3. After the Davis Cup success, *Spalding's 1915 Annual* said, "[I]n McLoughlin America undoubtedly has the greatest tennis player of all time."[11]

Writing in 1920, Fred Hawthorne said that McLoughlin "was undoubtedly known to more people, in and out of tennis, than any player who ever trod the courts ... because of his terrific and awe-inspiring smash." "Maury" could hit his whirlwind smash from any position on the court. Although "Red Mac" had a limited assortment of ground strokes, the "instinct of self-preservation cautioned McLoughlin's opponents to keep" him "away from the net at all costs, and if they could not do this by driving, they fell back on the lob." However, it made no difference to McLoughlin whether the lob was short or deep. If the former, he would rush in from the baseline to crack it for a kill and, if the latter, "he would go racing back, watching the ball in its flight, and then, when it came within the swing of his racquet, hurl himself bodily off the ground and upward, and whip his racquet arm forward and downward in a curving parabola that sent the ball cannonading back into the opposing court."[12]

McLoughlin's book, *Tennis As I Play It*, published in 1915 with a preface by Dick Williams, was dedicated to Dr. Sidney R. Marvin, who helped develop and encourage many successful Golden Gate Park players. After losing handily to George Church in the fourth round of the 1916 U.S. Championships, Maury was absent from the 1917 and 1918 nationals while in the U.S. Navy during World War I. He married Helen Mears of Pasadena in 1918,[13] came back for a go in 1919, and lost decisively to Dick Williams in the U.S. quarterfinals. Some believed McLoughlin's game, like that of Lin Murray's, was too strenuous. He never fully recovered from his Davis Cup wins over Brookes and Wilding[14] and was only a shell of his former self after the war.

He left the tennis scene for golf, where he soon was shooting in the low seventies,[15] while engaged in real estate and other businesses. Maury and Helen had three children, one son and two daughters. A longtime resident of Pasadena and then of Hermosa Beach, the Comet was inducted into the National Tennis Hall of Fame in 1957 and died of heart disease on December 10 of that year.[16–17]

Nathaniel (Nat) W. Niles

Nat Niles was born July 5, 1886, in Boston. He won the 1904 and 1905 U.S. interscholastic singles for Boston Latin and then won the 1907 intercollegiate doubles for Harvard with A. S. Dabney and the 1908 intercollegiate singles. In the 1908 International tennis tournament at Niagara-on-the-Lake, Niles defeated Wallace Johnson of Philadelphia, 6–4, 6–4, 2–6, 8–6, in the final and Irving Wright, 1–6, 2–6, 6–4, 6–4, 6–4, in the challenge round.[1] He liked Niagara Falls so well he came back to win the title in 1909 and 1910.[2–3] He also won the 1910 and 1911 Great Lakes Championship in Buffalo during the challenge round days, the first over the titleholder W. Johnson (U.S. no. 3) by 4–6, 7–5, 6–2, 7–5, the second over C. Benton of Cleveland in three easy sets.[4–5]

In the U.S. Championships Niles paired with Edith Rotch to win the 1908 mixed doubles. He beat Leonard Beekman to reach the 1913 U.S. semifinals where he lost to Dick Williams, 6-4, 7-5, 3-6, 6-1, and defeated U.S. no. 1 Williams in the 1917 U.S. "Patriotic" semis where he lost to Lindley Murray in the final.

As late as 1920 Niles again defeated Wallace Johnson (U.S. no. 5) in the fourth round of the Longwood Club tournament in a desperately fought five-set match. In the fourth set, when leading two sets to one, the Philadelphian needed only one point to take the fourteenth game—and the set and match—but failed to get it. The final score was 2–6, 6–1, 6–8, 12–10, 6–3.[6] Ten times he was ranked in the U.S. top ten: 1908 to '13, '15, '18, '20, and '21. Nat Niles was inducted into the USTA New England Hall of Fame in 2000.

Although his tennis accomplishments were significant, Niles is probably better known as a figure skater. He won the U.S. Figure Skating Championships three times (1918, '25, and '27) and placed second five times (1920 to '22, '24, and '26). He was even more successful in pairs skating with Theresa Weld-Blanchard. They placed first in the national pairs nine successive times from 1918 to 1927 (there was no competition 1919) and second three times. Blanchard and Niles won the North American Championships in 1925 and also won a further five national titles in ice dancing. At the 1920 Olympic Games, Niles placed sixth in men's single skating and fourth with Blanchard in pairs skating. Niles died July 11, 1932, at the age of forty-six. Earlier that year he and Blanchard had competed at the World Figure Skating Championships.[7]

Theodore Roosevelt Pell*

Theodore Pell, a slender six-foot New Yorker, made his mark inside, winning the U.S. Indoor singles in 1907, '09, and '11; he was runner-up in 1908 to Wylie Grant. He won the doubles four times between 1905 and 1912, in 1905 with H. F. Allen, in 1909 with Wylie Grant, and in 1911 and 1912 with Fred Alexander.[1–2] The only U.S. tennis player at the 1912 Olympics, he lost to Ludwig Heyden of Germany in the round of sixteen who next lost to gold medalist Charles Winslow of South Africa in Winslow's only five-setter.

Pell also won four successive New England titles at Hartford from 1907 to 1910 and four successive doubles titles from 1906 to 1909, in 1906 with Wylie Grant, in 1907 with Robert LeRoy, in 1908 with T. R. Gross, and in 1909 again with Wylie Grant.[3] This was the same tournament in which Lindley Murray captured the singles in 1914 and the doubles with Stanford teammate Herbert Hahn.

As was Lin Murray by his mother Nella Howland Gifford through Sarah Allen, Theodore Roosevelt Pell was one of the Howland heirs through John H. Howland. He was the son of John Howland Pell and Caroline E. Hyatt. Born at Yonkers, New York, May 12, 1878, Pell was a member of the real estate firm of Pell and Tibbits, New York City. He married Florence Cramp and had no children.[4]

Pell had a particularly strong backhand and was ranked in the U.S. top ten five times between 1910 and 1918, no. 5 in 1913 and 1915. Allison Danzig wrote that Pell "unsheathed a backhand that was as much of a sensation as Donald Budge's was to become a generation later."[5] Pell won the 1913 Seabright Invitation for the Achelis Cup over Nat Niles, 6–3, 4–6, 6–2, 4–6, 8–6,[6] and was doubles finalist with Karl Behr in 1914, losing to Maurice McLoughlin and Thomas Bundy, national champions, 12–10, 7–5, 4–6, 7–9, 7–5.[7] The Pell-Behr combination won the 1914 Eastern doubles title and the 1914 and 1915 Middle States doubles titles.[8] Pell captured the Middle States singles title in 1916 and was runner-up to Karl Behr in 1914.[9]

In the 1910 nationals he upset the Pennsylvania State champion, Wallace Johnson, 7–5, 8–6, 6–4.[10] His best showing at the nationals was in 1915 when he defeated in succession Watson Washburn, Charles Bull, and Irving Wright in straight sets, before losing to "the Comet," Maurice McLoughlin, in the semis. Pell was elected to the National Tennis Hall of Fame in 1966 and died a year later, on August 18, 1967, in Sands Point, New York.[11]

Eleonora Randolph Sears*

Eleonora "Eleo" Sears was born on September 28, 1881, into wealth and the highest strata of society. She was the great-great-granddaughter of Thomas Jefferson and granddaughter of Thomas Jefferson Coolidge, ambassador to France and founder of the First National Bank.[1] Her father, Fred Sears, a shipping and real estate tycoon, was the first person on record to play tennis in the United States, with Dr. James Dwight at Nahant in 1874. Her uncle, Dick Sears, won the first seven U.S. singles championships and six of the first seven doubles titles. Eleo was a beautiful and popular society woman at night and a daring and talented athlete by day.

Eleo attended the balls, debuts, weddings, and other events that were considered *de rigueur* for a woman of her day and position. Over the 1904 Christmas holidays she attended a dinner dance in New York celebrating the debut of President Roosevelt's niece, Corinne Douglass Robinson, and sat at a table presided over by Miss Eleanor Roosevelt,[2] Corinne's first cousin. (Eleanor married Franklin on March 17, 1905.[3]) In June of 1905 she was a member of the wedding party of Grace Dabney and four-time U.S. singles tennis champion Robert Wrenn. By August 15, 1905, she was playing singles and doubles at a lawn tennis tournament on the Newport Casino courts arranged by Mrs. John Jacob Astor.[4] By the end of 1905 she was planning a visit to her friend Alice Roosevelt, Theodore's eldest daughter.[5] "Sometime in 1905 or 1906, Eleonora started 'being seen with' the young Harold Vanderbilt, heir to the Vanderbilt fortune, who shared many of Eleo's sporting proclivities," but the pair eventually drifted apart.[6]

Eleo would go on to become the first great multi-sport woman of the twentieth century. Having bred, rode, and trained show horses all her life she was a determined and independent sportswoman. She rode in steeplechases and on a bet one winter's morning in 1912, drove a four-in-hand coach (akin to a stagecoach or tallyho) down Fifth Avenue.[7] "During a 1912 stay in California, she won a quarter horse race in San Diego and fielded a women's polo team at the Hotel Del Monte,"[8] the site of several Pacific Coast tennis championships.

Like her namesake, Eleanor of Aquitaine, the queen consort of France and England who rode into the Second Crusade with her ladies-in-waiting dressed as Amazons, Eleonora Sears was the first woman known to have worn pants for sporting purposes when in 1909 at the Burlingame Country Club, south of San Francisco, she rode out onto the "men only" polo field shockingly riding her horse astride in breeches and a cutaway coat and asked if she could join in a practice session with the visiting British international team.[9–10] She was promptly ordered to leave the field and the fictitious "Burlingame Mothers' Club" passed a resolution stating: "Such unconventional trousers and clothes of the masculine sex are contrary to the hard and fast customs of our ancestors. It is immodest and wholly unbecoming a woman, having a bad effect on the sensibilities of our boys and girls."[11] Nevertheless, she became the first woman to ride astride at the National Horse Show in 1915.

In tennis, Eleonora reached the U.S. singles final in 1912, losing to Mary K. Browne, but she was most successful in doubles. She won four U.S. women's doubles titles, two with Hazel Hotchkiss-Wightman (1911 and 1915) and two with Molla Bjurstedt (1916 and 1917), as well as the mixed with Willis Davis in 1916. Eleo ranked in the U.S. top ten twice, in 1914 and 1916, and entered the National Tennis Hall of Fame in 1968.[12]

On the water Eleo skippered a yacht that raced Alfred Vanderbilt's *Walthra*—and won. She also raced speedboats and was the first person of either gender to swim from Bailey's Beach to First Beach in Newport, Rhode Island, a distance of four and a half miles.[13]

Eleo was also known for her marathon walks. She frequently walked from Boston to Providence, a distance of about forty-four miles that she covered in less than ten hours in 1926. She once walked from Newport to Boston, seventy-three miles, in seventeen hours. During her 1912 California visit, she walked from the Burlingame Country Club to the Hotel del Monte, 109 miles, in forty-one hours.[14] She usually had a chauffer tag along with a thermos and sandwiches.

In a kindred racket sport, Eleonora was a frequent guest at the all-men's Harvard Club where in 1918 she learned to play squash.[15] In 1928 Eleo helped to found the U.S. Women's Squash Racquets Association becoming its first singles champion that inaugural year at age forty-six. She later served as its president and was captain of the U.S. national team.[16]

Eleo was an excellent golfer and played baseball and football, as fullback. She played field hockey and was one of New England's best trap shooters. "She was one of the first women to fly in a plane (in 1910 with pilot [and English aviation pioneer] Claude Grahame-White) and to race a car."[17] Kihm Winship wrote that "she was summoned to appear in court for driving a 'high-power roadster' on the roads of Massachusetts" in the summer of 1913. "The police presented the summons at Miss Sears' home, presumably because they could not catch her on the open road."[18]

Eleonora had many male companions but never married, possibly because she never met a man who could keep up with her. One might think, given her athletic prowess and more than 240 trophies, that Sears was a tomboy, "but in fact, she was a great beauty and, after dark, every inch the socialite."[19] "She frequently topped New York's '10-best dressed' list."[20] After spending a packed day in Boston hunting by day at Myopia and dancing by night with the debutantes in 1924, Edward, the Prince of Wales, who would later marry Wallis Simpson and abdicate the British throne, was said to be so charmed by Eleo that he spent much of the evening as her dancing partner, although thirteen years her junior.[21] The beautiful and controversial trendsetter died on March 16, 1968, at age eighty-six.[22]

John R. Strachan

John Strachan, another San Franciscan trained at the Golden Gate Junior Tennis Club, reached the finals of three singles and four doubles tournaments in 1913 California as a teenager, each time losing to sixteen-year-old Bill Johnston in singles and to Johnston and partner in doubles. At the Coronado Country Club championship in February, he lost to Johnston, 8–6, 6–3, in singles and to Johnston and Nat Browne, 6–1, 6–2, 6–2, in the doubles paired with Clarence Griffin.[1] At the Ojai Valley championship in April, Strachan lost to Johnston, 6–4, 6–8, 6–2, in singles and to Johnston and Elia Fottrell, 6–4, 8–6, in the doubles paired with Rosenberg.[2] In the Pacific States championship in June, he lost to Johnston, 6–1, 6–1, 3–6, 4–6, 6–4, in singles and to Johnston and Fottrell, 10–8, 6–0, 2–6, 6–3, in the doubles event paired with Griffin.[3] The two pairs collided again at the California State championship in September. Strachan and Griffin's losing score in the finals was 6–3, 6–4, 6–2.[4]

Strachan won the 1913 National Clay Court singles over Walter Merrill Hall, 6–0, 6–4, 4–6, 6–4, and paired again with Clarence Griffin to win the doubles. Strachan and Griffin paired so well together they reached the finals of the 1913 U.S. men's doubles at Newport, where they lost to Tom Bundy and Maurice McLoughlin, 6–4, 7–5, 6–1. His best showing in the nationals was in the 1917 "Patriotic" tournament. He defeated Charles Garland, 6–1, 2–6, 6–2, 6–3, in the quarters before losing to eventual winner Lindley Murray, 4–6, 6–3, 6–3, 6–1, in the semis. He was ranked in the U.S. top ten in 1913.

William Tatem Tilden II*

Writing a short biography on William Tatem Tilden II, or "Big Bill," would be difficult enough if one were just to concentrate on his tennis accomplishments. The many adjectives that have been used by writers to describe Tilden in alphabetical order include: arrogant, artistic, belligerent, carping, cerebral, charming, conceited, contemptuous, demanding, dramatic, egotistical, faultfinding, flamboyant, generous, gracious, inconsiderate, inglorious, insufferable, intelligent, opinionated, self-destructive, strategical, temperamental, theatrical—and in the late 1940s, homosexual.

He was born February 10, 1893, into a wealthy Philadelphia family that had lost three infant children to a diphtheria epidemic in 1884. After his mother contracted Bright's disease in 1908, Tilden was shipped to Germantown Academy and lived with his mother's sister, Betsy Hey, and her niece, Selina, a few houses away. He would retain his room in that house until 1941 when he was forty-eight. His mother suffered a stroke and died on May 2, 1911. His father fell ill with kidney trouble, compounded by uremic poisoning, and died on July 29, 1915. His older brother Herbert "caught a cold" swimming at Cape May, New Jersey, and died a few days later of pneumonia, September 15, 1915. Herbert was twenty-nine, and Bill was twenty-two.[1–3]

Tilden's early tennis days were none too promising. He was not no. 1 at his prep school, nor did he make the University of Pennsylvania tennis team in his first try. Bill dropped out of Penn and began to practice against a backboard.[4] He played in the 1912 U.S. Championships at Newport, losing in his first match to Wallace Johnson, 6–2, 6–3, 6–4. In 1916 he lost in the first round to Harold Throckmorton, 4–6, 6–4, 6–2, 8–6, and in 1917 and 1918 to Lin Murray. In the meantime Bill won the 1913 and 1914 U.S. mixed titles with Mary Browne, and was a finalist in 1916, '17, and '19 with Florence Ballin. He paired with Vinnie Richards to win the

1918 men's doubles and was runner-up in 1919. Bill was therefore quite successful at doubles; in singles he won the 1918 U.S. Clay Court and the 1919 Seabright invitational tournaments.

"Johnston came out of the service and Tilden beat him two or three times in the summer of 1919" and on the grass at Newport a couple of weeks before the U.S. Championships at Forest Hills.[5] Tilden beat the famous Australian Norman Brookes in the quarters and Dick Williams in straight sets in the semis, and he really believed his time had come. Little Bill, the gallery favorite, toppled Tilden in the final, 6–4, 6–4, 6–3. At twenty-six—the age when Bjorn Borg lost his fourth U.S. Open final to John McEnroe in 1981 and walked off court and out of the stadium before the ceremonies and press conference had begun, literally retiring from the game—Tilden's career had just begun. Little Bill said he sent most of his shots down the middle and came to the net. Big Bill thought that Johnston had done him in by exploiting the one loophole in his game, his backhand. His backhand slice was defensive, and Johnston pounded it to death.

Instead of foregoing the game as Borg later did at twenty-six, Tilden made arrangements with an insurance executive named Mr. John D. E. Jones of Providence, Rhode Island, who happened to own one of the few indoor courts in the country. Bill gave tennis lessons to Jones's son Arnold W., the national sixteen-and-under champion, in exchange for practice time. Arnold would go on to become a member of the 1928 U.S. Davis Cup team.[6] During the winter of 1919–20, Bill Tilden hit backhand after backhand alone or with young Jones at the indoor facility, or chopped wood to build muscle and gain strength. His Hall of Fame write-up said, "He emerged with a brand new, fearsome, multifaceted backhand and complete game, and was ready to conquer the world."[7]

He did just that for the next decade. In 1920 Tilden became the first American male to win Wimbledon, defeating Gerald Patterson of Australia in the challenge round. Already theatrical at the 1920 U.S. final, Tilden and Johnston took to the court after a rain delay under gray, forbidding skies—Tilden in his camel's hair coat with a big sash and an armful of rackets, and Johnston with two. It was then called the greatest U.S. final in history.[8] Tilden defeated Johnston, 6–1, 1–6, 7–5, 5–7, 6–3, in a match that was interrupted after four sets. A single-engine Curtiss airplane made several passes over the stadium when it choked out and plummeted to the ground barely two hundred feet from the stands. As about a third of the people in the stadium left their seats for the crash site, the two Bills got on with their brilliant contest. Big Bill came to the net to shake Little Bill's hand as the two bodies were extricated from the wreckage.[9]

Tilden would win six consecutive U.S. singles titles from 1920 through 1925 in five finals against Johnston and in 1921 against Wallace Johnson, as well as a record-tying seventh in 1929. Allison Danzig pointed out: "It was Johnston's misfortune that he was a contemporary of Tilden. Had their career's not coincided, 'Little Bill' might have won the championship eight times instead of twice."[10] The only year Johnston didn't make the final was 1921 when he lost to Tilden in the fourth round.

Tilden also won Wimbledon in 1920 and 1921. He decided not to cross the pond on a slow boat to compete from 1922 to 1926 largely because the Davis Cup was being played in the United States. The next three years he lost in the semifinals before winning again in 1930 against fellow American Wilmer Allison. Wimbledon was his first major at age twenty-seven and his last at age thirty-seven, giving him a total of ten major singles titles. Counting men's and mixed doubles, his total major count is twenty-one. He was also a major finalist on thirteen other occasions. In the U.S. Championships Tilden won sixty-nine matches and a record forty-two straight between 1920 and 1926.

According to his Hall of Fame write-up, "[n]obody had a more devastating service than Tilden's cannonball, or a more challenging second serve than his kicking American twist. No player had a stronger combination of forehand and backhand drives, supplemented by a forehand chop and backhand slice … [T]he backcourt game was where Tilden played tennis. He was no advocate of the 'big game,' the big serve and rush for the net for the instant volley coup. He relished playing tennis as a game of chess, matching wits as well as physical prowess. The drop shot, at which he was particularly adroit, and the lob were among his disconcerting weapons."[11]

Tilden won seven U.S. clay court titles, five U.S. doubles titles, four U.S. mixed titles, and four national indoor titles.[12] His concentration could be awesome: he didn't lose a match in 1924 and won fifty-seven straight games during a two-tournament stretch in 1925 at Glen Cove, New York, and Newport. Trailing Alfred Chapin 3–4 in the final at Nassau, he ran it out, 6–4, 6–0, 6–0, and on the next stop won three straight 6–0, 6–0 matches. He then came up against his old protégé Carl Fischer, and won the first set at love, but at 30–all in the first game of the second set, Fischer said that Tilden received an atrocious call against him, and lost the next point and record streak. He then ran off six more games and another 6–1 set[13-14] made it sixty-nine of seventy-one games. It was little known at the time, but in 1922 the tip of Tilden's right middle finger became infected and was amputated. He simply modified his grip and continued to play at the same level at which he had played before.

Led by Tilden and Johnston, the United States won seven consecutive Davis Cup challenge rounds between 1920 and 1926 over Australia, Japan, and France. Tilden won thirteen straight singles victories, his only loss being to Rene Lacoste in 1926. The United States lost the Cup to France by 3–2 in 1927. Constantly wrangling with USLTA officers and committeemen on Davis Cup policy and enforcement of the amateur rule, Tilden became front-page news in 1928 when he was removed as captain and star player of the Davis Cup team and suspended from amateur competition for six months, charged with violating the amateur rule by writing articles about the Wimbledon championships in which he was competing.

When the French heard that "Teelden" would not be playing in their new sold-out Roland Garros Stadium, they sent diplomats to ask then U.S. President Calvin Coolidge to allow Tilden to play. The president told the American ambassador in Paris, Myron T. Herrick, to disregard the U.S. Davis Cup captain, and Tilden played, beating Rene Lacoste in the opening match "with a display of versatility that has never been equaled," wrote George Lott. "Lacoste at this time had beaten Tilden on several occasions and was a 2–1 favorite. Tilden defeated this great baseliner with chops, slices, drop shots, lobs and power shots, conceived and executed by the greatest tennis brain of all time."[15] On Tilden's return home, he was found guilty and suspended from playing the U.S. Championships that year. Eligible for the U.S. title in 1929, he won the crown for the seventh time, defeating his doubles partner Frank Hunter.[16–17]

His showmanship occasionally veered into what his opponents called gamesmanship; he tried to give his paying audience its money's worth and threw the early sets of a match in order to prolong the battle. According to Allison Danzig, "[Tilden's] idea of a good time was to get the gallery seething with excitement by giving his opponent a dangerous lead and then, with the stage properly set and the crowd won over to his side by the seeming desperateness of his plight, come on in a cyclonic rally to victory."[18]

In the 1925 Illinois State championship at the Skokie Country Club, Tilden played Howard Kinsey, the no. 4 player in the country and 1924 National doubles champion with his brother, Robert. Allison Danzig described a specific example of confidence and theatrical showmanship.

> After winning the first two sets, Tilden lost the next two. Leading 2–0 in the fifth set, he then lost the next five games. The crowd of 5,000 buzzed with excitement. Could it be that the great Tilden was going down in defeat?
>
> The court was close to Lake Michigan and a cold wind was blowing. The spectators were bundled in coats and blankets. As the players changed sides with the score 2–5, Tilden took off his sweater for the first time, picked up a pitcher of ice water at the umpire's chair and poured it over his head.
>
> A shiver went through the crowd. Tilden kept them waiting as he carefully dried his head and hands. Finally he walked to the base line and prepared to serve. Then, adding to the suspense, he beckoned to a ball boy to bring him a towel with the imperious gesture he used so often when holding court before his tennis audiences.
>
> Meticulously, he wiped the last bit of moisture from his hands. By now the gallery was limp from tension. With the stage set as he wanted it, Tilden picked up racket and balls and cut loose. Kinsey could win only one more game—after Tilden had won four. Final score: 8–6. The cheers for Big Bill at the end were wild.[19]

In 1923 Brian "Babe" Norton of South Africa was quoted in the *New York Times* as saying that he was confident he could win the U.S. Nationals if he defeated Dick Williams the next day in the quarterfinals at Germantown, Pennsylvania, Tilden's home turf. Tilden was so infuriated that he threatened to withdraw from the tournament if Norton did not apologize to him for the implied slight. Norton did beat Williams, 1–6, 6–3, 6–4, 3–6, 6–4, and Tilden polished off Norton in straight sets in the semis, 6–3, 7–5, 6–2, before again conquering Bill Johnston.[20] Tilden had paired with Norton that year to win the U.S. doubles, the first time in history the national doubles title-winning team was hybrid.

Tilden could be brutal against any opponent he personally disliked or that had offended him and there were those who strived to get his goat like Jean Borotra and George Lott. Frank Deford told a story in which John Hennessy of Indianapolis, then ranked fifth, especially irked Tilden in April of 1928. Big Bill "had been made Davis Cup captain that year, and he brought Hennessey [and] six other candidates … to Augusta,

Georgia, to compete for positions in the upcoming zone matches held in Mexico City."[21] On the day of the tournament Hennessey came down to breakfast and apparently annoyed Tilden by asking what the dress would be in Mexico City. Tilden decided to change the draw and play Hennessey himself.

On a cool afternoon a very bulky Hennessey walked on the court to face Tilden with two to three hundred people in attendance. As Bill watched suspiciously "Hennessey took off his coat, twanged his racket strings a la Tilden, and picked one." Midway through practice Hennessey held up a hand, walked to the side and took off Arnold Jones's blue Yale sweater, revealing another one with a big burnt-orange *T*, a University of Texas sweater he had borrowed from Wilmer Allison. "The crowd snickered appreciatively while Tilden began to fume. Then, just as Big Bill was to serve to open the match, Hennessey summoned a halt again, went back to the sideline and took off his Texas sweater, going down to the P" for the black and orange Princeton sweater he had borrowed from John Van Ryn. This brought even more applause and laughter from the audience.

> Tilden was so furious that he spent the whole first game trying to slam balls at Hennessey, who won just by ducking nimbly.
>
> He only played one game in the Princeton sweater before getting down to his regulation white shirt, but Tilden never really simmered down the whole match. Once, Hennessey pulled off a beautiful sweeping crosscourt forehand, slashing it on a dead run for a winner. "Whee!" he called out with excitement.
>
> Tilden came to the net and addressed him sternly across it. "I wish you wouldn't whee me," he said.
>
> "Why not?" Hennessey asked.
>
> "Because it just isn't done in international tennis," Tilden huffed, and then turned and stormed back to the baseline. Hennessey beat him 8–6 in the fifth. John McGraw, the famous baseball manager of the Giants, was watching. He turned to his companion, William Fox, the movie producer, shook his head and said, "I've never seen such psychology in forty years of baseball."[22]

Tilden disliked authority and frequently clashed with USLTA officials. In one famous conflict, described by Frayne, Tilden was scheduled to play doubles in the 1927 Davis Cup challenge round with Frank Hunter. They had already won Wimbledon and Forest Hills, but for unknown reasons, on the morning of the match the officials changed their minds and declared that Dick Williams would be Tilden's partner. Obviously annoyed, he said, "Splendid, I'll be playing bridge in the clubhouse. When you've regained your sanity, come and advise me." Tilden calmly went and played bridge, impervious to the demands, threats, and pleadings of officials. At one point he asked them to stop interrupting his game while the sellout crowd at Germantown noisily demanded to see Tilden play. The officials gave in, and Tilden played—after he had finished his hand. Tilden and Hunter won their match against Jean Borotra and Jacques Brugnon, 3–6, 6–3, 6–3, 4–6, 6–0, but the Davis Cup was lost to France that year by 3–2.[23]

After the 1930 U.S. Championships, in which he was beaten in the semifinals by eventual champion, twenty-one-year-old and U.S. no. 3 John Doeg, 10–8, 6–3, 3–6, 12–10, Tilden turned pro. He made his professional debut early in 1931 in Madison Square Garden against Karel Kozeluh, the 1929 U.S. Pro champion and subsequent Hall of Famer. A crowd of 13,500 paid a grand sum of thirty-six thousand dollars to watch Tilden defeat the Czech player, 6–4, 6–2, 6–4. The pro champion was the player who won the World Championship Series. The other major pro titles were the British, French, and U.S. Pro titles. Tilden won the U.S. Pro title in 1931 and 1935, the French Pro title in 1933 and 1934, and the World Championship Series from 1931 through 1933. On turning pro, that year's top amateur signing would take on the reigning pro champion in a series of one-night stands known as the World Championship Series. In 1931 Tilden played Kozeluh, while Frank Hunter and Emmet Pare played the preliminary. Big Bill won the first sixteen matches and ended up with a 63–13 edge before playing a shorter series against Vinnie Richards, winning all ten.[24] The following year Tilden defeated twenty-two-year-old Hans Nusslein, a future Hall of Famer from Germany.

In 1934 Ellsworth Vines, U.S. titlist in 1931 and 1932 and 1932 Wimbledon titlist, defeated Tilden 47–26.[25] In Vines's professional debut at the Garden before a crowd of sixteen thousand on January 10, 1934, Big Bill clobbered him, 8–6, 6–3, 6–2. Vines was twenty-two, Tilden almost forty-one.[26] A little later in Los Angeles, Big Bill battled Vines for three hours before yielding. The score was 6–0, 21–23, 7–5, 3–6, 6–2.[27] In 1945 the fifty-two-year-old Tilden and his longtime doubles partner Vinnie Richards won the professional doubles championship—after winning the U.S. amateur title twenty-seven years earlier in 1918.[28] Bobby Riggs wrote that Tilden, at age fifty-two, had pushed him to the limit in a tournament match.

In 1950, during an era of closed minds and sexual conservatism, Big Bill Tilden was overwhelmingly voted the greatest tennis player of the first half of the twentieth century in an Associated Press poll only six weeks after being released from prison for the second time on a conviction of sexual misbehavior with teenage boys.[29] He was shunned in public, his name removed from the alumni files of Penn, and his photos removed from the walls of his home club, the Germantown Cricket Club.[30]

Tilden died of coronary thrombosis at age sixty on June 5, 1953, in Los Angeles. His bag was packed for a trip to Cleveland to play in the U.S. Pro Championships.[31] Although it was estimated he made more than a half-million dollars on tour between 1931 and 1937, he had a mere $282.11 in cash and traveler's checks in his apartment and a refund due of six dollars; two hundred dollars was returned to a student for lessons never given, leaving Big Bill's net worth at $88.11.[32]

Of course, in 1959, he entered the National Tennis Hall of Fame.[33]

Martin L. Tressel

In 1924 Martin Tressel came to Niagara Falls as an engineer for the Aluminum Company of America. Tressel had graduated from Massachusetts Tech (MIT) in 1924, where as captain of the tennis team he had captured the New England intercollegiate doubles title and dominated city tennis from 1924 through 1930, except for in 1927 when he didn't compete. Tressel captured the first Buffalo Muny singles title in 1923. In 1925, in arguably the best city singles final Niagara Falls had seen, Martin Tressel defeated Vinton Vernon from Cleveland, second only to Ohio State champion Kirk Reid, 6–1, 5–7, 6–3, 8–6. Tressel then paired with Vernon to win the city doubles against Lindley Murray and A. M. Hamann of Niagara Electrochemical Corporation. In 1946 and 1947, Tressel won the men's 45 USTA Clay Court doubles tournament, the former with Kirk Reid and the latter with Harold Hodge, defeating Jack Castle and Kirk Reid in the 1947 finals.

In 1961 Martin L. Tressel was awarded the "Samuel Hardy Award" for long and outstanding service to the sport of tennis. The recipients must exemplify those qualities of personal unselfishness and devotion to the game that have been an inspiration to others.[1]

The "Ralph W. Westcott USTA Family of the Year Award" was initiated in 1965 by Tressel, president of the USTA from 1965 to 1966, to emphasize the theme, "Tennis Is a Family Game."[2]

The West Penn tennis tournament began in 1889, with a women's singles division added in 1910. The tournament location bounced back and forth between a variety of Pittsburgh venues, including the Pittsburgh Lawn and Tennis Club, Pittsburgh Athletic Association, Shady Side Academy, and University of Pittsburgh. Then in 1967, Mt. Lebanon resident and USTA president, Martin Tressel, got involved and recruited the West Penn to its permanent home in Mt. Lebanon. At that time, the tournament was still a tri-state competition. But in 1969 Tressel revamped it into a collegiate championship with members of the Junior Davis Cup and Junior Wightman Cup teams among the competitors. In 1975 the West Penn joined with the National Amateur Clay Court championships—a natural fit, as the former was often used as a warm-up for the latter.[3]

The first men's final in the 1968 West Penn and National Amateur tournament featured two local players, the Reverend Bob Hetherington from Sewickley (who would later relocate to Buffalo and become a champion there) and Jack Waltz, a previous West Penn champion who had won the title in 1961 and 1962. Both men had starred on the Yale tennis team, although in different eras. Waltz used great strategy in winning the title in two hard-fought sets and later confessed that he knew it would have been impossible for him to win if the match had gone to three sets.

S. Howard Voshell

S. Howard Voshell was a southpaw from Kew Gardens, Long Island. In the semifinal round of the 1915 Rockaway Hunting Club tourney of Cedarhurst, Long Island, Voshell earned the right to play against Theodore Pell in the final by defeating Alrick Man, former captain of the Yale team, 6–2, 8–6, 6–2.[1] He won the 1915 Northeastern Pennsylvania championship at the Country Club of Scranton, Pennsylvania, over Cedric Major, 1–6, 7–5, 6–2, 6–8, 6–4, in September and paired with Major to win the doubles title.[2]

He defeated the brilliant young Californian, Clifton Herd, 7–5, 6–3, 6–3, for the 1917 U.S. Indoor title.[3] "The manner in which Voshell blocked the fast service of the Pacific coast star was a revelation. He slashed through wonderful crossing volleys when Hurd tried to make his assaults at the net. In every department of the game Voshell outplayed the Californian."[4] He also beat internationalist Fred Alexander for the 1918 title.[5] Voshell was a finalist with Sam Hardy to Bill Tilden and Vinnie Richards in the 1919 U.S. Indoor and paired with Richards to win the 1920 title over Fred Anderson and Benjamin Letson, 6–4, 6–4, 6–2.[6-7]

Voshell won the first grass court tennis event of the 1917 season at the Westchester Country Club invitation on June 16 by defeating national junior champion Harold Throckmorton of Elizabeth, New Jersey, 6–4, 7–5, 6–3, Throckmorton being within a point of the second set.[8] Voshell also won the 1917 Southampton tournament at the Meadow Club by defeating John Strachan of San Francisco in the morning by a score of 2–6, 6–0, 6–4, and Throckmorton in the afternoon, 6–4, 6–4. This was Strachan's first defeat since his Eastern invasion.[9]

At the 1921 Metropolitan clay court championship in June, Voshell again paired with Vinnie Richards to beat A. J. Ostendorf and E. H. Binzen, 6–1, 6–3, 6–4.[10] In July of 1924 at Glen Cove, Long Island, Voshell upset Australian Davis Cup player Pat O'Hara Wood in the finals of an invitation tournament.[11]

At the U.S. Championships Voshell lost to Lin Murray in the 1918 semis. Voshell was in the U.S. top ten in 1918 and 1921.

Watson McLean Washburn*

Watson Washburn was born in New York on June 13, 1894.[1] As a six-foot, right-handed Harvard man, he won the 1913 intercollegiate doubles championship with J. J. Armstrong, while teammate Dick Williams won the singles title. At Narragansett Washburn captured the 1914 Point Judith Country Club open singles title over Elia Fottrell, 6–2, 6–2, 3–6, 9–7, becoming possessor of the Point Judith Challenge Cup, having won three seasons in succession.[2]

He served in the U.S. Army in World War I and subsequently played his best tennis. While Bill Johnston and Bill Tilden were winning their singles matches in the 1921 Davis Cup challenge round against Japan, Washburn and Williams won the Cup-clinching doubles match over Ichiya Kumagae and Zenzo Shimizu, 6–2, 7–5, 4–6, 7–5.

With Dick Williams as a partner, Washburn was a doubles finalist at the 1921 and 1923 U.S. Championships and at Wimbledon in 1924. He ranked seven times in the U.S. top ten between 1914 and 1922, no. 5 in

1921. In contrast to Murray, Watson played a never-hurried game. With no spectacular single shot, his strength was in his persistence of attack, strategy, and coolness under pressure—he was always dangerous.[3]

Washburn continued to play well into his fifties, winning the 1940 USTA Men's 45 Grass Court singles champiosnhip and the 1940, '42, and '44 USTA Men's 45 Grass Court doubles events. He was a USTA committee member, inducted into the National Tennis Hall of Fame in 1965. He died in New York, on December 2, 1973.[4]

Richard Norris Williams II*

Dick Williams, usually listed as R. Norris Williams, was born in Geneva, Switzerland, on January 29, 1891. "He was a fourth great-grandson of Benjamin Franklin and the only child of Charles Duane Williams, a Philadelphia lawyer who resided in Switzerland for health reasons, and Lydia Biddle (White) Williams. Taught tennis by" his father "and French professionals, he recorded his first win in the 1904 Geneva Cup open singles" competition[1] and subsequently won the Swiss title.[2] Williams had one of the most incredible life experiences of any of the top tennis players.

It was "A Night to Remember" when, at age twenty-one, Dick and his father embarked first-class on the RMS *Titanic* back to the United States for a visit to Philadelphia to take part in tournaments in America before going on to study at Harvard. After the ship collided with the iceberg on April 14, 1912, the pair left their stateroom on C Deck and saw a steward trying to open the door of a cabin behind which a panicking passenger was trapped. When Williams put his shoulder to the door and broke in, the steward threatened to report him for destroying White Star Line property, an event that inspired a scene in James Cameron's 1997 film *Titanic*.[3]

According to a family member, at around midnight the two men went to the bar and found it closed. They asked the steward if he could open it up, but the steward said it was against regulations. The two men wandered the decks as the ship sank under them. They entered the gymnasium at the top of the grand staircase and, despite the severe slant of the ship, pedaled stationary bicycles to keep warm. By then the angle of the deck was so steep that people were sliding off into the water, the stern tilting ever higher into the air.[4]

Richard and Charles, wearing life preservers under their heavy fur coats, watched the lifeboats loaded and lowered, women and children first.

"After the last of the lifeboats had been loaded, ... the situation turned ominous" and "Dick realized it was time to swim for it."[5] In two articles by Bud Collins, author and tennis commentator for NBC Sports, we learn of Dick's experience by what he later wrote:

> As the bow of the ship went down, my father and myself were on the boat deck, beside the captain's deck. The bow went first. It did not seem as if the boat was sinking but as if the water was rising. The first onrush of water separated us, and I never saw my father again. (C. Duane Williams was crushed beneath a collapsing funnel). I believe at that time the stern broke off, for the bow suddenly began to rise out of the water until at least two of her decks were out of the water again. As my father was gone, I jumped. It was only about 15 feet, so I got into the water all right.[6]

A collapsible boat was also swept into the water, and Williams swam twenty yards for it after discarding his fur coat and patent leather shoes.[7-8] Williams held on to the side of the waterlogged collapsible for quite a while before getting in. Even standing inside he was waist-deep in water. Dick estimated that thirty others clung with him to the collapsible before the eleven who survived were "picked up by a lifeboat. All the others died from the cold."[9]

Gripping the raft, Williams "saw the *Titanic* take her last plunge," he would write. "I turned towards the ship. It was an extraordinary sight. As the bow went under, the stern lifted higher and higher into the air, then pivoted and swung slowly over my head. Had it come down then I would have been crushed. Looking straight up I saw the three propellers and the rudder distinctly outlined against the clear sky. She slid into the ocean. No suction. No noise. Stillness."[10] "Then came the terrible part—hundreds and hundreds of people in the water crying for help."[11] "They were not drowning, for the life belts held them up. They were dying from the cold, gradually freezing to death. As they did their cries grew weaker and weaker. In another five to ten minutes everything was quiet, the ocean calm—a deathly stillness."[12] Of the 2,223 passengers and crew, all but 706 perished.

The ordeal left his legs so severely frozen that the *Carpathia's* doctor wanted to amputate them, but Richard refused. He exercised daily and eventually his legs recovered, a choice which worked out well, as only about two months later he won his first U.S. title, the mixed doubles with Mary K. Browne at Philadelphia; later at Newport, he lost in the quarters in five to the champ, Maurice McLoughlin. In his first season of play Williams earned a national ranking second only to McLoughlin. From then until 1925 he was ranked in the U.S. top ten eleven times (including time out for wartime combat service in France with the army, when he earned the French Chevalier de la Legion d'Honneur and Croix de Guerre medals).

Williams used the continental grip and hit his ground strokes with underspin. According to *New York Times* tennis critic Allison Danzig, "Williams ... was a player of breathtaking daring in his tactics and stroke production, who either beat his opponent with his sheer brilliance of stroke in taking the ball on the rise or defeated himself with his errors if his touch was lacking. Never content to play safe or to win with prosaic measures, he might scale the heights or plumb the depths. At his best Williams ... [left] galleries spellbound with the volleys and half-volleys that rippled off his racket with the minimum margin of safety,... hitting to the hilt on every shot with complete disregard for the consequences."[13] When he had the feel and touch, Dick was unbeatable against any and all, and once he won a set over Bill Tilden in five minutes.

As a Harvard undergraduate he won the intercollegiate singles championships in 1913 and 1915 and the doubles with Richard Harte in 1914 and 1915. In 1913 he was a runner-up at Newport to McLoughlin, but in 1914 he beat the Comet in three sets, 6–3, 8–6, 10–8. In 1916 he won the U.S. title again, this time over "Little Bill" Johnston, and attained the no. 1 ranking. Beginning in 1913 he played on five winning Davis Cup teams (there was no competition from 1915 to 1918) and captained six Cup winners from 1921 to 1926, plus the 1934 team. He was victorious in each of the four Cup doubles matches he played, a volleyer whose doubles titles were numerous.

He won the 1924 Olympic gold in the mixed event alongside Hazel Wightman. Dick said, "I had a sprained ankle and suggested to her that we default. Not on your life with her. She told me to stay at the net, and she'd do the running." It worked, as they defeated Marion Jessup and Vinnie Richards, 6–2, 6–3, even though Dick was thirty-four and Hazel thirty-seven.[14]

He made the World top ten (there were no rankings from 1915 to 1918) in 1913 and 1914 (no. 5), 1919 to '22 and '23 (no. 4), and 1925 (no. 5); and the U.S. top ten eleven times between 1912 and 1925 (no. 1 in 1916, no. 2 from 1912 to 1915, and no. 3 in 1920 and 1923). Williams won six majors—1912 U.S. mixed with Mary Browne, 1914 and 1916 U.S. singles, 1920 Wimbledon doubles with Chuck Garland and 1925 and 1926 U.S. doubles with Vinnie Richards. He was a U.S. singles finalist in 1913 to "the Comet" McLoughlin and a U.S. doubles finalist three times, in 1921 and 1923 with Watson Washburn and in 1927 with Bill Johnston. In 1957 he was elected to the National Tennis Hall of Fame[15] and in 1984 to the ITA Hall of Fame.

Williams went on to become a successful investment banker in Philadelphia and was for twenty-two years the president of the Historical Society of Pennsylvania. He died of emphysema on June 2, 1968, at the age of seventy-seven.

Appendix

Advent of Tiebreak Scoring

The eighty-two game contest in 1918 between Throckmorton and Taylor was eclipsed in the 1969 Wimbledon championship when Pancho Gonzales took 112 games to defeat Charlie Pasarell in the first round, 22–24, 1–6, 16–14, 6–3, 11–9, in a match lasting five hours and twelve minutes over two days.

Jimmy Van Alen, President of the Newport Casino in 1952 and founder of the National Tennis Hall of Fame in 1954 came up with the tiebreak scoring system in 1965.[1] The old system's death-knell was the Gonzales-Pasarell match. "The tiebreak was introduced at the 1970 U.S. Open and was used in sets other than the last that were even at 8-8." It was sudden death in that the first player to reach five points won the set. "In 1979, the tiebreak rule was changed to the current standard—in sets other than the final set that were tied at 6-6 with the first player to seven points with a two-point lead."[2]

The purpose of the tiebreak was to both reduce the duration of a match and the number of games played. The US Open is unique in that there are final-set tiebreaks whereas advantage sets are still used in the final sets of the Australian Open, French Open, Wimbledon, Davis Cup, and Fed Cup.[3] While longer tiebreak matches have been played than the 1969 Wimbledon match, the almost impossible happened while this book was out for editing.

At the 2010 Wimbledon, John Isner defeated Nicolas Mahut in a first-round match by the score of 6–4, 3–6, 6–7(7), 7–6(3), 70–68. It was the longest professional match in terms of both total games (183) and playing time (eleven hours and five minutes), and took three days to complete. The match was called due to darkness after four sets, and again after 118 games of the fifth set on the second day which lasted seven hours and six minutes, longer than any previous match. The fifth set alone lasted eight hours and eleven minutes.[4] We'll see what the future holds for final advantage sets.

1. "RI—Newport: International Tennis Hall of Fame—Jimmy Van Alen." Retrieved August 9, 2010, from http://www.flickr.com/photos/wallyg/1218836384/.
2. "History of Tiebreak in Tennis." Retrieved August 9, 2010, from http://tennisracquetsport.suite101.com/article.cfm/history_of_tiebreak_in_tennis.
3. "Tennis score." Retrieved August 9, 2010, from http://en.wikipedia.org/wiki/Tennis_score.
4. "Longest tennis match records." Retrieved June 29, 2010, from http://en.wikipedia.org/wiki/Longest_tennis_match_records.

Chemical Industry Medal Speech by R. Lindley Murray

(April 27, 1956)

Decisions, of course, must pay off. And for us, our most important decisions have paid off in growth. Our research program now has us doing any number of things which we could scarcely have imagined in the early 1930s. Above all, it has given us scores of new products which have given us a powerful push in the direction of rapid growth.

Another, perhaps more unusual, reason for our growth is that over the years we have kept an especially watchful eye on growth regions, and have located plants in several of these areas. The Pacific Northwest is a case in point.

Still another, and to us quite interesting, reason for our growth concerns some of our financial friends who are here tonight—the security analysts. Until a decade ago Hooker stock was unlisted and closely held. But by the end of World War II it became clear that capital requirements for our expansion would necessitate listing our stock on the exchange. This was done in November 1947. Within a short time substantial blocks of our stock had been bought by investment houses, and we found ourselves with some new owners who had a keen professional interest in our progress. We quickly discovered that their representatives—the security analysts—had had rather lofty ideas of where we were going and how soon we would get there. The representatives of investment houses, we find, act as a spur to management. This has been a quite unexpected advantage of being publicly owned.

All of these factors—plus our management training program, our process study group, our grass roots budgetary control system, our general development department and many more—have helped to make us somewhat out of the ordinary—a growth company. And as I have mentioned earlier a growth company makes out-of-the-ordinary demands upon its management.

In this respect, a growth company bears about the same relation to a non-growth company that chess bears to checkers or jai alai to ping pong—one is vastly more demanding than the other and you must work proportionately harder to succeed.

Any company which intends to stay in business must, of course, keep an eye on industrial trends, technological advances, and shifts in population and consumer preferences. A growth company, we feel, must do a little extra homework in this direction.

A growth company's management must also undergo a certain amount of financial brainwashing. Rapid growth very quickly plunges management into what is too often a bewildering world of 'convertible debentures,' 'paid-in-surpluses,' and 'miscellaneous accruals.' There are no route markers through this maze. The only way out is by management putting an end to its financial innocence.

Management would be remiss, too, if it failed to study possible future acquisitions. There are some chemical lines in which sound growth can be achieved quickly only by merger with companies already solidly established in those lines. Durez in phenolics and Niagara Alkali in potassium chemicals are two examples with which we, of course, are familiar.

In solving these problems (of growth), we run the risk of what Time magazine has called 'the perils of table sitting.' The perils of table sitting, of course, are not peculiar to growth companies. Because of the complexity of modern business it has become increasingly difficult for executives to make decisions individually. A great number of decisions must be made around the conference table. The peril, of course, is that while conferees sit, the wheels of production will grind to a halt. Because of the unusually large number of problems which face a growth company it runs the risk of table sitting almost precisely in proportion to its growth. Its management must be especially artful in avoiding this built-in pitfall.

But the central over-riding problem of a growth company is to maintain its stature. It must keep growing—and at a rate significantly above the average. To do so, as I have tried to indicate, requires a tremendous amount of plain hard work.

I would not like to leave you, however, with the impression that managing a growth company is all work and no play, or at any rate, no pleasure. A growth company offers management quite out-of-the-ordinary rewards—rewards commensurate with its out-of-the-ordinary burdens.

Western New York Championship (Great Lakes Championship after 1911)

Year	Event	Results
1909	Men's singles	Wallace Johnson
	Ladies' singles	May Sutton
1910	Men's singles	Nat Niles d. Harold Hodge, 6-1, 10-8, 6-1
	Challenge round	Nat Niles (U.S. #4) d. Wallace Johnson (U.S. #3), 4-6, 7-5, 6-2, 7-5
	Men's doubles	Baird-H. Hodge d. Jones-Hoerr, 6-3, 4-6, 6-3, 1-6, 6-4
	Ladies' singles	Lois Moyes (Canadian champion) d. Edith Rotch (Boston), 6-2, 6-0
	Challenge round	Lois Moyes d. May Sutton, default
	Mixed doubles	Mrs. Rice-Hoerr d. Edith Rotch-Harry Kirkover (Buffalo), 7-5, 6-3
1911	Men's singles	C. Benton (Cleveland) d. F.H. Harris, 9-7, 3-6, 6-3, 1-6, 6-4
	Challenge round	Nat Niles (holder) d. C. Benton (challenger)
	Men's doubles	Harris-Benton d. Hamlin-Russell, default
	Ladies' singles	May Sutton d. Florence Sutton, 6-2, 6-1
	Challenge round	May Sutton d. Lois Moyes (Canadian champion), 6-2, 6-0
	Ladies' doubles	Florence Sutton-Lois Moyes d. May Sutton-H. Bissell, 6-2, 6-3

	Mixed doubles	May Sutton-Harry Kirkover d. Florence Sutton-F.H. Harris, 9-7, 9-7
1912	Men's singles	R.N. Williams d. W.S. McEllroy, 6-1, 6-2, 6-3
	Challenge round	R.N. Williams (challenger) d. Nat W. Niles (holder)
	Men's doubles	Gus Touchard-R.N. Williams d. Beals C. Wright-Harry Kirkover, 2-6, 6-4, 7-5, 7-5
	Ladies' singles	Mary K. Browne (U.S. champion) d. Dorothy Green, 8-6, 6-1
	Mixed doubles	Lois Moyes (Canadian champ)-F.C. Inman d. Dorothy Green-H. Kirkover, 6-2, 6-3
1913	Men's singles	R. Chauncey Seaver (Boston) d. T.W. Hendrick (Buffalo), 6-3, 6-1, 6-2
	Men's doubles	Hendrick-A.T. Spaulding (Buffalo) d. R.C. Seaver-H. Hodge, 6-0, 2-6, 6-0, 5-7, 6-2
	Ladies' singles	Mary K. Browne (U.S. champion) d. Edith Rotch, 6-8, 6-3, 6-3
	Ladies' doubles	Edith Rotch-Mrs. C.N. Beard d. Mrs. R.H. Williams-Mary Browne, 6-3, 6-4, 6-1
	Mixed doubles	Mary Browne-R.C. Seaver d. Mrs. R.H. Williams-T.W. Hendrick, 6-1, 6-1
1914	Men's singles	Clarence J. Griffin d. R.C. Seaver, 6-4, 5-7, 6-3, 6-1
	Challenge round	Clarence J. Griffin d. R.C. Seaver, 6-2, 6-2, 6-1
	Men's doubles	Harry D. Kirkover-Robert Baird d. Clarence Griffin-William Swift, 6-3, 6-1, 7-5
	Ladies' singles	Edith Rotch d. Mrs. R.H. Williams, 6-2, 6-3
	Challenge round	Mary K. Browne (U.S. champion) d. Edith Rotch, 6-4, 6-2
	Ladies' doubles	Mary Browne-Mrs. R.H. Williams d. Clare Cassel-Edith Rotch, 6-3, 7-5
	Mixed doubles	Edith Rotch-Robert Baird d. Mary K. Browne-Harry D. Kirkover, 2-6, 6-3, 6-4
1915	Men's singles	Vanderbilt B. Ward d. L.F. Gilbert (Buffalo), 6-3, 6-1, 6-2
	Men's doubles	Sidney Thayer-V.B. Ward d. A.T. Spaulding-T.W. Hendrick, 1-6, 7-5, 6-3, 7-5

	Ladies' singles	Edith Rotch (U.S. #5) d. Buda Stephens, 4-6, 6-4, 6-2
	Ladies' doubles	Mrs. H. Bickle-Miss Best d. Edith Rotch-Buda Stephens, 6-2, 6-3
	Mixed doubles	Mrs. H. Bickle-Reed d. Florence Ballin-T.W. Hendrick, 6-3, 5-7, 6-2
1916	Men's singles	H.V.D. Johns (San Francisco) d. Lester F. Gilbert, 10-8, 6-1, 0-6, 6-3
	Men's singles	H.V.D. Johns d. Vanderbilt B. Ward, default
	Men's doubles	T.W. Hendrick-A.T. Spaulding d. H.V.D. Johns-J.R. Pratt, 6-4, 1-6, 6-2, 6-4
	Ladies' singles	Molla Bjurstedt (U.S. champion) d. Edith Rotch (Boston), 6-2, 6-1
	Ladies' doubles	Molla Bjurstedt-Bull d. Mrs. H. Bickle-F. Best, 5-7, 6-3, 6-3
	Mixed doubles	Molla Bjurstedt-H.V.D. Johns d. Florence Ballin-T.W. Hendrick, 6-4, 6-2
1917	Men's singles	R. Lindley Murray d. Charles Garland (Pittsburgh), 9-7, 6-1, 6-4
	Men's doubles	C.S. Garland-J.E. McLain d. T.W. Hendrick-A.T. Spaulding, 5-7, 7-9, 6-4, 6-1, 7-5
	Ladies' singles	Molla Bjurstedt d. E. Best, 6-2, 6-3
	Ladies' doubles	E. Best-MacDonald d. Molla Bjurstedt-Moes, 6-4, 6-2
	Mixed doubles	MacDonald-R.L. Murray d. E. Best-Charles S. Garland, 6-2, 4-6, 10-8
1918	Men's singles	A.J. Veysey (Montreal) d. A.V. Duncan (Los Angeles), 2-6, 9-7, 7-5, 6-3
	Men's doubles	A.J. Vesey-T.C. Fulton d. A.V. Duncan-T.W. Hendrick, 6-1, 3-6, 7-5, 6-8, 6-2
	Ladies' singles	Molla Bjurstedt d. Eleanora Sears, 6-4, 6-1
	Ladies' doubles	M. Bjurstedt-E. Sears d. E. Best-McDonald, 6-3, 6-4
	Men's singles (e)	William Tilden d. R.L. Murray, 7-5, 6-1, 6-4
	Men's doubles (e)	T.C. Fulton-R.L. Murray d. W.T. Tilden-A.J. Vesey, 6-4, 6-3
	Mixed doubles (e)	Molla Bjurstedt-R.L. Murray d. Florence Ballin-W.T. Tilden, 10-8, 6-4

1919	Men's singles	Ichiya Kumagae d. William Tilden, 6-2, 10-8, 8-6 and A.J. Vesey, 6-1, 6-3, 6-3
	Men's doubles	I. Kumagae-Harold Taylor d. Eric Hedstrom-R.L. Murray, 7-5, 6-2, 6-4
1920	Men's singles	R. Lindley Murray d. Walter Wesbrook, 6-2, 6-3, 6-2
	Men's doubles	R.L. Murray-Eric Hedstrom d. Jack Castle-Gowans, 6-4, 7-5, 6-2
	Ladies' singles	Marion Zinderstein d. E. Tennant, 6-4, 6-1
1922	Men's singles	R. Lindley Murray d. Kirk Reid (Cleveland), 1-6, 6-1, 6-2, 6-4
	Men's doubles	Murray-Gerald Emerson d. Reid-Henry Wick, 6-4, 2-6, 10-8, 3-6, 6-2
1923	Men's singles	William Tilden d. Manuel Alonso, 7-5, 6-3, 6-3
	Men's doubles	William Tilden-Sandy Weiner d. Manuel Alonso-Chuck Garland, 6-1, 6-1, 7-5
	Ladies' singles	Miss MacDonald d. Miss Scharman, 7-5, 1-6, 6-4
	Ladies' doubles	Mrs. Leachman- Miss Sigourney d. Miss MacDonald-Miss Scharman, 6-1, 6-0
	Mixed doubles	Miss MacDonald-Jack Castle d. Miss Sigourney-Walter Misner, 6-1, 7-5
	Boy's singles	Weiner d. Marynowski, 7-5, 4-6, 6-3
1924	Men's singles	William T. Tilden d. Alex H. Chapin, 3-6, 7-5, 6-1, 4-6, 8-6
	Men's doubles	R.Lindley Murray-Sam Hardy d. Gerald Emerson-Alex Chapin, 6-2, 7-5, 1-6, 6-2

Niagara International Tennis Tournament

Year	Event	Results
1893	Men's singles	F.K. Ward (Rochester) d. H. Avery (Canadian champion), 6-1, 6-0, 7-5
	Challenge round	F.K. Ward (challenger) d. A.F. Fuller (holder), 8-6, 2-6, 6-4, 6-0
	Men's doubles	F.K. Ward-W.A. Boys d. Coldham brothers (Toledo), 6-4, 6-2, 7-5
	Ladies' singles	Maude Delano Osborne (Canadian titlist) d. Mrs. Sydney Smith, 6-8, 6-3, 6-3
	Ladies' doubles	M.D. Osborne-Mrs. Smith d. Bernard (England)-Nay, 6-2, 7-5
	Mixed doubles	M. Osborne-Gordon Mackenzie d. Miss Coldham-Ashton Coldham, 6-4, 6-3
1894	Men's singles	Malcom G. Chace (Yale) d. A.E. Foote (Yale), 6-0, 6-1, retired
	Challenge round	M.G. Chace (challenger) d. Fitz Ward (holder), 6-3, 6-1, 8-6
	Men's doubles	M.G. Chace-A.E. Foote d. R.W.P. Matthews-H.E. Avery, 6-3, 6-1, 6-3
	Ladies' singles	Maude Delano Osborne (Canadian titlist) d. Mrs. Whitehead, 4-6, 6-3, 6-4
	Mixed doubles	Hollister (Buffalo)-M.G. Chace d. M.D. Osborne-Matthews, 3-6, 8-6, 9-7

1895	Men's singles	Carr Neel
1896	Men's singles	F.K. Ward (Rochester) d. Leo Ware, 6-3, 6-2, 3-6, 7-5
	Challenge round	Carr Neel (holder) d. F.K. Ward (challenger), 6-2, 6-3, 6-3
	Men's doubles	L. Ware-Malcolm Whitman d. C. Neel-George Wrenn, 6-1, 1-6, 9-7, 3-6, 7-5
	Ladies' singles	Juliette Atkinson d. Kathleen Atkinson
1898	Challenge round	Billy Bond (Chicago)
	Men's doubles	Billy Bond-Eddie Fischer
	Ladies' singles	Juliette Atkinson (U.S. champion) d. Marie Wimer
	Men's handicap	E. Langton d. Peter Porter
1899	Men's singles	R.D. Little (Princeton) d. E.P. Fischer, 6-3, 5-7, 6-4, 1-6, 7-5
	Challenge round	R.D. Little (challenger) d. W.S. Bond (holder), 6-2, 5-7, 6-4, 2-6, 6-4
	Men's doubles	E.P. Fischer-W.S. Bond d. P. Porter-P. Wright, 6-0, 6-4, 6-1
	Ladies' singles	Parker d. Champlain, 4-6, 6-4, 6-2, 4-6, 6-2
	Challenge round	Parker (challenger) d. Juliette Atkinson (U.S. runner-up), default
1900	Men's singles	Harold H. Hackett (Yale) d. E.P. Fischer (New York), 7-5, 1-6, 6-1, 6-4
	Ladies' singles	Marie Wimar (Washington) d. Parker (Chicago), 9-7, 3-6, 6-3, 6-2
1901	Men's singles	Ray D. Little
1902	Men's singles	Beals C. Wright d. Harold H. Hackett, 4-6, 6-4, 4-6, 6-1, 6-1
	Challenge round	Beals C. Wright (challenger) d. Ray D. Little (holder), default.
	Men's doubles	B.C. Wright-Kriegh Collins d. E.P. Fischer-Robert LeRoy, 6-4, 6-3, 6-1
	Men's handicap	H.E. Avery (owe ½15) d. Ralph Burns (owe 15), 6-2, 4-6, 6-3, 6-4
1903	Men's singles	E.P. Fischer

1904	Men's singles	A.E. Bell (Los Angeles) d. Robert LeRoy (New York), 7-5, 6-4, 4-6, 4-6, 6-2
	Men's doubles	Holt-Dewhurst d. LeRoy-Bell, 7-5, 6-4, 6-8, 5-7, default (darkness)
	Canadian singles	Paterson d. W.A. Boys, 6-2, 6-3, 6-2
	Challenge round	Paterson (challenger) d. Burns (holder), 6-0, 8-6, 6-3
	Men's handicap	Kirkover (Buffalo) d. McDonnell (Toronto)
1905	Men's singles	Irving C. Wright
1906	Men's singles	Johnson (Boston) d. Burns (Toronto), 6-3, 6-3, 1-6, 4-6, 6-4
	Challenge round	Irving C. Wright (holder) d. Johnson (challenger), default
	Men's doubles	I.C. Wright-Johnson d. Dewhurst-H.D. Kirkover, 6-2, 9-7, 6-1
	Men's handicap	H.D. Kirkover (Buffalo) d. W.A. Boys (Barrie, owe ½15), 7-5, 6-4
1907	Men's singles	J.F. Foulkes (Canadian champion) d. Nat Niles, 6-2, 2-6, 2-6, 8-6, 6-4
	Challenge round	Irving C. Wright (holder) d. J.F. Foulkes (challenger), 6-1, 6-4, 6-2
	Men's doubles	I.C. Wright-N.W. Niles d. Chase-H.D. Kirkover, 6-4, 6-2, 6-4
	Ladies' singles	May Sutton (Wimbledon champion) d. Edith Rotch, 6-2, 6-1
	Mixed doubles	Edith Rotch-Niles d. Bessie Moore-Wright, 3-6, 6-4, 6-3
	Canadian singles	J.F. Foulkes (Ottawa) d. Burns, 6-3, 6-8, 6-3, 6-4
	Canadian doubles	Burns-Glassco (holders) d. Brown-Campbell (challengers), 7-5, 6-3, 6-3
	Canadian singles	Lois Moyes (holder) d. Hague (challenger), 3-6, 6-4, 6-3
1908	Men's singles	Nat Niles (Harvard) d. Wallace Johnson (Philadelphia), 6-4, 6-4, 2-6, 8-6
	Challenge round	Nat Niles (challenger) d. Irving Wright (holder), 1-6, 2-6, 6-4, 6-4, 6-4
	Men's doubles	Wright-Emerson d. Niles-Wagner, 6-4, 6-4, 11-13, 6-4

	Ladies' singles	Marie Wagner (New York) d. Lois Moyes, 6-4, 6-2
1909	Men's singles	George Janes d. Simpson S. Sinsabaugh, 6-4, 6-3, defaulted
	Challenge round	Nat W. Niles (holder) d. George Janes (challenger), 6-1, 6-1, 6-1
	Men's doubles	Beals C. Wright-Ray D. Little d. Janes-Sinsabaugh, 6-4, 8-6, 6-4
	Ladies' singles	May Sutton d. Mrs. J.H. Hannam, 6-3, 6-3
1910	Men's singles	Wick d. Drummond Jones, 6-3, 8-6, 6-3
	Challenge round	Nat Niles (holder) d. Wick (challenger), 6-1, 6-4, 6-0
	Men's doubles	Drummond Jones-Hoerr d. Burns-Carroll, 6-2, 6-3, 6-2
	Ladies' singles	Lois Moyes (Canadian champion) d. Mrs. Beard, 6-3, 6-4
	Ladies' doubles	Lois Moyes-Fairbairn d. Steever-Craven, 6-1, 4-6, 7-5
	Mixed doubles	Steever-Hoerr d. Fairbairn-Burns, 6-0, 2-6, 7-5
1911	Men's singles	Edwin H. Whitney (Boston) d. Harris (Dartmouth), 6-2, 6-2, 5-7, 4-6, 6-3
	Men's doubles	Sherwood-Baird (Toronto) d. Benton (Cleveland)-Marty (Cincinnati), 3-6, 5-7, 6-3, 8-6, 6-4
	Ladies' singles	Hazel Hotchkiss d. May Sutton, 0-6, 7-5, 6-0
	Mixed doubles	Hazel Hotchkiss-Harris d. Florence Sutton-Baird, 2-6, 7-5, 6-4
1912	Men's singles	R.N. Williams d. W.S. McEllroy, 6-3, 6-3, 6-4
	Men's doubles	Gus F. Touchard-R.N. Williams d. R. Baird-T.Y. Sherwell, 6-3, 4-6, 6-4, 6-3
	Ladies' singles	Mary K. Browne (U.S. champion) d. Dorothy Green, 6-2, 7-5
	Mixed doubles	Mary K. Browne-G.F. Touchard d. Dorothy Green-H.C. Johnson, 6-4, 2-6, 7-5
1913	Men's singles	Clarence J. Griffin d. E.H. Whitney, 9-7, 1-6, 6-2, 9-7
	Men's doubles	C.J. Griffin-W.M. Johnston d R.C. Seaver-E.H. Whitney, 6-2, 6-3, 6-3

	Ladies' singles	Mrs. Robert Williams d. Mary K. Browne (U.S. champion), 8-6, 3-6, 6-4
	Mixed doubles	M.K. Browne-Johnston d. Mrs. Robert Williams-Griffin, 4-6, 6-3, 6-4
1914	Men's singles	Clarence J. Griffin d. George M. Church, 3-6, 6-1, 6-2, 6-2
	Men's doubles	Griffin-E.R. McCormick d. Elia Fottrell-Irving Wright, 3-6, 6-0, 5-7, 6-1, 6-4
	Ladies' singles	Mrs. J.H. Bickle d. Edith Rotch, 6-0, 6-4
	Mixed doubles	Mrs. J.H. Bickle-W. Merrill Hall d. Mrs. Vanvoorhis-R. Baird, 11-9, 6-2
1920	Men's singles	Harold Taylor d. J. Weber, 6-3, 3-6, default
	Men's doubles	R. Lindley Murray-R. Innes Taylor d. Harold Taylor-J. Weber, default
	Ladies' singles	Mrs. H. Bickle d. F. Best, 6-4, 6-3
	Ladies' doubles	Mrs. H. Bickle-F. Best d. Brock-Davidson
	Mixed doubles	F. Best-J. Weber d. Mrs. H. Bickle-H. Taylor, 6-3, 4-6, 6-4
1921	Men's singles	R. Lindley Murray d. Clifford B. Herd (Chicago), 7-5, 8-6, 6-3
	Men's doubles	Murray-Herd d. Frank Anderson-Walter Wesbrook, 9-7, 6-4, 8-10, 6-3
1922	Men's singles	R. Lindley Murray d. Armand Bruneau (Brooklyn), 6-2, 6-2, 6-2
1923	Men's singles	R. L. Murray d. Herbert Bowman (New York City), 6-2, 4-6, 6-2, 3-6, 6-3

References

Part I: The First Forty Years of American Tennis

Preface

1. Parke Cummings. *American Tennis: The Story of a Game.* Boston: Little, Brown & Company, 1957, p. 25.
2. Cummings, op. cit., p. 29.
3. Cummings, op. cit., pp. 36–37.

Chapter 1: Beginnings

1. "Real Tennis." Retrieved August 25, 2009, from http://en.wikipedia.org/wiki/Real_tennis.
2. Heiner Gillmeister. *Tennis: A Cultural History.* London: Leicester University Press, 1997, p. 105.
3. Gillmeister, op. cit., p. 106.
4. "Battle of Agincourt." Retrieved October 14, 2009, from http://en.wikipedia.org/wiki/Battle_of_Agincourt.
5. Gillmeister, op. cit., p. 112.
6. Gillmeister, op. cit., p. 113.
7. Gillmeister, op. cit., p. 115.
8. Max Robertson and Jack Kramer (eds.). *The Encyclopedia of Tennis.* New York: Viking Press, Inc., 1974, p. 14.
9. "Real Tennis." Retrieved August 25, 2009, from http://en.wikipedia.org/wiki/Real_tennis.
10. Bud Collins. *The Bud Collins History of Tennis: An Authoritative Encyclopedia and Record Book.* Washington, DC: New Chapter Press, 2008, p. 4.

11. Gillmeister, loc. cit.
12. Gillmeister, op. cit., p. 121.
13. Gillmeister, op. cit., p. 122.
14. Ibid.
15. Gillmeister, op. cit., p. 126.
16. Ibid.
17. Ibid.
18. Gillmeister, op. cit., pp. 126–27.
19. Gillmeister, op. cit., p. 127.
20. Gillmeister, op. cit., pp. 127–28.
21. "Rackets (sport)." Retrieved August 25, 2009, from http://en.wikipedia.org/wiki/Rackets_(sport).
22. "Badminton." Retrieved August 25, 2009, from http://en.wikipedia.org/wiki/Badminton.
23. Robertson and Kramer, op. cit., p. 22.
24. Parke Cummings. *American Tennis: The Story of a Game.* Boston: Little, Brown & Company, 1957, pp. 23–24.
25. Cummings, op. cit., pp. 24–25.
26. Cummings, op. cit., pp. 26–27.
27. Bud Collins, op. cit., p. 6.
28. J. Parmly Paret. *Lawn Tennis: Its Past, Present, and Future.* New York: Macmillan Company, 1904, p. 6.
29. Robertson and Kramer, op. cit., pp. 22–23.
30. "*The Field* (magazine)." Retrieved August 28, 2009, from http://en.wikipedia.org/wiki/The_Field_(magazine). "In March 1874 Gerald D. Fitzgerald wrote to the *Field* to inform readers about a new game called sphairstike, or Lawn Tennis. Over ensuing years the minutiae of the rules were subsequently thrashed out through the letters pages of the magazine, culminating with the printing of the rules of Lawn Tennis on June 16, 1877, followed by the inaugural Lawn Tennis Championship in 1877 where players competed for The Field Cup. The Field Cup is still on permanent display at Wimbledon Museum."
31. Robertson and Kramer, op. cit., pp. 24–25.
32. Cummings, op. cit., p. 27.
33. Spencer W. Gore. "A Reminiscence of Fifteen Years of Lawn Tennis," in *Tennis: Lawn Tennis: Rackets: Fives* by J. M. Heathcote, C. G. Heathcote, E. O. P-Bouverie, A. C. Ainger. The Badminton Library of Sports and Pastimes. Southampton, UK: Ashford Press

Publishing, 1987, pp. 280, 282. (First published in 1903; first edition 1890 by Longmans, Green, and Co., London, 484 pages.)

34. *Fifty Years of Lawn Tennis in the United States.* United States Lawn Tennis Association, New York, 1931, p. 18.
35. Gore, op. cit., p. 292.
36. Gore, op. cit., p. 289.
37. Robertson and Kramer, op. cit., p. 24.
38. Paret, op. cit., p. 14.
39. "William Charles Renshaw, 'Willie.'" Retrieved August 28, 2009, from http://www.tennisfame.com/famer.aspx?pgID=867&hof_id =213.

Chapter 2: American Men's Tennis

1. Max Robertson and Jack Kramer (eds.). *The Encyclopedia of Tennis.* New York: Viking Press, Inc., 1974, p. 26.
2. USLTA. *Fifty Years of Lawn Tennis in the United States.* New York: United States Lawn Tennis Association, 1931, p. 13.
3. Gianna Clerici. *Tennis.* London: Octopus Books Limited, 1976, p. 80.
4. *Fifty Years,* op. cit., p. 229.
5. "Mary Ewing Outerbridge 'Mother of Tennis.'" Retrieved August 13, 2009, from http://www.tennisfame.com/famer.aspx?pgID= 867&hof_id=231.
6. Heiner Gillmeister. *Tennis: A Cultural History.* London: Leicester University Press, 1997, pp. 208–9.
7. Gillmeister, op. cit., p. 209.
8. *Fifty Years,* op. cit., p. 13.
9. Martha Summerhayes. *Vanished Arizona: Recollections of the Army Life of a New England Woman*, 2nd ed. Salem, MA: Salem Press Co., 1911, pp. 92–93.
10. Summerhayes, op. cit., p. 22.
11. Warren Kimball. "The 'first' lawn tennis game in American story." Retrieved November 18, 2009, from http://www.usta.com/ USTA/Global/About_Us/Organization/Feature/History/Martha_ Summerhayes.
12. C. R. Yates. "Lawn Tennis on the Pacific Coast," in *Outing for July*, 1890, pp. 271–72.
13. Parke Cummings. *American Tennis: The Story of a Game.* Boston: Little, Brown & Company, 1957, p. 33.

14. Gillmeister, op. cit., p. 207.
15. *Fifty Years*, op. cit., p. 16.
16. *Fifty Years*, op. cit., p. 19.
17. Cummings, op. cit., pp. 30–32.
18. Bud Collins. "Death of the Longwood Grass, Alas," in *The Fireside Book of Tennis*. Edited by Allison Danzig and Peter Schwed. New York: Simon and Schuster, 1972, p. 99.
19. "Longwood Cricket Club." Retrieved May 12, 2009, from http://en.wikipedia.org/wiki/Longwood_Cricket_Club.
20. Ibid.
21. Malcolm D. Whitman. *Tennis Origins and Mysteries*. Mineola, NY: Dover Publications, Inc., 2004, p. 115. (Originally published by Derrydale Press, New York, in 1932, the Dover edition contains all of the author's text and all illustrations, but leaves out the historical bibliography by Robert W. Henderson, which comprised ninety-two pages of the original edition. The index has been corrected and its pages renumbered, and a few of the illustrations have been moved.)
22. Whitman, op. cit., p. 117.
23. *Fifty Years*, op. cit., p. 15.
24. Ibid.
25. "Drugs, Contraband Smuggled Into Jail in Tennis Balls." Retrieved November 19, 2009, from http://www.wdsu.com/news/21319658/detail.html.
26. Bud Collins. *The Bud Collins History of Tennis: An Authoritative Encyclopedia and Record Book*. Washington, DC: New Chapter Press, 2008, p. 5.
27. Martyn Kendrick. *Advantage Canada: A Tennis Centenary*. Toronto: McGraw-Hill Ryerson Limited, 1990, p. 10.
28. Whitman, op. cit., pp. 116–19.
29. Whitman, op. cit., pp. 120–21.
30. Whitman, op. cit., p. 121.
31. Robertson and Kramer, op. cit., pp. 26–27.
32. Kendrick, loc. cit.
33. Cummings, op. cit., p. 35.
34. Cummings, op. cit., p. 36.
35. Cummings, op. cit., pp. 36–37.
36. "James Gordon Bennett, Jr." Retrieved September 1, 2009, from http://en.wikipedia.org/wiki/James_Gordon_Bennett_Jr.

37. Cummings, op. cit., p. 39.
38. Information Research Center. Retrieved November 19, 2009, from http://www.tennisfame.com/tennisfame.aspx?pgID=880.
39. International Tennis Hall of Fame Museum. Retrieved November 19, 2009. from http://www.tennisfame.com/tennisfame.aspx?pgID=878.
40. Cummings, op. cit., p. 65.
41. "The Newport Casino." Retrieved September 26, 2009, from http://www.tennisfame.com/tennisfame.aspx?pgID=882.
42. Eric Tucker. "Historic RI theater to reopen after restoration." Retrieved September 26, 2009, from http://www.google.com/hostednews/ap/article/ALeqM5gbYwhXG9sRKPNk-t9dU_aBFvo...
43. Cummings, op. cit., pp. 63–64.
44. "International Tennis Hall of Fame." Retrieved November 19, 2009, from http://en.wikipedia.org/wiki/International_Tennis_Hall_of_Fame.
45. International Tennis Hall of Fame. Retrieved November 19, 2009, from http://www.tennisfame.com/tennisfame.aspx?pgID=866.
46. Kat Anderson. "USA Today Article Identifies International Tennis Hall of Fame as One of the '10 Great Places to Indulge Your Love for Tennis.'" Posted March 6, 2009, on Internet. Contact kat@tennisfame.com.
47. *Fifty Years*, op. cit., pp. 21–22.
48. "Former Newports," *American Lawn Tennis*, vol. 1, no. 13, p. 195.
49. "Former Newports," op. cit., p. 194.
50. *Fifty Years*, op. cit., p. 22.
51. Ibid.
52. *Fifty Years*, op. cit., pp. 22–23.
53. "Former Newports," op. cit., pp. 195–96.
54. "How Good Was William Renshaw?" Retrieved September 27, 2009, from http://tt.tennis-warehouse.cpm/showthread.php?p=3866003.
55. J. Parmly Paret. *Lawn Tennis: Its Past, Present, and Future*. New York: Macmillan Company, 1904, p. 58.
56. Paret, op. cit., p. 60.
57. Paret, op. cit., pp. 63–66.
58. Paret, op. cit., p. 66.
59. Paret, op. cit., pp. 62–63.
60. Paret, op. cit., p. 63.

61. "Larned, William 1872–1926." Retrieved September 30, 2009, from http://www.encyclopedia.com/doc/1G2-3468300318.html.
62. *Fifty Years*, op. cit., p. 23.
63. *Fifty Years*, op. cit., p. 32.
64. Robertson and Kramer, op. cit., p. 28.
65. *Fifty Years*, op. cit., p. 34.
66. *Fifty Years*, op. cit., p. 24.
67. *Fifty Years*, op. cit., p. 28.
68. Google grandslamtennis.freeukisp.co.uk.
69. Bud Collins, op. cit., p. 7.
70. *Wright & Ditson's Lawn Tennis Guide for 1891*. Boston: Wright & Ditson, Publishers, p. 142.
71. *Fifty Years*, op. cit., p. 24.
72. *Fifty Years*, op. cit., p. 25.
73. *Fifty Years*, op. cit., p. 27.
74. Ibid.
75. *Wright & Ditson's 1891 Guide*, op. cit. p. 16.
76. *Fifty Years*, op. cit., p. 47.
77. Cummings, op. cit., pp. 37–38.
78. "Former Newports," op. cit., p. 193.
79. *Fifty Years*, loc. cit.
80. "Oliver Samuel Campbell." Retrieved September 16, 2009, from http://www.tennisfame.com/famer.aspx?pgID=867&hof_id=67.
81. *Fifty Years*, op. cit., pp. 56–57.
82. *Fifty Years*, op. cit., p. 57.
83. *Fifty Years*, op. cit., p. 60.
84. *Fifty Years*, op. cit., pp. 73–74.
85. *Fifty Years*, op. cit., pp. 74, 76.
86. *Fifty Years*, op. cit., p. 76.
87. *Fifty Years*, op. cit., p. 77.
88. *Fifty Years*, op. cit., pp. 69–70.
89. *Fifty Years*, op. cit., p. 77.
90. *Fifty Years*, op. cit., pp. 83, 85.
91. *Fifty Years*, op. cit., p. 85.
92. A. Wallis Meyers. "1900: The First Davis Cup Matches," in *The Fireside Book of Tennis*. Edited by Allison Danzig and Peter Schwed. New York: Simon and Schuster, 1972, p. 504.
93. Cummings, op. cit., p. 74.
94. Ibid.

95. Cummings, op. cit., p. 38.
96. Cummings, op. cit., p. 74.
97. Meyers, loc. cit.
98. *Fifty Years*, op. cit., pp. 78, 80–81
99. *Fifty Years*, op. cit., p. 125.
100. *Fifty Years*, op. cit., p. 127.
101. "William Augustus Larned 'Bill.'" Retrieved September 30, 2009, from http://www.tennisfame.com/famer.aspx?pgID=867&hof_id=184.
102. "Larned, William 1872–1926." Retrieved September 30, 2009, from http://www.encyclopedia.com/doc/1G2-3468300318.html.
103. "William Larned." Retrieved September 30, 2009, from http://en.wikipedia.org/wiki/William_Larned.
104. "Maurice Evans McLoughlin 'Red, California Comet.'" Retrieved October 2, 2009, from http://www.tennisfame.com/famer.aspx?pgID=867&hof_id=207.
105. *Fifty Years*, op. cit., p. 131.
106. *Fifty Years*, op. cit., p. 130.
107. *Fifty Years*, op. cit., pp. 130–31.
108. *Fifty Years*, op. cit., p. 133.
109. *Fifty Years*, op. cit., p. 156.
110. Ibid.
111. *Fifty Years*, op. cit., p. 144.
112. *Fifty Years*, op. cit., p. 158.
113. *Fifty Years*, op. cit., p. 157.
114. Ibid.
115. Ibid.
116. "Williams Brings National Title East Again." *New York Times*, September 6, 1916.
117. *Fifty Years*, op. cit., p. 169.
118. "William M. Johnston 'Little Bill.'" Retrieved September 26, 2008, from http://www.tennisfame.com/famer.aspx?pgID=867&hof_id=163.
119. *Fifty Years*, op. cit., p. 172.
120. Ibid.
121. Ibid.
122. *Fifty Years*, op. cit., p. 186.

Chapter 3: Women's Tennis

1. Walter Wingfield. *The Game of* Sphairistike *or Lawn Tennis.* London: Harrison and Sons, 1874, p. 6.
2. Ibid.
3. Heiner Gillmeister. *Tennis: A Cultural History.* London: Leicester University Press, 1997, p. 202.
4. Gillmeister, op. cit., pp. 202–3.
5. Gillmeister, op. cit., p. 206.
6. Ibid.
7. Parke Cummings. *American Tennis: The Story of a Game.* Boston: Little, Brown & Company, 1957, p. 53.
8. "Charlotte Dod 'Lottie, The Little Wonder.'" Retrieved September 17, 2009, from http://www.tennisfame.com/famer.aspx?pgID=867&hof_id=89.
9. Miss L. Dod. "Ladies' Lawn Tennis," in *Tennis: Lawn Tennis: Rackets: Fives* by J. M. Heathcote, C. G. Heathcote, E. O. P-Bouverie, A. C. Ainger. The Badminton Library of Sports and Pastimes. Southampton, UK: Ashford Press Publishing, 1987, p. 312. (First published in 1903; first edition 1890 by Longmans, Green, and Co., London, 484 pages.)
10. Miss L. Dod, op. cit., p. 308.
11. Miss L. Dod, op. cit., p. 311.
12. Miss L. Dod, op. cit., pp. 310–11.
13. USLTA. *Fifty Years of Lawn Tennis in the United States.* New York: United States Lawn Tennis Association, 1931, p. 37.
14. *Fifty Years*, op. cit., pp. 38, 40–41.
15. *Fifty Years*, op. cit., p. 66.
16. Ibid.
17. *Fifty Years*, op. cit., p. 67.
18. Ibid.
19. Ibid.
20. *Fifty Years*, op. cit., p. 120.
21. Ibid.
22. "Maud Barger-Wallach." Retrieved September 10, 2009, from http://www.tennisfame.com/famer.aspx?pgID=867&hof_id=50.
23. *Fifty Years*, op. cit., p. 137.
24. Ibid.
25. *Fifty Years*, op. cit., pp. 137–38.
26. *Fifty Years*, op. cit., p. 138.

27. *Fifty Years*, op. cit., p. 139.
28. Ibid.
29. *Wright & Ditson's Official Lawn Tennis Guide for 1912*. Boston: Wright & Ditson, Publishers, pp. 206–7.
30. *Fifty Years*, loc. cit.
31. "Hazel Virginia Hotchkiss Wightman 'Lady Tennis.'" Retrieved September 12, 2009, from http://www.tennisfame.com/famer.aspx?pgID=867&hof_id=152.
32. Ibid.
33. Ibid.
34. *Fifty Years*, op. cit., p. 141.
35. Ibid.
36. *Fifty Years*, op. cit., p. 143.
37. Ibid.
38. Ibid.
39. Ibid.
40. *Fifty Years*, op. cit., p. 144.
41. Ibid.
42. *Fifty Years*, op. cit., p. 145.
43. "Elizabeth Montague Ryan 'Bunny.'" Retrieved September 12, 2009, from http://www.tennisfame.com/famer.aspx?pgID=867&hof_id=152.
44. Ibid.
45. *Fifty Years*, op. cit., p. 162.
46. *Fifty Years*, op. cit., pp. 162–63.
47. *Fifty Years*, op. cit., p. 163.
48. Ibid.
49. Ibid.

Chapter 4: California Tennis

1. C. R. Yates. "Lawn Tennis on the Pacific Coast," in *Outing for July*. New York: Outing Publishing Company, 1890, pp. 271–72.
2. "Lawn Tennis in California," in *American Lawn Tennis*, vol. 2, no. 1. Cambridge: University Press, February 9, 1899, pp. 28–29.
3. Yates, op. cit., pp. 273–74.
4. *American Lawn Tennis*, op. cit., pp. 136–38.
5. Parke Cummings. *American Tennis: The Story of a Game*. Boston: Little, Brown & Company, 1957, p. 59.

6. *American Lawn Tennis*. Cambridge: University Press, April 15, 1908, p. 12.
7. *Wright & Ditson's Lawn Tennis Guide for 1897*. Boston: Wright & Ditson, Publishers, pp. 38–40.
8. Don E. Liebendorfer. *The Color of Life Is Red: A History of Stanford Athletics 1892–1972*. Palo Alto: National Press, 1972, p. 263.
9. *Spalding's Lawn Tennis Annual for 1900*. New York: American Sports Publishing Co., pp. 27–29.
10. "Marion Jones (tennis)." Retrieved October 26, 2009, from http://wikipedia.org/wiki/Marion_Jones_(tennis).
11. "Marion Jones." Retrieved October 26, 2009, from http://www.sports-reference.com/olympics/athletes/jo/marion-jones-1.html.
12. "Farquhar, Marion." Retrieved October 26, 2009, from http://www.tennisticketnews.com/farquhar-marion-527.html.
13. "Charlotte Cooper (tennis)." Retrieved October 27, 2009, from http://wikipedia.org/wiki/Charlotte_Cooper_(tennis_player).
14. "Marion Jones." Retrieved October 26, 2009, from http://www.sports-reference.com/olympics/athletes/jo/marion-jones-1.html.
15. "Lawn Tennis in California," op. cit., pp. 27–28.
16. *Spalding's 1900 Annual*, op. cit., pp. 37–39.
17. *Wright & Ditson's Lawn Tennis Guide for 1905*. Boston: Wright & Ditson, Publishers, pp. 219–20, 226–27.
18. "May Godfrey Sutton Bundy." Retrieved August 20, 2009, from http://www.tennisfame.com/famer.aspx?pgID=867&hof_id=144.
19. USLTA. *Fifty Years of Lawn Tennis in the United States*. New York: United States Lawn Tennis Association, 1931, p. 112.
20. "Gussie Moran Faces Test in Wimbledon." *Niagara Falls Gazette*, June 22, 1949.
21. "Ted Tinling." Retrieved October 3, 2009, from http://en.wikipedia.org/wiki/Ted_Tinling.
22. *Wright & Ditson's 1905 Guide*, op. cit., pp. 215–16, 218, 223, 225.
23. Cummings, op. cit., p. 91.
24. *Spalding's Lawn Tennis Annual 1919*. New York: American Sports Publishing Company, pp. 277–79.
25. *Spalding's Lawn Tennis Annual 1906*. New York: American Sports Publishing Company, p. 103.
26. "The NTRP." Retrieved October 28, 2009, from http://www.1stserve.com/ntrp.asp.
27. *Spalding's 1906 Annual*, loc. cit.

28. *Spalding's 1906 Annual*, op. cit., p. 104.
29. *Wright & Ditson's Lawn Tennis Guide for 1907.* Boston: Wright & Ditson, Publishers, pp. 279–80, 282.
30. "Sherman Day Thacher." Retrieved August 8, 2010, from http://en.wikipedia.org/wiki/Sherman_Day_Thacher.
31. "The Ojai." Retrieved September 25, 2009, from http://ojaitourney.org/history.shtml.
32. *Wright & Ditson's 1907 Guide*, op. cit., pp. 272, 275.
33. *Wright & Ditson's 1907 Guide*, op. cit., pp. 269–71.
34. *Wright & Ditson's 1907 Guide*, op. cit., p. 275.
35. *Wright & Ditson's 1907 Guide*, op. cit., p. 270.
36. *Wright & Ditson's Lawn Tennis Guide for 1908.* Boston: Wright & Ditson, Publishers, pp. 216–17.
37. "Elizabeth Montague Ryan 'Bunny.'" Retrieved September 12, 2009, from http://www.tennisfame.com/famer.aspx?pgID=867&hof_id=180.
38. *Wright & Ditson's 1908 Guide*, op. cit., pp. 210, 213.
39. *Wright & Ditson's 1908 Guide*, op. cit., pp. 209–10, 214–16.
40. *Wright & Ditson's 1908 Guide*, op. cit., pp. 202, 205–6.
41. *Wright & Ditson's 1908 Guide*, op. cit., pp. 209–10.
42. *Wright & Ditson's Lawn Tennis Guide for 1909.* Boston: Wright & Ditson, Publishers, pp. 163, 170.
43. *Wright & Ditson's 1909 Guide*, op. cit., p. 160.
44. *Wright & Ditson's 1909 Guide*, op. cit., p. 162.
45. *Wright & Ditson's 1909 Guide*, op. cit., pp. 163–64, 166, 168, 170.
46. *Wright & Ditson's 1909 Guide*, op. cit., pp. 154, 156.
47. *Wright & Ditson's 1909 Guide*, op. cit., pp. 156–57.
48. *Wright & Ditson's 1909 Guide*, op. cit., p. 157.
49. *Spalding's Official Lawn Tennis Annual 1910.* New York: American Sports Publishing Company, pp. 77–78.
50. *Spalding's 1910 Annual*, op. cit., pp. 44–47.
51. *Wright & Ditson's Official Lawn Tennis Guide for 1911.* Boston: Wright & Ditson, Publishers, pp. 176–77.
52. *Wright & Ditson's 1911 Guide*, op. cit., p. 178.
53. *Wright & Ditson's 1911 Guide*, op. cit., p. 177.
54. *Wright & Ditson's 1911 Guide*, op. cit., pp. 174–76.
55. *Wright & Ditson's 1911 Guide*, op. cit., pp. 169, 171–72.
56. *Wright & Ditson's 1911 Guide*, op. cit., pp. 34, 36, 38.

57. *Wright & Ditson's Official Lawn Tennis Guide for 1912*. Boston: Wright & Ditson, Publishers, pp. 197, 199, 201.
58. *Wright & Ditson's 1912 Guide*, op. cit., p. 204.
59. *Wright & Ditson's 1912 Guide*, op. cit., p. 203.
60. *Wright & Ditson's Official Lawn Tennis Guide for 1913*. Boston: Wright & Ditson, Publishers, p. 195.
61. *Wright & Ditson's 1913 Guide*, op. cit., pp. 192, 194.
62. *Wright & Ditson's 1913 Guide*, op. cit., p. 192.
63. *Wright & Ditson's 1913 Guide*, op. cit., pp. 194–95.
64. *Wright & Ditson's Official Lawn Tennis Guide for 1914*. Boston: Wright & Ditson, Publishers, p. 183.
65. *Wright & Ditson's 1914 Guide*, op. cit., pp. 182–83.
66. *Wright & Ditson's 1914 Guide*, op. cit., pp. 174, 176–77.
67. *Wright & Ditson's 1914 Guide*, op. cit., pp. 180–82.
68. *Wright & Ditson's 1914 Guide*, op. cit., pp. 178–79.
69. "Tennis." *Stanford Quad, 1915*, p. 221.
70. *Spalding's Official Lawn Tennis Annual 1915*. New York: American Sports Publishing Company, p. 91.
71. *Wright & Ditson's Official Lawn Tennis Guide for 1915*. Boston: Wright & Ditson, Publishers, p. 195.
72. *Wright & Ditson's 1915 Guide*, op. cit., pp. 188, 190, 192.
73. *Wright & Ditson's 1915 Guide*, op. cit., pp. 193–94.
74. *Wright & Ditson's Officially Adopted Lawn Tennis Guide for 1916*. Boston: Wright & Ditson, Publishers, pp. 113–14.
75. *Wright & Ditson's 1916 Guide*, op. cit., pp. 130–31.
76. *Wright & Ditson's 1916 Guide*, op. cit., pp. 128–29.
77. *Wright & Ditson's 1916 Guide*, op. cit., pp. 109–10.
78. *Wright & Ditson's 1916 Guide*, op. cit., p. 114.
79. *Wright & Ditson's Officially Adopted Lawn Tennis Guide for 1917*. Boston: Wright & Ditson, Publishers, p. 127.
80. *Wright & Ditson's 1917 Guide*, op. cit., pp. 129–30, 132.
81. *Wright & Ditson's 1917 Guide*, op. cit., p. 131.
82. "Girls in Long Match." *New York Times*, June 20, 1916.
83. *Wright & Ditson's 1917 Guide*, op. cit., pp. 153–54, 156–57.
84. *Wright & Ditson's 1917 Guide*, op. cit., pp. 259–60.
85. *Wright & Ditson's Officially Adopted Lawn Tennis Guide for 1918*. Boston: Wright & Ditson, Publishers, pp. 100–101.
86. *Wright & Ditson's 1918 Guide*, op. cit., pp. 103–4.
87. *Wright & Ditson's 1918 Guide*, op. cit., pp. 106–7.

88. *Wright & Ditson's 1918 Guide*, op. cit., pp. 119–22, 124.
89. *Spalding's Lawn Tennis Annual 1919.* New York: American Sports Publishing Company, p. 131.
90. *Wright & Ditson's Officially Adopted Lawn Tennis Guide for 1920.* Boston: Wright & Ditson, Publishers, p. 55.
91. *Wright & Ditson's 1920 Guide*, op. cit., p. 56.
92. *The Brooklyn Daily Eagle Almanac*, 1922, p. 474.
93. "Phil Neer." Retrieved August 13, 2009, from http://www.answers.com/topic/phil-neer.
94. *Wright & Ditson's 1920 Guide*, op. cit., p. 50.
95. *Wright & Ditson's 1920 Guide*, op. cit., p. 53.
96. Ibid.
97. *Wright & Ditson's 1920 Guide*, op. cit., pp. 49–50.
98. *Wright & Ditson's 1920 Guide*, op. cit., pp. 54–55.
99. *Wright & Ditson's 1920 Guide*, op. cit., p. 57.
100. "Gerald Patterson." Retrieved October 3, 2009, from http://en.wikipedia.org/wiki/Gerald_Paterson.
101. "Howard Kinsey." Retrieved October 3, 2009, from http://en.wikipedia.org/wiki/Howard_Kinsey.
102. "Howard Kinsey, 66, a Tennis Champion." *New York Times*, July 28, 1966.

Chapter 5: A Few Notes on Men's Doubles

1. Parke Cummings. *American Tennis: The Story of a Game.* Boston: Little, Brown & Company, 1957, p. 63.
2. Bud Collins. *The Bud Collins History of Tennis: An Authoritative Encyclopedia and Record Book.* Washington, DC: New Chapter Press, 2008, pp. 442–43.
3. "Sites of the U.S. Open Championships." Retrieved September 16, 2009, from http://www.usopen.org/en_US/about/history/anec_sites.html.
4. Bud Collins, op. cit., p. 443.
5. "Sites of the U.S. Open Championships." Retrieved September 16, 2009, from http://www.usopen.org/en_US/about/history/anec_sites.html.
6. Max Robertson and Jack Kramer (eds.). *The Encyclopedia of Tennis.* New York: Viking Press, Inc., 1974, p. 370.
7. Bud Collins, loc. cit.
8. Ibid.

9. Robertson and Kramer, op. cit., pp. 364–65.
10. USLTA. *Fifty Years of Lawn Tennis in the United States.* New York: United States Lawn Tennis Association, 1931, p. 27.
11. R. D. Sears. "Lawn Tennis in America," in *Tennis: Lawn Tennis: Rackets: Fives* by J. M. Heathcote, C. G. Heathcote, E. O. P-Bouverie, A. C. Ainger. The Badminton Library of Sports and Pastimes. Southampton, UK: Ashford Press Publishing, 1987, pp. 325–28. (First published in 1903; first edition 1890 by Longmans, Green, and Co., London, 484 pages.)
12. *Wright & Ditson's Lawn Tennis Guide for 1891.* Boston: Wright & Ditson, Publishers, pp. 41, 43, 46.
13. *Wright & Ditson's Lawn Tennis Guide for 1897.* Boston: Wright & Ditson, Publishers, p. 37.
14. "Tennis Season Reviewed." *New York Times*, September 18, 1892.
15. "Sites of the U.S. Open Championships." Retrieved September 16, 2009, from http://www.usopen.org/en_US/about/history/anec_sites.html.
16. *Wright & Ditson's Official 1894 Lawn Tennis Guide.* Boston: Wright & Ditson, Publishers, pp. 36–38.
17. "Today in Tennis History." Retrieved September 16, 2009, from http://www.historyorb.com/sport/tennis.
18. *Wright & Ditson's Lawn Tennis Guide for 1895.* Boston: Wright & Ditson, Publishers, pp. 44–47.
19. "Western Tennis Players Won." *New York Times*, August 18, 1894.
20. Wright & *Ditson's 1897 Guide*, op. cit., pp. 38–40.
21. "Tennis at Longwood." *New York Times*, August 1, 1897.
22. "Lawn Tennis Records." *The World Almanac and Book of Facts 1897.* New York: Press Publishing Co., p. 220.
23. *Wright & Ditson's Lawn Tennis Guide for 1899.* Boston: Wright & Ditson, Publishers, pp. 36–40.
24. *American Lawn Tennis*, vol. 1, no. 9, July 21, 1898, p. 132; vol. 1, no. 11, August 4, 1898, pp. 164–65.
25. *Spalding's Lawn Tennis Annual for 1900.* New York: American Sports Publishing Co., pp. 27–29.
26. *Spalding's 1900 Annual*, op. cit., p. 22–24.
27. *Spalding's 1900 Annual*, op. cit., p. 18.
28. *Spalding's Lawn Tennis Annual 1904.* New York: American Sports Publishing Company, pp. 13, 17.

29. *Spalding's Lawn Tennis Annual 1906*. New York: American Sports Publishing Company, p. 15.
30. *Wright & Ditson's Lawn Tennis Guide for 1906*. Boston: Wright & Ditson, Publishers, p. 67.
31. *Wright & Ditson's Lawn Tennis Guide for 1908*. Boston: Wright & Ditson, Publishers, p. 65.
32. *Wright & Ditson's Lawn Tennis Guide for 1909*. Boston: Wright & Ditson, Publishers, p. 47.
33. *Wright & Ditson's Officially Adopted Lawn Tennis Guide for 1918*. Boston: Wright & Ditson, Publishers, p. 292.
34. "Sites of the U.S. Open Championships." Retrieved September 16, 2009, from http://www.usopen.org/en_US/about/history/anec_sites.html.
35. *Spalding's Official Lawn Tennis Annual 1910*. New York: American Sports Publishing Company, pp. 47–48.
36. *Spalding's 1910 Annual*, op. cit., p. 34.
37. *Wright & Ditson's Official Lawn Tennis Guide for 1911*. Boston: Wright & Ditson, Publishers, pp. 172–73.
38. *Wright & Ditson's 1911 Guide*, op. cit., p. 12.
39. *Wright & Ditson's Official Lawn Tennis Guide for 1912*. Boston: Wright & Ditson, Publishers, p. 201.
40. *Wright & Ditson's 1912 Guide*, op. cit., p. 13.
41. *Spalding's Official Lawn Tennis Annual 1913*. New York: American Sports Publishing Company, p. 20.
42. *Spalding's 1913 Annual*, op. cit., p. 15.
43. *Wright & Ditson's Official Lawn Tennis Guide for 1914*. Boston: Wright & Ditson, Publishers, p. 177.
44. *Wright & Ditson's 1914 Guide*, op. cit., p. 11.
45. *Spalding's Official Lawn Tennis Annual 1915*. New York: American Sports Publishing Company, p. 89.
46. *Wright & Ditson's Official Lawn Tennis Guide for 1915*. Boston: Wright & Ditson, Publishers, p. 11.
47. *Wright & Ditson's Officially Adopted Lawn Tennis Guide for 1916*. Boston: Wright & Ditson, Publishers, p. 112.
48. *Wright & Ditson's 1916 Guide*, op. cit., p. 13.
49. *Wright & Ditson's 1916 Guide*, op. cit., p. 40.
50. *Wright & Ditson's Officially Adopted Lawn Tennis Guide for 1917*. Boston: Wright & Ditson, Publishers, pp. 133–34.
51. *Wright & Ditson's 1917 Guide*, op. cit., pp. 14–15.

52. *Wright & Ditson's 1917 Guide*, op. cit., p. 13.
53. *The Wright & Ditson Officially Adopted Lawn Tennis Guide for 1921.* Boston: Wright & Ditson, Publishers, p. 52.
54. *The Wright & Ditson 1921 Guide*, op. cit., p. 173.
55. *The Wright & Ditson 1921 Guide*, op. cit., pp. 8, 12.
56. *The Wright & Ditson 1921 Guide*, op. cit., p. 29.

Part II: Robert Lindley Murray

Chapter 6: Family Genealogy

1. "Welcome to Blair Castle." Retrieved February 26, 2010, from http://www.blair-castle.co.uk/.
2. The Murray Genealogy. Unpublished document, pp. 1–2.
3. Charles Monaghan. *The Murrays of Murray Hill.* Brooklyn, NY: Urban History Press, 1998, p. 11.
4. The Murray Genealogy, op. cit., p. 2.
5. Monaghan, loc. cit.
6. "Mary Lindley Murray." Retrieved February 11, 2010, from http://www.nwhm.org/Education/biography_mmurray.html.
7. Monaghan, op. cit., pp. 12–13.
8. Charles Monaghan. "Lindley Murray and the Enlightenment." Retrieved February 27, 2010, from http://faculty.ed.uiuc.edu/westbury/paradigm/monaghan2.html.
9. Ibid.
10. The Murray Genealogy, loc. cit.
11. Monaghan, op. cit., p. 17.
12. Monaghan, op. cit., pp. 15–16.
13. Monaghan, op. cit., p. 16.
14. Monaghan, op. cit., p. 17.
15. Monaghan, op. cit., p. 18.
16. Charles Monaghan. "Lindley Murray and the Enlightenment." Retrieved February 27, 2010, from http://faculty.ed.uiuc.edu/westbury/paradigm/monaghan2.html.
17. Monaghan, op. cit., p. 3.
18. Letter from John Murray Huneke to Michael V. Wilcox, November 14, 2003.
19. The Murray Genealogy, loc. cit.
20. "Nathan Hale." Retrieved February 26, 2010, from http://www.sonofthesouth.net/revolutionary-war/patriots/nathan-hale.htm.

21. Anonymous. *Under His Wings. A Sketch of the Life of Robert Lindley Murray.* New York: Anson D. F. Randolph & Company, 1876, p. 11.
22. Sarah S. Murray. *In the Olden Time: A Short History of the Descendants of John Murray the Good With Memories of More Recent Date.* New York: Stettiner, Lambert & Co., 1894, p. 16.
23. The Murray Genealogy, loc. cit.
24. "Mary Lindley Murray." Retrieved February 11, 2010, from http://www.nwhm.org/Education/biography_mmurray.html.
25. Monaghan, op. cit., p. 10.
26. "Lindley Murray." Retrieved February 27, 2010, from http://en.wikipedia.org/wiki/Lindley_Murray.
27. Monaghan, op. cit., p. 26.
28. Monaghan, op. cit., pp. 27–28.
29. Monaghan, op. cit., p. 28.
30. Monaghan, op. cit., pp. 30–31.
31. Monaghan, op. cit., p. 32.
32. Monaghan, op. cit., p. 43.
33. Monaghan, op. cit., p. 45.
34. Monaghan, op. cit., p. 46.
35. Monaghan, op. cit., p. 47.
36. "Townshend Acts." Retrieved March 5, 2010, from http://en.wikipedia.org/wiki/Townshend_Acts.
37. Monaghan, op. cit., p. 48.
38. Monaghan, op. cit., pp. 47–48.
39. Monaghan, op. cit., p. 48.
40. Monaghan, op. cit., p. 49.
41. Monaghan, op. cit., pp. 51–52.
42. Monaghan, op. cit., p. 52.
43. Monaghan, op. cit., pp. 52–53.
44. Philip Papas. *That Ever Loyal Island: Staten Island and the American Revolution.* New York: New York University Press, 2007, p. 29.
45. Monaghan, op. cit., p. 53.
46. Monaghan, op. cit., pp. 53–54.
47. Monaghan, op. cit., p. 54.
48. Monaghan, op. cit., pp. 57–58.
49. Monaghan, op. cit., p. 56.
50. Monaghan, op. cit., p. 72.
51. Monaghan, op. cit., p. 74.

52. Monaghan, op. cit., pp. 75, 77.
53. Monaghan, op. cit., p. 79.
54. Monaghan, op. cit., p. 80.
55. Monaghan, op. cit., p. 82.
56. Monaghan, op. cit., p. 81.
57. Monaghan, op. cit., p. 84.
58. Monaghan, op. cit., pp. 92–93.
59. Monaghan, op. cit., p. 94.
60. "Lindley Murray." Retrieved February 22, 2010, from http://www.answers.com/topic/lindley-murray.
61. Monaghan, op. cit., p. 95.
62. "Lindley Murray." Retrieved February 22, 2010, from http://www.answers.com/topic/lindley-murray.
63. Sarah S. Murray, op. cit., p. 47.
64. The Murray Genealogy, op. cit., p. 3.
65. "John Bowne House." Retrieved March 1, 2010, from http://en.wikipedia.org/wiki/John_Bowne_House.
66. The Murray Genealogy, loc. cit.
67. "John Bowne House." Retrieved March 1, 2010, from http://en.wikipedia.org/wiki/John_Bowne_House.
68. The Murray Genealogy, loc. cit.
69. Sarah S. Murray, op. cit., p. 53.
70. Monaghan, op. cit., pp. 107–8.
71. Sarah S. Murray, op. cit., pp. 54–55.
72. Sarah S. Murray, op. cit., p. 55.
73. Sarah S. Murray, op. cit., p. 56.
74. Sarah S. Murray, op. cit., p. 57.
75. Sarah S. Murray, op. cit., pp. 58–59.
76. The Murray Genealogy, loc. cit.
77. Thomas Eddy. *Memoir of the Late John Murray, Jun., Read Before the Governors of The New-York Hospital, 9th Month, 14th, 1819.*
78. Sarah S. Murray, op. cit., p. 82.
79. Sarah S. Murray, op. cit., p. 83.
80. Sarah S. Murray, op. cit., p. 86.
81. The Murray Genealogy, loc. cit.
82. "Cadwallader D. Colden." Retrieved March 1, 2010, from http://en.wikipedia.org/wiki/Cadwallader_D._Colden.
83. "Cadwallader Colden." Retrieved March 1, 2010, from http://en.wikipedia.org/wiki/Cadwallader_Colden.

84. "List of colonial governors of New York." Retrieved March 2, 2010, from http://en.wikipedia.org/wiki/List_of_colonial_governors_of_New_York.
85. Sarah S. Murray, op. cit., p. 93.
86. Sarah S. Murray, op. cit., p. 125.
87. Sarah S. Murray, op. cit., p. 92.
88. Sarah S. Murray, op. cit., pp. 122–23.
89. Although the author is listed as anonymous in *Under His Wings* of 1876, it has much the same phraseology as the last chapter ("Robert Lindley Murray," pp. 169–77) of *In the Olden Time* of 1894 by Sarah S. Murray.
90. Sarah S. Murray, op. cit., p. 128.
91. Sarah S. Murray, op. cit., p. 169.
92. Sarah S. Murray, op. cit., p. 170.
93. "Haverford College." Retrieved March 2, 2010, from http://en.wikipedia.org/wiki/Haverford_College.
94. The Murray Genealogy, loc. cit.
95. *New Bedford, Massachusetts: Its History, Industries, Institutions, and Attractions*. New Bedford: Mercury Publishing Company, 1889, pp. 245–46.
96. "Frederick Douglass and the Quakers." Retrieved March 2, 2010, from http://www2.gol.com/users/quakers/frederick_douglas_the_quakers.htm.
97. The Murray Genealogy, loc. cit.
98. Allen C. Thomas, A.M., '65, ed. *Biographical Catalogue of the Matriculates of Haverford College, 1833–1900*. Philadelphia, 1900, pp. 23–24.
99. Anonymous, op. cit., pp. 74–76.
100. Anonymous, op. cit., pp. 77–78.
101. Sarah S. Murray, op. cit., pp. 174–77.
102. The Murray Genealogy, loc. cit.
103. Thomas, op. cit., pp. 3, 7.
104. Thomas, op. cit., p. 87.
105. Stanford University Department of Classics. Retrieved September 29, 2008, from www.classics.stanford.edu/home/Community/community_dept_hist.html.
106. The Murray Genealogy, op. cit., p. 5.
107. Stanford University, Office of the President. Resolutions Adopted by the Academic Council. April 5, 1940, pp. 2–3.

108. "Memorial Resolution Augustus Taber Murray." Retrieved September 29, 2008, from www.histsoc.stanford.edu/pdfmem/MurrayA.pdf.
109. Stanford University, Office of the President. Resolutions Adopted by the Academic Council. April 5, 1940, p. 4.
110. "Special Residential Programs." Retrieved April 3, 2010, from http://www.stanford.edu/dept/resed/Program/SpecialProg.html.
111. "Welcome to Murray House!" Retrieved April 3, 2010, from http://www.stanford.edu/group/resed/govco/murray/Murray%2Home.html.
112. William M. Emery and William W. Crapo. *The Howland Heirs: Being the Story of a Family and a Fortune and the Inheritance of a Trust.* New Bedford, MA: E. Anthony & Sons, Inc., 1919, pp. 1–2.
113. Notes by John Murray Huneke, November 14, 2003.
114. Notes by Doug Murray, March 2001.
115. Emery, op. cit., p. 349.
116. "Fred Murray." Retrieved March 11, 2010, from www.sports-reference.com/olympics/athletes/mu/fred-murray-1.html.
117. Emery, loc. cit.
118. "World Record Progression: 110 m. hurdles men." Retrieved March 11, 2010, from http://www.athletix.org/statistics/wr110hurdmen.html.
119. Emery, loc. cit.
120. "USA Outdoor Track & Field Champions." Retrieved March 11, 2010, from http://www.woodhurdles.com/200meterLowHurdles/2.html.
121. Emery, loc. cit.
122. "Feg (Frederic) (Seymour) Murray." Retrieved March 12, 2010, from http://www.askart.com/ascart/m/feg_frederic_seymour_murray.
123. "Feg Murray." Retrieved March 12, 2010, from http://lambiek.net/artists/m/murray_feg.htm.
124. "Fred Murray." Retrieved March 11, 2010, from www.sports-reference.com/olympics/athletes/mu/fred-murray-1.html.
125. Notes by Doug Murray, March 2001.
126. *Time* Archive. Retrieved September 28, 2008, from www.time.com/time/magazine/article/0,9171,881817,00/.html.
127. Notes by Doug Murray, March 2001.
128. Emery, op. cit., p. 350.
129. Notes by Doug Murray, March 2001.

130. "Deaths." Retrieved September 29, 2008, from www.paloaltoonline.com/weekly/morgue/community_pulse/1996_Feb_14.OBITS14.
131. Notes by John Murray Huneke, November 14, 2003.
132. Notes by Doug Murray, March 2001.
133. "Deaths." Retrieved September 29, 2008, from www.paloaltoonline.com/weekly/morgue/community_pulse/1996_Feb_14.OBITS14.

Chapter 7: Robert Lindley "Lin" Murray at Stanford

1. H. R. Spence. "1912 Track Season." *Stanford Quad, 1913*, p. 417.
2. E. C. Behrens. "The 1913 Intercollegiate Track Meet." *Stanford Quad, 1914*.
3. "Mile run world record progression." Retrieved April 26, 2010, from http://en.wikipedia.org/wiki/Mile_run_world_record_progression.
4. Behrens, loc. cit.
5. Stanford University Interscholastic Athletic Association. Referee and timers certification sheet, March 21, 1914.
6. "Tennis." *Stanford Quad, 1911*, p. 428.
7. "Myth #113—A Tennis Great's Life Started in Carson City." Retrieved February 12, 2010, from http://nevadaculture.org/nsla/index.php?option=com_content&task=view&id=794&Itemi...
8. "Tennis." *Stanford Quad, 1911*, p. 429.
9. Don E. Liebendorfer. *The Color of Life Is Red: A History of Stanford Athletics 1892–1972*. Palo Alto, CA: National Press, 1972, p. 263.
10. "The 1910 Tennis Season." *Stanford Quad, 1912*.
11. "Intercollegiate Tennis." *Stanford Quad, 1913*.
12. Ibid.
13. Liebendorfer, loc. cit.
14. *Wright & Ditson's Official Lawn Tennis Guide for 1913*. Boston: Wright & Ditson, Publishers, p. 195.
15. Liebendorfer, loc. cit.
16. *Wright & Ditson's Official Lawn Tennis Guide for 1914*. Boston: Wright & Ditson, Publishers, pp. 182–83.
17. "Tennis." *Stanford Quad, 1915*, p. 220.
18. Ibid.
19. Ibid.
20. "Tennis." *Stanford Quad, 1915*, pp. 220–21.
21. Liebendorfer, loc. cit.

22. Philip Neer. "Tennis at Stanford." *Stanford Illustrated Review*. Published by the Students and Alumni of Stanford University, November 1919, p. 93.
23. *Wright & Ditson's Official Lawn Tennis Guide for 1912*. Boston: Wright & Ditson, Publishers, p. 201.
24. *Wright & Ditson's 1914 Guide*, op. cit., p. 182.
25. *Wright & Ditson's 1914 Guide*, op. cit., p. 178.

Chapter 8: The 1914 Eastern Invasion

1. "Tennis." *Stanford Quad, 1915*, p. 221.
2. *Wright & Ditson's Official Lawn Tennis Guide for 1915*. Boston: Wright & Ditson, Publishers, p. 122.
3. "Leland Stanford Tennis Victory." *New York Times*, May 28, 1914.
4. "Californians Beat Amherst at Tennis." *New York Times*, May 29, 1914.
5. *Spalding's Official Lawn Tennis Annual 1915*. New York: American Sports Publishing Company, p. 109.
6. "California Wins Tennis Title." *New York Times*, June 14, 1914.
7. *Wright & Ditson's 1915 Guide*, op. cit., pp. 77–79.
8. "California Tennis Player Wins Title." *New York Times*, June 21, 1914.
9. *Spalding's 1915 Annual*, op. cit., pp. 97–99.
10. *Spalding's 1915 Annual*, op. cit., p. 99.
11. "Western Players on Davis Cup Team." *New York Times*, June 22, 1914.
12. "Murray Defaults in Tennis Match." *New York Times*, June 24, 1914.
13. *Wright & Ditson's 1915 Guide*, op. cit., pp. 146–47.
14. *Wright & Ditson's Official Lawn Tennis Guide for 1914*. Boston: Wright & Ditson, Publishers, pp. 136–37.
15. *Wright & Ditson's 1915 Guide*, op. cit., p. 147.
16. "California Offers Another New Tennis Marvel." *New York Times*, July 5, 1914.
17. Ibid.
18. Ibid.
19. Ibid.
20. Ibid.
21. Ibid.
22. Ibid.

23. "Lindley Murray, the New Boy Tennis Wonder From Out of the West." *Ohio State Journal*, July 26, 1914.
24. *Wright & Ditson's 1915 Guide*, op. cit., pp. 67–68.
25. *Wright & Ditson's 1915 Guide*, op. cit., pp. 68–69.
26. "Tennis Players Overcome by Heat." *New York Times*, July 17, 1914.
27. *Wright & Ditson's 1915 Guide*, op. cit., pp. 61–62.
28. *Spalding's 1915 Annual*, op. cit., pp. 117–18.
29. "M'Loughlin to Play Murray for Title." *New York Times*, August 5, 1914.
30. *Spalding's 1915 Annual*, op. cit., p. 117.
31. "Murray Easy for 'Champ' M'Loughlin." *New York Times*, August 20, 1914.
32. *Spalding's 1915 Annual*, op. cit., p. 107.
33. "Tennis Champions Win in Doubles." *New York Times*, August 22, 1914.
34. *Spalding's 1915 Annual*, op. cit., pp. 107–8.
35. *Wright & Ditson's 1915 Guide*, op. cit., p. 9.
36. Ibid.
37. *Wright & Ditson's 1915 Guide*, op. cit., p. 10.
38. "Why M'Loughlin Was Ranked First." *New York Times*, December 20, 1914.
39. *Wright & Ditson's 1915 Guide*, op. cit., pp. 193–94.
40. *Spalding's 1915 Annual*, op. cit., p. 7.
41. William M. Emery and William W. Crapo. *The Howland Heirs: Being the Story of a Family and a Fortune and the Inheritance of a Trust.* New Bedford, MA: E. Anthony & Sons, Inc., 1919, p. 348.

Chapter 9: The 1915 Season

1. *Spalding's Official Lawn Tennis Annual 1915*. New York: American Sports Publishing Company, p. 89.
2. "East's Tennis Team Expects a Victory." *New York Times*, July 11, 1915.
3. "Eastern Tennis Stars Invade West." *Niagara Falls Gazette*, July 9, 1915.
4. *Wright & Ditson's Officially Adopted Lawn Tennis Guide for 1916.* Boston: Wright & Ditson, Publishers, p. 225.
5. "Williams Beats Murray." *New York Times*, July 14, 1915.
6. Ibid.

7. "Williams Loses in Coast Tennis." *New York Times*, July 15, 1915.
8. *Wright & Ditson's 1916 Guide*, op. cit., p. 128.
9. *Wright & Ditson's 1916 Guide*, op. cit., p. 114.
10. *Wright & Ditson's 1916 Guide*, op. cit., p. 113.
11. *Wright & Ditson's 1916 Guide*, op. cit., p. 109.
12. *Wright & Ditson's 1916 Guide*, op. cit., pp. 25–28.
13. "Johnston Gets Two 'Firsts' in Tennis." *New York Times*, December 5, 1915.
14. *Wright & Ditson's 1916 Guide*, op. cit., pp. 203–4.
15. *Wright & Ditson's 1916 Guide*, op. cit., pp. 136–37.
16. Frank Deford. *Big Bill Tilden: The Triumphs and the Tragedy*. Toronto: Sport Media Publishing, Inc., 1975, p. 163.
17. *Wright & Ditson's 1916 Guide*, op. cit., p. 245.
18. *Wright & Ditson's 1916 Guide*, op. cit., p. 234.
19. Bob Watson. "Bounce of Tennis Ball Set up Hooker President for Job With Company." *Buffalo Evening News Magazine*, March 19, 1955.
20. "Western Tennis Star Here." *New York Times*, October 28, 1915.

Chapter 10: The 1916 U.S. Indoor Championship

1. "Murray's Smashes Tell." *New York Times*, February 6, 1916.
2. "Murray Captures Trio of Matches." *New York Times*, February 13, 1916.
3. "Murray Keeps up Keen Tennis Play." *New York Times*, February 17, 1916.
4. "Grant and Man in Tennis Semi-Final." *New York Times*, February 18, 1916.
5. "Murray and Man in Tennis Final." *New York Times*, February 20, 1916.
6. "Tennis Title Won by Lindley Murray." *New York Times*, February 23, 1916.
7. "Murray Keeps up Keen Tennis Play." *New York Times*, February 17, 1916.
8. "Murray's Tennis Victory." *New York Times*, February 28, 1916.
9. "Williams Beats Murray." *New York Times*, February 27, 1916.
10. "Singles Final Won by Miss Bjurstedt." *New York Times*, March 12, 1916.
11. "Miss Weber and McNeil Win." *New York Times*, April 23, 1916.

12. "Murray Defeats LeRoy on Courts." *New York Times*, May 28, 1916.
13. "Murray Outplayed by Throckmorton." *New York Times*, May 29, 1916.
14. "Davis Is Winner at Sleepy Hollow." *New York Times*, May 31, 1916.
15. "Tennis Surprises on Nassau Courts." *New York Times*, July 3, 1916.
16. "Murray Smashes Way to Victory." *New York Times*, July 5, 1916.
17. "Behr and Murray Rout Coast Stars." *New York Times*, July 23, 1916.
18. "East Routes West on Tennis Courts." *New York Times*, August 5, 1916.
19. "Murray to Meet Church in Final." *New York Times*, August 11, 1916.
20. "Attack of Church Lays Murray Low." *New York Times*, August 12, 1916.
21. "Murray Once More Conquers Kumagae." *New York Times*, August 14, 1916.
22. "Indoor Champion Murray Decides to Enter Tennis Classic for City Title." *Niagara Falls Gazette*, September 20, 1916.
23. William T. Tilden. *The Art Of Lawn Tennis*. London: Methuen & Co. Ltd., 1921, pp. 53–55.
24. "Williams to Meet Johnston in Final." *New York Times*, September 5, 1916.
25. Ibid.
26. Ibid.
27. "Williams Brings National Tennis Title East Again." *New York Times*, September 6, 1916.

Chapter 11: Hooker Electrochemical Company

1. Robert E. Thomas. *Salt & Water, Power & People: A Short History of Hooker Electrochemical Company*. New York: Appleton, Parsons & Company, Inc., 1955, p. 4.
2. Thomas, op. cit., pp. 5–6.
3. Thomas, op. cit., p. 6.
4. Ibid.
5. Ibid.
6. Thomas, op. cit., p. 7.

7. Thomas, op. cit., p. 11.
8. Thomas, op. cit., p. 10.
9. Thomas, op. cit., p. 14.
10. Ibid.
11. Thomas, op. cit., pp. 16–17.
12. Thomas, op. cit., p. 20.
13. Thomas, op. cit., p. 21.
14. Thomas, op. cit., pp. 21, 23.
15. Thomas, op. cit., pp. 23–24.
16. Thomas, op. cit., p. 25.
17. Thomas, op. cit., p. 29.
18. Thomas, op. cit., p. 31.
19. Ibid.
20. Thomas, op. cit., p. 33.
21. Ibid.
22. Thomas, op. cit., p. 34.
23. Ibid.
24. Thomas, op. cit., p. 35.
25. Thomas, op. cit., p. 37.
26. Thomas, op. cit., p. 38.
27. Ibid.
28. Thomas, op. cit., p. 41.
29. Ibid.
30. "Board Chairman at Hooker Retires." *Niagara Falls Gazette*, December 15, 1959.
31. Bob Watson. "Bounce of Tennis Ball Set up Hooker President for Job With Company." *Buffalo Evening News Magazine*, March 19, 1955.
32. Ibid.

Chapter 12: The 1917 Patriotic Tournaments

1. Paul Benjamin Williams and George Townsend Adee. *United States Lawn Tennis Association and the World War (1921)*. New York: Robert Hamilton Company, 1921, p. 2.
2. Williams, Adee, op. cit., p. 3.
3. Williams, Adee, op. cit., p. 29.
4. *Wright & Ditson's Officially Adopted Lawn Tennis Guide for 1918*. Boston: Wright & Ditson, Publishers, p. 9.

5. "Tennis Body Agrees to Award No Titles." *New York Times*, April 22, 1917.
6. Williams, Adee, op. cit., p. 17.
7. Ibid.
8. "French Open." Retrieved October 31, 2009, from http://en.wikipedia.org/wiki/French_Open.
9. *Wright & Ditson's Officially Adopted Lawn Tennis Guide for 1916.* Boston: Wright & Ditson, Publishers, p. 234.
10. Williams, Adee, op. cit., pp. 19–20.
11. Williams, Adee, op. cit., pp. 29, 31–32.
12. Williams, Adee, op. cit., p. 31.
13. *Wright & Ditson's 1918 Guide*, op. cit., pp. 72–73.
14. Williams, Adee, loc. cit.
15. Williams, Adee, op. cit., p. 27.
16. Williams, Adee, op. cit., p. 20.
17. Williams, Adee, op. cit., pp. 33–34.
18. Williams, Adee, op. cit., p. 36.
19. "Murray Twice Victor in Buffalo Tourney." *Niagara Falls Gazette*, July 3, 1917.
20. "Murray May Figure in Patriotic Tennis Finals." *Niagara Falls Gazette*, July 5, 1917.
21. "Murray vs. Garland in Tennis Finals Today." *Niagara Falls Gazette*, July 6, 1917.
22. "R. L. Murray Wins Great Lakes Tennis Title." *Niagara Falls Gazette*, July 9, 1917.
23. *Wright & Ditson's 1918 Guide*, op. cit., p. 89.
24. "R. L. Murray Wins Great Lakes Tennis Title." *Niagara Falls Gazette*, July 9, 1917.
25. "Local Tennis Champion Entered in Utica Tourney." *Niagara Falls Gazette*, July 19, 1917.
26. "Murray Victorious in Utica Tennis Tourney." *Niagara Falls Gazette*, July 21, 1917.
27. "Murray Victorious in Utica Tournament." *Niagara Falls Gazette*, July 23, 1917.
28. "Miss Browne and R. L. Murray Win Brilliant Mixed Doubles Match." *New York Times*, July 30, 1917.
29. "Murray May Figure in Forest Hills Tourney." *Niagara Falls Gazette*, July 14, 1917.
30. *Wright & Ditson's 1918 Guide*, op. cit., p. 11.

31. "Murray May Figure in Forest Hills Tourney." *Niagara Falls Gazette*, July 14, 1917.
32. "Local Tennis Champion Entered in Utica Tourney." *Niagara Falls Gazette*, July 19, 1917.
33. "Ranking Players Triumph in Third Round Matches of National Net Tourney." *New York Times*, August 22, 1917.
34. "Williams and Murray Have Close Call in National Tennis Tournament." *New York Times*, August 23, 1917.
35. "Murray Defeats Strachan in Fast Lawn Tennis Battle at Forest Hills." *New York Times*, August 25, 1917.
36. "Murray New Leader of Tennis Cohorts." *New York Times*, August 26, 1917.
37. "Murray Crowned National Tennis King at Forest Hills." *Niagara Falls Gazette*, August 27, 1917.
38. *Wright & Ditson's 1918 Guide*, loc. cit.
39. Ibid.
40. Ibid.
41. USLTA. *Fifty Years of Lawn Tennis in the United States*. New York: United States Lawn Tennis Association, 1931, pp. 173–74.
42. "Murray Able Holder of National Single Title." *Niagara Falls Gazette*, September 7, 1917.
43. "Murray New Leader of Tennis Cohorts." *New York Times*, August 26, 1917.
44. "Hooker Officials Honor R. Lindley Murray." *Niagara Falls Gazette*, August 28, 1917.
45. "Expect Record Crowd at Patriotic Tennis Tournament." *Niagara Falls Gazette*, August 29, 1917.
46. "Murray vs. Strachan in Feature Match Labor Day." *Niagara Falls Gazette*, August 30, 1917.
47. "Expect Record Crowd at Patriotic Tennis Tournament." *Niagara Falls Gazette*, August 29, 1917.
48. "Murray vs. Strachan in Feature Match Labor Day." *Niagara Falls Gazette*, August 30, 1917.
49. Ibid.
50. "Strain Tells on Players." *New York Times*, August 29, 1917.
51. "Patriotic Tennis Tournament Proves Big Success." *Niagara Falls Gazette*, September 4, 1917.
52. Ibid.

53. "Murray Tennis King of Present Season." *Niagara Falls Gazette*, September 5, 1917.
54. Ibid.

Chapter 13: The 1918 U.S. Championships

1. *Spalding's Lawn Tennis Annual 1919*. New York: American Sports Publishing Company, pp. 92–93.
2. *Wright & Ditson's Official Lawn Tennis Guide for 1912*. Boston: Wright & Ditson, Publishers, p. 181.
3. *Spalding's 1919 Annual*, op. cit., p. 93.
4. "Murray Out of Nationals." *New York Times*, July 24, 1918.
5. "The Story of the 37th Championship." *American Lawn Tennis*, September 15, 1918, p. 239.
6. USLTA. *Fifty Years of Lawn Tennis in the United States*. New York: United States Lawn Tennis Association, 1931, p. 174.
7. *Fifty Years*, op. cit., p. 176.
8. "PowerLabs Picric Acid Synthesis." Retrieved October 6, 2009, from http://www.powerlabs.org/chemlabs/picric.htm.
9. *Fifty Years*, loc. cit.
10. Ibid.
11. *Fifty Years*, op. cit., pp. 176–77.
12. "Tilden and Pell Reach Net Final." *New York Times*, August 24, 1918.
13. "Murray Loses to Tilden in Semi-Finals." *Niagara Falls Gazette*, August 24, 1918.
14. "Tilden and Pell Reach Net Final." *New York Times*, August 24, 1918.
15. "Tilden Beats Pell in Straight Sets." *New York Times*, August 25, 1918.
16. "Net Experts Begin Title Play Today." *New York Times*, August 26, 1918.
17. "Greetings From Williams." *New York Times*, August 25, 1918.
18. "Net Experts Begin Title Play Today." *New York Times*, August 26, 1918.
19. *Fifty Years*, op. cit., p. 177.
20. "Match of Eighty-Two Games Inaugurates National Tennis Singles Championship Tourney." *New York Times*, August 27, 1918.
21. "Thrilling Matches Played in National Tennis Tourney." *New York Times*, August 29, 1918.

22. "Rain Halts Tennis Tournament, But Holds off Long Enough for Murray to Defeat Alexander." *Niagara Falls Gazette*, August 30, 1918.
23. "Murray Defeats Alexander in Match Abounding in Sharp Tennis." *New York Times*, August 30, 1918.
24. "Murray, Tilden, and Kumagae Win in Tennis Title Fray." *New York Times*, August 31, 1918.
25. *Fifty Years*, loc. cit.
26. "Murray, Tilden, and Kumagae Win in Tennis Title Fray." *New York Times*, August 31, 1918.
27. "Murray in Final of Tennis Tourney." *New York Times*, September 1, 1918.
28. "Tilden's Racquet Tangles Kumagae." *New York Times*, September 3, 1918.
29. *Fifty Years*, loc. cit.
30. Ibid.
31. "Murray Easily Beats Tilden in Final for National Tennis Title." *New York Times*, September 4, 1918.
32. "R. Lindley Murray Defeats Tilden and Wins National Title." *Niagara Falls Gazette*, September 4, 1918.
33. Frank Deford. *Big Bill Tilden: The Triumphs and the Tragedy*. Toronto: Sport Media Publishing, Inc., 1975, p. 20.
34. *Fifty Years*, op. cit., pp. 177–78.
35. *Fifty Years*, op. cit., p. 178.

Chapter 14: Family, Exhibitions, and Local Events

1. "Believe Murray's Form Was Spoiled by His Honeymoon." *Niagara Falls Gazette*, June 17, 1916.
2. "Murray Forsakes New York." *New York Times*, September 6, 1916.
3. "Murray, California Tennis Star to Locate at Falls." *Niagara Falls Gazette*, September 8, 1916.
4. "State OKs eminent domain for Niagara Falls land sought by Senecas." Retrieved February 18, 2010, from http://www.propertyrightsresearch.org/2005/articles12/state_oks_eminent_domain_for_Nia….
5. Notes by Doug Murray, March 2001 and telecom March 25, 2010.

6. “R. L. Murray Dies; Retired Industrialist.” *Niagara Falls Gazette*, January 18, 1970.
7. *Mid-York Weekly*, April 7, 1988, p. 2.
8. “Augustus T. Murray.” *Niagara Falls Gazette*, June 25, 1978.

1919

1. “Mary Kendall Browne.” Retrieved July 10, 2009, from http://www.tennisfame.com/famer.aspx?pgID=867&hof_id=61.
2. “C. C. Pyle.” Retrieved January 5, 2010, from http://en.wikipedia.org/wiki/C._C._Pyle.
3. “Alexander Beats Murray.” *New York Times*, March 23, 1919.
4. “Lindley Murray to Compete in Buffalo Tournament Today.” *Niagara Falls Gazette*, March 22, 1919.
5. “R. Lindley Murray and Hendricks Lose to Brooklyn Stars.” *Niagara Falls Gazette*, March 24, 1919.
6. “Hall and Voshell Win.” *New York Times*, May 4, 1919.
7. “Kumagae Victor Again.” *New York Times*, June 1, 1919.
8. “Murray to Captain Selected Eastern Team at Cincinnati.” *Niagara Falls Gazette*, July 2, 1919.
9. “Victories of Murray and Johnson Put East Even With West in Tennis Tournament.” *New York Times*, July 12, 1919.
10. “Murray Displays Real Form in Winning First Match at Cincinnati.” *Niagara Falls Gazette*, July 12, 1919.
11. *The Wright & Ditson Officially Adopted Lawn Tennis Guide for 1920*. Boston: Wright & Ditson, Publishers, pp. 101–2.
12. “Kumagae Unable to Solve Murray’s Terrific Service and Loses Special Match in Two Sets.” *Niagara Falls Gazette*, July 15, 1919.
13. *The Wright & Ditson 1920 Guide*, op. cit., pp. 106–8.
14. “Walter Wesbrook.” Retrieved July 12, 2009, from http://en.wikipedia.org/wiki/Walter_Wesbrook.
15. *The Wright & Ditson 1920 Guide*, op. cit., pp. 107–8.
16. “Open Greenwich Tourney.” *New York Times*, July 18, 1919.
17. “Williams and Murray Win.” *New York Times*, July 19, 1919.
18. “Lindley Murray Wins From Kumagae After Five Spectacular Sets.” *Niagara Falls Gazette*, July 28, 1919.
19. “Kumagae’s Keen Eye Wins Him Victory Over Lindley Murray.” *Niagara Falls Gazette*, August 8, 1919.
20. “Murray Displays ‘Pep’ in Initial Work Out at Down River Courts.” *Niagara Falls Gazette*, August 15, 1919.

21. “Murray Brings McNeil to the Falls as Guest.” *Niagara Falls Gazette*, August 13, 1919.
22. “Murray Displays ‘Pep’ in Initial Work Out at Down River Courts.” *Niagara Falls Gazette*, August 15, 1919.
23. “Williams Victor at Net.” *New York Times*, August 17, 1919.
24. “Pell and Behr Victors.” *New York Times*, August 18, 1919.
25. “R. Murray Wins Match Against Dr. Rosenbaum in First Round Play.” *Niagara Falls Gazette*, August 27, 1919.
26. “Murray Conquers Mathey on Court.” *New York Times*, August 28, 1919.
27. “Murray Again Wins His Match With Ease at National Tourney.” *Niagara Falls Gazette*, August 29, 1919.
28. “Tilden, Williams, Johnston, and Johnson Semi-Finalists for National Tennis Title.” *New York Times*, August 31, 1919.
29. Ibid.
30. William T. Tilden. *The Art Of Lawn Tennis*. London: Methuen & Co. Ltd., 1921, pp. 124–25.
31. Tilden, op. cit., pp. 133–34.
32. “Employees Are Lauded for Role in Growth of Chemical Firm; Leadership Training Is Cited.” *Niagara Falls Gazette*, March 19, 1955.

1920

1. “R. Lindley Murray and Ichiya Kumagae to Play Here Saturday.” *Niagara Falls Gazette*, June 8, 1920.
2. “Murray Advances Into Fifth Round.” *New York Times*, July 15, 1920.
3. “Squair Defeats Murray.” *New York Times*, July 17, 1920.
4. “Roberts Wins Clay Court Tennis Title.” *New York Times*, July 19, 1920.
5. “Murray Defeats Tilden.” *New York Times*, October 4, 1920.
6. “R. L. Murray Defeats William Tilden in Exhibition Match.” *Niagara Falls Gazette*, October 5, 1920.

1921

1. “Murray Trims Jack Castle.” *Niagara Falls Gazette*, July 8, 1921.
2. “R. Lindley Murray Wins State Title.” *New York Times*, July 9, 1921.

3. *The Wright & Ditson Officially Adopted Lawn Tennis Guide for 1922.* Boston: Wright & Ditson, Publishers, p. 166.
4. "International Tennis Title to Lindley Murray of Buffalo." *New York Times*, August 14, 1921.

1922

1. "Richards Defeats Tilden in Final." *New York Times*, April 2, 1922.
2. "Murray Defeats Jack Castle at Country Club." *Niagara Falls Gazette*, June 5, 1922.
3. "Murray Defeats Reid in Great Match at C. C." *Niagara Falls Gazette*, July 3, 1922.
4. "Murray in Action at Buffalo Today—Miss Hooker Wins." *Niagara Falls Gazette*, July 6, 1922.
5. "Easy for Murray—Women's Finals at Buffalo Tomorrow." *Niagara Falls Gazette*, July 7, 1922.
6. "Ray Johnson Proved Easy for Lindley Murray in Semi-Finals—Meets Reid in Finals Today." *Niagara Falls Gazette*, July 8, 1922.
7. "R. Lindley Murray Showed Great Form to Trim Kirk Reid." *Niagara Falls Gazette*, July 10, 1922.
8. *The Wright & Ditson Officially Adopted Lawn Tennis Guide for 1923.* Boston: Wright & Ditson, Publishers, p. 155.
9. "Murray Not to Defend Title." *Niagara Falls Gazette*, July 15, 1922.
10. "R. L. Murray Beats Charles Garland." *Niagara Falls Gazette*, July 24, 1922.
11. "Ira Reindel Was Easy for Murray in Buffalo Play." *Niagara Falls Gazette*, August 5, 1922.
12. "Buffalo Tennis Team Easily Won Over Cleveland." *Niagara Falls Gazette*, August 7, 1922.
13. "Tennis Stars Clash Tomorrow in Exhibition." *Niagara Falls Gazette*, August 12, 1922.
14. "Pittsburgh Star Gives Falls Man Terrific Game." *Niagara Falls Gazette*, August 14, 1922.
15. "Is International Winner." *New York Times*, August 27, 1922.
16. "Murray Again Holder of I. L. Tennis Title." *Niagara Falls Gazette*, August 28, 1922.
17. "Australian Star Beats Falls Man in Great Contest." *Niagara Falls Gazette*, September 18, 1922.

18. "Tennis Stars in Exhibition Here Tomorrow." *Niagara Falls Gazette*, September 23, 1922.
19. "Little Bill Had Great Battle to Beat Falls Man." *Niagara Falls Gazette*, September 25, 1922.
20. "Bill Tilden in Great Victory Over Johnston." *Niagara Falls Gazette*, September 18, 1922.
21. Ibid.
22. Allison Danzig. "Try, Try Again," in *The Fireside Book of Tennis*. Edited by Allison Danzig and Peter Schwed. New York: Simon and Schuster, 1972, pp. 158–59.
23. "Murray Defeats Wm. Johnston in Toronto Match." *Niagara Falls Gazette*, September 26, 1922.

1923

1. "William Tilden 2d vs. Lindley Murray—Sunday." *Niagara Falls Gazette*, May 16, 1923.
2. "Tilden Loses in Doubles." *New York Times*, May 29, 1922.
3. "Tilden in Top Form for Game With L. Murray." *Niagara Falls Gazette*, May 19, 1923.
4. "Tilden, Tennis Champion, Wins Over L. Murray." *Niagara Falls Gazette*, May 21, 1923.
5. "Murray–Hardy Victors Over Tilden–Crocker." *Niagara Falls Gazette*, June 5, 1923.
6. "Begin Clay Court Tourney." *New York Times*, July 2, 1918.
7. "Hardy and Voshell Victors at Tennis." *New York Times*, April 3, 1920.
8. "The Samuel Hardy Award." Retrieved October 12, 2008, from www.usta.com/USTA/Global/Archive/News/Community%20Tennis/Volunteers/10....
9. "Murray in Great Lakes Tourney." *Niagara Falls Gazette*, June 13, 1923.
10. "Lindley Murray to Meet Tilden in Tournament." *Niagara Falls Gazette*, June 19, 1923.
11. "Tennis Stars Battle Today in Tournament." *Niagara Falls Gazette*, June 20, 1923.
12. "Great Lakes Champion Defeats Buffalo Stars in Easy Fashion on Second Day of Tournament." *Niagara Falls Gazette*, June 22, 1923.

13. "Lindley Murray Continues Star Form at Tourney." *Niagara Falls Gazette*, June 23, 1923.
14. Ibid.
15. *The Wright & Ditson Officially Adopted Lawn Tennis Guide for 1924*. Boston: Wright & Ditson, Publishers, p. 148.
16. "International Lawn Tennis Tourney Will Get Underway Monday With Gala List of Well-Known Players on Hand." *Niagara Falls Gazette*, August 4, 1923.
17. "Bowman, State Champion, Defeats Wesbrook, Michigan Title-Holder, in International Open Singles." *Niagara Falls Gazette*, August 10, 1923.
18. "Local Tennis Champion Renews International Laurels, Winning Most Spectacular Court Battle." *Niagara Falls Gazette*, August 13, 1923.
19. *The Wright & Ditson 1924 Guide*, loc. cit.

1924

1. *The Wright & Ditson Officially Adopted Lawn Tennis Guide for 1925*. Boston: Wright & Ditson, Publishers, p. 143.
2. "Sport: Intercollege Tennis." *Time*, July 9, 1923. Retrieved January 14, 2010, from http://www.time.com/time/printout/0,8816,716124,00.html.
3. "Tilden–Chapin Play Today for Great Lakes Title." *Niagara Falls Gazette*, June 20, 1924.
4. "George Lott." Retrieved January 14, 2010, from http://en.wikepedia.org/wiki/George_Lott.
5. *The Wright & Ditson 1925 Guide*, loc. cit.
6. Ibid.
7. "National Lawn Tennis Doubles to Open Today." *Niagara Falls Gazette*, August 19, 1924.
8. "Jacques Brugnon 'Toto.'" Retrieved July 4, 2009, from http://www.tennisfame.com/famer.aspx?pgID=867&hof_id=62.
9. "Jean Robert Borotra 'Bounding Basque from Biarritz.'" Retrieved July 4, 2009, from http://www.tennisfame. com/famer.aspx?pgID=867&hof_id=62
10. "French Tennis Stars Win Over Marsh–Murray." *Niagara Falls Gazette*, September 15, 1924.

1925

1. "Manuel Alonso, Tennis Champion of Spain, Will Play R. Lindley Murray at Country Club Sunday." *Niagara Falls Gazette*, June 5, 1925.
2. "Spanish Ace Lauds American Tennis." *New York Times*, September 12, 1922.
3. "Manuel Alonso." Retrieved January 26, 2009, from http://www.tennisfame.com/famer.aspx?pgID=867&hof_id=43.
4. "Murray–Alonso Thrill Tennis Fans at C. C." *Niagara Falls Gazette*, June 8, 1925.
5. "Niagara Falls Tennis Star Shows Fine Performance at Great Lakes Tourney at Buffalo; Murray In." *Niagara Falls Gazette*, June 9, 1925.
6. "R. Lindley Murray and Jack Castle in Double Semi-Finals of Great Lakes Tennis Tourney; Tressel in Singles." *Niagara Falls Gazette*, June 12, 1925.
7. "Murray–Castle Win Doubles Championship." *Niagara Falls Gazette*, June 15, 1925.

1926

1. "Murray Defeats Tressel in First Match of New Evershed Tennis Club." *Niagara Falls Gazette*, June 8, 1926.
2. "Murray–Castle Repeat Victory in Doubles Also." *Niagara Falls Gazette*, July 26, 1926.

Chapter 15: Niagara Falls, Frontier, and Industrial Tennis

1. *The Park Country Club of Buffalo, 1903–2003*. Williamsville, NY: Park Country Club of Buffalo, Inc., 2003, pp. 17, 20, 22.
2. *Wright & Ditson's Lawn Tennis Guide for 1899*. Boston: Wright & Ditson, Publishers, p. 123.
3. *Wright & Ditson's Lawn Tennis Guide for 1901*. Boston: Wright & Ditson, Publishers, pp. 181, 184.
4. A. Wallis Meyers. "1900: The First Davis Cup Matches," in *The Fireside Book of Tennis*. Edited by Allison Danzig and Peter Schwed. New York: Simon and Schuster, 1972, p. 504.
5. *Wright & Ditson's 1901 Guide*, op. cit., p. 186.
6. *Wright & Ditson's Official Lawn Tennis Guide for 1914*. Boston: Wright & Ditson, Publishers, pp. 186–87.
7. *Wright & Ditson's 1914 Guide*, op. cit., p. 185.

8. *Wright & Ditson's 1914 Guide*, op. cit., pp. 187–88.
9. "Niagara's Tennis Tourney." *New York Times*, August 26, 1900.
10. "Good Work, Porter." *Niagara Falls Gazette*, September 18, 1900.
11. "May Godfray Sutton Bundy." Retrieved August 20, 2009, from http://www.tennisfame.com/famer.aspx?pgID=867&hof_id=144.
12. "Beals Coleman Wright." Retrieved May 12, 2009, from http://www.tennisfame.com/famer.aspx?pgID=867&hof_ id=83.
13. "Raymond D. Little." Retrieved January 14, 2010, from http://en.wikipedia.org/wiki/Raymond_D._Little.

Tennis Club Development in Niagara Falls

1. "Over the Net." *Niagara Falls Gazette*, May 28, 1892.
2. "To Play Tennis. The Courts of the Local Club Will Be Open Tomorrow." *Niagara Falls Gazette*, May 28, 1897.
3. "Tennis Match." *Niagara Falls Gazette*, May 29, 1899.
4. "Tennis Match Was a Tie." *Niagara Falls Gazette*, June 1, 1899.
5. "Falls Tennis Players Won." *Niagara Falls Gazette*, June 19, 1899.
6. "Falls Team Won. Local Players Were Victorious in Tennis Match at Tonawanda Saturday." *Niagara Falls Gazette*, August 13, 1900.
7. "Country Club and Tennis Club Consolidate." *Niagara Falls Gazette*, April 22, 1901.
8. Thomas J. Sheeran. *The Niagara Falls Country Club: 100 Years, 1901–2001*. The Niagara Falls Country Club, 2001, p. 3.
9. Sheeran, op. cit., p. 4.
10. "Tilden, Johnston and Richards Lead." *New York Times*, January 2, 1922.
11. "Bartlett Wins First Country Club Tourney." *Niagara Falls Gazette*, September 5, 1922.
12. "Open New Tennis Court at Institute." *Niagara Falls Gazette*, June 19, 1929.
13. "Address, Parade, Athletic Meet Features of Formal Dedication of Hyde Park, City Playground." *Niagara Falls Gazette*, September 9, 1929.
14. "Tennis Club to Officially Open Courts Tomorrow." *Niagara Falls Gazette*, June 27, 1930.
15. "City's New Clay Tennis Courts at Hyde Park to Be Officially Opened." *Niagara Falls Gazette*, May 23, 1941.

Industrial Tennis League

1. "Central Industrial Athletic Association to Be Formed at Meeting in Y. M. C. A. Tonight." *Niagara Falls Gazette*, April 3, 1919.
2. "Sixteen Teams Ready for Opening Industrial League Sets Tomorrow." *Niagara Falls Gazette*, June 13, 1919.
3. "Organization Meeting for Industrial Tennis League Monday Night." *Niagara Falls Gazette*, June 7, 1919

Chapter 16: Lin Murray, the Industrialist

1. "Bob Kay and 'Tad' Murray Seeking District High School Golf Title." *Niagara Falls Gazette*, June 9, 1937.
2. "Falls High Golf Team Wins Title in District Scholastic Tourney." *Niagara Falls Gazette*, June 14, 1937.
3. "Kay Breaks Record With Round of 64." *Niagara Falls Gazette*, August 7, 1947.
4. "Bob Kay Wins Shore Line Open; Beats Julius Boros." *Niagara Falls Gazette*, July 19, 1952.
5. "Murrays Capture Father, Son Play." *Niagara Falls Gazette*, July 16, 1937.
6. "Tower, Murray Gain Finals in Junior Tourney." *Niagara Falls Gazette*, September 4, 1937.
7. "Murray Defeats Tower in Finals of Junior Event." *Niagara Falls Gazette*, September 7, 1937.
8. "Murray, Faill Tied on Links." *Niagara Falls Gazette*, June 10, 1940.
9. "Murray Wins Top Golfing Honors." *Niagara Falls Gazette*, July 29, 1940.
10. "Murray Takes Country Club Golf Tourney." *Niagara Falls Gazette*, September 6, 1945.
11. "Hooker Group Honors Retiring Members." *Niagara Falls Gazette*, January 1, 1951.
12. "Central Industrial Athletic Association to Be Formed at Meeting in Y. M. C. A. Tonight." *Niagara Falls Gazette*, April 3, 1919.
13. "2 Top Officials of Hooker Firm Get New Posts." *Niagara Falls Gazette*, January 18, 1951.
14. Ibid.
15. Ibid.
16. "Chemists' Award to Be Presented to R. L. Murray." *Niagara Falls Gazette*, January 23, 1953.

17. "Murray Is Named to Receive Chemical Industry Medal for 1956." *Niagara Falls Gazette*, December 10, 1956.
18. "2 Top Officials of Hooker Firm Get New Posts." *Niagara Falls Gazette*, January 18, 1951.
19. "Jacob F. Schoellkopf Medal Award." Retrieved October 14, 2009, from http://pubs.acs.org/appl/literatum/publisher/achs/journals/production/iechad/1931/iechad.1...
20. "Chemists' Award to Be Received by Hooker President." *Niagara Falls Gazette*, January 23, 1953.
21. "R. Lindley Murray Honored by Institute of Chemists." *Niagara Falls Gazette*, February 5, 1953.
22. Bob Watson. "Bounce of Tennis Ball Set up Hooker President for Job With Company." *Buffalo Evening News Magazine*, March 19, 1955.
23. "Employees Are Lauded for Role in Growth of Chemical Firm; Leadership Training Is Cited." *Niagara Falls Gazette*, March 19, 1955.
24. Watson, loc. cit.
25. "Employees Are Lauded for Role in Growth of Chemical Firm; Leadership Training Is Cited." *Niagara Falls Gazette*, March 19, 1955.
26. Ibid.
27. Ibid.
28. "R. Lindley Murray Elected Board Chairman of Hooker." *Niagara Falls Gazette*, June 22, 1955.
29. Ibid.
30. "Hooker, Niagara Alkali Boards Approve Merger." *Niagara Falls Gazette*, October 6, 1955.
31. "Durez and Niagara Alkali Mergers Boost Hooker's Net Worth 75 Per Cent in Year." *Niagara Falls Gazette*, October 8, 1955.
32. "Hooker Executive Honored." *Niagara Falls Gazette*, April 25, 1956.
33. "Hooker Board Chairman to Receive 1956 Medal of Chemistry Industry." *Niagara Falls Gazette*, April 25, 1956.
34. "Firm That Grows Poses Out-of-ordinary Burdens, Murray Says in Accepting Medal." *Niagara Falls Gazette*, April 28, 1956.
35. "Hooker Firm Is Certified as 'Excellently Managed.'" *Niagara Falls Gazette*, January 7, 1956.

36. "Merger Plans Readied by Hooker, Oldbury; Negotiations Begin." Undetermined, July 12, 1956.
37. "Erection of $6–8 Million Research Center Reported Being Planned for Grand Island." *Niagara Falls Gazette*, January 21, 1956.
38. "Hooker Considering Grand Island Plant." *Niagara Falls Gazette*, January 27, 1956.
39. "Hooker Research Center on Island Seen as Tax Boon." *Niagara Falls Gazette*, January 30, 1956.
40. "Chamber to Hear Talk on Research Center Proposal." *Niagara Falls Gazette*, February 21, 1956.
41. "Hooker Planning No Production at Island Center." *Niagara Falls Gazette*, February 29, 1956.
42. "Island Building Boom Continues, Permits Indicate." *Niagara Falls Gazette*, May 5, 1956.
43. "Hooker Shifts Lab Staff to Island Center." *Niagara Falls Gazette*, January 25, 1959.
44. Ibid.
45. Ibid.
46. "Hooker Lab Dedicated to Murray by Rocky." *Niagara Falls Gazette*, June 2, 1959.
47. Ibid.
48. "Hooker Chairman Retires." *New York Times*, Dec 16, 1959.

Hall of Fame

1. "Four Ex-Champions Enter Tennis Hall of Fame." *New York Times*, August 10, 1958.
2. Ibid.
3. Letter from Tad Murray to James Van Alen, August 17, 1966.
4. "The Newport Invitation." *World Tennis*, October, 1958, pp. 10–11.
5. Letter from Lin Murray to James Van Alen, August 14, 1963.
6. "Industrialist's Wife, 79, Dies." *Niagara Falls Gazette*, April 2, 1965.
7. "Augustus G. Porter, Descendant of First Falls Settler, Dies," *Niagara Falls Gazette*, August 4, 1950.
8. Letter from Lin Murray to James Van Alen, August 14, 1963.
9. "Industrialist's Wife, 79, Dies." *Niagara Falls Gazette*, April 2, 1965.
10. Letter from Tad Murray to James Van Alen, August 17, 1966.

11. "History of Tiebreak in Tennis." Retrieved December 12, 2009, from http://tennisracquetsports.suite101.com/article.cfm/history_of_tiebreak_on_tennis.
12. Letter from Molla Mallory to Mr. Heffernan, July 16, 1958.
13. Letter from Molla Mallory to Mr. Heffernan, July 22, 1958.
14. Letter from Molla Mallory to Mr. Heffernan, July 31, 1958.
15. "Queen of Courts Smokes and Crochets While Waiting Turn With Racquet." *Niagara Falls Gazette*, July 7, 1916.
16. Billie Jean King with Cynthia Starr. *We Have Come a Long Way: The Story of Women's Tennis.* New York: McGraw-Hill, 1988, p. 29.
17. Letter from Julian S. Myrick to Mr. Henry Heffernan November 21, 1958.
18. Remarks by Julian S. Myrick, Chairman of the Board, National Tennis Hall of Fame and Tennis Museum, Inc. William M. Johnston Memorial Dinner. Friday, January 30, 1959, Olympic Country Club.

Part III: Players During Murray's Era

Frederik Beasley Alexander*

1. "Frederik Beasley Alexander." Retrieved January 10, 2009, from http://www.tennisfame.com/famer.aspx?pgID=867&hof_id=117.
2. "Fred Alexander." Retrieved July 4, 2009, from http://en.wikipedia.org/wiki/Fred_Alexander.
3. "Frederik Beasley Alexander." Retrieved January 10, 2009, from http://www.tennisfame.com/famer.aspx?pgID=867&hof_id=117.

Manuel Alonso*

1. "Manuel Alonso." Retrieved January 26, 2009, from http://www.tennisfame.com/famer.aspx?pgID=867&hof_id=43.
2. "Manuel Alonso." Retrieved January 26, 2009, from http://en.wikipedia.org/wiki/Manuel_Alonso.
3. "Algernon Kingscote." Retrieved July 6, 2009, from http://en.wikipedia.org/wiki/Algernon_Kingscote.
4. "Strachan Defeated by Howard Voshell." *New York Times*, August 11, 1917.
5. "Manuel Alonso." Retrieved January 26, 2009, from http://www.tennisfame.com/famer.aspx?pgID=867&hof_id=43.

James Outram Anderson

1. "Anderson, James Outram (1894–1973)." Retrieved August 17, 2010, from http://adbonline.anu.edu.au/biogs/A130060b.htm.
2. Ibid.
3. "James Anderson (tennis)." Retrieved January 26, 2009, from http://en.wikipedia.org/wiki/James_Anderson_(tennis).

Karl Howell Behr*

1. "Karl Behr." Retrieved February 22, 2009, from http://en.wikipedia.org/wiki/Karl_Howell_Behr.
2. "Karl Howell Behr." Retrieved February 23, 2009, from http://www.tennisfame.com/famer.aspx?pgID=867&hof_id=52.
3. "Karl Behr." Retrieved February 22, 2009, from http://en.wikipedia.org/wiki/Karl_Howell_Behr.
4. "Mr Karl Howell Behr." Retrieved February 22, 2009, from http://www.encyclopedia-titanica.org/titanic-biography/karl-howell-behr.html.
5. "Karl Howell Behr." Retrieved February 23, 2009, from http://www.tennisfame.com/famer.aspx?pgID=867&hof_id=52.
6. "M'Loughlin Loses to Karl H. Behr." *New York Times*. August 14, 1915.

Molla Bjurstedt-Mallory*

1. Per Gramsborg. "Eight-Time American Singles Champion." *Norseman*, September, 1988, p. 20.
2. Ibid.
3. Ibid.
4. Billie Jean King with Cynthia Starr. *We Have Come a Long Way: The Story of Women's Tennis*. New York: McGraw-Hill, 1988, p. 29.
5. Emma Harrison. "You've Got to Hit the Ball Hard," in *The Fireside Book of Tennis*. Edited by Allison Danzig and Peter Schwed. New York: Simon and Shuster, 1972, pp. 154–55.
6. "Anna Margarethe Bjurstedt Mallory 'Molla.'" Retrieved July 8, 2009, from http://www.tennisfame.com/famer.aspx?pgID=867&hof_id=174.
7. "Molla Mallory—Great American Tennis Champion." Retrieved July 8, 2009, from http://www.all-about-tennis.com/molla-mallory.html.

8. "Anna Margarethe Bjurstedt Mallory 'Molla.'" Retrieved July 8, 2009, from http://www.tennisfame.com/famer.aspx?pgID=867&hof_id=174.
9. King with Starr, op. cit., pp. 28–29.
10. "Molla Mallory." Retrieved July 8, 2009, from http://en.wikipedia.org/wiki/Molla_Mallory.
11. King with Starr, op. cit., p. 31.
12. "French Court Star Found Her American Opponent in Great Form—Molla Won the First Set." *Niagara Falls Gazette*, August 17, 1921.
13. "Mlle. Lenglen's One Ambition to Meet Mrs. Mallory." *Niagara Falls Gazette*, August 18, 1921.
14. "Helen Moody Defaults Match to Helen Jacobs After Two-set Play." *Niagara Falls Gazette*, August 28, 1933.
15. "Molla Mallory." Retrieved July 8, 2009, from http://en.allexperts.com/e/m/mo/molla_mallory.htm.
16. "Pete Sampras and Molla Mallory Inducted Into US Open Court of Champions." Retrieved July 8, 2009, from http://2008.usopen.org/en_US/news/articles/2008-09-07/200809071220842763343.html.

Mary Kendall Browne*

1. "Mary Kendall Browne." Retrieved July 10, 2009, from http://www.tennisfame.com/famer.aspx?pgID=867&hof_id=61.
2. Peter Schwed. "The Unsinkable Mary K. Browne." *World Tennis*, p. 76.
3. "Mary Browne Quits Game." *New York Times*, February 5, 1918.
4. Schwed, loc. cit.
5. "Glenna Collett—Part 2." Retrieved July 10, 2009, from http://www.1920-30.com/sports/glenna-collett-part2.html.
6. "Glenna Collett Vare." Retrieved July 10, 2009, from http://www.wgv.com/hof/member.php?member=1119.
7. "Mary Kendall Browne." Retrieved July 10, 2009, from http://www.tennisfame.com/famer.aspx?pgID=867&hof_id=61.
8. Susan E. Cayleff. *Babe: The Life and Legend of Babe Didrikson Zaharias*. Chicago: University of Illinois Press, 1954, p. 125.
9. Excerpts from *Top Flite Tennis* by Mary K. Browne. Retrieved July 10, 2009, from http://tennis.quickfound.net/training/mary_k_browne.html.

10. "Lake Erie College—Hall of Fame—1991." Retrieved July 10, 2009, from http://www.lec.edu/athletics/hall_of_fame/1991.
11. "Cleveland Women's Golf Association." Retrieved July 10, 2009, from http://www.cwga.net/History.html.
12. "Lake Erie College—Hall of Fame—1991." Retrieved July 10, 2009, from http://www.lec.edu/athletics/hall_of_fame/1991.
13. Schwed, op. cit., p. 77.
14. Ibid.
15. Ibid.
16. "Cleveland Women's Golf Association." Retrieved July 10, 2009, from http://www.cwga.net/History.html.
17. "Lake Erie College—Hall of Fame—1991." Retrieved July 10, 2009, from http://www.lec.edu/athletics/hall_of_fame/1991.
18. "Mary Kendall Browne." Retrieved July 10, 2009, from http://www.tennisfame.com/famer.aspx?pgID=867&hof_id=61.

Jack Castle

1. "Little Man With Big Game." *Buffalo Evening News*, March 5, 1950.
2. Ibid.
3. "Jack Castle Moves Forward in Pro Tennis Tournament After Winning 4-Set Match." *Buffalo Evening News*, August 21, 1934.
4. "Spirited Tennis Matches Thrill Buffalo Society." *Buffalo Courier-Express*, January 21, 1939.

George Myers Church

1. "Tennis". Retrieved July 20, 2009, from http://etcweb.princeton.edu/CampusWWW/Companion/tennis.html.
2. *Wright & Ditson's Official Lawn Tennis Guide for 1914*. Boston: Wright & Ditson, Publishers, p. 136.
3. *Wright & Ditson's Official Lawn Tennis Guide for 1915*. Boston: Wright & Ditson, Publishers, pp. 146–47.
4. "Williams Loses in College Tennis." *New York Times*, September 19, 1914.
5. "Clay Court Tennis Final." *New York Times*, July 2, 1915.
6. "Cleveland History." Retrieved July 20, 2009, from http://ech.cwru.edu/ech-cgi/article.pl?id=T3.

7. "George M. Church." Retrieved July 20, 2009, from http://www.zoominfo.com/Search/ReferencesView.aspx?PersonID=324574540.
8. *Spalding's Lawn Tennis Annual 1919.* New York: American Sports Publishing Company, p. 96.
9. "Church Cup." Retrieved July 20, 2009, from http://www.usta.com/USTA/Global/About_Us/Yearbook/ Yearbook2/23088_2008_...

William Jackson Clothier*

1. "William Jackson Clothier." Retrieved July 22, 2009, from http://www.tennisfame.com/famer.aspx?pgID=867& hof_id=75.
2. "Clothier, William." Retrieved July 22, 2009, from www.tennisticketnews.com/clothier-william-469.html.

Willis E. Davis

1. "New Tennis Star From the Coast." *New York Times*, May 23, 1915.
2. Ibid.
3. "Titleholder Loses at Meadow Club." *New York Times*, August 9, 1922.

Charles Stedman Garland*

1. "Charles Stedman Garland 'Chuck.'" Retrieved July 3, 2009, from http://www.tennisfame.com/famer.aspx?pgID =867&hof id=117.
2. *Wright & Ditson's Official Lawn Tennis Guide for 1916.* Boston: Wright & Ditson, Publishers, p. 73.
3. *Wright & Ditson's 1916 Guide*, op. cit., pp. 152–53.
4. "Kumagae Retains New York State Tennis Title, Defeating Garland Easily in Final." *New York Times*, July 20, 1919.
5. "Garland Beats Davis, Conqueror of Brookes, in Lawn Tennis Final at Southampton." *New York Times*, August 24, 1919.
6. William T. Tilden. *The Art of Lawn Tennis.* London: Methuen & Co. Ltd., 1921, pp. 130–31.
7. "Charles Stedman Garland 'Chuck.'" Retrieved July 3, 2009, from http://www.tennisfame.com/famer.aspx?pgID=867&hof_id=117.

Clarence James "Peck" Griffin*

1. "Clarence James Griffin 'Peck.'" Retrieved February 25, 2009, from http://www.tennisfame.com/famer.aspx?pgID=867&hof_id=130.

2. *Wright & Ditson's Official Lawn Tennis Guide for 1914*. Boston: Wright & Ditson, Publishers, p. 183
3. *Wright & Ditson's 1914 Guide*, op. cit., pp. 174–75.
4. *Wright & Ditson's 1914 Guide*, op. cit., pp. 178–79.
5. *Wright & Ditson's 1914 Guide*, op. cit., pp. 184–85.
6. "Tri-State Tennis Titles." *New York Times*, September 19, 1915.
7. "Clarence James Griffin 'Peck.'" Retrieved February 25, 2009, from http://www.tennisfame.com/famer.aspx?pgID=867&hof_id=130.

Wallace F. Johnson

1. "Sports Briefs: Thursday, June 3, 1999." Retrieved July 2, 2009, from http://media.www.dailypennsylvanian.com/ media/storage/paper 882/news/1999/06/03/Reso....
2. "Wallace Johnson Wins." *New York Times*, September 14, 1909.
3. "Wallace F. Johnson." Retrieved July 2, 2009, from http://en.wikipedia.org/wiki/Wallace_F._Johnson.
4. *Wright & Ditson's Official Lawn Tennis Guide for 1915*. Boston: Wright & Ditson, Publishers, pp. 179–80.
5. "Wallace Johnson Returns." *New York Times*, August 11, 1913.
6. "Sports Briefs: Thursday, June 3, 1999." Retrieved July 2, 2009, from http://media.www.dailypennsylvanian.com/media/storage/paper 882/news/1999/06/03/Reso....
7. "Wallace F. Johnson." Retrieved July 2, 2009, from http://en.wikipedia.org/wiki/Wallace_F._Johnson.

William M. Johnston*

1. "William M. Johnston 'Little Bill.'" Retrieved February 22, 2009, from http://www.tennisfame.com/famer.aspx?pgID=867&hof_id=163.
2. "Johnston, William M. 'Billy' 'Little Billy.'" *Tennis*, p. 361.
3. Ibid.
4. *Wright & Ditson's Official Lawn Tennis Guide for 1914*. Boston: Wright & Ditson, Publishers, pp. 58–60.
5. *Wright & Ditson's 1914 Guide*, op. cit., pp. 122–23.
6. *Tennis*, op. cit., pp. 361–62.
7. "Bill Johnston." Retrieved February 22, 2009, from http://en.wikipedia.org/wiki/Bill_Johnston.

8. "William M. Johnston 'Little Bill.'" Retrieved February 22, 2009, from http://www.tennisfame.com/famer.aspx?pgID=867&hof_id=163.
9. *Tennis*, op. cit., p. 362.
10. Ibid.
11. Steve Flink. "Tilden, Johnston and How Tournament Seedings Began," p. 21 (source unknown).
12. *American Tennis*, p. 117.
13. Steve Flink, loc. cit.
14. "World Hard Court Championships." Retrieved February 22, 2009, from http://en.wikipedia.org/wiki/World_Hard_Court_Championships.
15. *Tennis*, op. cit., p. 363.
16. "William M. Johnston 'Little Bill.'" Retrieved February 22, 2009, from http://www.tennisfame.com/famer.aspx?pgID=867&hof_id=163.
17. *Tennis*, loc. cit.
18. Remarks by Julian S. Myrick, Chairman of the Board, National Tennis Hall of Fame and Tennis Museum, Inc. William M. Johnston Memorial Dinner. Friday, January 30, 1959, Olympic Country Club.

Ichiya Kumagae

1. "Ichiya Kumagae." Retrieved October 15, 2008, from http://en.wikipedia.org/wiki/Ichiya_Kumagae.
2. "Jersey Net Stars in Orient Tourney." *New York Times*, October 19, 1916.
3. "Kumagae on Way East." *New York Times*, July 14, 1918.
4. "Local Tennis Title Goes to Nipponese." *New York Times*, August 5, 1918.
5. William T. Tilden. *The Art of Lawn Tennis*. London: Methuen & Co. Ltd., 1921, p. 149.
6. Tilden, op. cit., p. 150.
7. "Ichiya Kumagae." Retrieved October 15, 2008, from http://en.wikipedia.org/wiki/Ichiya_Kumagae.

Melville H. Long

1. AAA Tennis Boys Annual Champions.

2. "Myth #113—A Tennis Great's Life Started in Carson City." Retrieved February 12, 2010, from http://nevadaculture.org/nsla/index.php?option=com_content&task=view&id=794&Itemi....
3. USLTA. *Fifty Years of Lawn Tennis in the United States.* New York: United States Lawn Tennis Association, 1931, pp. 130–31.
4. "Wallace Johnson Wins." *New York Times*, September 14, 1909.
5. Samuel J. Brookman. "Man From the West," in *The Fireside Book of Tennis.* Edited by Allison Danzig and Peter Schwed. New York: Simon and Schuster, 1972, p. 81.
6. "Long Wins Tennis Title." *New York Times*, August 7, 1910.
7. "Official Athletic Site of the University of California." Retrieved August 10, 2009, from http://www.calbears.com/sports/m-tennis/archive/cal-m-tennis-alltimeawards.html.
8. "TheBuzz: Stories Behind the Headlines." Retrieved August 10, 2009, from http://thebuzz.hellotennis.com/2008/06/16/mustreads.aspx.
9. Unknown newspaper, 1969.

Dean Mathey

1. "Mathey, Dean." Retrieved December 15, 2009, from http://etcweb.princeton.edu/CampusWWW/Companion/mathey_dean.html.
2. *Wright & Ditson's Official Lawn Tennis Guide for 1913*, Boston: Wright & Ditson, Publishers, pp. 137–38.
3. *Wright & Ditson's Official Lawn Tennis Guide for 1914*, Boston: Wright & Ditson, Publishers, p. 66.
4. *Wright & Ditson's 1914 Guide*, op. cit., pp. 62–63.
5. *Spalding's Official Lawn Tennis Annual 1915.* New York: American Sports Publishing Company, pp. 97–99.
6. "Dean Mathey Wins State Tennis Title." *New York Times*, June 21, 1920.
7. "Mathey, Dean." Retrieved December 15, 2009, from http://etcweb.princeton.edu/CampusWWW/Companion/mathey_dean.html.
8. "Mathey College History." Retrieved December 15, 2009, from http://web.princeton.edu/sites/mathey/History.htm.
9. "Mathey, Dean." Retrieved December 15, 2009, from http://etcweb.princeton.edu/CampusWWW/Companion/mathey_dean.html.
10. Ibid.
11. "Mathey College History." Retrieved December 15, 2009, from http://web.princeton.edu/sites/mathey/History.htm.

12. As the Past Catches up With Us AMIB Benefits From a Major Charitable Remainder Unitrust. Posted on Internet.
13. "Mathey College History." Retrieved December 15, 2009, from http://web.princeton.edu/sites/mathey/History.htm.
14. "Pretty Brook Tennis Club Facilities." Retrieved December 17, 2009, from http://www.prettybrook.com/club/scripts/section.asp?GRP=13053&NS=F.
15. "Winans Family Genealogy." Retrieved December 15, 2009, from http://cwcfamily.org/egyc1.htm.
16. "Mathey Halts Savitt in Junior Tennis Play." *New York Times*, July 14, 1944.
17. "Dick Savitt." Retrieved December 16, 2009, from http://en.wikipedia.org/wiki/Dick_Savitt.
18. "USTA Boys Tournament History." Retrieved December 15, 2009, from http://ustaboys.com/tournament_history.html.
19. "Miss Helen Monypeny Newsom." Retrieved December 15, 2009, from http://www.encyclopedia-titanica.org/titanic-biography/helen-monypeny-newsom.html.

Maurice Evans McLoughlin*

1. "McLoughlin, Maurice Evans 'Mac' 'Maury.'" *Tennis*, p. 371.
2. "Myth #113—A Tennis Great's Life Started in Carson City." Retrieved February 12, 2010, from http://nevadaculture.org/nsla/index.php?option=com_content&task=view&id=794&Itemid...
3. *Tennis*, loc. cit.
4. "Lowell High School (San Francisco)." Retrieved January 8, 2010, from http://en.wikipedia.org/wiki/Lowell_High_School_(San_Francisco).
5. "William T. Tilden." *The Art of Lawn Tennis*. London: Methuen & Co. Ltd., 1921, p. 124.
6. "Maurice Evans McLoughlin 'Red, California Comet.'" Retrieved June 25, 2009, from http://www.tennisfame.com/famer.aspx?pgID=867&hof_id=207.
7. "McLoughlin, Maurice." Retrieved February 23, 2009, from http://www.tennisticketnews.com/mcloughlin-maurice-638.html.
8. "'The California Comet'—Maurice McLoughlin '09." Posted on Internet.

9. "Maurice Evans McLoughlin 'Red, California Comet.'" Retrieved June 25, 2009, from http://www.tennisfame.com/famer.aspx?pgID=867&hof_id=207.
10. *Spalding's Official Lawn Tennis Annual 1915*. New York: American Sports Publishing Company, p. 8.
11. *Spalding's 1915 Annual*, op. cit., p. 9.
12. Fred Hawthorne. "The Winning Tennis Punch," in *American Golfer*, August 14, 1920, p. 9.
13. *Tennis*, op. cit, p. 372.
14. Ibid.
15. "Maurice Evans McLoughlin 'Red, California Comet.'" Retrieved June 25, 2009, from http://www.tennisfame.com/famer.aspx?pgID=867&hof_id=207.
16. Ibid.
17. *Tennis*, loc. cit.

Nathaniel (Nat) W. Niles

1. *Wright & Ditson's Official Lawn Tennis Guide for 1909*. Boston: Wright & Ditson, Publishers, pp. 175–76.
2. *Spalding's Official Lawn Tennis Annual 1910*. New York: American Sports Publishing Company, pp. 57, 59.
3. *Wright & Ditson's Official Lawn Tennis Guide for 1911*. Boston: Wright & Ditson, Publishers, p. 183.
4. *Wright & Ditson's 1911 Guide*, op. cit., pp. 65–66.
5. *Wright & Ditson's Official Lawn Tennis Guide for 1912*. Boston: Wright & Ditson, Publishers, p. 75.
6. "Niles Vanquishes Wallace Johnson." *New York Times*, July 23, 1920.
7. "Nathaniel Niles (figure skater)." Retrieved June 10, 2010, from http://en.wikipedia.org/wiki/Nathaniel_Niles_(figure_skater).

Theodore Roosevelt Pell*

1. "Theodore Roosevelt Pell." Retrieved April 23, 2009, from http://www.tennisfame.com/famer.aspx?pgID=867&hof_id=236.
2. William M. Emery and William W. Crapo. *The Howland Heirs: Being the Story of a Family and a Fortune and the Inheritance of a Trust*. New Bedford, MA: E. Anthony & Sons, Inc., 1919, p. 402.
3. *The Wright & Ditson Officially Adopted Lawn Tennis Guide for 1921*. Boston: Wright & Ditson, Publishers, p. 37.

4. Emery and Crapo, op. cit., p. 401.
5. Allison Danzig. "The Top Shotmakers," in *The Fireside Book of Tennis.* Edited by Allison Danzig and Peter Schwed. New York: Simon and Schuster, 1972, p. 177.
6. *Wright & Ditson's Official Lawn Tennis Guide for 1914*. Boston: Wright & Ditson, Publishers, p. 65.
7. "Tennis Champions Win Hard Match." *New York Times,* July 19, 1914.
8. Emery and Crapo, op. cit., p. 402.
9. *Wright & Ditson's 1921 Guide*, op. cit., p. 38.
10. "Upset at Tennis in Newport Tourney." *New York Times,* August 17, 1910.
11. "Theodore Roosevelt Pell." Retrieved April 23, 2009, from http://www.tennisfame.com/famer.aspx?pgID=867&hof_id=236.

Eleonora Randolph Sears*

1. Joanna Davenport. "Personal Recollections of Biographical Research." Auburn University, Auburn, Alabama 36849, pp. 47–48. Posted on Internet.
2. "Eleanora [*sic*] Randolph Sears." Retrieved October 31, 2009, from http://boston1905.blogspot.com/2008/08/eleanora-randolph-sears.html.
3. "Eleanor Roosevelt." Retrieved November 7, 2009, from http://en.wikipedia.org/wiki/Eleanor_Roosevelt.
4. "Eleanora [*sic*] Randolph Sears." Retrieved October 31, 2009, from http://boston1905.blogspot.com/2008/08/eleanora-randolph-sears.html.
5. "Eleanor Roosevelt." Retrieved November 7, 2009, from http://en.wikipedia.org/wiki/Eleanor_Roosevelt.
6. "Eleanora [*sic*] Randolph Sears." Retrieved October 31, 2009, from http://boston1905.blogspot.com/2008/08/eleanora-randolph-sears.html.
7. "Eleonora Sears." Retrieved November 7, 2009, from http://home.earthlink.net?-ggghostie/eleonorasears.html.
8. Ibid.
9. "Eleanora [*sic*] Randolph Sears." Retrieved October 31, 2009, from http://boston1905.blogspot.com/2008/08/eleanora-randolph-sears.html.

10. “Eleonora Sears.” Retrieved November 7, 2009, from http://home.earthlink.net?~ggghostie/eleonorasears.html.
11. Ibid.
12. “Eleonora Randolph Sears ‘Eleo.’” Retrieved November 6, 2009, from http://www.tennisfame.com/famer.aspx? pgID=867&hof_id=167.
13. “Eleonora Sears.” Retrieved November 7, 2009, from http://home.earthlink.net?~ggghostie/eleonorasears.html.
14. Ibid.
15. “Eleonora R. Sears (1881–1968).” Retrieved November 1, 2009, from http://www.nwhm.org/Education/biography_esears.html.
16. “Eleanora [*sic*] Randolph Sears.” Retrieved October 31, 2009, from http://boston1905.blogspot.com/2008/08/eleanora-randolph-sears.html.
17. “Eleonora Sears.” Retrieved November 7, 2009, from http://home.earthlink.net?~ggghostie/eleonarasears.html.
18. Ibid.
19. Ibid.
20. “Eleonora R. Sears (1881–1968).” Retrieved November 1, 2009, from http://www.nwhm.org/Education/biography_esears.html.
21. “Eleanora [*sic*] Randolph Sears.” Retrieved October 31, 2009, from http://boston1905.blogspot.com/2008/08/eleanora-randolph-sears.html.
22. “Eleonora Randolph Sears ‘Eleo.’” Retrieved November 6, 2009, from http://www.tennisfame.com/famer.aspx?pgID=867&hof_id=167.

John R. Strachan

1. *Wright & Ditson's Official Lawn Tennis Guide for 1914*. Boston: Wright & Ditson, Publishers, p. 183.
2. *Wright & Ditson's 1914 Guide*, op. cit., p. 182.
3. *Wright & Ditson's 1914 Guide*, op. cit., pp. 174–75.
4. *Wright & Ditson's 1914 Guide*, op. cit., pp. 178–79.

William Tatem Tilden II*

1. “Bill Tilden.” Retrieved July 23, 2009, from http://en.wikipedia.org/wiki/Bill_Tilden.

2. Ron Borges. "Tilden brought theatrics to tennis." Retrieved July 23, 2009, from http://espn.go.com/sportscentury/features/00016509.html.
3. Frank Deford. *Big Bill Tilden: The Triumphs and the Tragedy.* Toronto: Sport Media Publishing, Inc., 1975, pp. 162–63.
4. "Bill Tilden." Retrieved July 23, 2009, from http://www.answers.com/topic/bill-tilden.
5. Deford, op. cit., p. 20.
6. "Welcome to the Indoor Tennis Court." Retrieved July 23, 2009, from http://t47usa.tripod.com/history.html.
7. "William Tatem Tilden 'Bill, Big Bill.'" Retrieved July 23, 2009, from http://www.tennisfame.com/famer.aspx?pgID=867&hof_id=140.
8. Deford, op. cit., p. 22.
9. Deford, op. cit., pp. 23–24.
10. Allison Danzig. "The Greatest of All Time," in *The Fireside Book of Tennis.* Edited by Allison Danzig and Peter Schwed. New York: Simon and Schuster, 1972, p. 174.
11. "William Tatem Tilden 'Bill, Big Bill.'" Retrieved July 23, 2009, from http://www.tennisfame.com/famer.aspx?pgID=867&hof_id=140.
12. "Ron Borges. Tilden brought theatrics to tennis." Retrieved July 23, 2009, from http://espn.go.com/sportscentury/features/00016509.html.
13. Deford, op. cit., p. 73.
14. "William Tatem Tilden 'Bill, Big Bill.'" Retrieved July 23, 2009, from http://www.tennisfame.com/famer.aspx?pgID=867&hof_id=140.
15. George Lott. "The Records Prove It," in *The Fireside Book of Tennis.* Edited by Allison Danzig and Peter Schwed. New York: Simon and Schuster, 1972, p. 167.
16. "William Tatem Tilden 'Bill, Big Bill.'" Retrieved July 23, 2009, from http://www.tennisfame.com/famer.aspx?pgID=867&hof_id=140.
17. "Bill Tilden." Retrieved July 23, 2009, from http://www.answers.com/topic/bill-tilden.
18. Allison Danzig. "Man of the Half Century," in *The Fireside Book of Tennis.* Edited by Allison Danzig and Peter Schwed. New York: Simon and Schuster, 1972, p. 179.
19. Allison Danzig. "The Greatest of All Time," in *The Fireside Book of Tennis.* Edited by Allison Danzig and Peter Schwed. New York: Simon and Schuster, 1972, p. 173.
20. Danzig, op. cit., p. 175.

21. Deford, op. cit., p. 46.
22. Deford, op. cit., pp. 47–48.
23. “Bill Tilden.” Retrieved July 23, 2009, from http://www.answers.com/topic/bill-tilden.
24. Deford, op. cit., p. 129.
25. “Professional Tennis.” Retrieved July 23, 2009, from http://grandslamtennis.freeukisp.co.uk/aboutprotennis.htm.
26. Deford, op. cit., p. 130.
27. Danzig, op. cit., p. 176.
28. “Bill Tilden.” Retrieved July 23, 2009, from http://en.wikipedia.org/wiki/Bill_Tilden.
29. Ron Borges. “Tilden brought theatrics to tennis.” Retrieved July 23, 2009, from http://espn.go.com/sportscentury/features/00016509.html.
30. “Bill Tilden.” Retrieved July 23, 2009, from http://en.wikipedia.org/wiki/Bill_Tilden.
31. “William Tatem Tilden ‘Bill, Big Bill.’” Retrieved July 23, 2009, from http://www.tennisfame.com/famer.aspx?pgID=867&hof_id=140.
32. Ron Borges. “Tilden brought theatrics to tennis.” Retrieved July 23, 2009, from http://espn.go.com/sportscentury/features/00016509.html.
33. “William Tatem Tilden ‘Bill, Big Bill.’” Retrieved July 23, 2009, from http://www.tennisfame.com/famer.aspx?pgID=867&hof_id=140.

Martin L. Tressel

1. “The Samuel Hardy Award.” Retrieved October 12, 2008, from http://www.usta.com/USTA/Global/Get_Involved/Awards/Information/107711_The_Sam....
2. “Ralph W. Westcott USTA Family of the Year Award.” Retrieved October 12, 2008, from http://www.usta.com/USTA/Global/Get_Involved/ Awards/Information/108544_Ralph_W….
3. “112 Years of West Penn Play.” Retrieved October 12, 2008, from http:/mtlebanontennis.com/history/.

S. Howard Voshell

1. “Pell and Voshell for Tennis Final.” *New York Times*, July 23, 1915.
2. *Wright & Ditson’s Official Lawn Tennis Guide for 1916*. Boston: Wright & Ditson, Publishers, pp. 171–72.

3. "Voshell Defeats Herd for the National Indoor Title." *New York Times*, February 23, 1917.
4. "Voshell Wins Singles Championship." *Deseret News*, February 23, 1917.
5. *The Wright & Ditson Officially Adopted Lawn Tennis Guide for 1921.* Boston: Wright & Ditson, Publishers, pp. 35–36.
6. *The Wright & Ditson Officially Adopted Lawn Tennis Guide for 1921.* Boston: Wright & Ditson, Publishers, p. 36.
7. *The Brooklyn Daily Eagle Almanac*, 1922, p. 473.
8. "Throckmorton Is Voshell's Victim." *New York Times*, June 17, 1917.
9. "Strachan Defeated by Howard Voshell." *New York Times*, August 11, 1917.
10. *The Brooklyn Daily Eagle Almanac*, loc. cit.
11. "Tennis." *Time*. July 14, 1924. Retrieved January 11, 2010, from http://www.time.com/time/printout/0,8816,736323,00.html.

Watson McLean Washburn*

1. "Watson Washburn 'Watty.'" Retrieved January 8, 2010, from http://www.tennisfame.com/famer.aspx?pgID=867&hof_id=108.
2. "At Narragansett Pier." *New York Times*, September 2, 1914.
3. "William T. Tilden." *The Art of Lawn Tennis.* London: Methuen & Co. Ltd., 1921, pp. 134–35.
4. "Watson Washburn 'Watty.'" Retrieved January 8, 2010, from http://www.tennisfame.com/famer.aspx?pgID=867&hof_id=108.

Richard Norris Williams II*

1. Williams, Richard Norris II 'Dick.'" *Tennis*, p. 416.
2. Bud Collins. "R. Norris Williams," p. 13 (source unknown).
3. "R. Norris Williams: Encyclopedia." Retrieved June 26, 2009, from http://en.allexperts.com/e/r/r/r._norris_williams.htm.
4. "Mr Richard Norris II Williams." Retrieved February 22, 2009, from http://www.encyclopedia-titanica.org/titanic-biography/richard-norris-williams.html.
5. Bud Collins. "Tennis Was Easy After the Titanic." *Sports Illustrated*, April 6, 1998.
6. Bud Collins. "R. Norris Williams," p. 13 (source unknown).
7. Ibid.

8. "Mr Richard Norris II Williams." Retrieved February 22, 2009, from http://www.encyclopedia-titanica.org/titanic-biography/richard-norris-williams.html.
9. Bud Collins. "R. Norris Williams," p. 13 (source unknown).
10. Bud Collins. "Tennis Was Easy After the Titanic." *Sports Illustrated*, April 6, 1998.
11. Bud Collins. "R. Norris Williams," p. 13 (source unknown).
12. Bud Collins. "Tennis Was Easy After the Titanic." *Sports Illustrated*, April 6, 1998.
13. Allison Danzig. "Richard Norris Williams 2d," in *The Fireside Book of Tennis*. Edited by Allison Danzig and Peter Schwed. Simon and Schuster, New York, 1972, p. 194.
14. "Richard Norris Williams II 'Dick.'" Retrieved February 22, 2009, from http://www.tennisfame.com/famer.aspx?pgID=867&hof_id=97.
15. Ibid.